# THE COMPLETE STEP-BY-STEP BAKING COOKBOOK

General editor: GINA STEER

FLAME TREE
PUBLISHING

# Contents

## Baking Basics. . . . . . . . . . . . . . . . 6–29

Make sure your cupboard is stocked with the essential baking ingredients and check whether you have the necessary equipment and utensils – you might not get very far without them! Basic techniques are also explained here, along with extra information on working with chocolate, and basic recipes, from making pastry to caramel. Culinary terms and useful conversions complete this invaluable reference section.

## Breads & Scones . . . . . . . . . . . 30–51

Nothing beats the smell of freshly baked bread filling the air and it is easy to make. Choose a Classic White Loaf or go for something a little more hearty with Rustic Country Bread, or branch out and try Rosemary & Olive Focaccia. Let's not forget those homely Traditional Oven Scones or, for the sweet-toothed, try Maple, Pecan & Lemon Loaf.

## Cakes, Brownies & Buns. . . . . 52–95

Homemade cake is a real treat, but with these easy-to-follow recipes it can be a more frequent one! Familiar classics are included, such as Fruit Cake and Carrot Cake, while some have a twist, such as Victoria Sponge with Mango & Mascarpone. Sink your teeth into the Chunky Chocolate Muffins, indulge in Triple Chocolate Brownies or tantalize the taste buds with Lemon & Ginger Buns.

## Special Cakes & Gateaux. . . 96–135

More tempting cakes but on a richer, creamier or grander scale. Many of these cakes are so indulgently moist that they need to be eaten with a fork – all the more to prolong the delight! Some are more ambitious versions of classics, such as Celebration Fruit Cake, some are divine as desserts, such as White Chocolate & Raspberry Mousse Gateau and some are simply naughty, such as Rich Devil's Food Cake.

## Biscuits & Cookies. . . . . . . . . 136–71

Whether you have been inspired while in Italy to make your own Biscotti to go with your coffee, or crave the cosy Oatmeal Raisin Cookies mum used to make, you will find it here. Try the classic Chocolate Chip Cookies, the delectable Pecan Caramel Millionaire's Shortbread or the more fruity flavours of Fig & Chocolate Bars or Spiced Palmier Biscuits with Apple Pureé.

# Sweet Pastry, Tarts & Pies . . 172–205

You do not have to be a pastry whizz to make these delicious tarts and pies – a lot of the recipes can be made using bought ready-made pastry. Create melt-in-the-mouth confections ranging from the fresh flavours of Goats' Cheese and Lemon Tart to the sugary goodness of Lattice Treacle Tart. Rejoice in the heartiness of Rich Double-crust Plum Pie and indulge in Triple Chocolate Cheesecake.

# Baked Puddings & Desserts . . 206–45

Traditional puddings will always be firm favourites – this selection includes the classics Jam Roly Poly, Rice Pudding and Golden Castle Pudding. Try something a little different with Baked Stuffed Amaretti Peaches or delight your dinner guests with Raspberry & Hazelnut Meringue Cake – you cannot go wrong with cream, raspberries and meringue!

# Savoury Pastry & Pizzas . . . . 246–77

Let's not forget the wonderfully tasty savoury dishes that can be made using dough and pastry, from moreish Smoked Mackerel Vol-au-Vents and rich Luxury Fish Pasties to hearty Beef & Red Wine Pie and fragrant Tomato & Courgette Herb Tart. Making pizza from scratch can be very rewarding – try Roquefort, Parma & Rocket Pizza.

# Baked Fish & Seafood . . . . 278–301

Baking fish can be one of the healthiest and easiest ways to cook it, not to mention one of the tastiest. This section provides all sorts of variations, from Zesty Whole-baked Fish to Saucy Cod & Pasta Bake.

# Baked Meat & Poultry . . . . . 302–27

This section is packed with mouthwatering recipes for beef, lamb, pork, chicken and turkey – there is even one for Duck Lasagne. Fill your belly with that family favourite, Shepherd's Pie, or try a fruity twist with Sausage & Redcurrant Bake.

# Baked Vegetable Dishes . . . 328–49

You will not miss meat with these hearty dishes, such as Vegetable Cassoulet with a crispy topping or Courgette Lasagne. Cheese fans can try Cheese & Onion Oat Pie and Baked Macaroni Cheese – yum!

# Index . . . . . . . . . . . . . . . . . . . 350–52

# Baking Basics

Make sure your cupboard is stocked with the essential baking ingredients and check whether you have the necessary equipment and utensils – you might not get very far without them! Basic techniques are also explained here, along with extra information on working with chocolate, and basic recipes, from making pastry to caramel. Culinary terms and useful conversions complete this invaluable reference section.

# Essential Ingredients

## Fat

Butter and firm block margarine are the fats most commonly used in baking. Others can also be used, such as white vegetable fat, lard and oil. Low–fat spreads are not recommended as they break down when cooked at a high temperature. Often it is a matter of personal preference which fat you choose when baking, but there are a few guidelines that are important to remember.

### Butter and Margarine

Unsalted butter is the fat most commonly used in cake making, especially in rich fruit cakes and the heavier sponge cakes such as Madeira or chocolate torte. Unsalted butter gives a distinctive flavour to the cake. Some people favour margarine, which imparts little or no flavour to the cake. As a rule, firm margarine and butter should not be used straight from the refrigerator but allowed to come to room temperature before using. Also, it should be beaten by itself first before creaming or rubbing in. Soft margarine is best suited to one–stage recipes.

### Oil

Oil is sometimes used instead of solid fats. However, if oil is used, care should be taken – it is a good idea to follow a specific recipe as the proportions of oil to flour and eggs are different.

### Fat in Pastry-making

Fat is an integral ingredient when making pastry, again there are a few specific guidelines to bear in mind. For shortcrust pastry, the best results are achieved by using equal amounts of lard or white vegetable fat with butter or block margarine. The amount of fat used is always half the amount of flour. Other pastries use differing amounts of ingredients. Pâte sucrée (a sweet flan pastry) uses all butter with eggs and a little sugar, while flaky or puff pastry uses a larger proportion of fat to flour and relies on the folding and rolling during making to ensure that the pastry rises and flakes well.

## Flour

### Flour Types

We can buy a wide range of flour all designed for specific jobs. Strong ('bread') flour, which is rich in gluten, whether it is white or brown (this includes granary and stoneground), is best kept for bread and Yorkshire pudding. It is also recommended for steamed suet puddings as well as puff pastry. '00' flour is designed for pasta making and there is no substitute for this flour. Ordinary flour or weak flour is best for cakes, biscuits and sauces as it absorbs the fat easily and gives a soft light texture. This flour comes in plain white/all-purpose, self–raising (which has the raising agent already incorporated) and wholemeal varieties. Plain flour can be used for all types of baking and sauces.

### Flour and Raising Agents

If using plain flour for scones or cakes and puddings, unless otherwise stated in the recipe, use 1 teaspoon baking powder to 225 g/8 oz/1¾ cups plain flour. With sponge cakes and light fruit cakes, where it is important that an even rise is achieved, it is best to use self–raising flour because, since the raising agent has already been added, there is no danger of using too much – which can result in a sunken cake with a sour taste. There are other raising agents that are also used. Some cakes use bicarbonate of soda/baking soda with or without cream of tartar (both these

compounds are typical ingredients in baking powder), blended with warm or sour milk. Whisked eggs also act as a raising agent as the air trapped in the egg ensures that the mixture rises. Generally, no other raising agent is required.

## Other Flours

Flour also comes ready sifted. There is even a special sponge flour designed especially for whisked sponges. Also, it is possible to buy flours that contain no gluten and so cater for coeliacs. Buckwheat, soya and chick pea flours are also available.

# Eggs

When a recipe states 1 egg, it is generally accepted this refers to a medium ('large' in the USA) egg. Over the past few years, the grading of eggs has changed. For years, in the UK, eggs were sold as small, standard and large, then this method changed and they were graded in numbers with 1 being the largest. The general feeling by the public was that this system was misleading, so now we buy our eggs as small, medium and large. Due to the slight risk of salmonella, all eggs are now sold date stamped to ensure that the eggs are used in their prime. This applies even to farm eggs, which are no longer allowed to be sold straight from the farm. Look for the lion quality

stamp (on 85% of all eggs sold in the UK) which guarantees that the eggs come from hens vaccinated against salmonella, have been laid in the UK and are produced to the highest food safety and standards. All of these eggs carry a best before date.

## Sizes

The sizing of eggs in the USA does not quite match that of the UK: a small egg in the UK is anything under 53 g, which covers 'peewee' and 'small' in the USA and, at a push, 'medium'; a medium egg in the UK most closely corresponds to a 'large' in the USA, and a large UK egg is equivalent to an 'extra-large' American egg – hence our use of 'small', 'medium/large' and 'large/extra-large' for the recipes in this book, where the first word refers to the UK and the second to the USA.

## Types

There are many types of eggs sold and it really is a question of personal preference which ones are chosen. All offer the same nutritional benefits. More than half of the eggs sold in the UK are from caged hens. These are the cheapest eggs and the hens have been fed on a manufactured mixed diet. Barn eggs are from hens kept in barns who are free to roam within the barn. However, their diet is similar to caged hens and the barns may be overcrowded.

## Free-range

It is commonly thought that free-range eggs are from hens that lead a much more natural life and are fed natural foods. This, however, is not always the case and in some instances they may still live in a crowded environment and be fed the same foods as caged and barn hens. However, it is good that the production of eggs from caged hens is steadily decreasing in favour of free-range eggs – with more and more shops selling only free-range.

## Four-grain and Organic

Four-grain eggs are from hens that have been fed on grain and no preventative medicines have been included in their diet. Organic eggs are from hens that live in a flock, whose beaks are not clipped and who are completely free to roam. Obviously, these eggs are much more expensive than the others.

## Storage

Store eggs in the refrigerator with the round end uppermost (as packed in the egg boxes). Allow to come to room temperature before using. Do remember, raw or semi-cooked eggs should not be given to babies, toddlers, pregnant women, the elderly and those suffering from a recurring illness

## Sugar

Sugar not only offers taste to baking but also adds texture and volume to the mixture. It is generally accepted that caster/superfine sugar is best for sponge cakes, puddings and meringues. Its fine granules disperse evenly when creaming or whisking. Granulated sugar is used for more general cooking, such as stewing fruit, whereas demerara/turbinado sugar, with its toffee taste and crunchy texture, is good for sticky puddings and cakes such as flapjacks. For rich fruit cakes, Christmas puddings and cakes, use the muscovado sugars (dark brown or golden brown) which give a rich intense molasses or treacle flavour.

Icing/confectioners' (powdered) sugar is used primarily for icings and can be used in meringues and in fruit sauces when the sugar needs to dissolve quickly. For a different flavour, try flavouring your own sugar. Place a vanilla pod in a screw-top jar, fill with caster sugar, screw down the lid and leave for 2–3 weeks before using. Top up after use or use thinly pared lemon or orange rind in the same manner.

### Reducing Sugar Intake

If trying to reduce sugar intake, then use the unrefined varieties, such as golden/unrefined granulated, golden caster/unrefined superfine, unrefined demerara and the muscovado sugars. All of these are a little sweeter than their refined counterparts, so less is required. Alternatively, clear honey or fructose (fruit sugar) can reduce sugar intake as they have similar calories to sugar, but are twice as sweet. Also, they have a slow release, so their effect lasts longer. Dried fruits can also be included in the diet to top up sugar intake.

## Yeast

There is something very comforting about the aroma of freshly baked bread and the taste is far different and superior to commercially made bread. Bread making is regarded by some as being a time-consuming process but, with the advent of fast-acting yeast, this no longer applies. There are three types of yeast available: fresh yeast, which can now be bought in the instore bakery department of many supermarkets (fresh yeast freezes well), dried yeast (which is available in tins) and quick-acting yeast, which comes in packets.

### Fresh

Fresh yeast should be bought in small quantities; it has a putty-like colour and texture with a slight wine smell. It should be creamed with a little sugar and some warm liquid before being added to the flour.

### Dried

Dried yeast can be stored for up to six months and comes in small hard granules. It should be sprinkled onto warm liquid with a little sugar, then left to stand, normally between 15–20 minutes, until the mixture froths. When replacing the fresh yeast with dried yeast, use 1 tablespoon dried yeast for 25 g/1 oz fresh yeast.

### Quick-acting

Quick-acting yeast cuts down the time of bread making, as it eliminates the need for proving the bread twice and can be added straight to the flour without it needing to be activated. When replacing quick-acting yeast for dried yeast, you will need double the amount. When using yeast, the most important thing to remember is that yeast is a living plant and needs food, water and warmth to work.

# Equipment

Nowadays, you can get lost in the cookware sections of some of the larger stores – they really are a cook's paradise with gadgets, cooking tools and state-of-the-art electronic blenders, mixers and liquidizers. A few, well-picked, high-quality utensils and pieces of equipment will be frequently used and will therefore be a much wiser buy than cheaper gadgets.

Cooking equipment not only assists in the kitchen, but can make all the difference between success and failure. Take the humble cake tin/pan: although a very basic piece of cooking equipment, it plays an essential role in baking. Using the incorrect size can mean disaster – a tin that is too large, for example, will spread the mixture too thinly and the result will be a flat, limp-looking cake. On the other hand, cramming the mixture into a tin which is too small will result in the mixture rising up and out of the tin.

## Baking Tins & Utensils

To ensure successful baking, it is worth investing in a selection of high quality tins, which, if looked after properly, should last for many years. Follow the manufacturer's instructions when first using and ensure that the tins are thoroughly washed and dried after use and before putting away.

### Deep Cake Tins

With these, it is personal choice whether you buy round or square tins and they vary in size from 12.5–35.5 cm/5–14 inches (a useful size is 20.5 cm/8 inches), with a depth of between 12.5–15 cm/5–6 inches. A deep cake tin, for everyday fruit or Madeira cake, is a must.

### Sandwich/layer-cake Tins

Perhaps the most useful of tins for baking are sandwich/layer-cake tins, ideal for classics such as Victoria sponge, Genoese and coffee and walnut cake. You will need two tins, normally 18 cm/7 inches or 20.5 cm/8 inches in diameter and about 5–7.5cm/2–3 inches deep. They are often nonstick.

### Loaf Tins

Loaf tins are used for bread, fruit or tea breads and terrines and normally come in two sizes: 450 g/1 lb and 900 g/2 lb.

### Baking Sheets and Trays

Good baking sheets and trays are a must for all cooks. Dishes that are too hot to handle, such as apple pies, should be placed directly onto a baking sheet. Meringues, biscuits and cookies are cooked on the sheet. Though the terms are often used interchangeably, the difference between baking 'sheets' and baking 'trays', or specific Swiss/jelly-roll tins, is that the latter have sides all around, whereas a sheet only has one raised side, or none.

### Other Tins and Dishes

Square or oblong shallow baking tins are also very useful for making traybakes, fudge brownies, flapjacks and shortbread. Then there are patty tins, which are ideal for making small buns, jam tarts or mince pies; and individual Yorkshire pudding tins, muffin tins or flan tins/tart pans. They are available in a variety of sizes.

There are plenty of other tins to choose from, ranging from themed tins, such as Christmas tree shapes, numbers from 1–9 and tins shaped as petals, to ring-mould tins (tins with a hole in the centre) and spring-form tins, where the sides release after cooking, allowing the finished cake to be removed easily.

A selection of different-sized roasting tins (i.e. deep baking trays) are also a worthwhile investment, as they can double up as a bain marie, or for cooking larger quantities of cakes such as gingerbread. A few different tins and dishes are required if baking crumbles, soufflés and pies. Ramekin dishes and small pudding basins can be used for a variety of different recipes, as can small tartlet tins and dariole moulds.

## Cooling Racks

Another piece of equipment which is worth having is a wire cooling rack. It is essential when baking to allow biscuits and cakes to cool (either in their tins and/or after being removed from their tins), and a wire rack protects your kitchen surfaces from the heat as well as allowing air to circulate around the goodies, speeding cooling and preventing soggy bottoms.

## Rolling Pin

When purchasing your implements for baking, perhaps the rolling pin is one of the most important. Ideally it should be long and thin, and heavy enough to roll the pastry out easily, but not so heavy that it is uncomfortable to use. Pastry needs to be rolled out on a flat surface and, although a lightly floured flat surface will do, a marble slab will ensure that the pastry is kept cool and ensures that the fats do not melt while being rolled. This helps to keep the pastry light, crisp and flaky rather than heavy and stodgy, which happens if the fat melts before being baked.

## Other Tools

Other useful basic pastry implements are tools such as a pastry brush (which can be used to wet pastry or brush on a glaze), a pastry wheel

for cutting and a sieve to remove impurities and also to sift air into the flour, encouraging the pastry or mixture to be lighter in texture.

Basic mixing cutlery is also essential, such as a wooden spoon (for mixing and creaming), a spatula (for transferring the mixture from the mixing bowl to the baking tins and spreading the mixture once it is in the tins) and a palette knife (to ease cakes and breads out of their tins before placing them on the wire rack to cool). Scales and measuring jugs, or measuring spoons and cups, are essential for accurate measuring of both dry and wet ingredients. Three to four different sizes of mixing bowls are also very useful.

# Electrical Equipment

Nowadays, help from time-saving gadgets and electrical equipment make baking far easier and quicker. Equipment can be used for creaming, mixing, beating, whisking, kneading, grating and chopping. There is a wide choice of machines available, from the most basic to the very sophisticated.

## Food Processors

First decide what you need your processor to do when choosing a machine. If you are a novice to baking, it may be a waste to start with a machine which offers a wide range of implements and functions. This can be off-putting and result in you not using the machine to its fullest. In general, while styling and product design play a role in the price, the more you pay, the larger the machine will be, with a bigger bowl capacity and many more gadgets attached. Nowadays, you can chop, shred, slice, chip, blend, purée, knead, whisk and cream anything. However, just what basic features should you ensure your machine has before buying it?

blades of this blender are at the bottom of the goblet with measurements up the sides. The second blender is portable. It is hand-held and should be placed in a bowl to blend.

## Food Mixers

These are ideally suited to mixing cakes and kneading dough, either as a table-top mixer or a hand-held mixer. Both are extremely useful and based on the same principle of mixing or whisking in an open bowl to allow more air to get to the mixture and therefore give a lighter texture.

The table-top mixers are freestanding and are capable of dealing with fairly large quantities of mixture. They are robust machines, capable of easily dealing with kneading dough and heavy cake mixing as well as whipping cream, whisking egg whites or making one-stage cakes. These mixers also offer a wide range of attachments ranging from liquidizers, mincers, juicers, can openers and many more and varied attachments.

Hand-held mixers are smaller than freestanding mixers and often come with their own bowl and stand from which they can be lifted off and used as hand-held devices. They have a motorized head with detachable twin whisks. These mixers are particularly versatile as they do not need a specific bowl in which to whisk. Any suitable mixing bowl can be used.

When buying a food processor, look for measurements on the side of the processor bowl and machines with a removable feed tube which allows food or liquid to be added while the motor is still running. Look out for machines that have the facility to increase the capacity of the bowl (ideal when making soup) and have a pulse button for controlled chopping. For many, storage is also an issue, so reversible discs and flex storage or, on more advanced models, a blade storage compartment or box, can be advantageous.

It is also worth thinking about machines that offer optional extras that can be bought as your cooking requirements change. Mini-chopping bowls are available for those wanting to chop small quantities of food. If time is an issue, dishwasher-friendly attachments may be vital. Citrus presses, liquidizers and whisks may all be useful attachments for the individual cook.

## Blenders

Blenders often come as attachments to food processors and are generally used for liquidizing and puréeing foods. There are two main types of blender. The first is known as a goblet blender. The

# Basic Techniques

There is no mystery to successful baking, it really is easy providing you follow a few simple rules and guidelines. First, read the recipe right through before commencing. There is nothing more annoying than getting to the middle of a recipe and discovering that you are minus one or two of the ingredients. Until you are confident, follow a recipe, do not try a short cut, otherwise you may find that you have left out a vital step which means that the recipe really cannot work. Most of all, have patience, baking is easy – if you can read, you can bake.

## Working with Pastry

Pastry dough needs to be kept as cool as possible throughout. Cool hands help, but are not essential. Use cold or iced water, but not too much as pastry does not need to be wet. Make sure that your fat is not runny or melted but firm (this is why block fat is the best). Avoid using too much flour when rolling out as this alters the proportions, and also avoid handling the dough too much. Roll in one direction as this helps to ensure that the pastry does not shrink. Allow the pastry to rest, preferably in the refrigerator, after rolling. If you follow these guidelines but still your pastry is not as good as you would like it to be, then make in a processor instead.

### Lining a Flan Dish

It is important to choose the right dish or tin/pan to bake with. You will often find that a loose-bottomed metal flan tin is the best option, as it conducts heat more efficiently and evenly than a ceramic dish. It also has the added advantage of a removable base which makes the transfer of the final flan or tart a much simpler process; it simply lifts out, keeping the pastry intact.

Roll the pastry dough out on a lightly floured surface, ensuring that it is a few inches larger than the flan tin. Wrap the pastry round the rolling pin, lift and place in the tin. Carefully ease the pastry into the base and sides of the tin, ensuring that there are no gaps or tears in the pastry. Allow to rest for a few minutes, then trim the edge either with a sharp knife or by rolling a rolling pin across the top of the flan tin.

### Baking Blind

The term 'baking blind' means cooking the pastry case/pie crust without the filling, resulting in a crisp pastry shell that is either partially or fully cooked, depending on whether the filling needs any cooking. Pastry shells can be prepared ahead of time as they last for several days if stored correctly in an airtight container, or longer if frozen.

To bake blind, line a tin or dish with the prepared pastry dough and allow to rest in the refrigerator for 30 minutes. This will help to minimize shrinkage while it is being cooked. Remove from the refrigerator and lightly prick the base all over with a fork (do not do this if the filling is runny). Brush with a little beaten egg if desired or simply line the case with a large square of greaseproof paper, big enough to cover both the base and sides of the pastry case. Fill with ceramic baking beans/pie weights, dried beans or rice. Place on a baking sheet and bake in a preheated oven, generally at 200°C/400°F/Gas Mark 6, remembering that ovens can take at least 15 minutes to reach this heat (unless they are fan/convection ovens, see page 16). Cook for 10–12 minutes, then remove from the oven, discard the paper and beans. Return to the oven and continue to cook for a further 5–10 minutes, depending on whether the filling needs cooking. Normally, unless otherwise stated, individual pastry tartlet cases also benefit from baking blind.

## Covering a Pie with a Pastry Lid

To cover a pie, roll out the pastry dough until it is about two inches larger than the circumference of the dish. Cut a 2.5 cm/1 inch strip from around the outside of the pastry and then moisten the edge of the pie dish you are using. Place the strip on the edge of the dish and brush with water or beaten egg. Generously fill the pie dish until the surface is slightly rounded. Using the rolling pin, lift the remaining pastry and cover the pie dish. Press together, then seal. Using a sharp knife, trim off any excess pastry from around the edges. Try to avoid brushing the edges of the pastry, especially puff pastry, as this prevents the pastry rising evenly. Before placing in the oven, make a small hole in the centre of the pie to allow the steam to escape.

The edges of the pie can be forked by pressing the back of a fork around the edge of the pie or instead crimp by pinching the edge crust, holding the thumb and index finger of your right (or left) hand against the edge while gently pushing with the index finger of your left (or right) hand. Other ways of finishing the pie are to knock up

(achieved by gently pressing your index finger down onto the rim and, at the same time, tapping a knife horizontally along the edge, giving it a flaky appearance), or fluting the edges by pressing your thumb down on the edge of the pastry while drawing the blunt edge of a knife inwards, against your thumb for about 1 cm/½ inch, and repeating around the rim. Experiment by putting leaves and berries made out of leftover pastry to finish off the pie, then brush the top of the pie with beaten egg.

## Lining Cake Tins

If a recipe states that the tin needs lining, do not be tempted to ignore this. Rich fruit cakes and other cakes that take a long time to cook benefit from the tin being lined so that the edges and base do not burn or dry out. Greaseproof paper or baking parchment is ideal for this. It is a good idea to have the paper at least double thickness, or preferably 3–4 thicknesses. Sponge cakes and other cakes that are cooked in 30 minutes or less are also better if the bases are lined, as it is far easier to remove them from the tin.

The best way to line a round or square tin is to lightly draw around the base and then cut just inside the markings, making it easy to sit in the tin. Next, lightly oil the paper so that it will easily peel away from the cake. If the sides of the tin also need to be lined, then cut a strip of paper long enough for the tin. This can be measured by wrapping a piece of string around the rim of the tin. Once again, lightly oil the paper, push against the tin and oil once more, as this will hold the paper to the sides of the tin. Steamed puddings usually need only a disc of greaseproof paper at the bottom of the dish, as the sides come away easily.

# Hints for Successful Baking

## Measurements

Ensure that the ingredients are accurately measured. A cake that has too much flour or insufficient egg will be dry and crumbly. Take care when measuring the raising agent if used, as too much will mean that the cake will rise too quickly and then sink. Insufficient raising agent means the cake will not rise in the first place.

## Oven Temperature

Ensure that the oven is preheated to the correct temperature; it can take 10 minutes to reach 180°C/350°F/Gas Mark 4. You may find that an oven thermometer is a good investment. Cakes are best if cooked in the centre of the preheated oven. Do try to avoid the temptation of opening the oven door at the beginning of cooking, as a draught can make the cake sink. *Important:* If using a fan/convection oven, then refer to the manufacturer's instructions, as they normally cook 10–20° hotter than conventional ovens and often do not need preheating.

## Testing for Doneness

Check that the cake is thoroughly cooked by removing from the oven and inserting a clean skewer into the cake. Leave for 30 seconds and remove. If the skewer is completely clean, then the cake is cooked; if there is a little mixture left on the skewer, then return to the oven for a few minutes.

## Problems

Other problems that you may encounter while cake making are insufficient creaming of the fat and sugar or a curdled creamed mixture (which will result in a densely textured and often fairly solid cake). Flour that has not been folded in carefully enough or has not been mixed with enough raising agent may also result in a fairly heavy consistency. It is very important to try to ensure that the correct size of tin is used, as you may end up either with a flat, hard cake or one which has spilled over the edge of the tin. Another tip to be aware of (especially when cooking with fruit) is that, if the consistency is too soft, the cake will not be able to support the fruit.

## Cooling and Storing

Finally, when you take your cake out of the oven, unless the recipe states that it should be left in the tin until cold, leave for a few minutes, then loosen the edges and turn out onto a wire rack to cool. Cakes which are left in the tin for too long, unless otherwise stated, tend to sink or slightly overcook. Make sure the cake is completely cold before storing an airtight tin or plastic container.

# Equipment for Chocolate

Chocolate has a reputation for being difficult to work with but a few pieces of well–chosen equipment make the job much easier. Although you can get by with just a selection of basic items, the following list provides a more comprehensive set of equipment for the serious chocolatier.

**Bowls**  Bowls in a variety of sizes in glass, ceramic and metal are all suitable for working with chocolate, as these materials distribute the heat well and are suitable for use on the hob and over hot water. Glass and ceramic can be used in the microwave too. Plastic is less versatile, as it can only be used in the microwave.

**Saucepans**  All kitchens will have a set of saucepans, but for chocolate cooking they need to be fairly small so that a bowl can sit snugly on top without touching the bottom of the pan. Alternatively, glass double boilers are very useful. The top pan sits in the bottom one, with a large gap for water between them. They were designed for making sauces such as hollandaise which did not require the bottom of the pan to get any direct heat and so are perfect for melting chocolate.

**Microwave oven**  This is very good for melting chocolate. Most packets of chocolate will have instructions for melting using a microwave, but you will need to know the power of your oven. This is usually indicated on the door panel or on the control panel and will either be a letter rating or a number indicating wattage. It is important, as with all methods, not to overheat the chocolate, so the best method is to use the microwave in bursts of about 30 seconds, stirring well between bursts.

**Candy thermometer**  This is very useful, especially if tempering chocolate (see Working with Chocolate, page 19).

**Cake-cooling rack**  As we have seen, this has a multitude of uses, not just for chocolate, and is essential if you are going to do any kind of baking. If items are left to cool in tins or on baking sheets, they are likely to create steam as they cool, which will be trapped by the tin or baking sheet. Biscuits and cookies will not be crisp and cakes may become soggy.

**Fine-mesh cooling rack**  This is great for setting dipped items. Put coated items on it to drain and set, putting the rack over a plate or tray to catch any drips. Larger-meshed cake-cooling racks are not really suitable but can be adapted by being covered with nonstick baking parchment.

**Kitchen forks/skewers**  These are a much more affordable alternative to specialist chocolate forks. Kitchen forks and skewers can both be used to handle dipped items. Using skewers, items can be speared before being dipped (fruit or truffles, for example). Harder items such as biscuits should be dipped using two kitchen forks. Both items are more likely to leave marks on the chocolate than specialist forks.

**Chocolate forks**  These are very fine forks, similar to fondue forks, but with longer prongs. Sometimes the points of the prongs are joined and curved. They are very useful for coating truffles and handling chocolate–dipped items. They are also very expensive, however, and are really only for the dedicated chocolate maker.

**Large sharp knife**  Good for cutting shapes out of a set sheet of chocolate or for making chocolate caraque.

**Paint scraper**  A clean paint scraper is the best tool for making chocolate curls. It is worth purchasing one and keeping it specially for the purpose.

**Vegetable peeler**  This is excellent for making chocolate curls quickly from a bar of chocolate. They will be smaller and coarser than curls made using set chocolate, but can be an effective decoration on top of a cake.

**Pastry cutters**  These are mainly useful for cutting shapes out of chocolate that has set in a sheet. These can then be used for sandwiching a filling or for decorating cakes.

**Petit-four cutters**  As with pastry cutters, these are very useful for making small shapes for use as decorations.

**Grater**  The coarser side of a box grater is very useful for making chocolate decorations.

**Small paintbrush/pastry brush**  Brushes are most useful for making moulded chocolates in unusual shapes, but are also good for painting the insides of pastry cases with chocolate before filling with fruit or cream.

**Greaseproof/waxed paper and nonstick baking parchment**
As we have seen, these are both essential items for baking, to line cake tins. Also available are reusable nonstick mats which can be cut to size and used again and again. Nonstick baking parchment is good for making small disposable piping bags, which are perfect for drizzling chocolate or icing onto cakes and biscuits. Take a piece of paper, about 20.5 cm/8 inches square, and fold it in half diagonally to make a double triangle. Fold the paper round to form a cone. Tighten the cone until all the points meet, then fold the points of paper down into the top of the cone. You can now fill the cone and then snip off the bottom to make a piping bag.

**Piping bag with nozzle**  This is a small nylon piping bag with a variety of nozzles that is very useful for decorating cakes and, when fitted with a plain nozzle, for drizzling chocolate.

**Marble slab**  This is also useful in pastry making, as it stays cool regardless of the kitchen temperature. Melted chocolate can be poured directly onto the marble, either in a sheet for making curls or caraque, or for making shapes.

**Metal spatulas**  These are long thin blades with rounded ends, though they come in different sizes. The blades are flexible and are very useful for spreading melted chocolate, either onto cakes or biscuits or onto marble slabs for making chocolate decorations.

**Rubber spatulas**  These are available in small, medium and large sizes, including one that is spoon shaped.

**Moulds**  A large variety of moulds for making chocolates is available from specialist shops and by mail order. Sometimes made

of rigid material, flexible plastic moulds are the easiest to use. There are three methods for using the moulds, depending on the desired result. Method 1 is to pour melted chocolate into the mould and leave until set. This is the best method for making small chocolate shapes. Method 2 is to pour chocolate into the mould until about one-third full, then tilt the mould until the inside is completely coated with a layer of chocolate, then pour off any excess. This is the best method for making large hollow shapes, such as Easter eggs. Method 3 is to use a paintbrush dipped in melted chocolate to paint the inside of the mould with a thin layer. Repeat the process using thin layers until the chocolate is set firm. This is the best method to use if your mould is unconventional, a paper fairy cake case, for example. The plastic moulds can then simply be bent and flexed until the chocolate comes loose. These produce excellent results and the chocolate emerges from the mould with a beautiful shiny surface. If using something like a paper fairy cake case, it will need to be removed carefully, possibly in strips.

**Petit-four cases**  These are available in supermarkets and kitchenware shops and come in a variety of sizes and colours. They are perfect for displaying handmade chocolates, especially if they are being packed in a box.

**Sieve**  This is useful for sifting cocoa powder and icing sugar, both of which are a bit sticky and may have lumps that need removing.

**Dredger**  This is useful both for icing sugar and cocoa powder and is less messy than using a sieve. Dredgers are also good for dusting finished chocolates or cakes.

# Working with Chocolate & Caramel

There are a few useful techniques for working with chocolate. None of them is very complicated and all can be mastered easily with a little practice. These general guidelines apply equally for all types of chocolate.

## Melting Chocolate

All types of chocolate are sensitive to temperature, so care needs to be taken during the melting process. It is also worth noting that different brands of chocolate have different consistencies when melting and when melted. Experiment with different brands to find one that you prefer.

### No Water

As a general rule, it is important not to allow any water to come into contact with the chocolate. In fact, a drop or two of water is more dangerous than larger amounts, which may blend in. The melted chocolate will seize and it will be impossible to bring it back to a smooth consistency.

### Gently Does It

Do not overheat chocolate or melt it by itself in a pan over a direct heat. Always use either a double boiler or a heatproof bowl set over a saucepan of water, but do not allow the bottom of the bowl to come into contact with the water, as this would overheat the chocolate. Keep an eye on the chocolate, checking it every couple of minutes and reducing or extinguishing the heat under the saucepan, as necessary. Stir the chocolate once or twice during melting until it is smooth and no lumps remain. Do not cover the bowl once the chocolate has melted or condensation will form, water will drop into it and it will be ruined. If the chocolate turns from a glossy, liquid mass into a dull, coarse, textured mess, you will have to start again.

### Microwaving

Microwaving is another way of melting chocolate but, again, caution is required. Follow the oven manufacturer's instructions together with the instructions on the chocolate and proceed with care. Melt the chocolate in bursts of 30 or so seconds, stirring well between bursts, until the chocolate is smooth. If possible, stop microwaving before all the chocolate has melted and allow the residual heat in the chocolate to finish the job. The advantage of microwaving is that you do not need to use a saucepan, making the whole job quicker and neater.

## Making Chocolate Decorations

**Curls and caraque** Chocolate curls are made using a clean paint scraper. They are usually large, fully formed curls which are useful for decorating gateaux and cakes. Caraque are long thin curls which can be used in the same way, but are less dramatic. To make either shape, melt the chocolate following your preferred method and then spread it in a thin layer over a cool surface, such as a marble slab, ceramic tile or piece of granite. Leave until just set but not hard.

To make curls, take a clean paint scraper and set it at an angle to the surface of the chocolate, then push, taking a layer off the surface. This will curl until you release the pressure. Alternatively, you can make curled shapes by painting melted chocolate onto pieces of kitchen foil, shaping accordingly and chilling until set (*see* page 131).

To make caraque, use a large sharp knife and hold it at about a 45-degree angle to the chocolate. Hold the handle and the tip and scrape the knife towards you, pulling the handle but keeping the tip more or less in the same place. This method makes thinner, tighter, longer curls.

**Shaved chocolate**  Using a vegetable peeler, shave a thick block of chocolate to make mini-curls. These are best achieved if the chocolate is a little soft, otherwise it has a tendency to break into little flakes.

**Chocolate shapes**  Spread a thin layer of chocolate, as described in the instructions for chocolate curls, and allow to set as before. Use shaped cutters or a sharp knife to cut out shapes. Use to decorate cakes.

**Chocolate leaves**  Many types of leaf are suitable, but ensure they are not poisonous before using. Rose leaves are easy to find and make good shapes. Wash and dry the leaves carefully before using. Melt chocolate following the instructions given at the beginning of the section. Using a small paintbrush, paint a thin layer of chocolate onto the back of the leaf. Allow to set before adding another thin layer. When set, carefully peel off the leaf. Chocolate leaves are also very attractive when made using two different types of chocolate, white and dark chocolate, for example. Paint half the leaf first with one type

of chocolate and allow to set before painting the other half with the second chocolate. Leave to set, then peel off the leaf as above.

**Chocolate lace**  Make a nonstick baking parchment piping bag (*see* Equipment for Chocolate, page 17). Draw an outline of the required shape onto some nonstick baking parchment, a triangle, for example. Pipe chocolate evenly onto the outline, fill in the centre with lacy squiggles and leave until set. Remove the paper to use.

**Chocolate squiggles**  Use a teaspoon of melted chocolate to drizzle random shapes onto nonstick baking parchment. Leave to set and remove the paper to use. Alternatively, pipe a zigzag line about 5 cm/2 inches long onto a piece of nonstick baking parchment. Pipe a straight line slightly longer at either end down the middle of the zigzag.

**Chocolate butterflies**  Draw a butterfly shape on a piece of nonstick baking parchment. Fold the paper down the middle of the body of the butterfly to make a crease, then open the paper out flat. Pipe chocolate onto the outline of the butterfly, then fill in the wings with loose zigzag lines. Carefully fold the paper so the wings are at right-angles, supporting them from underneath in the corner of a large tin or with some other support, and leave until set. Peel away the paper to use.

**Chocolate modelling paste** To make chocolate modelling paste (very useful for cake coverings and for making heavier shapes, such as ribbons) put 200 g/7 oz plain chocolate in a bowl and add 3 tablespoons of liquid glucose. Set the bowl over a pan of gently simmering water. Stir until the chocolate is just melted, then remove from the heat. Beat until smooth and leave the mixture to cool. When cool enough to handle, knead to a smooth paste on a clean work surface. The mixture can now be rolled and cut to shape. If the paste hardens, wrap it in clingfilm/plastic wrap and warm it in the microwave for a few seconds on low.

## Caramel and Praline Decorations

### Caramel

To make caramel, put 75 g/3 oz/⅓ cup granulated sugar into a heavy-based saucepan with about 3 tablespoons cold water. Over a low heat, stir well until the sugar has dissolved completely. If any sugar clings to the pan, brush it down using a wet brush. Bring the mixture to the boil and cook, without stirring, until the mixture turns golden. You may need to tilt the pan carefully to ensure the sugar colours evenly. As soon as the desired colour is reached, remove the pan from the heat and plunge the base of the pan into cold water to stop it from cooking further.

**Caramel-dipped nuts** Make the caramel, remove the pan from the heat and plunge into cold water as described earlier. Using two skewers or two forks, dip individual nuts into the hot caramel, lift out carefully, allowing excess to run off, then transfer to a foil-covered tray until set. If the caramel becomes too sticky or starts making a lot of sugar strands, reheat gently until liquid again.

**Caramel shapes** Make the caramel, remove the pan from the heat and plunge into cold water as described earlier. Using a teaspoon, drizzle or pour spoonfuls of caramel onto an oiled baking sheet. Leave to set before removing from the tray. Do not refrigerate caramel shapes as they will liquefy.

**Caramel lace** Follow the method for caramel shapes, but use the teaspoon to drizzle threads in a random pattern onto an oiled tray. When set, break into pieces for decorations. Do not refrigerate.

### Praline

To make praline, follow the instructions as for caramel, but do not plunge the pan into cold water. Add nuts to the caramel mixture. Do not stir, but pour immediately onto an oiled baking sheet. Leave to set at room temperature. Once cold, the praline can be chopped or broken into pieces as required. Keep leftover praline in a sealed container. It will keep for several months stored this way.

# Basic Recipes: Pastry

## Shortcrust Pastry

Makes 225 g/8 oz

225 g/8 oz/2 cups plain/all–purpose white flour
pinch salt
50 g/2 oz/4 tbsp white vegetable fat/shortening or lard
50 g/2 oz/½ stick butter or block margarine

Sift the flour and salt into a mixing bowl. Cut the fats into small pieces and add to the bowl. Rub the fats into the flour using your fingertips until the mixture resembles fine breadcrumbs. Add 1–2 tablespoons cold water and, using a knife or your hands if easier, mix to form a soft, pliable dough. Knead gently on a lightly floured surface until smooth and free from cracks, then wrap and chill for 30 minutes before rolling out on a lightly floured surface. Use as required. Cook in a preheated hot oven (200°C/400°F/Gas Mark 6).

## Sweet Shortcrust Pastry (Pâte Sucrée)

Makes 225 g/8 oz

225 g/8 oz/2 cups plain/all–purpose white flour
150 g/5 oz/1¼ sticks unsalted butter, softened
2 tbsp caster/superfine sugar
1 egg yolk

Sift the flour into a mixing bowl, cut the fat into small pieces, add to the bowl and rub into the flour. Stir in the sugar, then mix to form a pliable dough with the egg yolk and about 1 tablespoon cold water. Wrap, chill and use as required.

## Cheese Pastry

Follow the recipe for sweet shortcrust pastry, but omit the sugar and add 1 teaspoon dried mustard powder and 50 g/2 oz/½ cup mature grated Cheddar cheese.

## Rough Puff Pastry

Makes 225 g/8 oz

225 g/8 oz/2 cups plain/all–purpose white flour
pinch salt
150 g/5 oz/1¼ sticks butter, block margarine or lard
squeeze lemon juice

Sift the flour and salt together in a mixing bowl. Cut up the fat, add to the bowl. Add the lemon juice and 6–7 tablespoons cold water. Mix with a fork until it is a fairly stiff mixture. Turn out onto a lightly floured surface. Roll into an oblong. Fold the bottom third up to the centre, bring the top third down to the centre. Gently press the edges together. Give the pastry a half turn, roll the pastry out again into an oblong. Repeat the folding, turning and rolling at least four times. Wrap. Leave to rest in a cool place for at least 30 minutes. Cook as directed by your recipe, in a preheated oven at 220°C/425°F/Gas Mark 7.

## Choux Pastry

Makes 225 g/8 oz

50 g/2 oz/½ stick butter
75 g/3 oz/¾ cup plain/all–purpose white flour
pinch salt
2 eggs, beaten

Place the butter and 150 ml/5 fl oz/²/₃ cup water in a heavy–based saucepan. Heat gently, stirring until the butter has melted, and bring to the boil. Draw off the heat and add the flour and salt all at once. Beat with a wooden spoon until the mixture forms a ball in the centre. Cool for 5 minutes. Gradually add the eggs, beating well after each addition, until a stiff mixture is formed. Either place in a piping/decorating bag fitted with a large nozzle/tip, or shape using two spoons. Cook in a preheated oven at 200°C/400°F/Gas Mark 6 for 15–25 minutes, depending on size. Remove and make a small slit in the side, then return to the oven and cook for a further 5 minutes. Remove and cool before filling.

## Hot Water Crust Pastry

Makes 450 g/1 lb

450 g/1 lb/4 cups plain/all–purpose white flour
1 tsp salt
125 g/4 oz/7 tbsp lard or white vegetable fat/shortening
150 ml/¹/₄ pt/²/₃ cup milk and water, mixed

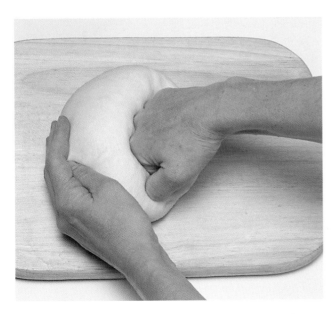

Sift the flour and salt together and reserve. Heat the lard or white vegetable fat/shortening until melted. Bring to the boil. Pour immediately into the flour along with some of the milk and water and, using a wooden spoon, mix together and beat until the mixture comes together and forms a ball, using more milk and water as needed. When cool enough to handle, knead lightly until smooth and pliable. Use as required, covering the dough with a clean cloth before use. Bake in a preheated oven at 220°C/425°F/Gas Mark 7, or as directed.

# Basic Recipes: Batters

## Pouring Batter for Yorkshire Puddings and Pancakes

125 g/4 oz/1 cup plain/all–purpose white flour
pinch salt
2 eggs
300 ml/¹/₂ pint/1¹/₄ cups whole milk and water, mixed
1 tbsp vegetable oil

Sift the flour and salt into a mixing bowl and make a well in the centre. Drop the eggs into the well with a little milk. Beat the eggs into the flour, gradually drawing the flour in from the sides of the bowl. Once half the milk has been added, beat well until smooth and free from lumps. Stir in the remaining milk and leave to stand for 30 minutes. Stir before using. Heat 1 tablespoon oil in a roasting tin/pan or individual Yorkshire pudding tins/pans in an oven preheated to 220°C/425°F/Gas Mark 7. When the oil is almost smoking, stir the batter, then pour it into the hot oil. Cook for 30–40 minutes for a large pudding and 18–20 minutes for individual puddings. This batter can also be used for pancakes and, if liked, 2 tbsp caster/superfine sugar can be added.

## Coating Batter for Fritters

125 g/4 oz/1 cup plain/all–purpose white flour
pinch salt
1 tbsp sunflower/corn oil
150 ml/¹/₄ pint/²/₃ cup water
2 egg whites

Sift the flour and salt into a mixing bowl and make a well in the centre. Add the oil and half the water and beat until smooth and free from lumps. Gradually beat in the remaining water. Just before using, whisk the egg whites until stiff, then stir into the batter and use immediately.

# Basic Recipes: Meringues

Meringue is made from egg whites and caster/superfine sugar. As a general rule, allow 1 egg white to 50 g/2 oz/¼ cup caster sugar. If liked, add a pinch of salt at the start of whisking.

## Making Meringue

Place the egg whites in a clean mixing bowl (any grease in the bowl will prevent the egg white from whisking). Use a balloon or wire whisk if whisking by hand, or an electric mixer fitted with a balloon whisk if not. Whisk the egg whites until stiff. To test if they are stiff enough, turn the bowl upside down – if the egg white does not move, it is ready. Slowly add half the sugar, 1 teaspoon at a time, whisking well after each addition. Once half the sugar has been added, add the remaining sugar and gently stir it in with a metal spoon. Take care not to over-mix.

Spoon the meringue onto a baking sheet lined with nonstick baking parchment. Shape the meringue according to preference or the recipe – such as in a round 'case' – and typically bake in a preheated oven at 150°C/300°F/Gas Mark 2 for 1½ hours, or until set and firm to the touch. Remove from the oven, leave until cold before using or storing in an airtight container.

## Whipped Cream
### (to accompany the meringues)

Whipping cream, double/heavy cream or a combination of single/light cream and double cream will all whip. For the combination option, use one third single cream and two thirds double cream.

Place the cream in a mixing bowl and use a balloon whisk, wire whisk or electric mixer fitted with the balloon whisk attachment. Place the bowl on a damp cloth if whipping by hand. Whip until thickened and soft peaks are formed – this is when the whisk, if dragged gently through the cream and lifted out, leaves soft peaks in the cream. Whipped cream is ideal for using in soufflés, mousses and other cream desserts. For piping/decorating and to use as a filling, whip for a little longer until the cream is slightly stiffer. If using only double cream, take care that you do not over-whip, as it will curdle.

# Basic Recipes: Fruit & Icings

## Poaching Fruit

This method is suitable for plums, apricots, damsons, greengages, peaches, nectarines, cherries, raspberries, strawberries, blackberries and currants, cored and sliced cooking apples, peeled and cored pears and rhubarb. Poached fruit can be used in pies or wrapped in pastry, but is also delicious served with cream or sauce.

Place 75 g/3 oz/¹/₃ cup sugar in a heavy-based saucepan with 150 ml/¹/₄ pint/²/₃ cup water. Place over a gentle heat and stir occasionally until the sugar has dissolved. Bring to the boil and boil steadily for 5 minutes, or until a syrup is formed. Pour into a frying pan, or, if the pan is large enough, keep the syrup in the pan. Prepare the fruit to be poached by rinsing and cutting in half and discarding the stones. Add to the syrup and poach gently for 8–10 minutes until just cooked. Remove from the heat and gently transfer to a serving dish.

Alternatively, the fruits can be gently poached without sugar. Prepare as required and rinse lightly. Half-fill a frying pan with water or a mixture of orange juice and water and bring to the boil. Reduce the heat to a simmer, then add the fruits and cook for 5–10 minutes until just tender.

## Icings

### Butter Cream

125 g/4 oz/1 stick unsalted butter or margarine, softened
1 tsp vanilla extract
225 g/8 oz/2 cups icing/confectioners' sugar, sifted

Cream the butter or margarine with the vanilla extract until soft and creamy. Add the icing/confectioners' sugar, 1 tablespoon at a time,

and beat well. Continue until all the icing sugar is incorporated. Beat in 1–2 tablespoons slightly cooled boiled water or fruit juice to give a smooth, spreadable consistency.

**Chocolate butter cream**  Melt 50 g/2 oz/2 squares dark/bittersweet chocolate. Stir into the prepared butter cream, omitting the hot water. Or, if preferred, replace 1 tablespoon of the icing/confectioners' sugar with 1 tablespoon cocoa.

**Orange/lemon butter cream**  Beat 1 tablespoon finely grated orange or lemon zest into the butter cream and replace the water with fruit juice.

**Coffee butter cream**  Dissolve 1 tablespoon coffee granules in a little very hot water. Omit the vanilla extract and stir in the coffee in place of the hot water.

**Mocha butter cream**  Make the coffee butter cream as above and replace 1 tablespoon of the icing sugar with 1 tablespoon unsweetened cocoa powder, or use melted chocolate.

### Glacé Icing

Sift 225 g/8 oz/2 cups icing/confectioners' sugar into a mixing bowl, then slowly stir in 2–3 tablespoons hot water. Blend to form a spreadable consistency – the icing should coat the back of a wooden spoon. Other flavours can be made by adding 1 tablespoon cocoa to the sugar or 1 tablespoon coffee granules, dissolved in hot water. Or use orange or lemon juice, such as with Bakewell Tart. For a coloured icing, add a few drops of food colouring.

# Culinary Terms Explained

At a glance, here are some of the key terms you will come across when baking. Some we may have discussed already, some may be new to you.

**Baking parchment** Sometimes called 'baking parchment paper' or just 'baking paper'. Used for wrapping food to be cooked (en papillote) and for lining cake tins/pans to prevent sticking. Usually comes as nonstick, in theory avoiding the need to grease or oil the paper.

**Greaseproof/waxed paper** Paper that tends to be relatively nonstick and which is used to line tins/pans to prevent cakes and puddings from sticking, and for wrapping food such as packed lunches or fatty foods. Historically, unlike baking parchment, if greaseproof paper was used in the oven, it would smoke, so the batter or cake mixture had to cover it entirely. However, today, greaseproof paper and baking parchment are often able to be used in the same way – check the packaging.

**En papillote** A French term used to describe food which is baked, but is wrapped in baking parchment before cooking. This works well with fish, as the aroma from the different herbs or spices and the fish are contained during cooking and not released until the paper parcel is opened.

**Rice paper** This edible paper is made from the pith of a Chinese tree and can be used as a base on which to bake sticky cakes and biscuits such as almond macaroons.

**Centigrade** This is a metric scale for measuring the temperature within the oven (usually known as Celsius).

**Baking blind** The method often used for cooking the pastry case/pie crust of flans and tarts before the filling is added. After lining the tin/pan with the uncooked pastry, it is then covered with a sheet of greaseproof/waxed paper or baking parchment and weighed down with either ceramic baking beans/pie weights, dried beans or rice and is baked in the oven as directed in the recipe.

**Baking powder** A raising agent which works by producing carbon dioxide as a consequence of a reaction caused by the acid and alkali ingredients, which expand during the baking process and make the breads and cakes rise.

**Bicarbonate of soda/baking soda** This alkali powder acts as a raising agent in baking when combined with an acid or acid liquid (cream of tartar, lemon juice, yogurt, buttermilk, cocoa or vinegar, for example).

**Cream of tartar** An acid raising agent (potassium hydrogen tartrate) often present in both self-raising flour and baking powder. Activates the alkali component of baking powder.

**Fermenting** A term used during bread, beer or wine making to note the chemical change brought about through the use of a fermenting or leavening agent, such as yeast.

**Unleavened** Often refers to bread which does not use a raising agent and is therefore flat, such as Indian naan bread.

**Cornflour/cornstarch** Used to thicken consistency and can also be used in meringue making to prevent the meringue becoming hard and brittle and to enhance its chewiness.

**Pasteurizing** The term given when milk and eggs are heated to destroy bacteria.

**Curdling** When the milk separates from a sauce through acidity or excessive heat. This can also happen to creamed cake mixtures that have separated due to the eggs being too cold or added too quickly.

**Sifting** The shaking of dry ingredients (primarily flour) through a metal or nylon sieve to remove impurities before using in baking.

**Binding** Adding liquid or egg to bring a dry mixture together. Normally, this entails using either a fork, spoon or your fingertips.

**Blending** When two or more ingredients are thoroughly mixed together.

**Creaming** The method by which fat and sugar are beaten together until lighter in colour and fluffy. By creaming the fat in cake mixtures, air is incorporated into the fairly high fat content. It thus lightens the texture of cakes and puddings.

**Folding** A method of combining creamed fat and sugar with flour in cake and pudding mixes, usually by carefully mixing with a large metal spoon, either by cutting and folding, or by doing a figure of eight in order to maintain a light texture.

**Rubbing in** The method of combining fat into flour for crumble toppings, shortcrust pastry, biscuits and scones.

**Beating** The method by which air is introduced into a mixture using a fork, wooden spoon, whisk or electric mixer. Beating is also used as a method to soften ingredients.

**Whipping/whisking** The term given to incorporating air rapidly into a mixture (either through using a manual whisk or an electric whisk).

**Dropping consistency** The consistency that a cake or pudding mixture reaches before being cooked. It tends to be fairly soft (but not runny) and should drop off a spoon in around five seconds when tapped lightly on the side of a bowl.

**Grinding** Reducing hard ingredients, such as nuts, to crumbs, normally by the use of a grinder or a pestle and mortar.

**Blender** An electric machine with rotating blades used mainly with soft and wet ingredients to purée and liquidize, although it can grind dry ingredients such as nuts and breadcrumbs.

**Dough** A dense mixture of flour, water and, often, yeast. Also used to describe raw pastry, scones and biscuit mixtures.

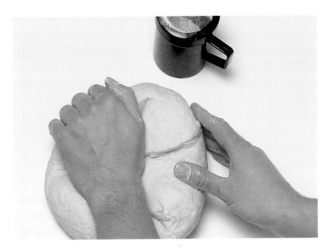

**Knead** The process of pummelling and working dough in order to strengthen the gluten in the flour and make the dough more elastic, thus giving a good rise. Also applies to pastry making: the dough is kneaded on a lightly floured surface to give a smooth and elastic pastry, making it easier to roll and ensuring an even texture after baking. In both cases, the outside of the dough is drawn into the centre.

**Proving** The term used in bread making when the bread is allowed to rise a second time after it has been kneaded once and then shaped before it is baked.

**Knock back** The term used for a second kneading after the dough has been allowed to rise. This is done to ensure an even texture and to disperse any large pockets of air.

**Crumb** The internal texture of a cake or bread as defined by the air pockets.

**En croûte** Used to describe food which is covered with raw pastry and then baked.

**Vol-au-vent** Meaning 'flying' or 'floating' on the wind, this small and usually round or oval puff pastry case is first baked and then filled with savoury meat, seafood or vegetable filling in a sauce.

**Choux**  A type of pastry, whose uncooked dough is rather like a glossy batter, which is piped into small balls onto a baking sheet and baked until light and airy. They can then be filled with cream or savoury fillings.

**Filo/Phyllo**  A type of pastry that is wafer-thin. Three to four sheets are usually used at a time in baking.

**Puff pastry**  Probably the richest of pastries. When making from the beginning, it requires the lightest of handling.

**Brioche**  A traditional bread eaten in France for breakfast, usually served warm. Brioche has a rich but soft texture, made from a very light yeast dough, and is baked in the shape of a small cottage loaf. A delicious substitute for bread in bread and butter pudding.

**Caramel**  Obtained by heating sugar at a very low heat until it turns liquid and deep brown in colour. This is used in dishes such as crème caramel, which is, in turn, baked in a *bain-marie*.

**Bain marie**  A French term, meaning water bath. A shallow tin/pan, often a roasting tin, is half-filled with water; smaller dishes of food are then placed in it, allowing them to cook at lower temperatures without over-heating. This method is often used to cook custards and other egg dishes or to keep some dishes warm.

**Ramekin**  An ovenproof, earthenware dish which provides an individual serving.

**Cocotte**  Another name for a ramekin.

**Dariole**  A small narrow mould with sloping sides used for making Madeleines. Darioles can also be used for individual steamed or baked puddings and jellies.

**Crimping**  The fluted effect used for the decoration on pies or tarts, created by pinching the edge crust with the thumb and index finger of your right (or left) hand and gently pushing against them with the index finger of your other hand.

**Scalloping**  The term given to a type of pie decoration achieved by horizontal cuts made in the pastry which is then pulled back with the knife to produce a scalloped effect.

**Dusting**  To sprinkle lightly, often with flour, sugar or icing/confectioners' sugar.

**Dredging**  The sprinkling of food with a coating (generally of flour or sugar). A board may be dredged with flour before the pastry is rolled out and cakes and biscuits can be dredged with sugar or icing/confectioners' sugar after baking.

**Glacé**  A French term meaning glossy or iced. Glacé icing is a quick icing often used to decorate cakes and biscuits. It is made using icing/confectioners' sugar and warm water.

**Piping**  A way in which cakes and desserts are decorated, or the method by which choux pastry is placed onto a baking sheet. This is achieved by putting cream, icing or mixture in a nylon bag (with a nozzle/tip attached), or an improvised piping bag made from a cone of greaseproof/waxed paper, and then slowly forcing through the nozzle and piping it onto the cake or baking sheet.

**Zest**  This can refer to the outer, coloured part of an orange, lemon or lime peel, or the very thin, long pieces of that peel. The zest contains the fruit oil, which is responsible for the citrus flavour. Normally, a zester is used to create the strips, as it removes the zest without any of the bitter white pith. Zest can also be grated on a grater into very small pieces, again taking care to only remove the very outer layer.

# Useful Conversions

## Liquid Measures
Metric, Imperial and US Cups/Quarts

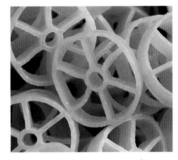

| | | | |
|---|---|---|---|
| 2.5 ml | ½ tsp | | |
| 5 ml | 1 tsp | | |
| 15 ml | 1 tbsp | | |
| 25 ml | 1 fl oz | ⅛ cup | 2 tbsp |
| 50 ml | 2 fl oz | ¼ cup | 3–4 tbsp |
| 65 ml | 2½ fl oz | ⅓ cup | 5 tbsp |
| 85 ml | 3 fl oz | ⅓ cup | 6 tbsp |
| 100 ml | 3½ fl oz | ⅓ cup | 7 tbsp |
| 125 ml | 4 fl oz | ½ cup | 8 tbsp |
| 135 ml | 4½ fl oz | ½ cup | 9 tbsp |
| 150 ml | 5 fl oz | ¼ pint | ⅔ cup |
| 175 ml | 6 fl oz | ⅓ pint | scant ¾ cup |
| 200 ml | 7 fl oz | ⅓ pint | ¾ cup |
| 250 ml | 8 fl oz | ⅜ pint | 1 cup |
| 275 ml | 9 fl oz | ½ pint | 1⅛ cups |
| 300 ml | 10 fl oz | ½ pint | 1¼ cups |
| 350 ml | 12 fl oz | ⅔ pint | 1½ cups |
| 400 ml | 14 fl oz | ⅝ pint | 1⅔ cups |
| 450 ml | 15 fl oz | ¾ pint | 1¾ cups |
| 475 ml | 16 fl oz | ⅞ pint | scant 2 cups |
| 500 ml | 18 fl oz | ⅞ pint | 2 cups |
| 600 ml | 20 fl oz | 1 pint | 2½ cups |
| 750 ml | 26 fl oz | 1¼ pints | 3¼ cups |
| 900 ml | | 1½ pints | scant 1 quart |
| 1 litre | | 2 pints | 1 quart |
| 1.25 litres | | 2¼ pints | 1¼ quarts |
| 1.3 litres | | 2⅓ pints | 1⅓ quarts |
| 1.5 litres | | 2½ pints | 1½ quarts |
| 1.6 litres | | 2¾ pints | 1¾ quarts |
| 1.7 litres | | 3 pints | 1¾ quarts |
| 1.8 litres | | 3⅛ pints | 1⅞ quarts |
| 1.9 litres | | 3⅓ pints | 2 quarts |
| 2 litres | | 3½ pints | 2 quarts |
| 2.25 litres | | 4 pints (½ gal) | 2¼ quarts |
| 2.5 litres | | 4¼ pints | 2½ quarts |
| 2.75 litres | | 5 pints | 3 quarts |
| 3 litres | | 5¼ pints | 3 quarts |
| 4.5 litres | | 8 pints (1 gal) | scant 5 quarts |

## Temperature Conversion

| | |
|---|---|
| –4°F | –20°C |
| 5°F | –15°C |
| 14°F | –10°C |
| 23°F | –5°C |
| 32°F | 0°C |
| 41°F | 5°C |
| 50°F | 10°C |
| 59°F | 15°C |
| 68°F | 20°C |
| 77°F | 25°C |
| 86°F | 30°C |
| 95°F | 35°C |
| 104°F | 40°C |
| 113°F | 45°C |
| 122°F | 50°C |
| 212°F | 100°C |

## Dry Weights
Metric/Imperial

| | |
|---|---|
| 10 g | ¼ oz |
| 15 g | ½ oz |
| 20 g | ¾ oz |
| 25 g | 1 oz |
| 40 g | 1½ oz |
| 50 g | 2 oz |
| 65 g | 2½ oz |
| 75 g | 3 oz |
| 100 g | 3½ oz |
| 125 g | 4 oz |
| 150 g | 5 oz |
| 165 g | 5½ oz |
| 175 g | 6 oz |
| 185 g | 6½ oz |
| 200 g | 7 oz |
| 225 g | 8 oz |
| 250 g | 9 oz |
| 275 g | 10 oz |
| 300 g | 11 oz |
| 325 g | 11½ oz |
| 350 g | 12 oz |
| 375 g | 13 oz |
| 400 g | 14 oz |
| 425 g | 15 oz |
| 450 g | 1 lb |

## Oven Temperatures
Bear in mind that if using a fan oven you should reduce the stated temperature by around 20°C – check the manufacturer's instructions.

| | | | |
|---|---|---|---|
| 110°C | 225°F | Gas Mark ¼ | Very slow (low) oven |
| 120/130°C | 250°F | Gas Mark ½ | Very slow oven |
| 140°C | 275°F | Gas Mark 1 | Slow oven |
| 150°C | 300°F | Gas Mark 2 | Slow oven |
| 160/170°C | 325°F | Gas Mark 3 | Moderate oven |
| 180°C | 350°F | Gas Mark 4 | Moderate oven |
| 190°C | 375°F | Gas Mark 5 | Moderately hot oven |
| 200°C | 400°F | Gas Mark 6 | Moderately hot oven |
| 220°C | 425°F | Gas Mark 7 | Hot oven |
| 230°C | 450°F | Gas Mark 8 | Hot oven |
| 240°C | 475°F | Gas Mark 9 | Very hot oven |

# Breads & Scones

**Nothing beats the smell of freshly baked bread filling the air and it is easy to make. Choose a Classic White Loaf or go for something a little more hearty with Rustic Country Bread, or branch out and try Rosemary & Olive Focaccia. Let's not forget those homely Traditional Oven Scones or, for the sweet-toothed, try Maple, Pecan & Lemon Loaf.**

# Quick Brown Bread

## Makes 2 x 450 g/1 lb loaves

**Ingredients**

700 g/1½ lb/4¾ cups strong wholemeal/whole-wheat flour

2 tsp salt

½ tsp caster/superfine sugar

1 tsp sachet easy-blend dried yeast

450 ml/¾ pint/2 cups warm water

**To finish:**

beaten egg, to glaze

1 tbsp plain/all-purpose white flour, to dust

**For onion and caraway seed rolls:**

1 small onion, peeled and finely chopped

1 tbsp olive oil

2 tbsp caraway seeds

milk, to glaze

Preheat the oven to 200°C/400°F/Gas Mark 6, 15 minutes before baking. Oil two 450 g/1 lb loaf tins/pans. Sift the wholemeal/whole-wheat flour, salt and sugar into a large bowl, adding the remaining bran in the sieve. Stir in the yeast, then make a well in the centre.

Pour the warm water into the dry ingredients and mix to form a soft dough, adding a little more water if needed. Knead on a lightly floured surface for 10 minutes until smooth and elastic. Divide in half, shape into two oblongs and place in the tins. Cover with oiled clingfilm/plastic wrap and leave in a warm place for 40 minutes, or until risen to the top of the tins.

Glaze one loaf with the beaten egg and dust the other loaf generously with the plain/all-purpose flour. Bake the loaves in the preheated oven for 35 minutes, or until well risen and lightly browned. Turn out of the tins and return to the oven for 5 minutes to crisp the sides. Cool on a wire rack.

This recipe can also be used to make onion and caraway seed rolls. For these, gently fry the onion in the oil until soft. Reserve until the onions are cool. Stir into the dry ingredients with 1 tablespoon of the caraway seeds. Make the dough as before.

Divide the dough into 16 pieces and shape into rolls. Put on two oiled baking trays, cover with oiled clingfilm and leave for 30 minutes. Glaze the rolls with milk and sprinkle with the rest of the seeds. Bake for 25–30 minutes, cool on a wire rack and serve.

## Difficulty Rating: 2 points

# Classic White Loaf

## Makes 1 x 900 g/2 lb loaf

**Ingredients**

700 g/1¹/₂ lb/6 cups strong white/bread flour

1 tbsp salt

25 g/1 oz/¹/₄ stick butter, cubed

1 tsp caster/superfine sugar

2 tsp easy-blend dried yeast

150 ml/¹/₄ pint/²/₃ cup milk

300 ml/¹/₂ pint/1¹/₄ cups warm water

1 tbsp plain/all-purpose flour, to dust

**For a light wholemeal variation:**

450 g/1 lb/4 cups strong wholemeal/whole-wheat flour

225 g/8 oz/2 cups strong white/bread flour

beaten egg, to glaze

1 tbsp kibbled wheat/wheat germ, to finish

Preheat the oven to 220°C/425°F/Gas Mark 7, 15 minutes before baking. Oil and line the base of a 900 g/2 lb loaf tin/pan with greaseproof/waxed paper. Sift the flour and salt into a large bowl. Rub in the butter, then stir in the sugar and yeast. Make a well in the centre and add the milk and the warm water. Mix to a soft dough, adding a little more water if needed. Turn out the dough and knead on a lightly floured surface for 10 minutes, or until smooth and elastic. Place the dough in an oiled bowl, cover with clingfilm/plastic wrap or a clean dishtowel and leave in a warm place to rise for 1 hour, or until doubled in size. Knead again for a minute or two to knock out the air. Shape the dough into an oblong and place in the prepared tin. Cover with oiled clingfilm and leave to rise for a further 30 minutes, or until the dough reaches the top of the tin.

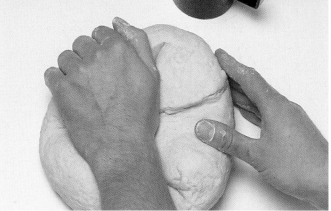

Dust the top of the loaf with flour or brush with the egg glaze and scatter with kibbled wheat/wheat germ if making the wholemeal version. Bake the loaf on the middle shelf of the preheated oven for 15 minutes. Turn down the oven to 200°C/400°F/Gas Mark 6. Bake the loaf for a further 20–25 minutes, or until well risen and hollow sounding when tapped underneath. Turn out, cool on a wire rack and serve.

## Difficulty Rating: 3 points

# Multigrain Bread

## Makes 1 large loaf

### Ingredients

350 g/12 oz/3 cups strong white/bread flour

2 tsp salt

225 g/8 oz/2 cups granary flour/granary bread flour
   or whole-wheat bread flour

125 g/4 oz/1 cup rye flour

25 g/1 oz/¼ stick butter, diced

2 tsp easy-blend dried yeast

25 g/1 oz/⅓ cup rolled oats/oatmeal

2 tbsp sunflower seeds

1 tbsp malt extract

450 ml/¾ pint/2 cups warm water

1 egg, beaten

Preheat the oven to 220°C/425°F/Gas Mark 7, 15 minutes before baking. Sift the white flour and salt into a large bowl. Stir in the granary and rye flours, then rub in the butter until the mixture resembles breadcrumbs. Stir in the yeast, oats and seeds and make a well in the centre.

Stir the malt extract into the warm water until dissolved. Add the malt water to the dry ingredients. Mix to a soft dough.

Turn the dough out onto a lightly floured surface and knead for 10 minutes until smooth and elastic. Put in an oiled bowl, cover with clingfilm/plastic wrap and leave to rise in a warm place for 1½ hours, or until doubled in size.

Turn out and knead again for a minute or two to knock out the air. Shape into an oval loaf about 30.5 cm/12 inches long and place on a well-oiled baking sheet. Cover with oiled clingfilm and leave to rise for 40 minutes, or until doubled in size.

Brush the loaf with beaten egg and bake in the preheated oven for 35–45 minutes, or until the bread is well risen, browned and sounds hollow when the base is tapped. Leave to cool on a wire rack, then serve.

## Difficulty Rating: 3 points

# Rustic Country Bread

## Makes 1 large loaf

**Ingredients**

**For the sourdough starter:**
225 g/8 oz/2 cups strong white/bread flour
2 tsp easy-blend dried yeast
300 ml/½ pint/1¼ cups warm water

**For the bread dough:**
350 g/12 oz/3 cups strong white/bread flour
3 tbsp rye flour
1½ tsp salt
½ tsp caster/superfine sugar
1 tsp dried yeast
1 tsp sunflower/corn oil
175 ml/6 fl oz/scant ¾ cup warm water

**To finish:**
2 tsp plain/all-purpose flour; 2 tsp rye flour

Preheat the oven to 220°C/425°F/Gas Mark 7, 15 minutes before baking. For the starter, sift the flour into a bowl. Stir in the yeast and make a well in the centre. Pour in the warm water and mix with a fork. Transfer to a saucepan, cover with a clean dishtowel and leave for 2–3 days at room temperature. Stir the mixture and spray with a little water twice a day.

For the dough, mix the dry ingredients in a bowl. Add 250 ml/8 fl oz/1 cup of the starter, the oil and the warm water. Mix to a soft dough. Knead on a lightly floured surface for 10 minutes until smooth and elastic. Put in an oiled bowl, cover and leave to rise in a warm place for about 1½ hours, or until doubled in size. Turn the dough out and knead for a minute or two. Shape into a round loaf. Place on an oiled baking sheet. Cover with oiled clingfilm/plastic wrap and leave to rise for 1 hour, or until doubled in size. Dust the loaf with flour. With a sharp knife, make slashes across the top. Slash across the loaf in the opposite direction to make a grid pattern. Bake in the oven for 40–45 minutes, or until golden brown and hollow sounding when tapped underneath. Cool on a wire rack and serve.

**Difficulty Rating: 4 points**

# Irish Soda Bread

## Makes 1 loaf

### Ingredients

400 g/14 oz/3¹⁄₂ cups plain/all-purpose white flour,
  plus 1 tbsp for dusting

1 tsp salt

2 tsp bicarbonate of soda/baking soda

15 g/¹⁄₂ oz/1 tbsp butter

50 g/2 oz/¹⁄₃ cup coarse oatmeal/quick oats

1 tsp clear honey

300 ml/¹⁄₂ pint/1¹⁄₄ cups buttermilk

2 tbsp milk

**For a wholemeal variation:**

400 g/14 oz/3¹⁄₂ cups plain wholemeal/whole-wheat flour,
  plus 1 tbsp for dusting

1 tbsp milk

## Difficulty Rating: 2 points

Preheat the oven to 200°C/400°F/Gas Mark 6, 15 minutes before baking. Sift the flour, salt and bicarbonate of soda/baking soda into a large bowl. Rub in the butter until the mixture resembles fine breadcrumbs. Stir in the oatmeal/quick oats and make a well in the centre.

Mix the honey, buttermilk and milk together and add to the dry ingredients. Mix to a soft dough.

Knead the dough on a lightly floured surface for 2–3 minutes until the dough is smooth. Shape into a 20.5 cm/8 inch round and place on an oiled baking sheet. Thickly dust the top of the bread with flour and, using a sharp knife, cut a deep cross on top, going about halfway through the loaf.

Bake in the preheated oven on the middle shelf for 30–35 minutes, or until the bread is slightly risen, golden and sounds hollow when tapped underneath. Cool on a wire rack. Eat on the day of making.

For a wholemeal soda bread, use all the wholemeal/whole-wheat flour instead of the white flour and add an extra tablespoon of milk when mixing together. Dust the top with wholemeal flour and bake as before.

# Soft Dinner Rolls

## Makes 16

**Ingredients**

50 g/2 oz/½ stick butter

1 tbsp caster/superfine sugar

225 ml/8 fl oz/1 cup milk

550 g/1¼ lb/4⅓ cups strong white/bread flour

1½ tsp salt

2 tsp easy-blend dried yeast

2 medium/large eggs, beaten

**To glaze and finish:**

2 tbsp milk

1 tsp sea salt

2 tsp poppy seeds

Preheat the oven to 220°C/425°F/Gas Mark 7, 15 minutes before baking. Gently heat the butter, sugar and milk in a saucepan until the butter has melted and the sugar has dissolved. Cool until tepid. Sift the flour and salt into a bowl, stir in the yeast and make a well in the centre. Reserve 1 tablespoon of the beaten eggs. Add the rest to the dry ingredients with the milk mixture. Mix to form a soft dough.

Knead the dough on a lightly floured surface for 10 minutes until smooth and elastic. Put in an oiled bowl, cover with clingfilm/plastic wrap and leave in a warm place to rise for 1 hour, or until doubled in size. Knead again for a minute or two, then divide into 16 pieces. Shape into balls, braids, coils, cottage buns, or whatever shape you want. Place on two oiled baking sheets, cover with oiled clingfilm and leave to rise for 30 minutes, or until doubled in size.

Mix the reserved beaten egg with the milk and brush over the rolls. Sprinkle some with sea salt, others with poppy seeds and leave some plain. Bake in the preheated oven for about 20 minutes, or until golden and hollow sounding when tapped underneath. Transfer to a wire rack. Cover with a clean dishtowel while cooling to keep the rolls soft, and serve.

## Difficulty Rating: 3 points

# Bagels

## Serves 4

### Ingredients

450 g/1 lb/3½ cups strong plain/bread flour
1½ tsp salt
2 tsp easy-blend dried yeast
2 medium/large eggs
1 tsp clear honey
2 tbsp sunflower/corn oil
250 ml/8 fl oz tepid water

**To finish:**
1 tbsp caster/superfine sugar
beaten egg, to glaze
2 tsp poppy seeds
½ small onion, peeled and finely chopped
2 tsp sunflower/corn oil

Preheat the oven to 200°C/400°F/Gas Mark 6, 15 minutes before baking. Sift the flour and salt into a large bowl. Stir in the yeast, then make a well in the centre. Whisk the eggs together with the honey and oil. Add to the dry ingredients with the tepid water and mix to form a soft dough. Knead the dough on a lightly floured surface for 10 minutes until smooth and elastic. Put in a bowl, cover with clingfilm/plastic wrap and leave in a warm place to rise for 45 minutes, or until doubled in size. Briefly knead the dough again to knock out the air. Divide into 12 pieces, form each into a 20.5 cm/8 inch roll, curve into a ring and pinch the edges to seal. Put the rings on an oiled baking sheet, cover with oiled clingfilm and leave to rise in a warm place for 20 minutes, or until risen and puffy.

Add the caster/superfine sugar to a large saucepan of water. Bring to the boil, then drop in the bagels, one at a time, and poach for 15 seconds. Lift out with a slotted spoon and return to the baking tray. Brush with beaten egg and sprinkle one–third with poppy seeds. Mix together the onion and oil and sprinkle over another third of the bagels. Leave the remaining third plain. Bake in the preheated oven for 12–15 minutes, or until golden brown. Transfer to a wire rack and serve when cool.

## Difficulty Rating: 4 points

# Sweet Potato Baps

## Makes 16

### Ingredients

225 g/8 oz/1¼ cups sweet potato, peeled and cut into chunks
15 g/½ oz/1 tbsp butter
freshly grated nutmeg
about 200 ml/7 fl oz/¾ cup milk
450 g/1 lb/4 cups strong white/bread flour
2 tsp salt
1 tsp easy-blend yeast
1 egg, beaten

### To finish:
beaten egg, to glaze
1 tbsp rolled oats

Preheat the oven to 200°C/400°F/Gas Mark 6, 15 minutes before baking. Cook the sweet potato in a saucepan of boiling water for 12–15 minutes, or until tender. Drain well and mash with the butter and nutmeg. Stir in the milk, then leave until barely warm.

Sift the flour and salt into a large bowl. Stir in the yeast. Make a well in the centre, then add the mashed sweet potato and beaten egg and mix to a soft dough. Add a little more milk if needed, depending on the moisture in the sweet potato.

Turn out the dough onto a lightly floured surface and knead for about 10 minutes, or until smooth and elastic. Place in a lightly oiled bowl, cover with clingfilm/plastic wrap and leave in a warm place to rise for about 1 hour, or until the dough doubles in size. Turn out the dough and knead for a minute or two until smooth. Divide into 16 pieces, shape into rolls and place on a large oiled baking sheet. Cover with oiled clingfilm and leave to rise for 15 minutes.

Brush the rolls with beaten egg, sprinkle half with rolled oats and leave the rest plain. Bake in the preheated oven for 12–15 minutes, or until they are well risen, lightly browned and sound hollow when the bases are tapped. Transfer to a wire rack and cover immediately with a dishtowel to keep the crusts soft.

## Difficulty Rating: 3 points

# Basic Focaccia with Antipasti

## Serves 4

### Ingredients

**For the antipasti:**

3 fresh figs, quartered

125 g/4 oz/1 cup green beans, cooked and halved

1 small head of radicchio, rinsed and shredded

125 g/4 oz/1 cup large prawns/shrimp, peeled and cooked

125 g/4 oz can sardines, drained

25 g/1 oz/¼ cup pitted black olives

25 g/1 oz/¼ cup stuffed green olives

125 g/4 oz mozzarella cheese, sliced (about 4 slices)

50 g/2 oz Italian salami sausage, thinly sliced (about 8 slices)

3 tbsp olive oil

**For the focaccia:**

275 g/10 oz/2 cups strong white/bread flour

pinch sugar

175 g/6 oz/⁴/₅ cup fine semolina

1 tsp salt

3 tsp easy-blend quick-acting yeast or 15 g/½ oz/1 cake fresh yeast

300 ml/½ pint/1¼ cups warm water

little extra olive oil, for brushing

1 tbsp coarse salt crystals

Preheat oven to 220°C/425°F/Gas Mark 7, 15 minutes before baking. Arrange the fresh fruit, vegetables, prawns/shrimp, sardines, olives, cheese and meat on a large serving platter. Drizzle over 1 tablespoon of the olive oil, then cover and chill in the refrigerator while making the bread.

If using dried yeast, sift the flour, sugar, semolina and salt into a large mixing bowl, then sprinkle in the yeast. Make a well in the centre and add the remaining 2 tablespoons of olive oil. Add the warm water, a little at a time, and mix together until a smooth, pliable dough is formed. If using fresh yeast, cream the yeast with the sugar, then gradually beat in half the warm water. Leave in a warm place until frothy, then proceed as for dried yeast. Place onto a lightly floured board and knead until smooth and elastic.

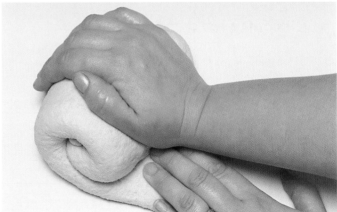

Place the dough in a lightly greased bowl, cover and leave in a warm place for 45 minutes.

Knead again and flatten the dough into a large, flat oval shape about 1 cm/½ inch thick. Place on a lightly oiled baking sheet. Prick the surface with the end of a wooden spoon and brush with olive oil. Sprinkle on the coarse salt and bake in the preheated oven for 25 minutes, or until golden. Serve the bread with the prepared platter of food.

## Difficulty Rating: 3 points

# Rosemary & Olive Focaccia

## Makes 2 loaves

### Ingredients

700 g/1½ lb/5½ cups strong white/bread flour

pinch salt

pinch caster/superfine sugar

7 g/¼ oz sachet easy-blend dried yeast

2 tsp freshly chopped rosemary

450 ml/¾ pint/1¾ cups warm water

3 tbsp olive oil

75 g/3 oz/½ cup pitted black olives, roughly chopped

rosemary sprigs, to garnish

To finish:

3 tbsp olive oil

coarse sea salt

freshly ground black pepper

## Difficulty Rating: 3 points

Preheat the oven to 200°C/400°F/Gas Mark 6, 15 minutes before baking. Sift the flour, salt and sugar into a large bowl. Stir in the yeast and rosemary. Make a well in the centre.

Pour in the warm water and the oil and mix to a soft dough. Turn out onto a lightly floured surface and knead for about 10 minutes until smooth and elastic.

Pat the olives dry on kitchen paper, then gently knead into the dough. Put in an oiled bowl, cover with clingfilm/plastic wrap and leave to rise in a warm place for 1½ hours, or until it has doubled in size.

Turn out the dough and knead again for a minute or two. Divide in half and roll out each piece to a 25.5 cm/10 inch circle. Transfer to oiled baking sheets, cover with oiled clingfilm and leave to rise for 30 minutes.

Using the fingertips, make deep dimples all over the dough. Drizzle with the oil and sprinkle with sea salt. Bake in the preheated oven for 20–25 minutes, or until risen and golden. Cool on a wire rack and garnish with sprigs of rosemary. Grind over a little black pepper before serving.

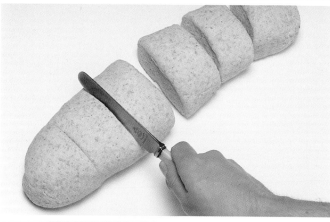

# Daktyla–style Bread

## Makes 1 loaf

**Ingredients**

350 g/12 oz/3 cups strong white/bread flour
125 g/4 oz/1 cup wholemeal/whole-wheat flour
1 tsp salt
50 g/2 oz/1 cup fine cornmeal
2 tsp easy-blend dried yeast
2 tsp clear honey
1 tbsp olive oil
4 tbsp milk
250 ml/8 fl oz/1 cup plus 1 tbsp water

**To glaze and finish:**
4 tbsp milk
4 tbsp sesame seeds

Preheat the oven to 220°C/425°F/Gas Mark 7, 15 minutes before baking. Sift the flours and salt into a large bowl, adding the bran left in the sieve. Stir in the cornmeal and yeast. Make a well in the centre.

Put the honey, oil, milk and water in a saucepan and heat gently until tepid. Add to the dry ingredients and mix to a soft dough, adding a little more water if needed. Knead the dough on a lightly floured surface for 10 minutes until smooth and elastic. Put in an oiled bowl, cover with clingfilm/plastic wrap and leave to rise in a warm place for 1½ hours, or until it has doubled in size.

Turn the dough out and knead for a minute or two. Shape into a long oval about 25.5 cm/10 inches long. Cut the oval into six equal pieces. Shape each piece into an oblong, then arrange in a row on an oiled baking sheet so that all the pieces of dough are touching. Cover with oiled clingfilm and leave for 45 minutes, or until doubled in size.

Brush the bread with milk, then scatter with sesame seeds. Bake the bread in the preheated oven for 40–45 minutes, or until golden brown and hollow sounding when tapped underneath. Cool on a wire rack and serve.

## Difficulty Rating: 3 points

# Spicy Filled Naan Bread

## Makes 6

### Ingredients

400 g/14 oz/3½ cups strong white/bread flour

1 tsp salt

1 tsp easy-blend dried yeast

1 tbsp ghee or melted unsalted butter

1 tsp clear honey

200 ml/7 fl oz/¾ cup warm water

### For the filling:

25 g/1 oz/2 tbsp ghee or unsalted butter

1 small onion, peeled and finely chopped

1 garlic clove, peeled and crushed

1 tsp ground coriander

1 tsp ground cumin

2 tsp grated fresh root ginger

pinch chilli powder

pinch ground cinnamon

salt and freshly ground black pepper

Preheat the oven to 230°C/450°F/Gas Mark 8, 15 minutes before baking and place a large baking sheet in to heat up. Sift the flour and salt into a large bowl. Stir in the yeast and make a well in the centre. Add the ghee or melted butter, honey and warm water and mix to a soft dough. Knead the dough on a lightly floured surface until smooth and elastic. Put in a lightly oiled bowl, cover with clingfilm/plastic wrap and leave to rise for 1 hour, or until doubled in size.

For the filling, melt the ghee or butter in a frying pan and gently cook the onion for about 5 minutes. Stir in the garlic and spices and season to taste with salt and pepper. Cook for a further 6–7 minutes until soft. Remove from the heat, stir in 1 tablespoon water and leave to cool.

Briefly knead the dough, then divide into six pieces. Roll out each piece of dough to 12.5 cm/5 inch rounds. Spoon the filling on to one half of each round. Fold over and press the edges together to seal. Re-roll to shape into flat ovals, about 16 cm/6½ inches long. Cover with oiled clingfilm and leave to rise for about 15 minutes.

Transfer the breads to the hot baking sheet and cook in the preheated oven for 10–12 minutes, until puffed up and lightly browned. Serve hot.

## Difficulty Rating: 3 points

# Bacon & Tomato Breakfast Twist

## Serves 8

### Ingredients

450 g/1 lb/3½ cups strong plain/bread flour
½ tsp salt
7 g/¼ oz sachet easy-blend dried yeast
300 ml/½ pint/1¼ cups warm milk
15 g/½ oz butter, melted

### For the filling:
225 g/8 oz back bacon, derinded
1 tbsp butter, melted
175 g/6 oz/1 cup ripe tomatoes, peeled, deseeded and chopped
freshly ground black pepper

### To finish:
beaten egg, to glaze
2 tsp medium-ground oatmeal

Preheat the oven to 200°C/400°F/Gas Mark 6, 15 minutes before baking. Sift the flour and salt into a large bowl. Stir in the yeast and make a well in the centre. Pour in the milk and butter and mix to a soft dough.

Knead on a lightly floured surface for 10 minutes until smooth and elastic. Put in an oiled bowl, cover with clingfilm/plastic wrap and leave to rise in a warm place for 1 hour, or until doubled in size.

Cook the bacon under a hot grill for 5–6 minutes, turning once, until crisp. Leave to cool, then chop roughly.

Knead the dough again for a minute or two. Roll it out to a 25.5 x 33 cm/10 x 13 inch rectangle. Cut in half lengthways. Lightly brush with butter, then scatter with the bacon, tomatoes and black pepper, leaving a 1 cm/½ inch margin around the edges.

Brush the edges of the dough with beaten egg, then roll up each rectangle lengthways. Place the two rolls side by side and twist together, pinching the ends to seal. Transfer to an oiled

baking sheet and loosely cover with oiled clingfilm. Leave to rise in a warm place for 30 minutes.

Brush with the beaten egg and sprinkle with the oatmeal. Bake in the preheated oven for about 30 minutes, or until golden brown and hollow sounding when tapped on the base. Serve the bread warm in thick slices.

## Difficulty Rating: 4 points

# Fruited Brioche Buns

## Makes 12

**Ingredients**

225 g/8 oz/1¾ cups strong white/bread flour

pinch salt

1 tbsp caster/superfine sugar

7 g/¼ oz sachet easy-blend dried yeast

2 large/extra-large eggs, beaten

50 g/2 oz/¼ cup butter, melted

beaten egg, to glaze

**For the filling:**

40 g/1½ oz/⅓ cup blanched almonds, chopped

50 g/2 oz/⅓ cup luxury mixed dried fruit

1 tsp soft light brown sugar

2 tsp orange liqueur or brandy

Preheat the oven to 220°C/425°F/Gas Mark 7. 15 minutes before baking. Sift the flour and salt into a bowl. Stir in the sugar and yeast. Make a well in the centre. Add the eggs, butter and 2 tablespoons warm water and mix to a soft dough. Knead the dough on a lightly floured surface for 5 minutes until smooth and elastic. Put in an oiled bowl, cover with clingfilm/plastic wrap and leave to rise in a warm place for 1 hour, or until it has doubled in size.

Mix the ingredients for the filling together, cover the bowl and leave to soak while the dough is rising.

Re-knead the dough for a minute or two, then divide into 12 pieces. Taking one at a time, flatten three quarters of each piece into a 6.5 cm/2½ inch round. Spoon a little filling in the centre, then pinch the edges together to enclose. Put seam-side down into a well-greased fluted 12-hole muffin tin/pan. Shape the smaller piece of dough into a round and place on top of the larger one.

Push a finger or floured wooden spoon handle through the middle of the top one and into the bottom one to join them together. Repeat with the remaining balls of dough. Cover the brioches with oiled clingfilm and leave for about 20 minutes, or until well risen.

Brush the brioches with beaten egg and bake in the preheated oven for 10–12 minutes, or until golden. Cool on a wire rack and serve.

## Difficulty Rating: 4 points

# Traditional Oven Scones

## Makes 8

### Ingredients

225 g/8 oz/2 cups self-raising flour

1 tsp baking powder

pinch salt

40 g/1½ oz/3 tbsp butter, cubed

1 tbsp caster/superfine sugar

150 ml/¼ pint/⅔ cup milk, plus 1 tbsp
   for brushing

1 tbsp plain/all-purpose flour, to dust

**For a lemon and sultana scone variation:**

50 g/2 oz/⅓ cup sultanas/golden raisins

finely grated zest of ½ lemon

beaten egg, to glaze

## Difficulty Rating: 2 points

Preheat the oven to 220°C/425°F/Gas Mark 7, 15 minutes before baking. Sift the self-raising flour, baking powder and salt into a large bowl. Rub in the butter until the mixture resembles fine breadcrumbs. Stir in the sugar and mix in enough milk to give a fairly soft dough.

Knead the dough on a lightly floured surface for a few seconds until smooth. Roll out until 2 cm/¾ inch thick and stamp out 6.5 cm/2½ inch rounds with a floured plain cutter.

Place on an oiled baking sheet and brush the tops with milk – do not brush it over the sides or the scones will not rise properly. Dust with a little plain/all-purpose flour.

Bake in the preheated oven for 12–15 minutes, or until well risen and golden brown. Transfer to a wire rack and serve warm or leave to cool completely. The scones are best eaten on the day of baking, but may be kept in an airtight tin for up to two days.

For lemon and sultana scones, stir in the sultanas/golden raisins and lemon zest with the sugar. Roll out until 2 cm/¾ inch thick and cut into eight fingers, 10 x 2.5 cm/4 x 1 inch in size. Bake the scones as before.

# Cheese-crusted Potato Scones

## Serves 4

### Ingredients

200 g/7 oz/1¾ cups self-raising flour

3 tbsp wholemeal/whole-wheat flour

½ tsp salt

1½ tsp baking powder

25 g/1 oz/¼ stick butter, cubed

5 tbsp milk

175 g/6 oz/¼ cup cold mashed potato

freshly ground black pepper

2 tbsp milk

40 g/1½ oz/6 tbsp mature Cheddar cheese, finely grated

paprika, to dust

basil sprig, to garnish

## Difficulty Rating: 3 points

Preheat the oven to 220°C/425°F/Gas Mark 7, 15 minutes before baking. Sift the flours, salt and baking powder into a large bowl. Rub in the butter until the mixture resembles fine breadcrumbs. Stir 4 tablespoons of the milk into the mashed potato and season with black pepper. Add the dry ingredients to the potato mixture, mixing together with a fork and adding the remaining 1 tablespoon of milk if needed.

Knead the dough on a lightly floured surface for a few seconds until smooth. Roll out to a 15 cm/6 inch round and transfer to an oiled baking sheet.

Mark the scone round into six wedges, cutting about halfway through with a small sharp knife. Brush with milk, then sprinkle with the cheese and a faint dusting of paprika.

Bake on the middle shelf of the preheated oven for 15 minutes, or until well risen and golden brown. Transfer to a wire rack and leave to cool for 5 minutes before breaking into wedges.

Serve warm or leave to cool completely. Once cool, store the scones in an airtight tin. Garnish with a basil sprig and serve split and buttered.

# Fruity Apple Tea Bread

## Cuts into 12 slices

### Ingredients

125 g/4 oz/1 stick plus 1 tbsp butter
125 g/4 oz/²/₃ cup soft light brown sugar
275 g/10 oz/2 cups sultanas/golden raisins
150 ml/¹/₄ pint/²/₃ cup apple juice
1 eating apple, peeled, cored and chopped
2 eggs, beaten
275 g/10 oz/2¹/₂ cups plain/all-purpose flour
¹/₂ tsp ground cinnamon
¹/₂ tsp ground ginger
2 tsp bicarbonate of soda/baking soda
butter curls, to serve

### To decorate:
1 eating apple, cored, sliced
1 tsp lemon juice
1 tbsp golden syrup or light corn syrup, warmed

Preheat the oven to 180°C/350°F/Gas Mark 4. Oil and line the base of a 900 g/2 lb loaf tin/pan with nonstick baking parchment.

Put the butter, sugar, sultanas/golden raisins and apple juice in a small saucepan. Heat gently, stirring occasionally, until the butter has melted. Tip into a bowl and leave to cool.

Stir in the chopped apple and beaten eggs. Sift the flour, spices and bicarbonate of soda/baking soda over the apple mixture. Stir into the sultana mixture, spoon into the prepared loaf tin and smooth the top level with the back of a spoon. Toss the apple slices in lemon juice and arrange on top.

Bake in the preheated oven for 50 minutes, or until a skewer inserted into the centre comes out clean. Cover with kitchen foil to prevent the top from browning too much. Leave in the tin for 10 minutes before turning out onto a wire rack to cool.

Brush the top with golden/corn syrup and leave to cool. Remove the lining paper, cut into thick slices and serve with curls of butter.

## Difficulty Rating: 2 points

# Maple, Pecan & Lemon Loaf

## Cuts into 12 slices

### Ingredients

350 g/12 oz/2³⁄₄ cups plain/all-purpose flour

1 tsp baking powder

175 g/6 oz/³⁄₄ cup butter, cubed

75 g/3 oz/¹⁄₃ cup caster/superfine sugar

125 g/4 oz/1¹⁄₄ cups pecan nuts, roughly chopped

3 medium/large eggs

1 tbsp milk

finely grated zest of 1 lemon

5 tbsp maple syrup

**For the icing:**

75 g/3 oz/³⁄₄ cup icing/confectioners' sugar

1 tbsp lemon juice

25 g/1 oz/¹⁄₄ cup pecans, roughly chopped

Preheat the oven to 170°C/325°F/Gas Mark 3, 10 minutes before baking. Lightly oil and line the base of a 900 g/2 lb loaf tin/pan with nonstick baking parchment.

Sift the flour and baking powder into a large bowl. Rub in the butter until the mixture resembles fine breadcrumbs. Stir in the caster/superfine sugar and pecan nuts.

Beat the eggs together with the milk and lemon zest. Stir in the maple syrup. Add to the dry ingredients and gently stir in until mixed thoroughly to make a soft dropping consistency.

Spoon the mixture into the prepared tin and level the top with the back of a spoon. Bake on the middle shelf of the preheated oven for 50–60 minutes, or until the cake is well risen and lightly browned. If a skewer inserted into the centre comes out clean, then the cake is ready. Leave the cake in the tin for about 10 minutes, then turn out and leave to cool on a wire rack. Carefully remove the lining paper.

Sift the icing/confectioners' sugar into a small bowl and stir in the lemon juice to make a smooth icing. Drizzle the icing over the top of the loaf, then scatter with the chopped pecans. Leave to set, slice thickly and serve.

## Difficulty Rating: 2 points

# Moist Mincemeat Tea Loaf

## Cuts into 10 slices

**Ingredients**

225 g/8 oz/2 cups self-raising flour

½ tsp ground mixed spice

125 g/4 oz/1 stick plus 1 tbsp cold butter, cubed

75 g/3 oz/¾ cup flaked almonds

25 g/1 oz/¼ cup glacé/candied cherries, rinsed,
   dried and quartered

75 g/3 oz/⅓ cup light muscovado/golden brown sugar

2 eggs

250 g/9 oz/2 cups prepared mincemeat/mince pie filling

1 tsp lemon zest

2 tsp brandy or milk

Preheat the oven to 180°C/350°F/Gas Mark 4, 10 minutes before cooking. Oil and line the base of a 900 g/2 lb loaf tin/pan with nonstick baking parchment.

Sift the flour and mixed spice into a large bowl. Add the butter and rub in until the mixture resembles breadcrumbs. Reserve 2 tablespoons of the flaked almonds and stir in the rest with the glacé/candied cherries and sugar.

Lightly whisk the eggs, then stir in the mincemeat/mince pie filling, lemon zest and brandy or milk. Make a well in the centre of the dry ingredients, add the egg mixture and fold together until blended. Spoon into the prepared loaf tin, smooth the top with the back of a spoon, then sprinkle over the reserved flaked almonds. Bake on the middle shelf of the preheated oven for 30 minutes. Cover with kitchen foil to prevent the almonds browning too much. Bake for a further 30 minutes, or until well risen and a skewer inserted into the centre comes out clean.

Leave the tea loaf in the tin for 10 minutes before removing and cooling on a wire rack. Remove the lining paper, slice thickly and serve.

## Difficulty Rating: 2 points

# Marbled Chocolate & Orange Loaf

## Cuts into 6 slices

**Ingredients**

50 g/2 oz plain dark chocolate, broken into squares,
   or ⅓ cup semisweet chocolate chips
125 g/4 oz/1 stick plus 1 tbsp butter, softened
125 g/4 oz/⅔ cup caster/superfine sugar
zest of 1 orange
2 eggs, beaten
125 g/4 oz/1 cup self-raising flour
2 tsp orange juice
1 tbsp cocoa powder (unsweetened), sifted

**To finish:**
1 tbsp icing/confectioners' sugar
1 tsp cocoa powder (unsweetened)

Preheat the oven to 180°C/350°F/Gas Mark 4. Lightly oil a 450 g/1 lb loaf tin/pan and line the base with a layer of nonstick baking parchment. Put the chocolate in a bowl over a saucepan of very hot water. Stir occasionally until melted. Remove and leave until just cool, but not starting to reset.

Meanwhile, cream together the butter, sugar and orange zest until pale and fluffy. Gradually add the beaten eggs, beating well after each addition. Sift in the flour, add the orange juice and fold with a metal spoon or rubber spatula. Divide the mixture in half into two separate bowls. Gently fold the cocoa powder and chocolate into one half of the mixture. Drop tablespoonfuls of each cake mixture into the prepared tin, alternating between the orange and chocolate mixtures. Briefly swirl the colours together with a knife to give a marbled effect. Bake in the preheated oven for 40 minutes, or until firm and a fine skewer inserted into the centre comes out clean. Leave in the tin for 5 minutes, then turn out and cool on a wire rack. Carefully remove the lining paper. Dust the cake with the icing/confectioners' sugar and then with the cocoa powder. Cut into thick slices and serve.

## Difficulty Rating: 2 points

# Cakes, Brownies & Buns

Homemade cake is a real treat, but with these easy-to-follow recipes it can be a more frequent one! Familiar classics are included, such as Fruit Cake and Carrot Cake, while some have a twist, such as Victoria Sponge with Mango & Mascarpone. Sink your teeth into the Chunky Chocolate Muffins, indulge in Triple Chocolate Brownies or tantalize the taste buds with Lemon & Ginger Buns.

# Chestnut Cake

## Serves 8–10

**Ingredients**

175 g/6 oz/1½ sticks butter, softened
175 g/6 oz/¾ cup caster/superfine sugar
250 g/9 oz can sweetened chestnut purée
3 eggs, lightly beaten
175 g/6 oz/1½ cups plain/all-purpose flour
1 tsp baking powder
pinch ground cloves
1 tsp fennel seeds, crushed
75 g/3 oz/½ cup raisins
50 g/2 oz/½ cup pine nuts, toasted
125 g/4 oz/1 cup icing/confectioners' sugar
5 tbsp lemon juice
strips pared lemon rind, to decorate

Preheat the oven to 150°C/300°F/Gas Mark 2. Oil and line a 23 cm/9 inch springform tin/pan. Beat together the butter and sugar until light and fluffy. Add the chestnut purée and beat. Gradually add the eggs, beating after each addition. Sift in the flour with the baking powder and cloves. Add the fennel seeds and beat. The mixture should drop easily from a wooden spoon when tapped against the side of the bowl. If not, add a little milk.

Beat in the raisins and pine nuts. Spoon the mixture into the prepared tin and smooth the top. Put in the centre of the preheated oven and bake for 55–60 minutes, or until a skewer inserted in the centre of the cake comes out clean. Remove from the oven and leave in the tin.

Meanwhile, mix together the icing/confectioners' sugar and lemon juice in a small saucepan until smooth. Heat gently until hot, but not boiling.

Using a cocktail stick/toothpick or skewer, poke holes into the cake all over. Pour the hot syrup evenly over the cake and leave to soak into the cake. Decorate with pared strips of lemon rind and serve.

## Difficulty Rating: 1 point

# Chocolate & Coconut Cake

## Cuts into 8 slices

### Ingredients

125 g/4 oz/5 squares dark/bittersweet chocolate, roughly chopped

175 g/6 oz/1½ sticks butter or margarine

175 g/6 oz/1 scant cup caster/superfine sugar

3 medium/large eggs, beaten

175 g/6 oz/1⅓ cups self-raising flour

1 tbsp cocoa powder (unsweetened)

50 g/2 oz/⅔ cup desiccated/shredded coconut

### For the icing:

125 g/4 oz/1 stick plus 1 tbsp butter or margarine

2 tbsp creamed coconut, grated (or ½ tbsp coconut cream)

225 g/8 oz/2¼ cups icing/confectioners' sugar

25 g/1 oz/⅓ cup desiccated/shredded coconut,
   lightly toasted

Preheat the oven to 180°C/350°F/Gas Mark 4, 10 minutes before baking. Melt the chocolate in a small bowl placed over a saucepan of gently simmering water, ensuring that the base of the bowl does not touch the water. When the chocolate has melted, stir until smooth and allow to cool.

Lightly oil and line the bases of two 18 cm/7 inch sandwich tins/layer–cake pans with greaseproof or baking paper. In a large bowl, beat the butter or margarine and sugar together with a wooden spoon until light and creamy. Beat in the eggs a little at a time, then stir in the melted chocolate. Sift the flour and cocoa powder together and gently fold into the chocolate mixture with a metal spoon or rubber spatula. Add the desiccated/shredded coconut and mix lightly. Divide between the two prepared tins and smooth the tops. Bake in the preheated oven for 25–30 minutes, or until a skewer comes out clean when inserted into the centre of the cake. Allow to cool in the tin for 5 minutes, then turn out, discard the lining paper and leave on a wire rack until cold.

Beat together the butter or margarine and creamed coconut until light. Add the icing/confectioners' sugar and mix well.

Spread half of the icing on one cake and press the cakes together. Spread the remaining icing over the top, sprinkle with the coconut and serve.

## Difficulty Rating: 1 point

# Citrus Cake

## Cuts into 6 slices

### Ingredients

175 g/6 oz/1 scant cup golden caster/superfine sugar

175 g/6 oz/1½ sticks butter or margarine

3 medium/large eggs

2 tbsp orange juice

175 g/6 oz/1⅓ cups self-raising flour

finely grated zest of 2 oranges

5 tbsp lemon curd

125 g/4 oz icing/confectioners' sugar

finely grated zest of 1 lemon

1 tbsp freshly squeezed lemon juice

## Difficulty Rating: 2 points

Preheat the oven to 190°C/375°F/Gas Mark 5, 10 minutes before baking. Lightly oil and line the base of a round 20.5 cm/8 inch deep cake tin/pan with baking parchment.

In a large bowl, cream the sugar and butter or margarine together until light and fluffy. Whisk the eggs together and beat into the creamed mixture a little at a time. Beat in the orange juice with 1 tablespoon of the flour.

Sift the remaining flour onto a large plate several times, then, with a metal spoon or rubber spatula, fold into the creamed mixture. Spoon into the prepared cake tin. Stir the finely grated orange zest into the lemon curd and dot randomly across the top of the mixture.

Using a fine skewer, swirl the lemon curd through the cake mixture. Bake in the preheated oven for 35 minutes, or until risen and golden. Allow to cool for 5 minutes in the tin, then turn out carefully onto a wire rack.

Sift the icing/confectioners' sugar into a bowl, add the grated lemon zest and juice and stir well to mix. When the cake is cold, cover the top with the icing and serve.

# Victoria Sponge with Mango & Mascarpone

## Cuts into 8 slices

### Ingredients

175 g/6 oz/³/₄ cup caster/superfine sugar, plus extra for dusting

175 g/6 oz/1¹/₂ cups self-raising flour, plus extra for dusting

175 g/6 oz/1¹/₂ sticks butter or margarine

3 large/extra-large eggs

1 tsp vanilla extract

25 g/1 oz/¹/₄ cup icing/confectioners' sugar

250 g/9 oz tub mascarpone cheese

1 large ripe mango, peeled

Preheat the oven to 190°C/375°F/Gas Mark 5, 10 minutes before baking. Lightly oil two 18 cm/7 inch sandwich tins/cake pans. Lightly dust with caster/superfine sugar and flour, tapping the tins to remove any excess.

In a large bowl, cream the butter or margarine and sugar together with a wooden spoon until light and creamy. In another bowl mix the eggs and vanilla extract together. Sift the flour several times onto a plate. Beat a little egg into the butter and sugar, then a little flour, and beat well.

Continue adding the flour and eggs alternately, beating between each addition, until the mixture is well mixed and smooth. Divide the mixture between the two prepared cake tins, level the surface, then, using the back of a large spoon, make a slight dip in the centre of each cake. Bake in the preheated oven for 25–30 minutes until the centre of the cake springs back when gently pressed with a clean finger. Turn out onto a wire rack and leave the cakes until cold.

Beat the icing/confectioners' sugar and mascarpone cheese together, then chop the mango into small cubes. Use half the mascarpone and mango to sandwich the cakes together. Spread the rest of the mascarpone on top, decorate with the remaining mango and serve. Otherwise cover lightly and store in the refrigerator. Use within 3–4 days.

## Difficulty Rating: 3 points

# Whisked Sponge Cake

## Cuts into 6 slices

**Ingredients**

125 g/4 oz/1 cup plain/all-purpose flour, plus 1 tsp

175 g/6 oz/1 scant cup caster/superfine sugar, plus 1 tsp

3 medium/large eggs

1 tsp vanilla extract

4 tbsp raspberry jam/jelly

50 g/2 oz (about 25) fresh raspberries, crushed

icing/confectioners' sugar, to dredge

Preheat the oven to 200°C/400°F/Gas Mark 6, 15 minutes before baking. Mix 1 teaspoon of the flour and 1 teaspoon of the sugar together. Lightly oil two 18 cm/7 inch sandwich tins/layer–cake pans and dust lightly with the sugar and flour.

Place the eggs in a large heatproof bowl. Add the sugar, then place over a saucepan of gently simmering water, ensuring that the base of the bowl does not touch the hot water. Using an electric whisk, beat the sugar and eggs until they become light and fluffy. (The whisk should leave a trail in the mixture when it is lifted out.)

Remove the bowl from the saucepan of water, add the vanilla extract and continue beating for 2–3 minutes. Sift the flour gently into the egg mixture and, using a metal spoon or rubber spatula, carefully fold in, taking care not to overmix and remove all the air that has been whisked in.

Divide the mixture between the two prepared cake tins. Tap lightly on the work surface to remove any air bubbles. Bake in the preheated oven for 20–25 minutes, or until golden. Test that the cake is ready by gently pressing the centre with a clean finger – it should spring back.

Leave to cool in the tins for 5 minutes, then turn out onto a wire rack. Blend the jam/jelly and the crushed raspberries together. When the cakes are cold, spread over the jam mixture and sandwich together. Dredge the top with icing sugar and serve.

## Difficulty Rating: 4 points

# Almond Cake

## Cuts into 8 slices

### Ingredients

225 g/8 oz/2 sticks butter or margarine

225 g/8 oz/1 heaped cup caster/superfine sugar

3 large/extra-large eggs

1 tsp vanilla extract

1 tsp almond extract

125 g/4 oz/1 cup self-raising flour

175 g/6 oz/2 scant cups ground almonds

50 g/2 oz/1/3 cup whole almonds, blanched

25 g/1 oz/1 square dark/bittersweet chocolate

Preheat the oven to 150°C/300°F/Gas Mark 2. Lightly oil and line the base of a 20.5 cm/8 inch deep round cake tin/pan with greaseproof/waxed paper or baking parchment.

Cream together the butter or margarine and sugar with a wooden spoon until light and fluffy.

Beat the eggs and extracts together. Gradually add to the sugar and butter mixture and mix well between each addition.

Sift the flour and mix with the ground almonds. Beat into the egg mixture until well mixed and smooth. Pour into the prepared cake tin.

Roughly chop the whole almonds and scatter over the cake. Bake in the preheated oven for 45 minutes, or until golden and risen and a skewer inserted into the centre of the cake comes out clean.

Remove from the tin and leave to cool on a wire rack. Melt the chocolate in a small bowl placed over a saucepan of gently simmering water, stirring until smooth and free of lumps. Drizzle the melted chocolate over the cooled cake and serve once the chocolate has set.

## Difficulty Rating: 1 point

# Lemon Drizzle Cake

## Cuts into 16 squares

**Ingredients**

125 g/4 oz/1 stick plus 1 tbsp butter or margarine
175 g/6 oz/1 scant cup caster/superfine sugar
2 large/extra-large eggs
175 g/6 oz/1½ cups self-raising flour
2 lemons, preferably unwaxed
50 g/2 oz/¼ cup granulated sugar

Preheat the oven to 180°C/350°F/Gas Mark 4, 10 minutes before baking. Lightly oil and line the base of an 18 cm/7 inch square cake tin/pan with baking parchment.

In a large bowl, cream the butter or margarine and caster/superfine sugar together until soft and fluffy.

Beat the eggs, then gradually add a little of the egg to the creamed mixture, adding 1 tablespoon of flour after each addition.

Finely grate the zest from one of the lemons and stir into the creamed mixture, beating well until smooth. Squeeze the juice from the lemon, strain, then stir into the mixture.

Spoon into the prepared tin, level the surface and bake in the preheated oven for 25–30 minutes.

Using a zester, remove the zest from the last lemon and mix with 25 g/1 oz of the granulated sugar and reserve.

Squeeze the juice into a small saucepan. Add the rest of the granulated sugar to the lemon juice and heat gently, stirring occasionally. When the sugar has dissolved, simmer gently for 3–4 minutes until syrupy.

Prick the cake all over with a cocktail stick/toothpick or fine skewer, to allow the syrup to soak in. Sprinkle the lemon zest and sugar over the top of the cake, drizzle over the syrup and leave to cool in the tin. Cut the cake into squares and serve.

## Difficulty Rating: 3 points

# Double Chocolate Cake with Cinnamon

## Cuts into 10 slices

### Ingredients

50 g/2 oz/²/₃ cup cocoa powder (unsweetened)

1 tsp ground cinnamon

225 g/8 oz/1³/₄ cups self-raising flour

225 g/8 oz/2 sticks unsalted butter or margarine

225 g/8 oz/1 heaped cup caster/superfine sugar

4 large/extra-large eggs

### For the filling:

125 g/4 oz/5 squares white chocolate

50 ml/2 fl oz/¹/₄ cup double/heavy cream

25 g/1 oz/1 square dark/bittersweet chocolate

Preheat the oven to 190°C/375°F/Gas Mark 5, 10 minutes before baking. Lightly oil and line the base of two 20.5 cm/8 inch sandwich tins/layer-cake pans with greaseproof/waxed paper or baking parchment. Sift the cocoa powder, cinnamon and flour together and reserve.

In a large bowl, cream the butter or margarine and sugar until light and fluffy. Beat in the eggs a little at a time until they are all incorporated and the mixture is smooth. (If it looks curdled at any point, beat in 1 tablespoon of the sifted flour.) Using a rubber spatula or metal spoon, fold the sifted flour and cocoa powder into the egg mixture until well mixed. Divide between the two prepared cake tins, and level the surface. Bake in the preheated oven for 25–30 minutes until springy to the touch and a skewer inserted into the centre of the cake comes out clean. Turn out onto a wire rack to cool.

To make the filling, coarsely break the white chocolate and heat the cream very gently in a small saucepan. Add the broken chocolate, stirring until melted. Leave to cool, then, using half of the cooled white chocolate, sandwich the cakes together. Top the cake with the remaining cooled white chocolate. Coarsely grate the dark/bittersweet chocolate over the top and serve.

## Difficulty Rating: 3 points

# Swiss Roll

## Cuts into 8 slices

**Ingredients**

75 g/3 oz/¹/₂ cup self-raising flour

3 large/extra-large eggs

1 tsp vanilla extract

100 g/3¹/₂ oz/scant ¹/₂ cup caster/superfine sugar

25 g/1 oz/¹/₄ cup hazelnuts, toasted and finely chopped

3 tbsp apricot jam/jelly

300 ml/¹/₂ pint/1¹/₄ cups double/heavy cream, lightly whipped

Preheat the oven to 220°C/425°F/Gas Mark 7, 15 minutes before baking. Lightly oil and line the base of a 23 x 33 cm/9 x 13 inch Swiss roll tin/jelly roll pan with a single sheet of greaseproof/waxed paper or baking parchment. Sift the flour several times, then reserve on top of the oven to warm a little.

Place a mixing bowl with the eggs, vanilla extract and sugar over a saucepan of hot water, ensuring that the base of the bowl is not touching the water. With the saucepan off the heat, whisk with an electric hand whisk until the egg mixture becomes pale and mousse–like and has increased in volume.

Remove the basin from the saucepan and continue to whisk for a further 2–3 minutes. Sift in the flour and very gently fold in using a metal spoon or rubber spatula, trying not to knock out the air already whisked in. Pour into the prepared tin, tilting to ensure that the mixture is evenly distributed. Bake in the preheated oven for 10–12 minutes, or until well risen, golden brown and the top springs back when touched lightly with a clean finger.

Sprinkle the toasted, chopped hazelnuts over a large sheet of greaseproof paper. When the cake has cooked, turn out onto the hazelnut–covered paper and trim the edges of the cake. Holding an edge of the paper with the short side of the cake nearest you, roll the cake up. When fully cold, carefully unroll and spread with the jam/jelly and then the cream. Roll back up and serve. Otherwise, store in the refrigerator and eat within two days.

## Difficulty Rating: 4 points

# Toffee Apple Cake

## Cuts into 6–8 slices

### Ingredients

2 small eating apples, peeled

50 g/2 oz/¼ cup soft dark brown sugar

175 g/6 oz/1½ sticks butter or margarine

175 g/6 oz/1 scant cup caster/superfine sugar

3 medium/large eggs

175 g/6 oz/1½ cups self-raising flour

150 ml/¼ pint/⅔ cup double/heavy cream

2 tbsp icing/confectioners' sugar

½ tsp vanilla extract

½ tsp ground cinnamon

## Difficulty Rating: 2 points

Preheat the oven to 180°C/350°F/Gas Mark 4, 10 minutes before baking. Lightly oil and line the bases of two 20.5 cm/8 inch sandwich tins/layer-cake pans with greaseproof/waxed paper or baking parchment. Thinly slice the apples, toss them in the brown sugar and arrange in the prepared tins. Reserve.

Cream together the butter or margarine and caster/superfine sugar until light and fluffy. Beat the eggs together in a small bowl. Gradually beat them into the creamed mixture, beating well between each addition.

Sift the flour into the mixture. With a metal spoon or rubber spatula, fold in. Divide the mixture between the two cake tins and level the surface. Bake in the preheated oven for 25–30 minutes until golden and well risen. Leave to cool.

Lightly whip the cream with 1 tablespoon of the icing/confectioners' sugar and vanilla extract. Sandwich the cakes together with the cream. Mix the remaining icing sugar and the ground cinnamon together, sprinkle over the top of the cake and serve.

# Marble Cake

## Cuts into 8 slices

**Ingredients**

225 g/8 oz/2 sticks butter or margarine

225 g/8 oz/1 cup caster/superfine sugar

4 eggs

225 g/8 oz/2 cups self-raising flour, sifted

finely grated zest and juice of 1 orange

25 g/1 oz cocoa powder (unsweetened), sifted

**For the topping:**

zest and juice of 1 orange

1 tbsp caster/superfine sugar

Preheat the oven to 190°C/375°F/Gas Mark 5, 10 minutes before baking. Lightly oil and line the base of a 20.5 cm/8 inch deep round cake tin/pan with greaseproof/waxed paper or baking parchment.

In a large bowl, cream the butter or margarine and sugar together until light and fluffy. Beat the eggs together. Beat into the creamed mixture a little at a time, beating well between each addition. When all the egg has been added, fold in the flour with a metal spoon or rubber spatula. Divide the mixture equally between two bowls. Beat the grated orange zest into one of the bowls with a little of the orange juice. Mix the cocoa with the remaining orange juice until smooth, then add to the other bowl and beat well. Spoon the mixture into the prepared tin, in alternate spoonfuls. When all the cake mixture is in the tin, take a skewer and swirl it in the two mixtures. Tap the base of the tin on the work surface to level the mixture. Bake in the preheated oven for 50 minutes, or until cooked and a skewer inserted into the centre of the cake comes out clean. Remove from the oven and leave in the tin for a few minutes before cooling on a wire rack. Discard the lining paper.

For the topping, place the orange zest and juice with the caster/superfine sugar in a small saucepan and heat gently until the sugar has dissolved. Bring to the boil and simmer gently for 3–4 minutes until the juice is syrupy. Pour over the cooled cake and serve when cool. Otherwise, store the marble cake in an airtight tin.

## Difficulty Rating: 2 points

# Honey Cake

## Cuts into 6 slices

**Ingredients**

50 g/2 oz/¼ cup butter

2 tbsp caster/superfine sugar

125 g/4 oz/⅓ cup clear honey

175 g/6 oz/1⅓ cups plain/all-purpose flour

½ tsp bicarbonate of soda/baking soda

½ tsp mixed/pumpkin pie spice

1 medium/large egg

2 tbsp milk

25 g/1 oz/¼ cup flaked almonds

1 tbsp clear honey, to drizzle

Preheat the oven to 180°C/350°F/Gas Mark 4, 10 minutes before baking. Lightly oil and line the base of an 18 cm/7 inch deep round cake tin/pan with lightly oiled greaseproof/waxed paper or baking parchment.

In a saucepan, gently heat the butter, sugar and honey until the butter has just melted.

Sift the flour, bicarbonate of soda/baking soda and mixed/pumpkin pie spice together into a bowl.

Beat the egg and the milk until mixed thoroughly.

Make a well in the centre of the sifted flour and pour in the melted butter and honey. Using a wooden spoon, beat well, gradually drawing in the flour from the sides of the bowl.

When all the flour has been beaten in, add the egg mixture and mix thoroughly. Pour into the prepared tin and sprinkle with the flaked almonds. Bake in the preheated oven for 30–35 minutes, or until well risen and golden brown and a skewer inserted into the centre of the cake comes out clean.

Remove from the oven, and cool for a few minutes in the tin before turning out and leaving to cool on a wire rack. Drizzle with the remaining tablespoon of honey and serve.

## Difficulty Rating: 1 point

# Fruit Cake

## Cuts into 10 slices

**Ingredients**

225 g/8 oz/2 sticks butter or margarine

200 g/7 oz/1 scant cup brown sugar

finely grated zest of 1 orange

1 tbsp black treacle/molasses

3 large/extra-large eggs, beaten

275 g/10 oz/2½ cups plain/all-purpose flour

¼ tsp ground cinnamon

½ tsp mixed/pumpkin pie spice

pinch freshly grated nutmeg

¼ tsp bicarbonate of soda/baking soda

75 g/3 oz/½ cup mixed peel/candied peel

50 g/2 oz/¼ cup glacé/candied cherries

125 g/4 oz/⅔ cup raisins

125 g/4 oz/⅔ cup sultanas/golden raisins

125 g/4 oz/⅔ cup ready-to-eat dried apricots, chopped

Preheat the oven to 150°C/300°F/Gas Mark 2, 10 minutes before baking. Lightly oil and line a 23 cm/9 inch deep round cake tin/pan with a double thickness of greaseproof/waxed paper.

In a large bowl, cream together the butter or margarine, sugar and orange zest until light and fluffy, then beat in the treacle/molasses. Beat in the eggs a little at a time, beating well between each addition. Reserve 1 tablespoon of the flour. Sift the remaining flour, the spices and bicarbonate of soda/baking soda into the mixture.

Mix all the fruits and the reserved flour together, then stir into the cake mixture. Turn into the prepared tin and smooth the top, making a small hollow in the centre of the cake mixture.

Bake in the preheated oven for 1 hour, then reduce the heat to 140°C/275°F/Gas Mark 1. Bake for a further 1½ hours, or until cooked and a skewer inserted into the centre comes out clean. Leave to cool in the tin, then turn the cake out and serve. Store in an airtight tin when cold.

## Difficulty Rating: 1 point

# Banana Cake

## Cuts into 8 slices

**Ingredients**

3 medium-sized ripe bananas

1 tsp lemon juice

150 g/5 oz/³⁄₄ cup brown sugar

75 g/3 oz/²⁄₃ stick butter or margarine

250 g/9 oz/2 cups self-raising flour

1 tsp ground cinnamon

3 medium/large eggs

50 g/2 oz/¹⁄₃ cup walnuts, chopped

1 tsp each ground cinnamon and caster/superfine sugar

fresh cream, to serve

Preheat the oven to 190°C/375°F/Gas Mark 5, 10 minutes before baking. Lightly oil and line the base of an 18 cm/7 inch deep round cake tin/pan with greaseproof/waxed paper or baking parchment.

Mash two of the bananas in a small bowl, sprinkle with the lemon juice and a heaped tablespoon of the brown sugar. Mix together lightly and reserve.

Gently heat the remaining brown sugar and butter or margarine in a small saucepan until the butter has just melted. Pour into a small bowl, then allow to cool slightly. Sift the flour and cinnamon into a large bowl and make a well in the centre.

Beat the eggs into the cooled sugar mixture, pour into the well of flour and mix thoroughly. Gently stir in the mashed banana mixture. Pour half of the mixture into the prepared tin. Thinly slice the remaining banana and arrange over the cake mixture. Sprinkle over the chopped walnuts, then cover with the remaining cake mixture.

Bake in the preheated oven for 50–55 minutes, or until well risen and golden brown. Allow to cool in the tin, turn out and sprinkle with the ground cinnamon and caster/superfine sugar. Serve hot or cold with a jug of fresh cream for pouring.

## Difficulty Rating: 2 points

# Coffee & Pecan Cake

## Cuts into 8 slices

### Ingredients

175 g/6 oz/1¹⁄₃ cups self-raising flour

125 g/4 oz/1 stick plus 1 tbsp butter or margarine

175 g/6 oz/1 scant cup golden caster/superfine sugar

1 tbsp instant coffee powder or granules

2 large/extra-large eggs

50 g/2 oz/¹⁄₂ cup pecans, roughly chopped

**For the icing:**

1 tsp instant coffee powder or granules

1 tsp cocoa powder (unsweetened)

75 g/3 oz/²⁄₃ stick unsalted butter, softened

175 g/6 oz/1³⁄₄ cups icing/confectioners' sugar, sifted

whole pecans, to decorate

Preheat the oven to 190°C/375°F/Gas Mark 5, 10 minutes before baking. Lightly oil and line the bases of two 18 cm/7 inch sandwich tins/layer-cake pans with greaseproof/waxed paper or baking parchment. Sift the flour and reserve.

Beat the butter or margarine and sugar together until light and creamy. Dissolve the coffee in 2 tablespoons hot water and allow to cool. Lightly mix the eggs with the coffee liquid.

Gradually beat into the creamed butter and sugar, adding a little of the sifted flour with each addition. Fold in the pecans, then divide the mixture between the prepared tins and bake in the preheated oven for 20–25 minutes, or until well risen and firm to the touch. Leave to cool in the tins for 5 minutes before turning out and cooling on a wire rack.

To make the icing, blend together the coffee and cocoa powder with enough boiling water to make a stiff paste. Beat into the butter and icing/confectioners' sugar.

Sandwich the two cakes together using half of the icing. Spread the remaining icing over the top of the cake and decorate with the whole pecans to serve. Store in an airtight container.

## Difficulty Rating: 2 points

# Gingerbread

## Cuts into 8 slices

### Ingredients

175 g/6 oz/1½ sticks butter or margarine

225 g/8 oz/²⁄₃ cup black treacle/molasses

50 g/2 oz/¼ cup dark muscovado/dark brown sugar

350 g/12 oz/3 cups plain/all-purpose flour

2 tsp ground ginger

150 ml/¼ pint/²⁄₃ cup milk, warmed

2 eggs

1 tsp bicarbonate of soda/baking soda

1 piece stem ginger in syrup

1 tbsp stem ginger syrup

## Difficulty Rating: 1 point

Preheat the oven to 150°C/300°F/Gas Mark 2, 10 minutes before baking. Lightly oil and line the base of a 20.5 cm/8 inch deep round cake tin/pan with greaseproof/waxed paper or baking parchment.

In a saucepan, gently heat the butter or margarine, black treacle/molasses and sugar, stirring occasionally, until the butter melts. Leave to cool slightly.

Sift the flour and ground ginger into a large bowl. Make a well in the centre, then pour in the treacle mixture. Reserve 1 tablespoon of the milk, then pour the rest into the treacle mixture. Stir together lightly until mixed.

Beat the eggs together, then stir into the mixture. Dissolve the bicarbonate of soda/baking soda in the remaining 1 tablespoon of warmed milk and add to the mixture. Beat the mixture until well combined and free of lumps. Pour into the prepared tin and bake in the preheated oven for 1 hour, or until well risen and a skewer inserted into the centre comes out clean. Cool in the tin, then remove. Slice the stem ginger into thin slivers and sprinkle over the cake. Drizzle with the syrup and serve.

# Moist Mocha & Coconut Cake

## Makes 9 squares (Pictured page 52)

### Ingredients

3 tbsp ground coffee; 5 tbsp hot milk
75 g/3 oz/²⁄₃ stick butter; 175 g/6 oz/¹⁄₂ cup golden/corn syrup
2 tbsp soft light brown sugar
40 g/1¹⁄₂ oz/¹⁄₂ cup desiccated/shredded coconut
150 g/5 oz/scant 1¹⁄₄ cups plain/all-purpose flour
25 g/1 oz/¹⁄₃ cup cocoa powder (unsweetened)
¹⁄₂ tsp bicarbonate of soda/baking soda
2 medium/large eggs, lightly beaten; 2 chocolate flakes, to decorate

### For the coffee icing:
225 g/8 oz/2¹⁄₄ cups icing/confectioners' sugar, sifted
125 g/4 oz/1 stick plus 1 tbsp butter, softened

Preheat the oven to 170°C/325°F/Gas Mark 3, 10 minutes before baking. Lightly oil and line a deep 20.5 cm/8 inch square tin/pan with nonstick baking parchment. Place the ground coffee in a small bowl and pour over the hot milk. Leave to infuse for 5 minutes, then strain through a tea-strainer or a sieve lined with muslin. You will end up with about 4 tablespoons of liquid. Reserve.

Put the butter, golden/corn syrup, sugar and coconut in a small heavy-based saucepan and heat gently until the butter has melted and the sugar dissolved. Sift the flour, cocoa powder and bicarbonate of soda/baking soda together and stir into the melted mixture with the eggs and 3 tablespoons of the coffee-infused milk. Pour the mixture into the prepared tin. Bake on the centre shelf of the preheated oven for 45 minutes, or until the cake is well risen and firm to the touch. Leave in the tin for 10 minutes to cool slightly, then turn out onto a wire rack to cool completely.

For the icing, gradually add the icing/confectioners' sugar to the softened butter and beat together well. Add the remaining 1 tablespoon of coffee-infused milk and beat until light and fluffy. Carefully spread the icing over the top of the cake, then cut into squares. Decorate with pieces of chocolate flake and serve.

## Difficulty Rating: 1 point

# Carrot Cake

## Cuts into 8 slices

### Ingredients

200 g/7 oz/1¹⁄₂ cups plain/all-purpose flour
¹⁄₂ tsp ground cinnamon
¹⁄₂ tsp freshly grated nutmeg
1 tsp baking powder
1 tsp bicarbonate of soda/baking soda
150 g/5 oz/³⁄₄ cup muscovado/dark brown sugar
200 ml/7 fl oz/1 scant cup vegetable oil
3 medium/large eggs
225 g/8 oz/1³⁄₄ cups carrots, peeled and roughly grated
50 g/2 oz/¹⁄₂ cup chopped walnuts

### For the icing:
175 g/6 oz/³⁄₄ cup cream cheese
finely grated zest of 1 orange; 1 tbsp orange juice
1 tsp vanilla extract
125 g/4 oz/1 cup icing/confectioners' sugar

Preheat the oven to 150°C/300°F/Gas Mark 2, 10 minutes before baking. Lightly oil and line the base of a 15 cm/6 inch deep square cake tin/pan with greaseproof/waxed paper or baking parchment. Sift the flour, spices, baking powder and bicarbonate of soda/baking soda together into a large bowl. Stir in the muscovado/dark brown sugar and mix together.

Lightly whisk the oil and eggs together, then gradually stir into the flour and sugar mixture. Stir well. Add the carrots and walnuts. Mix thoroughly, then pour into the prepared cake tin. Bake in the preheated oven for 1¹⁄₄ hours, or until light and springy to the touch and a skewer inserted into the centre of the cake comes out clean. Remove from the oven and allow to cool in the tin for 5 minutes before turning out onto a wire rack. Leave until cold.

To make the icing, beat together the cream cheese, orange zest, orange juice and vanilla extract. Sift the icing/confectioners' sugar and stir into the cream cheese mixture. When cold, discard the lining paper, spread the cream cheese icing over the top and serve cut into squares.

## Difficulty Rating: 1 point

# Chocolate Madeleines

## Makes 10

**Ingredients**

125 g/4 oz/1 stick plus 1 tbsp butter

125 g/4 oz/²⁄₃ cup soft light brown sugar

2 medium/large eggs, lightly beaten

1 drop almond extract

1 tbsp ground almonds

75 g/3 oz/²⁄₃ cup self-raising flour

20 g/³⁄₄ oz/¹⁄₄ cup cocoa powder (unsweetened)

1 tsp baking powder

**To finish:**

5 tbsp apricot conserve

1 tbsp amaretto liqueur, brandy or orange juice

50 g/2 oz/²⁄₃ cup desiccated/shredded coconut

10 large chocolate buttons (optional)

## Difficulty Rating: 3 points

Preheat the oven to 180°C/350°F/Gas Mark 4, 10 minutes before baking. Lightly oil 10 dariole moulds and line the bases of each with a small circle of nonstick baking parchment. Stand the moulds on a baking sheet. Cream the butter and sugar together until light and fluffy. Gradually add the eggs, beating well between each addition. Beat in the almond extract and ground almonds.

Sift the flour, cocoa powder and baking powder over the creamed mixture. Gently fold in using a metal spoon. Divide the mixture equally between the prepared moulds; each should be about half full. Bake on the centre shelf of the preheated oven for 20 minutes, or until well risen and firm to the touch. Leave in the moulds for a few minutes, then run a small palette knife round the edge and turn out onto a wire rack to cool. Remove the paper circles from the sponges.

Heat the conserve with the liqueur, brandy or juice in a small saucepan. Sieve to remove any lumps. If necessary, trim the sponge bases, so they are flat. Brush the tops and sides with warm conserve, then roll in the coconut. Top each with a chocolate button, fixed by brushing its base with conserve.

# Cappuccino Cakes

## Makes 6

### Ingredients

125 g/4 oz/1 stick plus 1 tbsp butter or margarine
125 g/4 oz/²/₃ cup caster/superfine sugar
2 medium/large eggs
1 tbsp strong black coffee
150 g/5 oz/scant 1¼ cups self-raising flour
125 g/4 oz/½ cup mascarpone cheese
1 tbsp icing/confectioners' sugar, sifted
1 tsp vanilla extract
sifted cocoa powder (unsweetened), to dust

Preheat the oven to 190°C/375°F/Gas Mark 5, 10 minutes before baking. Place six large paper muffin cases/baking cups into a muffin tin/pan or, alternatively, place onto a baking sheet.

Cream the butter or margarine and sugar together until light and fluffy. Break the eggs into a small bowl and beat lightly with a fork.

Using a wooden spoon, beat the eggs into the butter and sugar mixture a little at a time until they are all incorporated. If the mixture looks curdled, beat in a spoonful of the flour to return the mixture to a smooth consistency. Finally beat in the black coffee.

Sift the flour into the mixture, then, with a metal spoon or rubber spatula, gently fold in the flour.

Place spoonfuls of the mixture into the muffin cases and bake in the preheated oven for 20–25 minutes, or until risen and springy to the touch. Cool on a wire rack.

In a small bowl, beat together the mascarpone cheese, icing/confectioners' sugar and vanilla extract. When the cakes are cold, spoon the vanilla mascarpone onto the top of each one. Dust with cocoa powder and serve. Store in the refrigerator and eat within 24 hours .

## Difficulty Rating: 1 point

# Chunky Chocolate Muffins

## Makes 7

### Ingredients

50 g/2 oz/2 squares dark/bittersweet chocolate,
  roughly chopped
50 g/2 oz/¼ cup light muscovado/golden brown sugar
25 g/1 oz/¼ stick butter, melted
125 ml/4 fl oz/½ cup milk, at room temperature
½ tsp vanilla extract
1 medium/large egg, lightly beaten
150 g/5 oz/1¼ cups self-raising flour
½ tsp baking powder
pinch salt
75 g/3 oz/3 squares white chocolate, chopped
2 tsp icing/confectioners' sugar (optional)

Preheat the oven to 200˚C/400˚F/Gas Mark 6, 15 minutes before baking. Line a muffin tin/pan with seven paper muffin cases/baking cups, or else oil the individual compartments well. Place the dark/bittersweet chocolate in a large heatproof bowl set over a saucepan of very hot water. Stir occasionally until melted. Remove the bowl and leave to cool for a few minutes.

Stir the sugar and butter into the melted chocolate, then add the milk, vanilla extract and egg. Sift the flour, baking powder and salt in together. Add the chopped white chocolate. Using a metal spoon, fold together quickly, taking care not to overmix.

Divide the mixture between the paper cases, piling it up in the centre. Bake on the centre shelf of the preheated oven for 20–25 minutes, or until well risen and firm to the touch.

Lightly dust the tops of the muffins with icing/confectioners' sugar as soon as they come out of the oven, if wanted. Leave the muffins in the tray for a few minutes, then transfer to a wire rack. Serve either warm or cold.

## Difficulty Rating: 2 points

# Rich Chocolate Cup Cakes

## Makes 12

### Ingredients

175 g/6 oz/1½ cups self-raising flour

25 g/1 oz/¼ cup cocoa powder (unsweetened)

175 g/6 oz/1 scant cup demerara/turbinado sugar

75 g/3 oz/¾ stick butter, melted

2 eggs, lightly beaten

1 tsp vanilla extract

40 g/1½ oz/2 tbsp maraschino cherries,
    drained and chopped

### For the chocolate icing:

50 g/2 oz/2 squares dark/bittersweet chocolate

25 g/1 oz/¼ cup unsalted butter

25 g/1 oz/¼ cup icing/confectioners' sugar, sifted

### For the cherry icing:

125 g/4 oz/1 cup icing/confectioners' sugar

2 tbsp unsalted butter, melted

1 tsp syrup from the maraschino cherries

3 maraschino cherries, halved, to decorate

Preheat the oven to 180°C/350°F/Gas Mark 4, 10 minutes before baking. Line a 12 hole muffin tin/pan with paper muffin cases/baking cups. Sift the flour and cocoa powder into a bowl. Stir in the sugar, then add the melted butter, eggs and vanilla extract. Beat together with a wooden spoon for 3 minutes, or until well blended.

Divide half the mixture between six of the paper cases. Dry the cherries thoroughly on absorbent paper towels, then fold into the remaining mixture and spoon into the rest of the paper cases. Bake on the shelf above the centre of the preheated oven for 20 minutes, or until a skewer inserted into the centre of a cake comes out clean. Transfer to a wire rack and leave to cool.

For the chocolate icing, melt the chocolate and butter in a heatproof bowl set over a saucepan of hot water. Remove from the heat and leave to cool for 3 minutes, stirring occasionally. Stir in the icing/confectioners' sugar. Spoon over the six plain chocolate cakes and leave to set.

For the cherry icing, sift the icing sugar into a bowl. Stir in 1 tablespoon boiling water, the butter and cherry syrup. Spoon the icing over the remaining six cakes, decorate each with a halved cherry and leave to set.

## Difficulty Rating: 1 point

# Triple Chocolate Brownies

## Makes 15

### Ingredients

350 g/12 oz/12 squares dark/bittersweet chocolate,
   broken into pieces
225 g/8 oz/2 sticks butter, cubed
225 g/8 oz/1 cup caster/superfine sugar
3 large/extra-large eggs, lightly beaten
1 tsp vanilla extract
2 tbsp very strong black coffee
100 g/3½ oz/¾ cup self-raising flour
125 g/4 oz/1 cup pecans, roughly chopped
75 g/3 oz/3 squares white chocolate, roughly chopped
75 g/3 oz/3 squares milk/semisweet chocolate,
   roughly chopped

Preheat the oven to 190°C/375°F/Gas Mark 5, 10 minutes
before baking. Oil and line a 28 x 18 x 2.5 cm/11 x 7 x 1 inch
cake tin/pan with nonstick baking parchment. Place the dark/
bittersweet chocolate in a heatproof bowl with the butter over
a saucepan of almost boiling water. Stir occasionally until
melted. Remove from the heat and leave until just cool, but
not beginning to set.

Place the caster/superfine sugar, eggs, vanilla extract and coffee
in a large bowl and beat together until smooth. Gradually beat
in the chocolate mixture. Sift the flour into the chocolate
mixture. Add the pecans and the white and milk/semisweet
chocolate. Gently fold in until mixed thoroughly. Spoon the
mixture into the prepared tin and level the top.

Bake on the centre shelf of the preheated oven for 45 minutes,
or until just firm to the touch in the centre and crusty on top.
Leave to cool in the tin, then turn out onto a wire rack.
Trim off the crusty edges and cut into 15 squares. Store in
an airtight container.

## Difficulty Rating: 2 points

# Chocolate Fudge Brownies

## Makes 16

### Ingredients

125 g/4 oz/1 stick plus 1 tbsp butter
175 g/6 oz/7 squares dark/bittersweet chocolate, roughly
   chopped or broken
225 g/8 oz/1 heaping cup caster/superfine sugar
2 tsp vanilla extract
2 eggs, lightly beaten
150 g/5 oz/1 heaping cup plain/all-purpose flour
175 g/6 oz/1½ cups icing/confectioners' sugar
2 tbsp cocoa powder (unsweetened)
1 tbsp butter

Preheat the oven to 180°C/350°F/Gas Mark 4, 10 minutes
before baking. Lightly oil and line a 20.5 cm/8 inch square cake
tin/pan with greaseproof/waxed paper or baking parchment.

Slowly melt the butter and chocolate together in a heatproof
bowl set over a saucepan of simmering water. Transfer the
mixture to a large bowl. Stir in the sugar and vanilla extract, then
stir in the eggs. Sift over the flour and fold together well with a
metal spoon or rubber spatula. Pour into the prepared tin.

Transfer to the preheated oven and bake for 30 minutes until
just set. Remove the cooked mixture from the oven. Leave to
cool in the tin before turning it out onto a wire rack.

Sift the icing/confectioners' sugar and cocoa into a small bowl
and make a well in the centre. Place the butter in the well, then
gradually add about 2 tablespoons hot water. Mix to form a
smooth, spreadable icing.

Pour the icing over the cooked mixture. Allow the icing to set
before cutting into squares. Serve the brownies when they are
cold, or store in an airtight container.

## Difficulty Rating: 2 points

# Chocolate Nut Brownies

## Makes 16

**Ingredients**

125 g/4 oz/1 stick plus 1 tbsp butter

150 g/5 oz/³⁄₄ cup demerara/turbinado sugar

50 g/2 oz/2 squares dark/bittersweet chocolate,
  roughly chopped or broken

2 tbsp smooth peanut butter

2 eggs

50 g/2 oz/¹⁄₂ cup unsalted roasted peanuts,
  finely chopped

100 g/3¹⁄₂ oz/1 scant cup self-raising flour

**For the topping:**

125 g/4 oz/4 squares dark/bittersweet chocolate, roughly
  chopped or broken

50 ml/2 fl oz/¹⁄₄ cup sour cream

Preheat the oven to 180°C/350°F/Gas Mark 4, 10 minutes before baking. Lightly oil and line a 20.5 cm/8 inch square cake tin/pan with greaseproof/waxed paper or baking parchment. Combine the butter, sugar and chocolate in a small saucepan and heat gently until the sugar and chocolate have melted, stirring constantly. Reserve and cool slightly.

Mix together the peanut butter, eggs and peanuts in a large bowl. Stir in the cooled chocolate mixture. Sift in the flour and fold together with a metal spoon or rubber spatula until combined. Pour into the prepared tin and bake in the preheated oven for about 30 minutes, or until just firm. Cool for 5 minutes in the tin before turning out onto a wire rack to cool.

To make the topping, melt the chocolate in a heatproof bowl over a saucepan of simmering water, making sure that the base of the bowl does not touch the water. Cool slightly, then stir in the sour cream until smooth and glossy. Spread over the brownies, refrigerate until set, then cut into squares. Serve the brownies cold.

## Difficulty Rating: 2 points

# Fruit & Spice Chocolate Slice

## Makes 10 slices

### Ingredients

350 g/12 oz/2¾ cups self-raising flour

1 tsp mixed/pumpkin pie spice

175 g/6 oz/1½ sticks butter, chilled

125 g/4 oz/5 squares dark/bittersweet chocolate, roughly chopped

125 g/4 oz/1 scant cup dried mixed fruit

75 g/3 oz/½ cup dried apricots, chopped

75 g/3 oz/½ cup chopped mixed nuts

175 g/6 oz/1 scant cup demerara/turbinado sugar

2 medium/large eggs, lightly beaten

150 ml/¼ pint/⅔ cup milk

Preheat the oven to 180°C/350°F/Gas Mark 4, 10 minutes before baking. Oil and line a deep 18 cm/7 inch square tin/pan with nonstick baking parchment. Sift the flour and mixed/pumpkin pie spice into a large bowl. Cut the butter into small squares and, using your hands, rub in until the mixture resembles fine breadcrumbs.

Add the chocolate, dried mixed fruit, apricots and nuts to the dry ingredients. Reserve 1 tablespoon of the sugar, then add the rest to the bowl and stir together. Add the eggs and half of the milk and mix together, then add enough of the remaining milk to give a soft dropping consistency.

Spoon the mixture into the prepared tin, level the surface with the back of a spoon and sprinkle with the reserved demerara/turbinado sugar. Bake on the centre shelf of the preheated oven for 50 minutes. Cover the top with kitchen foil to prevent the cake from browning too much and bake for a further 30–40 minutes, or until it is firm to the touch and a skewer inserted into the centre of the cake comes out clean.

Leave the cake in the tin for 10 minutes to cool slightly, then turn out onto a wire rack and leave to cool completely. Cut into 10 slices and serve. Store in an airtight container.

## Difficulty Rating: 1 point

# Chocolate Pecan Traybake

## Makes 12

**Ingredients**

175 g/6 oz/1½ sticks butter

75 g/3 oz/¾ cup icing/confectioners' sugar, sifted

175 g/6 oz/1⅓ cups plain/all-purpose flour

3 tbsp self-raising flour

5 tbsp cocoa powder

**For the pecan topping:**

75 g/3 oz/⅔ stick butter

50 g/2 oz/¼ cup light muscovado/golden brown sugar

2 tbsp golden/corn syrup

2 tbsp milk

1 tsp vanilla extract

2 medium/large eggs, lightly beaten

125 g/4 oz/1¼ cups pecan halves

Preheat the oven to 180°C/350°F/Gas Mark 4, 10 minutes before baking. Lightly oil and line a 28 x 18 x 2.5 cm/11 x 7 x 1 inch cake tin/pan with nonstick baking parchment. Beat the butter and sugar together until light and fluffy. Sift in the flours and cocoa powder and mix together to form a soft dough.

Press the mixture evenly over the base of the prepared tin. Prick all over with a fork, then bake on the shelf above the centre of the preheated oven for 15 minutes.

Put the butter, sugar, golden/corn syrup, milk and vanilla extract in a small saucepan and heat gently until melted. Remove from the heat and leave to cool for a few minutes, then stir in the eggs and pour over the base. Sprinkle with the nuts.

Bake in the preheated oven for 25 minutes, or until dark golden brown but still slightly soft. Leave to cool in the tin. When cool, carefully remove from the tin, then cut into 12 squares and serve. Store in an airtight container.

## Difficulty Rating: 1 point

# Chocolate Brazil & Polenta Squares

## Makes 9 squares

**Ingredients**

125 g/4 oz/1 cup shelled Brazil nuts

150 g/5 oz/1⅓ sticks butter, softened

150 g/5 oz/¾ cup soft light brown sugar

2 medium/large eggs, lightly beaten

75 g/3 oz/⅔ cup plain/all-purpose flour

25 g/1 oz/⅓ cup cocoa powder (unsweetened)

¼ tsp ground cinnamon

1 tsp baking powder

pinch salt

5 tbsp milk

65 g/2½ oz/⅓ cup instant polenta

Preheat the oven to 180°C/350°F/Gas Mark 4, 10 minutes before baking. Oil and line a deep 18 cm/7 inch square tin/pan with nonstick baking parchment. Finely chop half of the Brazil nuts and reserve. Roughly chop the remainder. Cream the butter and sugar together until light and fluffy. Gradually add the eggs, beating well between each addition.

Sift the flour, cocoa powder, cinnamon, baking powder and salt into the creamed mixture and gently fold in using a large metal spoon or spatula. Add the milk, polenta and the roughly chopped Brazil nuts. Fold into the mixture.

Turn the mixture into the prepared tin, levelling the surface with the back of a spoon. Sprinkle the reserved finely chopped Brazil nuts over the top. Bake the cake on the centre shelf of the preheated oven for 45–50 minutes, or until well risen and lightly browned and when a clean skewer inserted into the centre of the cake for a few seconds comes out clean.

Leave the cake in the tin for 10 minutes to cool slightly, then turn out onto a wire rack and leave to cool completely. Cut the cake into nine equal squares and serve. Store in an airtight container.

## Difficulty Rating: 2 points

# Chocolate Walnut Squares

## Makes 24

### Ingredients

125 g/4 oz/1 stick plus 1 tbsp butter

150 g/5 oz/6 squares dark/bittersweet chocolate, broken into pieces

450 g/1 lb/2¼ cups caster/superfine sugar

½ tsp vanilla extract

200 g/7 oz/1½ cups plain/all-purpose flour

75 g/3 oz/⅓ cup self-raising flour

50 g/2 oz/½ cup cocoa powder (unsweetened)

225 g/8 oz/1 cup mayonnaise, at room temperature

### For the chocolate glaze:

125 g/4 oz/5 squares dark/bittersweet chocolate,
   broken into pieces

40 g/1½ oz/⅓ stick unsalted butter

24 walnut halves

1 tbsp icing/confectioners' sugar, for dusting

## Difficulty Rating: 2 points

Preheat the oven to 170°C/325°F/Gas Mark 3, 10 minutes before baking. Oil and line a 28 x 18 x 5 cm/11 x 7 x 2 inch cake tin/pan with nonstick baking parchment. Place the butter, chocolate, sugar, vanilla extract and 250 ml/8 fl oz cold water in a heavy-based saucepan. Heat gently, stirring occasionally, until the chocolate and butter have melted, but do not allow to boil.

Sift the flours and cocoa powder into a large bowl and make a well in the centre. Add the mayonnaise and about one third of the chocolate mixture and beat until smooth. Gradually beat in the remaining chocolate mixture. Pour into the prepared tin and bake on the centre shelf of the preheated oven for 1 hour, or until slightly risen and firm to the touch. Place the tin on a wire rack and leave to cool. Remove the cake from the tin and peel off the parchment.

To make the chocolate glaze, place the chocolate and butter in a small saucepan with 1 tablespoon water and heat very gently, stirring occasionally, until melted and smooth. Leave to cool until thickened, then spread evenly over the cake. Chill the cake in the refrigerator for about 5 minutes, then mark into 24 squares. Lightly dust the walnut halves with a little icing/confectioners' sugar and place one on the top of each square. Cut into pieces and store in an airtight container until ready to serve.

# Indulgent Chocolate Squares

## Makes 16

**Ingredients**

350 g/12 oz/14 squares dark/bittersweet chocolate
175 g/6 oz/1½ sticks butter, softened
175 g/6 oz/1 scant cup soft light brown sugar
175 g/6 oz/2 scant cups ground almonds
6 large/extra-large eggs, separated
3 tbsp cocoa powder (unsweetened), sifted
75 g/3 oz/1⅔ cups fresh brown breadcrumbs
125 ml/4 fl oz/½ cup double cream
50 g/2 oz/2 squares white chocolate, chopped
50 g/2 oz/2 squares milk/semisweet chocolate, chopped
few freshly sliced strawberries, to decorate

Preheat the oven to 180°C/350°F/Gas Mark 4, 10 minutes before baking. Oil and line a deep 20.5 cm/8 inch square cake tin/pan with nonstick baking parchment. Melt 225 g/8 oz of the dark/bittersweet chocolate in a heatproof bowl set over a saucepan of almost boiling water. Stir until smooth, then leave until just cool, but not beginning to set.

Beat the butter and sugar until light and fluffy. Stir in the melted chocolate, ground almonds, egg yolks, cocoa powder and breadcrumbs. Whisk the egg whites until stiff peaks form, then stir a large spoonful into the chocolate mixture. Gently fold in the rest, then pour the mixture into the prepared tin. Bake on the centre shelf in the preheated oven for 1¼ hours, or until firm, covering the top with foil after 45 minutes, to prevent it over–browning. Leave in the tin for 20 minutes, then turn out onto a wire rack and leave to cool.

Melt the remaining 125 g/4 oz dark chocolate with the cream in a heatproof bowl set over a saucepan of almost boiling water, stirring occasionally. Leave to cool for 20 minutes, or until thickened slightly. Spread the topping over the cake. Scatter over the white and milk/semisweet chocolate and leave to set. Cut into 16 squares and serve decorated with a few freshly sliced strawberries, then serve.

## Difficulty Rating: 3 points

# Crunchy-topped Citrus Chocolate Slices

## Makes 12 slices

### Ingredients

175 g/6 oz/1½ sticks butter
175 g/6 oz/¾ cup firmly packed muscovado/dark brown sugar
finely grated zest of 1 orange
3 eggs, lightly beaten
1 tbsp ground almonds
175 g/6 oz/1½ cups self-raising flour
¼ tsp baking powder
125 g/4 oz/4 squares dark/bittersweet chocolate,
    coarsely grated
2 tsp milk

### For the crunchy topping:
125 g/4 oz/⅔ cup caster/superfine sugar
juice of 2 limes
juice of 1 orange

Preheat the oven to 170°C/325°F/Gas Mark 3, 10 minutes before baking. Oil and line a 28 x 18 x 2.5 cm/11 x 7 x 1 inch cake tin/pan with nonstick baking parchment. Place the butter, sugar and orange zest into a large bowl and cream together until light and fluffy. Gradually add the eggs, beating after each addition, then beat in the ground almonds. Sift the flour and baking powder into the creamed mixture. Add the grated chocolate and milk, then gently fold in using a metal spoon. Spoon the mixture into the prepared tin.

Bake on the centre shelf of the preheated oven for 35–40 minutes, or until well risen and firm to the touch. Leave in the tin for a few minutes to cool slightly. Turn out onto a wire rack and remove the baking parchment.

For the topping, place the sugar and fruit juices into a small jug. Stir together. Drizzle over the hot cake, covering the whole surface. Leave until completely cold, then cut into 12 slices to serve.

## Difficulty Rating: 2 points

# All-in-one Chocolate Fudge Cakes

## Makes 15 squares

**Ingredients**

175 g/6 oz/1 scant cup soft dark brown sugar

175 g/6 oz/1½ sticks butter, softened

150 g/5 oz/scant 1¼ cups self-raising flour

25 g/1 oz/⅓ cup cocoa powder (unsweetened)

½ tsp baking powder

pinch salt

3 medium/large eggs, lightly beaten

1 tbsp golden/corn syrup

**For the fudge topping:**

75 g/3 oz/heaped ⅓ cup granulated sugar

150 ml/¼ pint/⅔ cup evaporated milk

175 g/6 oz/7 squares dark/bittersweet chocolate,
   roughly chopped

40 g/1½ oz/⅓ stick unsalted butter, softened

125 g/4 oz soft fudge sweets, finely chopped

Preheat the oven to 180°C/350°F/Gas Mark 4, 10 minutes before baking. Oil and line a 28 x 18 x 2.5 cm/11 x 7 x 1 inch cake tin/pan with nonstick baking parchment.

Place the soft brown sugar and butter in a bowl and sift in the flour, cocoa powder, baking powder and salt. Add the eggs and golden/corn syrup, then beat with an electric whisk for 2 minutes, before adding 2 tablespoons warm water and beating for a further 1 minute. Turn the mixture into the prepared tin and level the top with the back of a spoon. Bake on the centre shelf of the preheated oven for 30 minutes, or until firm to the touch. Turn the cake out onto a wire rack and leave to cool before removing the baking parchment.

To make the topping, gently heat the sugar and evaporated milk in a saucepan, stirring frequently, until the sugar has dissolved. Bring the mixture to the boil and simmer for 6 minutes without stirring.

Remove the mixture from the heat. Add the chocolate and butter and stir until melted and blended. Pour into a bowl and chill in the refrigerator for 1–2 hours until thickened. Spread the topping over the cake, then sprinkle with the chopped fudge. Cut the cake into 15 squares before serving.

## Difficulty Rating: 1 point

# Marbled Chocolate Traybake

## Makes 18 squares

**Ingredients**

175 g/6 oz/1½ sticks butter

175 g/6 oz/1 scant cup caster/superfine sugar

1 tsp vanilla extract

3 medium/large eggs, lightly beaten

200 g/7 oz/1½ cups self-raising flour

½ tsp baking powder

1 tbsp milk

1½ tbsp cocoa powder (unsweetened)

**For the chocolate icing:**

75 g/3 oz/3 squares dark/bittersweet chocolate, broken into pieces

75 g/3 oz /3 squares white chocolate, broken into pieces

Preheat the oven to 180°C/350°F/Gas Mark 4, 10 minutes before baking. Oil and line a 28 x 18 x 2.5 cm/11 x 7 x 1 inch cake tin/pan with nonstick baking parchment. Cream the butter, sugar and vanilla extract until light and fluffy. Gradually add the eggs, beating well after each addition. Sift in the flour and baking powder and fold in with the milk. Spoon half the mixture into the prepared tin, spacing the spoonfuls apart and leaving gaps in between. Blend the cocoa powder to a smooth paste with 2 tablespoons warm water. Stir this into the remaining cake mixture. Drop small spoonfuls between the vanilla cake mixture to fill in all the gaps. Use a knife to swirl the mixtures together a little.

Bake on the centre shelf of the preheated oven for 35 minutes, or until well risen and firm to the touch. Leave in the tin for 5 minutes to cool, then turn out onto a wire rack and leave to cool. Remove the parchment.

For the icing, place the plain and white chocolate in separate heatproof bowls and melt each over a saucepan of almost boiling water. Spoon into separate nonstick baking parchment piping bags, snip off the tips and drizzle over the top. Leave to set before cutting into squares.

## Difficulty Rating: 2 points

# Light White Chocolate & Walnut Blondies

## Makes 15

**Ingredients**

75 g/3 oz/²/₃ stick unsalted butter

200 g/7 oz demerara/turbinado sugar

2 large/extra-large eggs, lightly beaten

1 tsp vanilla extract

2 tbsp milk

125 g/4 oz/1 cup, plus 1 tbsp plain/all-purpose flour

1 tsp baking powder

pinch salt

75 g/3 oz/²/₃ cup walnuts, roughly chopped

125 g/4 oz/³/₄ cup white chocolate drops

1 tbsp icing/confectioners' sugar

Preheat the oven to 190°C/375°F/Gas Mark 5, 10 minutes before baking. Oil and line a 28 x 18 x 2.5 cm/11 x 7 x 1 inch cake tin/pan with nonstick baking parchment. Place the butter and demerara/turbinado sugar into a heavy-based saucepan and heat gently until the butter has melted and the sugar has started to dissolve. Remove from the heat and leave to cool.

Place the eggs, vanilla extract and milk in a large bowl and beat together. Stir in the butter and sugar mixture, then sift in the 125 g/4 oz/³/₄ cup of flour, the baking powder and salt. Gently stir the mixture twice.

Toss the walnuts and chocolate drops in the remaining 1 tablespoon of flour to coat. Add to the bowl and stir the ingredients together gently.

Spoon the mixture into the prepared tin and bake on the centre shelf of the preheated oven for 35 minutes, or until the top is firm and slightly crusty. Place the tin on a wire rack and leave to cool.

When completely cold, remove the cake from the tin and lightly dust the top with icing/confectioners' sugar. Cut into 15 blondies, using a sharp knife, and serve.

## Difficulty Rating: 2 points

# Apple & Cinnamon Crumble Bars

## Makes 16

### Ingredients

450 g/1 lb apples (ideally Bramley cooking apples), roughly chopped
50 g/2 oz/¹/₃ cup raisins
50 g/2 oz/¹/₄ cup caster/superfine sugar
1 tsp ground cinnamon
zest of 1 lemon
200 g/7 oz/1³/₄ cups plain/all-purpose flour
250 g/9 oz/1¹/₄ cups demerara/turbinado sugar
¹/₂ tsp bicarbonate of soda/baking soda
150 g/5 oz/2 cups rolled oats
150 g/5 oz/1¹/₃ sticks butter, melted
crème fraîche or whipped cream, to serve

Preheat the oven to 190°C/375°F/Gas Mark 5, 10 minutes before baking. Place the apples, raisins, sugar, cinnamon and lemon zest into a saucepan over a low heat. Cover and cook for about 15 minutes, stirring occasionally, until the apple is cooked through. Remove the cover and stir well with a wooden spoon to break up the apple completely. Cook for a further 15–30 minutes over a very low heat until reduced, thickened and slightly darkened. Allow to cool.

Lightly oil and line a 20.5 cm/8 inch square cake tin/pan with greaseproof/waxed paper or baking parchment.

Mix together the flour, sugar, bicarbonate of soda/baking soda, oats and melted butter until well combined and crumbly. Spread half of the flour mixture into the bottom of the prepared tin and press down. Pour over the apple mixture. Sprinkle over the remaining flour mixture and press down lightly. Bake in the preheated oven for 30–35 minutes until golden brown.

Remove from the oven and allow to cool before cutting into slices. Serve the bars warm or cold with crème fraîche or whipped cream.

## Difficulty Rating: 3 points

# Lemon Bars

## Makes 24

**Ingredients**

175 g/6 oz/1½ cups plain/all-purpose flour
125 g/4 oz/1 stick plus 1 tbsp butter
50 g/2 oz/¼ cup caster/superfine sugar
2 tbsp plain/all-purpose flour
½ tsp baking powder
¼ tsp salt
2 eggs, lightly beaten
juice and finely grated zest of 1 lemon
sifted icing/confectioners' sugar, to decorate

Preheat the oven to 170°C/325°F/Gas Mark 3, 10 minutes before baking. Lightly oil and line a 20.5 cm/8 inch square cake tin/pan with greaseproof/waxed paper or baking parchment.

Rub together the flour and butter until the mixture resembles breadcrumbs. Stir in 4 tablespoons of the caster/superfine sugar and mix. Turn the mixture into the prepared tin and press down firmly. Bake in the preheated oven for 20 minutes until pale golden.

Meanwhile, in a food processor, mix together the remaining sugar, the flour, baking powder, salt, eggs, lemon juice and zest until smooth. Pour over the prepared base.

Transfer to the oven and bake for a further 20–25 minutes until nearly set but still a bit wobbly in the centre. Remove from the oven and cool in the tin/pan on a wire rack. Dust with icing/confectioners' sugar and cut into squares. Serve cold and store in an airtight container.

## Difficulty Rating: 2 points

# Lemon-iced Ginger Squares

## Makes 12

**Ingredients**

225 g/8 oz/1 cup caster/superfine sugar
50 g/2 oz/½ stick butter, melted
2 tbsp black treacle/molasses
2 egg whites, lightly whisked
225 g/8 oz/2 cups plain/all-purpose flour
1 tsp bicarbonate of soda/baking soda
½ tsp ground cloves
1 tsp ground cinnamon
¼ tsp ground ginger
pinch salt
250 ml/8 fl oz/1 cup buttermilk
175 g/6 oz/1½ cups icing/confectioners' sugar
lemon juice

Preheat the oven to 200°C/400°F/Gas Mark 6, 15 minutes before baking. Lightly oil a 20.5 cm/8 inch square cake tin/pan and sprinkle with a little flour.

Mix together the caster/superfine sugar, butter and treacle/molasses. Stir in the egg whites.

Mix together the flour, bicarbonate of soda/baking soda, cloves, cinnamon, ginger and salt. Stir the flour mixture and buttermilk alternately into the butter mixture until well blended. Spoon into the prepared tin and bake in the preheated oven for 35 minutes, or until a skewer inserted into the centre of the cake comes out clean. Remove from the oven and allow to cool for 5 minutes in the tin before turning out onto a wire rack over a large plate. Using a cocktail stick/toothpick, make holes on the top of the cake.

Mix together the icing/confectioners' sugar with enough lemon juice to make a smooth, pourable icing. Carefully pour the icing over the hot cake, then leave until cold. Cut the ginger cake into squares and serve.

## Difficulty Rating: 3 points

# Fudgy & Top Hat Chocolate Buns

## Makes 12

### Ingredients

50 g/2 oz/¹/₂ cup self-raising flour

25 g/1 oz/¹/₄ cup cocoa powder (unsweetened)

¹/₂ tsp baking powder

75 g/3 oz/²/₃ stick butter, softened

75 g/3 oz/¹/₃ cup demerara/turbinado sugar

1 egg, lightly beaten

1 tbsp milk

### For the fudgy icing:

15 g/¹/₂ oz/1 tbsp unsalted butter, melted

1 tbsp milk

15 g/¹/₂ oz/2 tbsp cocoa powder (unsweetened), sifted

3 tbsp icing/confectioners' sugar, sifted

25 g/1 oz/1 square dark/bittersweet chocolate, coarsely grated

### For the top hat filling:

150 ml/¹/₄ pint/¹/₂ cup whipping cream

2 tsp orange liqueur

1 tbsp icing/confectioners' sugar, sifted

Preheat the oven to 190°C/375°F/Gas Mark 5, 10 minutes before baking. Sift the flour, cocoa powder and baking powder into a bowl. Add the butter, sugar, egg and milk. Beat for 2–3 minutes until light and fluffy.

Divide the mixture equally between 12 paper cases/baking cups arranged in a muffin tin/pan. Bake on the shelf above the centre in the preheated oven for 15–20 minutes, or until well risen and firm to the touch. Leave in the tin for a few minutes, then transfer to a wire rack and leave to cool completely.

For the fudgy icing, mix together the melted butter, milk, cocoa powder and icing/confectioners' sugar. Place a spoonful of icing on the top of six of the cakes, spreading out to a circle with the back of the spoon. Sprinkle with grated chocolate.

To make the top hats, use a sharp knife to cut and remove a circle of sponge, about 3 cm/1¹/₄ inch across from each of the six remaining cakes. Whip the cream, orange liqueur and 1 teaspoon icing sugar together until soft peaks form. Spoon the filling into a piping/decorating bag fitted with a large star nozzle/tip and pipe a swirl in the centre of each cake. Replace the tops, then dust with the remaining icing sugar and serve with the other buns.

## Difficulty Rating: 2 points

# Chocolate & Orange Rock Buns

## Makes 12

### Ingredients

200 g/7 oz/1¾ cups self-raising flour

25 g/1 oz/¼ cup cocoa powder (unsweetened)

½ tsp baking powder

125 g/4 oz/1 stick plus 1 tbsp butter

3 tbsp granulated sugar

50 g/2 oz/⅓ cup glacé/candied pineapple, chopped

50 g/2 oz/⅓ cup ready-to-eat dried apricots, chopped

50 g/2 oz/2 tbsp glacé/candied cherries, quartered

1 egg

finely grated zest of ½ orange

1 tbsp orange juice

2 tbsp demerara/turbinado sugar

Preheat the oven to 200°C/400°F/Gas Mark 6, 15 minutes before baking. Lightly oil two baking sheets, or line with nonstick baking parchment. Sift the flour, cocoa powder and baking powder into a bowl. Cut the butter into squares, add to the dry ingredients. Rub in until the mixture resembles fine breadcrumbs. Add the granulated sugar, pineapple, apricots and cherries. Stir to mix.

Lightly beat the egg together with the grated orange zest and juice. Drizzle the egg mixture over the dry ingredients. Stir to combine. The mixture should be fairly stiff but not too dry – add a little more orange juice if necessary.

Using two teaspoons, shape the mixture into 12 rough heaps on the prepared baking sheets. Sprinkle generously with the demerara/turbinado sugar. Bake in the preheated oven for 15 minutes, switching the baking sheets around after 10 minutes. Leave on the baking sheets for 5 minutes to cool slightly, then transfer to a wire rack to cool. Serve warm or cold.

## Difficulty Rating: 2 points

# Jammy Buns

## Makes 12

### Ingredients

175 g/6 oz/1½ cups plain/all-purpose flour

175 g/6 oz/1½ cups wholemeal/whole-wheat flour

2 tsp baking powder

150 g/5 oz/1¼ sticks butter or margarine

125 g/4 oz/⅔ cup demerara/turbinado sugar

50 g/2 oz/⅓ cup dried cranberries

1 large/extra-large egg, beaten

1 tbsp milk, plus more for brushing

4–5 tbsp seedless raspberry jam/jelly

Preheat the oven to 190°C/375°F/Gas Mark 5, 10 minutes before baking. Lightly oil a large baking sheet.

Sift the flours and baking powder together into a large bowl, then tip in the grains remaining in the sieve.

Add the butter to the flours. Cut the butter or margarine into small pieces. (It is easier to do this when the butter is in the flour, as it helps stop the butter from sticking to the knife.) Rub the butter into the flours until it resembles coarse breadcrumbs. Stir in the sugar and cranberries.

Using a round-bladed knife, stir in the beaten egg and the milk. Mix to form a firm dough. Divide the mixture into 12 and roll into balls. Place the dough balls on the baking tray, leaving enough space for expansion.

Press your thumb into the centre of each ball to make a small hollow. Spoon a little of the jam/jelly into each hollow, and brush the top of the buns lightly with milk. Bake in the preheated oven for 20–25 minutes until golden brown. Cool on a wire rack and serve.

## Difficulty Rating: 1 point

# Lemon & Ginger Buns

## Makes 15

**Ingredients**

175 g/6 oz/1½ sticks butter or margarine
350 g/12 oz/3 cups plain/all-purpose flour
2 tsp baking powder
½ tsp ground ginger
pinch salt
finely grated zest of 1 lemon
175 g/6 oz/¾ cup demerara/turbinado sugar
125 g/4 oz/⅔ cup sultanas/golden raisins
75 g/3 oz/½ cup chopped mixed/candied peel
25 g/1 oz/2 tbsp stem ginger, finely chopped
1 egg
juice of 1 lemon

Preheat the oven to 220°C/425°F/Gas Mark 7, 15 minutes before baking. Cut the butter or margarine into small pieces and place in a large bowl.

Sift the flour, baking powder, ginger and salt together. Add to the butter with the lemon zest. Using your fingertips, rub the butter into the flour and spice mixture until it resembles coarse breadcrumbs. Stir in the sugar, sultanas/golden raisins, chopped mixed/candied peel and stem ginger.

Add the egg and lemon juice to the mixture, then, using a round-bladed knife, stir well to mix. The mixture should be quite stiff and just holding together.

Place heaped tablespoons of the mixture onto a lightly oiled baking tray, making sure that the dollops of mixture are well apart. Using a fork, rough up the edges of the buns and bake in the preheated oven for 12–15 minutes.

Leave the buns to cool for 5 minutes before transferring to a wire rack until cold, then serve. Otherwise, store the buns in an airtight container and eat within 3–5 days.

## Difficulty Rating: 2 points

# Chocolate Chelsea Buns

## Makes 12

**Ingredients**

75 g/3 oz/¹/₂ cup dried pears, finely chopped

1 tbsp apple or orange juice

225 g/8 oz/1³/₄ cups strong white/bread flour

1 tsp ground cinnamon

¹/₂ tsp salt

40 g/1¹/₂ oz/¹/₃ stick butter

1¹/₂ tsp easy-blend dried yeast

125 ml/4 fl oz/¹/₂ cup warm milk

1 medium/large egg, lightly beaten

75 g/3 oz/3 squares dark/bittersweet chocolate, chopped

3 tbsp maple syrup

Preheat the oven to 190°C/375°F/Gas Mark 5, 10 minutes before baking. Lightly oil an 18 cm/7 inch square tin/pan. Place the pears in a bowl with the fruit juice, stir, then cover and leave to soak while making the dough.

Sift the flour, cinnamon and salt into a bowl, rub in just over half of the butter, then stir in the yeast and make a well in the centre. Add the milk and egg and mix to a soft dough. Knead on a floured surface for 10 minutes until smooth and elastic, then place in a bowl. Cover with clingfilm/plastic wrap and leave in a warm place to rise for 1 hour, or until doubled in size. Turn out onto a lightly floured surface and knead the dough lightly before rolling out to a rectangle, about 30.5 x 23 cm/12 x 9 inches. Melt the remaining butter and brush over. Spoon the pears and chocolate evenly over the dough, leaving a 2.5 cm/ 1 inch border, then roll up tightly, starting at a long edge. Cut into 12 equal slices, then place cut–side up in the tin. Cover and leave to rise for 25 minutes, or until doubled in size.

Bake on the centre shelf of the preheated oven for 30 minutes, or until well risen and golden brown. Cover with foil after 20 minutes if the filling is starting to brown too much. Brush with the maple syrup while hot, then leave in the tin for 10 minutes to cool slightly. Turn out onto a wire rack and leave to cool. Separate the buns and serve warm.

## Difficulty Rating: 4 points

# Special Cakes & Gateaux

**More tempting cakes but on a richer, creamier or grander scale. Many of these cakes are so indulgently moist that they need to be eaten with a fork – all the more to prolong the delight! Some are more ambitious versions of classics, such as Celebration Fruit Cake, some are divine as desserts, such as White Chocolate & Raspberry Mousse Gateau and some are simply naughty, such as Rich Devil's Food Cake.**

# Apricot & Almond Layer Cake

## Cuts into 8–10 slices

### Ingredients

150 g/5 oz/1⅓ stick unsalted butter, softened

125 g/4 oz/⅓ cup caster/superfine sugar

5 medium/large eggs, separated

150 g/5 oz/6 squares dark/bittersweet chocolate,
    melted and cooled

150 g/5 oz/1 heaped cup self-raising flour, sifted

50 g/2 oz/½ cup ground almonds

75 g/3 oz/¾ cup icing/confectioners' sugar, sifted

300 g/11 oz/1 cup apricot jam/jelly

1 tbsp amaretto liqueur

125 g/4 oz/1 stick plus 1 tbsp unsalted butter, melted

125 g/4 oz/5 squares dark/bittersweet chocolate, melted

Preheat the oven to 180°C/350°F/Gas Mark 4, 10 minutes before baking. Lightly oil and line two 23 cm/9 inch round cake tins/pans. Cream the butter and sugar together until light and fluffy, then beat in the egg yolks, one at a time, beating well after each addition. Stir in the cooled chocolate with 1 tablespoon cooled boiled water, then fold in the flour and ground almonds.

Whisk the egg whites until stiff, then gradually whisk in the icing/confectioners' sugar, beating well after each addition. Whisk until the egg whites are stiff and glossy, then fold the egg whites into the chocolate mixture in two batches.

Divide the mixture evenly between the prepared tins and bake in the preheated oven for 30–40 minutes until firm. Leave for 5 minutes before turning out onto wire racks. Leave to cool completely.

Split the cakes in half. Gently heat the jam/jelly, pass through a sieve and stir in the amaretto liqueur. Place one cake layer onto a serving plate. Spread with a little of the jam, then sandwich with the next layer. Repeat with all the layers and use any remaining jam to brush over the entire cake. Leave until the jam sets.

Meanwhile, beat the butter and chocolate together until smooth, then cool at room temperature until thick enough to spread. Cover the top and sides of the cake with the chocolate icing and leave to set before slicing and serving.

## Difficulty Rating: 4 points

# Sauternes & Olive Oil Cake

## Cuts into 8–10 slices

**Ingredients**

125 g/4 oz/1 cup plain/all-purpose flour, plus extra for dusting

4 eggs

125 g/4 oz/²/₃ cup caster/superfine sugar

grated zest of ¹/₂ lemon

grated zest of ¹/₂ orange

2 tbsp Sauternes or other sweet dessert wine

3 tbsp very best-quality extra virgin olive oil

4 ripe peaches

1–2 tsp soft brown sugar, or to taste

1 tbsp lemon juice

icing/confectioners' sugar, to dust

Preheat the oven to 140°C/275°F/Gas Mark 1. Oil and line a 25.5 cm/10 inch springform tin/pan. Sift the flour onto a large sheet of greaseproof/waxed paper. Reserve.

Using a freestanding electric mixer, if possible, whisk the eggs and sugar together until pale and stiff. Add the lemon and orange zest. Turn the speed to low and pour the flour from the paper in a slow, steady stream onto the eggs and sugar mixture. Immediately add the wine and olive oil and switch the machine off, as the olive oil should not be incorporated completely.

Using a rubber spatula, fold the mixture very gently three or four times, so that the ingredients are just incorporated. Pour the mixture immediately into the prepared tin and bake in the preheated oven for 20–25 minutes without opening the door for at least 15 minutes. Test if cooked by pressing the top lightly with a clean finger – if it springs back, remove from the oven. If not, bake for a little longer. Leave the cake to cool in the tin on a wire rack. Remove the cake from the tin when cool enough to handle.

Meanwhile, skin the peaches and cut into segments. Toss with the brown sugar and lemon juice and reserve. When the cake is cold, dust generously with icing/confectioners' sugar, cut into wedges and serve with the peaches.

## Difficulty Rating: 4 points

# Peach & White Chocolate Gateau

## Cuts into 8–10 slices

### Ingredients

175 g/6 oz/1½ sticks unsalted butter, softened

2 tsp grated orange zest

175 g/6 oz/1 scant cup caster/superfine sugar

3 medium/large eggs

100 g/3½ oz/4 squares white chocolate, melted and cooled

225 g/8 oz/1¾ cups self-raising flour, sifted

300 ml/½ pint/1¼ cups double/heavy cream

40 g/1½ oz/scant ½ cup icing/confectioners' sugar

125 g/4 oz/1 cup hazelnuts, toasted and chopped

### For the peach filling:

2 ripe peaches, peeled and chopped

2 tbsp peach or orange liqueur

300 ml/½ pint/1¼ cups double/heavy cream

40 g/1½ oz/scant ½ cup icing/confectioners' sugar

Preheat the oven to 170°C/325°F/Gas Mark 3, 10 minutes before baking. Lightly oil and line a deep 23 cm/9 inch round cake tin/pan. Cream the butter, orange zest and sugar together until light and fluffy. Add the eggs, one at a time, beating well after each addition, then beat in the cooled white chocolate. Add the flour and 175 ml/6 fl oz water in two batches. Spoon into the prepared tin and bake in the preheated oven for 1½ hours, or until firm. Leave to stand for at least 5 minutes before turning out onto a wire rack to cool completely.

To make the filling, place the peaches in a bowl and pour over the liqueur. Leave to stand for 30 minutes. Whip the cream with the icing/confectioners' sugar until soft peaks form, then fold in the peach mixture.

Split the cold cake into three layers, place one layer on a serving plate and spread with half the peach filling. Top with a second sponge layer and spread with the remaining peach filling. Top with the remaining cake.

Whip the cream and icing sugar together until soft peaks form. Spread over the top and sides of the cake, piping some onto the top if liked. Press the hazelnuts into the side of the cake and if liked sprinkle a few on top. Chill in the refrigerator until required. Serve cut into slices. Store the cake in the refrigerator.

## Difficulty Rating: 4 points

# Orange Fruit Cake

## Cuts into 10–12 slices

### Ingredients

225 g/8 oz/1³/₄ cups self-raising flour

2 tsp baking powder

225 g/8 oz/1 heaped cup caster/superfine sugar

225 g/8 oz/2 sticks butter, softened

4 large/extra-large eggs

grated zest of 1 orange

2 tbsp orange juice

2–3 tbsp Cointreau

125 g/4 oz/1 cup chopped nuts

Cape gooseberries/ground cherries, blueberries, raspberries
and mint sprigs, to decorate

icing/confectioners' sugar, to dust (optional)

### For the filling:

450 ml/³/₄ pint/1³/₄ cups double/heavy cream

50 ml/2 fl oz/¹/₄ cup plain Greek yogurt

¹/₂ tsp vanilla extract

2–3 tbsp Cointreau

1 tbsp icing/confectioners' sugar

450 g/1 lb orange fruits, such as mango, peach, nectarine,
papaya and yellow plums

Preheat the oven to 180°C/350°F/Gas Mark 4, 10 minutes
before baking. Lightly oil and line the base of a 25.5 cm/
10 inch deep cake tin/pan or springform tin with nonstick
baking parchment.

Sift the flour and baking powder into a large bowl and stir
in the sugar. Make a well in the centre and add the butter,
eggs, grated zest and orange juice. Beat until blended and
a smooth batter is formed. Turn into the tin and smooth
the top.

Bake in the preheated oven for 35–45 minutes, or until golden
and the sides begin to shrink from the edge of the tin. Cool
before removing from the tin and discard the lining paper.

Using a serrated knife, slice off the top third of the cake, cutting
horizontally. Sprinkle the cut sides with the Cointreau.

For the filling, whip the cream and yogurt with the vanilla extract,
Cointreau and icing/confectioners' sugar until soft peaks form.
Chop the orange fruit and fold into the cream. Spread some of this
mixture onto the bottom cake layer. Transfer to a serving plate.
Cover with the top layer of sponge and spread the remaining
cream mixture over the top and sides. Press the chopped nuts
into the sides of the cake and decorate the top with the berries.
If liked, dust the top with icing sugar before serving.

## Difficulty Rating: 4 points

# Lemony Coconut Cake

## Cuts into 10–12 slices

### Ingredients

275 g/9½ oz/2½ cups plain/all-purpose flour

2 tbsp cornflour/cornstarch

1 tbsp baking powder

1 tsp salt

150 g/5 oz/½ cup white vegetable fat/shortening or soft margarine

275 g/10 oz/1¼ cups caster/superfine sugar

grated zest of 2 lemons

1 tsp vanilla extract

3 large/extra-large eggs

150 ml/¼ pint/⅔ cup milk

4 tbsp Malibu or rum

450 g/1 lb jar lemon curd

lime zest, to decorate

### For the frosting:

275 g/10 oz/1¼ cups caster/superfine sugar

125 ml/4 fl oz/½ cup water

1 tbsp glucose

¼ tsp salt

1 tsp vanilla extract

3 large/extra-large egg whites

75 g/3 oz/½ cup desiccated/shredded coconut

Preheat the oven to 180°C/350°F/Gas Mark 4, 10 minutes before baking. Lightly oil and flour two 20.5 cm/8 inch nonstick cake tins/pans.

Sift the flour, cornflour/cornstarch, baking powder and salt into a large bowl and add the white vegetable fat/shortening or margarine, sugar, lemon zest, vanilla extract, eggs and milk. With an electric whisk on a low speed, beat until blended, adding a little extra milk if the mixture is very stiff. Increase the speed to medium and beat for about 2 minutes.

Divide the mixture between the tins and smooth the tops evenly. Bake in the preheated oven for 20–25 minutes, or until the cakes feel firm and are cooked. Remove from the oven and cool before removing from the tins.

Put all the ingredients for the frosting, except the coconut, into a heatproof bowl placed over a saucepan of simmering water. (Do not allow the base of the bowl to touch the water.) Using an electric whisk, blend the frosting ingredients on a low speed, then increase the speed to high and beat for 7 minutes until the whites are stiff and glossy. Remove the bowl from the heat and continue beating until cool. Cover with clingfilm/plastic wrap.

Using a serrated knife, split the cake layers horizontally in half and sprinkle each cut surface with the Malibu or rum. Sandwich the cakes together with the lemon curd and press lightly. Spread the top and sides generously with the frosting, swirling and peaking the top.

Sprinkle the coconut over the top of the cake and gently press onto the sides to cover. Decorate the coconut cake with the lime zest and serve.

## Difficulty Rating: 4 points

# Almond Angel Cake with Amaretto Cream

## Cuts into 10–12 slices

### Ingredients

175 g/6 oz/1¾ cups, plus 2–3 tbsp icing/confectioners' sugar

150 g/5 oz/1 heaped cup plain/all-purpose flour

350 ml/12 fl oz egg whites (about 10 large/extra-large egg whites)

1½ tsp cream of tartar

½ tsp vanilla extract

1 tsp almond extract

¼ tsp salt

200 g/7 oz/1 cup caster/superfine sugar

175 ml/6 fl oz/scant ¾ cup double/heavy cream

2 tbsp amaretto liqueur

fresh raspberries, to decorate

Preheat the oven to 180°C/350°F/Gas Mark 4, 10 minutes before baking. Sift together the 175 g/6 oz icing/confectioners' sugar and flour. Stir to blend, then sift again and reserve.

Using an electric whisk, beat the egg whites, cream of tartar, vanilla extract, ½ teaspoon of the almond extract and salt on medium speed until soft peaks form. Gradually add the caster/superfine sugar, 2 tablespoons at a time, beating well after each addition, until stiff peaks form.

Sift about one third of the flour mixture over the egg white mixture and, using a metal spoon or rubber spatula, gently fold into the egg white mixture. Repeat, folding the flour mixture into the egg white mixture in two more batches. Spoon gently into an ungreased angel–food cake tin/pan or 25.5 cm/10 inch tube tin. Bake in the preheated oven until risen and golden on top and the surface springs back quickly when gently pressed with a clean finger. Immediately invert the cake tin and cool completely in the tin.

When cool, carefully run a sharp knife around the edge of the tin and the centre ring to loosen the cake from the edge. Using the fingertips, ease the cake from the tin and invert onto a cake plate. Thickly dust the cake with the extra icing sugar.

Whip the cream with the remaining almond extract, amaretto liqueur and a little more icing sugar until soft peaks form. Fill a piping/decorating bag fitted with a star nozzle/tip with half the cream and pipe around the bottom edge of the cake. Decorate the edge with the fresh raspberries and serve the remaining cream separately.

## Difficulty Rating: 5 points

# Wild Strawberry & Rose Petal Jam Cake

## Cuts into 8 servings

### Ingredients

275 g/10 oz/2 heaped cups plain/all-purpose flour

1 tsp baking powder

¼ tsp salt

150 g/5 oz/1⅓ sticks unsalted butter, softened

200 g/7 oz/1 cup caster/superfine sugar

2 large/extra-large eggs, beaten

2 tbsp rosewater

125 ml/4 fl oz/½ cup milk

125 g/4 oz/⅓ cup rose petal or strawberry jam/jelly,
   slightly warmed

125 g/4 oz/1 scant cup wild strawberries, hulled, or baby
   strawberries, chopped

frosted rose petals, to decorate

### For the rose cream filling:

200 ml/7 fl oz/¾ cup double/heavy cream

25 ml/1 fl oz/2 tbsp plain Greek yogurt

2 tbsp rosewater

1–2 tbsp icing/confectioners' sugar

Preheat the oven to 180°C/350°F/Gas Mark 4, 10 minutes before baking. Lightly oil and flour a 20.5 cm/8 inch nonstick cake tin/pan. Sift the flour, baking powder and salt into a bowl and reserve.

Beat the butter and sugar until light and fluffy. Beat in the eggs, a little at a time, then stir in the rosewater. Gently fold in the flour mixture and milk with a metal spoon or rubber spatula and mix lightly together. Spoon the cake mixture into the tin, spreading evenly and smoothing the top. Bake in the preheated oven for 25–30 minutes, or until well risen and golden and the centre springs back when pressed with a clean finger. Remove and cool, then remove from the tin.

For the filling, whisk the cream, yogurt, 1 tablespoon of rosewater and 1 tablespoon of icing/confectioners' sugar until soft peaks form. Split the cake horizontally in half and sprinkle with the remaining rosewater.

Spread the warmed jam/jelly on the base of the cake. Top with half the whipped cream mixture, then sprinkle with half the strawberries. Place the remaining cake half on top. Spread with the remaining cream and swirl if desired. Decorate with the rose petals. Dust the cake lightly with a little icing/confectioners' sugar and serve.

## Difficulty Rating: 4 points

# Buttery Passion Fruit Madeira Cake

## Cuts into 8–10 slices

### Ingredients

210 g/7½ oz/1⅔ cups plain/all-purpose flour

1 tsp baking powder

175 g/6 oz/1½ sticks unsalted butter, softened

250 g/9 oz/1¼ cups, plus 1 tsp caster/superfine sugar

grated zest of 1 orange

1 tsp vanilla extract

3 medium/large eggs, beaten

2 tbsp milk

6 ripe passion fruits

50 g/2 oz/½ cup icing/confectioners' sugar

icing/confectioners' sugar, to dust

Preheat the oven to 180˚C/350˚F/Gas Mark 4, 10 minutes before baking. Lightly oil and line the base of a 23 x 12.5 cm/9 x 5 inch loaf tin/pan with greaseproof/waxed paper. Sift the flour and baking powder into a bowl and reserve.

Beat the butter, sugar, zest and vanilla extract until light and fluffy, then gradually beat in the eggs, 1 tablespoon at a time, beating well after each addition. If the mixture appears to curdle or separate, beat in a little of the flour mixture. Fold in the flour mixture with the milk until just blended. Do not overmix. Spoon lightly into the prepared tin and smooth the top evenly. Sprinkle lightly with the teaspoon of caster/superfine sugar. Bake in the oven for 55 minutes, or until well risen and golden brown. Remove from the oven and leave to cool for 15–20 minutes.

Cut the passion fruits in half and scoop out the pulp into a sieve set over a bowl. Press the juice through using a spatula or spoon. Add the icing/confectioners' sugar and stir to dissolve, adding a little extra sugar if necessary. Using a skewer, pierce holes all over the cake. Slowly spoon the passion fruit glaze over the cake and allow to seep in. Gently turn the cake out of the tin onto a wire rack and turn it back the right way up, discarding the lining paper. Dust with icing sugar and cool completely. Serve cold.

## Difficulty Rating: 3 points

# White Chocolate & Passion Fruit Cake

## Cuts into 8–10 slices

**Ingredients**

125 g/4 oz/5 squares white chocolate

125 g/4 oz/1 stick plus 1 tbsp butter

225 g/8 oz/1 heaped cup caster/superfine sugar

2 medium/large eggs

125 ml/4 fl oz/½ cup sour cream

200 g/7 oz/1½ cups plain/all-purpose flour, sifted

75 g/3 oz/scant ⅔ cup self-raising flour, sifted

125 g/4 oz/5 squares white chocolate, coarsely grated, to decorate

**For the syrup and icing:**

200 g/7 oz/1 cup caster/superfine sugar

4 tbsp passion fruit juice (about 8–10 passion fruit, sieved)

1½ tbsp passion fruit seeds

250 g/9 oz/2¼ sticks unsalted butter

Preheat the oven to 180°C/350°F/Gas Mark 4, 10 minutes before baking. Lightly oil and line two 20.5 cm/8 inch cake tins/pans. Melt the white chocolate in a heatproof bowl set over a saucepan of simmering water. Stir in 125 ml/4 fl oz/½ cup warm water and stir, then leave to cool.

Whisk the butter and sugar together until light and fluffy, add the eggs, one at a time, beating well after each addition. Beat in the chocolate mixture, sour cream and sifted flours. Divide the mixture into eight portions. Spread one portion into each of the tins. Bake in the preheated oven for 10 minutes, or until firm, then turn out onto wire racks. Repeat with the remaining mixture to make eight cake layers.

To make a thin syrup, place 125 ml/4 fl oz/½ cup water with 50 g/2 oz/¼ cup of the sugar in a saucepan. Heat gently, stirring, until the sugar has dissolved. Bring to the boil, simmer for 2 minutes. Remove from the heat and cool, then add 2 tablespoons of the passion fruit juice. Reserve.

To make the icing, blend the remaining sugar with 50 ml/2 fl oz/ ¼ cup water in a small saucepan and stir constantly over a low

heat, without boiling, until the sugar has dissolved. Remove from the heat and cool. Stir in the remaining passion fruit juice and the seeds. Cool, then strain. Using an electric whisk, beat the butter in a bowl until very pale. Gradually beat in the thick syrup. Place one layer of cake on a serving plate. Brush with the thin syrup and spread with a thin layer of icing. Repeat with the remaining cake, syrup and icing. Cover the cake with the remaining icing. Press the grated chocolate into the top and sides to decorate.

## Difficulty Rating: 5 points

# White Chocolate & Raspberry Mousse Gateau

## Cuts into 8 slices

### Ingredients

4 medium/large eggs

125 g/4 oz/²/₃ cup caster/superfine sugar

75 g/3 oz/scant ²/₃ cup plain/all-purpose flour, sifted

25 g/1 oz/scant ¹/₄ cup cornflour/cornstarch, sifted

3 gelatine leaves

450 g/1 lb/3²/₃ cups raspberries, thawed if frozen

400 g/14 oz/16 squares white chocolate

200 g/7 oz/1 scant cup plain fromage frais/Quark
    or Greek yogurt

2 medium/large egg whites

2 tbsp caster/superfine sugar

4 tbsp raspberry or orange liqueur

200 ml/7 fl oz/³/₄ cup double/heavy cream

fresh raspberries, halved, to decorate

Preheat the oven to 190°C/375°F/Gas Mark 5, 10 minutes before baking. Oil and line two 23 cm/9 inch cake tins/pans. Whisk the eggs and sugar until thick and creamy and the whisk leaves a trail in the mixture. Fold in the flour and cornflour/cornstarch, then divide between the tins. Bake in the preheated oven for 12–15 minutes, or until risen and firm. Cool in the tins, then turn out onto wire racks.

Place the gelatine with 4 tablespoons cold water in a dish and leave to soften for 5 minutes. Purée half the raspberries, press through a sieve, then heat until nearly boiling. Squeeze out excess water from the gelatine, add to the purée and stir until dissolved. Reserve.

Melt 175 g/6 oz/7 squares of the chocolate in a bowl set over a saucepan of simmering water. Leave to cool, then stir in the fromage frais and the purée. Whisk the egg whites until stiff and whisk in the sugar. Fold into the raspberry mixture with the rest of the berries.

Line the sides of a 23 cm/9 inch springform tin with nonstick baking parchment. Place one layer of sponge in the base and sprinkle with half the liqueur. Pour in the raspberry mixture and top

with the second sponge. Brush with the remaining liqueur. Press down and chill in the refrigerator for 4 hours. Unmould onto a plate. Cut a strip of double thickness nonstick baking parchment to fit around the cake and stand 1 cm/¹/₂ inch higher. Melt the remaining white chocolate and spread thickly onto the parchment. Leave until just setting. Wrap around the cake and freeze for 15 minutes. Peel away the parchment. Whip the cream until thick and spread over the top. Decorate with raspberries.

## Difficulty Rating: 5 points

# Cranberry & White Chocolate Cake

## Serves 4

**Ingredients**

225 g/8 oz/2 sticks butter, softened
250 g/9 oz/1 scant cup full fat soft cheese
150 g/5 oz/³⁄₄ cup soft light brown sugar
200 g/7 oz/1 cup caster/superfine sugar
grated zest of ¹⁄₂ orange
1 tsp vanilla extract
4 medium/large eggs
375 g/13 oz/3 cups plain/all-purpose flour
2 tsp baking powder
200 g/7 oz/2 cups cranberries, thawed if frozen
225 g/8 oz/9 squares white chocolate, coarsely chopped
2 tbsp orange juice

Preheat the oven to 180°C/350°F/Gas Mark 4, 10 minutes before baking. Lightly oil and flour a 23 cm/9 inch kugelhopf tin/pan or ring tin. Using an electric mixer, cream the butter and cheese with the sugars until light and fluffy. Add the grated orange zest and vanilla extract and beat until smooth, then beat in the eggs, one at a time.

Sift the flour and baking powder together and stir into the creamed mixture, beating well after each addition. Fold in the cranberries and 175 g/6 oz/7 squares of the white chocolate. Spoon into the prepared tin and bake in the preheated oven for 1 hour, or until firm and a skewer inserted into the centre comes out clean. Cool in the tin before turning out onto on a wire rack.

Melt the remaining white chocolate, stir until smooth, then stir in the orange juice and leave to cool until thickened. Transfer the cake to a serving plate and spoon over the white chocolate and orange glaze. Leave to set.

## Difficulty Rating: 3 points

# Luxury Carrot Cake

## Cuts into 12 slices

### Ingredients

275 g/10 oz/2 heaped cups plain/all-purpose flour

2 tsp baking powder

1 tsp bicarbonate of soda/baking soda

1 tsp salt

2 tsp ground cinnamon

1 tsp ground ginger

200 g/7 oz/1 cup soft dark brown sugar

100 g/3½ oz/½ cup caster/superfine sugar

4 large/extra-large eggs, beaten

250 ml/9 fl oz/1 cup sunflower/corn oil

1 tbsp vanilla extract

4 carrots, peeled and shredded (about 450 g/1 lb)

400 g/14 oz can crushed pineapple, well drained

125 g/4 oz/1¼ cups pecans or walnuts, toasted and chopped

### For the frosting:

175 g/6 oz/¾ cup cream cheese, softened

50 g/2 oz/¼ cup butter, softened

1 tsp vanilla extract

225 g/8 oz/2¼ cups icing/confectioners' sugar, sifted

1–2 tbsp milk

Preheat the oven to 180°C/350°F/Gas Mark 4, 10 minutes before baking. Lightly oil a 33 x 23 cm/13 x 9 inch baking tin/pan. Line the base with nonstick baking parchment, oil and dust with flour.

Sift the first six ingredients into a large bowl and stir in the sugars to blend. Make a well in the centre.

Beat the eggs, oil and vanilla extract together and pour into the well. Using an electric whisk, gradually beat, drawing in the flour mixture from the side until a smooth batter forms. Stir in the carrots, crushed pineapple and chopped nuts until blended. Pour into the prepared tin and smooth the surface evenly. Bake in the preheated oven for 50 minutes, or until firm and a skewer inserted into the centre comes out clean. Remove from the oven and leave to cool before removing from the tin and discarding the lining paper.

For the frosting, beat the cream cheese, butter and vanilla extract together until smooth, then gradually beat in the icing/confectioners' sugar until the frosting is smooth. Add a little milk if necessary. Spread the frosting over the top. Refrigerate for about 1 hour to set the frosting, then cut into squares and serve.

## Difficulty Rating: 2 points

# Celebration Fruit Cake

## Cuts into 16 slices

**Ingredients**

125 g/4 oz/1 stick plus 1 tbsp butter or margarine

125 g/4 oz/²/₃ cup soft dark brown sugar

400 g/13 oz canned crushed pineapple

150 g/5 oz/1 cup raisins

150 g/5 oz/1 cup sultanas/golden raisins

125 g/4 oz/³/₄ cup crystallized/candied ginger, finely chopped

125 g/4 oz/²/₃ cup glacé/candied cherries, coarsely chopped

125 g/4 oz/³/₄ cup mixed/candied cut peel

225 g/8 oz/1³/₄ cups self-raising flour

1 tsp bicarbonate of soda/baking soda

2 tsp mixed/pumpkin pie spice

1 tsp ground cinnamon

¹/₂ tsp salt

2 large/extra-large eggs, beaten

**For the topping:**

100 g/3¹/₂ oz/1 cup pecan or walnut halves, lightly toasted

125 g/4 oz/³/₄ cup red, green and yellow glacé/candied cherries

100 g/3¹/₂ oz/²/₃ cup small pitted prunes or dates

2 tbsp clear honey

Preheat the oven to 170°C/325°F/Gas Mark 3, 10 minutes before baking. Heat the butter and sugar in a saucepan until the sugar has dissolved, stirring frequently. Add the pineapple and juice, dried fruits and peel. Bring to the boil, simmer for 3 minutes, stirring occasionally, then remove from the heat to cool completely.

Lightly oil and line the base of a 20.5 x 7.5 cm/8 x 3 inch loose-bottomed cake tin/pan with nonstick baking parchment.

Sift the flour, bicarbonate of soda/baking soda, spices and salt into a bowl. Add the boiled fruit mixture to the flour with the eggs and mix. Spoon into the tin and smooth the top. Bake in the preheated oven for 1¹/₄ hours, or until a skewer inserted into the centre comes out clean. (If the cake is browning too quickly, cover loosely with kitchen foil and reduce the oven temperature.) Remove and cool completely before removing from the tin and discarding the lining paper.

Arrange the nuts, cherries and prunes or dates in an attractive pattern on top of the cake. Heat the honey and brush over the topping to glaze. Alternatively, toss the nuts and fruits in the warm honey and spread evenly over the top of the cake. Cool completely and store in a cake tin for a day or two before serving to allow the flavours to develop.

## Difficulty Rating: 2 points

# Italian Polenta Cake with Mascarpone Cream

## Cuts into 6–8 slices

### Ingredients

1 tsp butter and flour for the tin/pan
100 g/3$\frac{1}{2}$ oz/$\frac{3}{4}$ cup plain/all-purpose flour
40 g/1$\frac{1}{2}$ oz/$\frac{1}{4}$ cup polenta or yellow cornmeal
1 tsp baking powder
$\frac{1}{4}$ tsp salt
grated zest of 1 lemon
2 large/extra-large eggs
150 g/5 oz/$\frac{3}{4}$ cup caster/superfine sugar
5 tbsp milk
$\frac{1}{2}$ tsp almond extract
2 tbsp raisins or sultanas/golden raisins
75 g/3 oz/$\frac{2}{3}$ stick unsalted butter, softened
2 medium dessert pears, peeled, cored and thinly sliced
2 tbsp apricot jam/jelly
175 g/6 oz/$\frac{3}{4}$ cup mascarpone cheese
1–2 tsp sugar
50 ml/2 fl oz/$\frac{1}{4}$ cup double/heavy cream
2 tbsp amaretto liqueur or rum
2–3 tbsp toasted flaked almonds
icing/confectioners' sugar, to dust

Preheat the oven to 190°C/375°F/Gas Mark 5, 10 minutes before baking. Butter a 23 cm/9 inch springform tin/pan. Dust lightly with flour. Stir the flour, polenta or cornmeal, baking powder, salt and lemon zest together.

Beat the eggs and half the sugar until light and fluffy. Slowly beat in the milk and almond extract. Stir in the raisins or sultanas/golden raisins, then beat in the flour mixture and 50 g/2 oz/$\frac{1}{4}$ cup of the butter. Spoon into the tin and smooth the top evenly. Arrange the pear slices on top in overlapping concentric circles.

Melt the remaining butter and brush over the pear slices. Sprinkle with the rest of the sugar. Bake in the preheated oven for about 40 minutes until puffed and golden and the edges of the pears are lightly caramelized. Transfer to a wire rack. Reserve to cool in the tin for 15 minutes. Remove the cake from the tin.

Heat the apricot jam/jelly with 1 tablespoon water and brush over the top of the cake to glaze.

Beat the mascarpone cheese with the sugar to taste, the cream and amaretto or rum until smooth and forming a soft dropping consistency. When the cake is cool, sprinkle over the almonds and dust generously with the icing/confectioners' sugar. Serve the cake with the liqueur-flavoured mascarpone cream on the side.

## Difficulty Rating: 3 points

# Autumn Bramley Apple Cake

## Cuts into 8–10 slices

**Ingredients**

225 g/8 oz/2 cups self-raising flour

1½ tsp baking powder

150 g/5 oz/½ cup plus 2 tbsp margarine, softened

150 g/5 oz/¾ cup caster/superfine sugar, plus
   extra for sprinkling

1 tsp vanilla extract

2 large/extra-large eggs, beaten

1.1 kg/2½ lb Bramley apples/tart cooking apples, peeled,
   cored and sliced

1 tbsp lemon juice

½ tsp ground cinnamon

fresh custard or cream

Preheat the oven to 170°C/325°F/Gas Mark 3, 10 minutes before baking. Lightly oil and line the base of a 20.5 cm/8 inch deep cake tin/pan with nonstick baking parchment or greaseproof/waxed paper. Sift the flour and baking powder into a small bowl. Beat the margarine, sugar and vanilla extract in a larger bowl until light and fluffy. Gradually beat in the eggs a little at a time, beating well after each addition. Stir in the flour. Spoon about one third of the mixture into the tin, smoothing the surface.

Toss the apple slices in the lemon juice and cinnamon and spoon over the cake mixture, making a thick even layer. Spread the remaining mixture over the apple layer to the edge of the tin, making sure the apples are covered. Smooth the top with the back of a wet spoon and sprinkle generously with sugar. Bake in the preheated oven for 1½ hours, or until well risen and golden, the apples are tender and the centre of the cake springs back when lightly pressed. If the top browns too quickly, reduce the oven temperature slightly and cover the cake loosely with kitchen foil. Transfer to a wire rack and cool for about 20 minutes in the tin. Run a thin knife blade between the cake and the tin to loosen the cake and invert onto a paper-lined rack. Turn the cake the right way up and cool. Serve with the custard or cream.

## Difficulty Rating: 2 points

# Black & White Torte

## Cuts into 8–10 slices

### Ingredients

4 medium/large eggs

150 g/5 oz/³/₄ cup caster/superfine sugar

50 g/2 oz/¹/₃ cup cornflour/cornstarch

50 g/2 oz/¹/₃ cup plain/all-purpose flour

50 g/2 oz/¹/₃ cup self-raising flour

900 ml/1¹/₂ pints/1 scant quart double/heavy cream

150 g/5 oz/6 squares dark/bittersweet chocolate, chopped

300 g/11 oz/12 squares white chocolate, chopped

6 tbsp Grand Marnier, or other orange liqueur

cocoa powder (unsweetened), for dusting

Preheat the oven to 180 C/350 F/Gas Mark 4, 10 minutes before baking. Lightly oil and line a 23 cm/9 inch round cake tin/pan. Beat the eggs and sugar in a large bowl until thick and creamy. Sift together the cornflour/cornstarch, plain/all-purpose flour and self-raising flour three times, then lightly fold into the egg mixture. Spoon the mixture into the prepared tin and bake in the preheated oven for 35–40 minutes or until firm. Turn the cake out onto a wire rack and leave to cool.

Place 300 ml/¹/₂ pint/1¹/₄ cups of the double/heavy cream in a saucepan and bring to the boil. Remove from the heat and add the dark/bittersweet chocolate and a tablespoon of the liqueur. Stir until smooth. Repeat using the remaining cream, white chocolate and 2 tablespoons of the liqueur. Refrigerate for 2 hours, then whisk each mixture until thick and creamy.

Place the dark chocolate mixture in a piping/decorating bag fitted with a plain nozzle/tip and place half the white chocolate mixture in a separate piping bag fitted with a plain nozzle. Reserve the remaining white chocolate mixture. Split the cold cake horizontally into two layers. Brush or drizzle the remaining 3 tablespoons of liqueur over the cakes. Put one layer onto a serving plate. Pipe alternating rings of white and dark chocolate mixture to cover the first layer of cake. Use the reserved white chocolate mixture to cover the top and sides of the cake. Dust with cocoa powder, cut into slices and serve. Store in the refrigerator.

## Difficulty Rating: 4 points

# Mocha Truffle Cake

## Cuts into 8–10 slices

### Ingredients

3 medium/large eggs

125 g/4 oz/²/₃ cup caster/superfine sugar

40 g/1¹/₂ oz/¹/₃ cup cornflour/cornstarch

40 g/1¹/₂ oz/¹/₃ cup self-raising flour

2 tbsp cocoa powder (unsweetened)

2 tbsp milk

2 tbsp coffee liqueur

100 g/3¹/₂ oz/4 squares white chocolate, melted and cooled

200 g/7 oz/8 squares dark/bittersweet chocolate, melted and cooled

600 ml/1 pint/2¹/₂ cups double/heavy cream

200 g/7 oz/8 squares milk/semisweet chocolate

100 g/3¹/₂ oz/1 stick unsalted butter

Preheat the oven to 180°C/350°F/Gas Mark 4, 10 minutes before baking. Lightly oil and line a deep 23 cm/9 inch round cake tin/pan. Beat the eggs and sugar in a bowl until thick and creamy.

Sift together the cornflour/cornstarch, self-raising flour and cocoa powder and fold lightly into the egg mixture. Spoon into the prepared tin and bake in the preheated oven for 30 minutes, or until firm. Turn out onto a wire rack and leave until cold. Split the cold cake horizontally into two layers. Mix together the milk and coffee liqueur and brush onto the cake layers.

Stir the cooled white chocolate into one bowl and the cooled dark/bittersweet chocolate into another one. Whip the cream until soft peaks form, then divide between the two bowls and stir. Place one layer of cake in a 23 cm/9 inch springform tin. Spread with half the white chocolate cream. Top with the dark chocolate cream, then the remaining white chocolate cream. Finally, place the remaining cake layer on top. Chill in the refrigerator for 4 hours, or overnight, until set. When ready to serve, melt the milk/semisweet chocolate and butter in a heatproof bowl set over simmering water and stir until smooth. Remove from the heat and leave until thick enough to spread, then use to cover the top and sides of the cake. Leave to set at room temperature, then chill in the refrigerator. Cut the cake into slices and serve.

## Difficulty Rating: 4 points

# Chocolate Buttermilk Cake

## Cuts into 8–10 slices

**Ingredients**

175 g/6 oz/1½ sticks butter

1 tsp vanilla extract

350 g/12 oz/1¾ cups caster/superfine sugar

4 medium/large eggs, separated

100 g/3½ oz/¾ cup self-raising flour

40 g/1½ oz/½ cup cocoa powder (unsweetened)

175 ml/6 fl oz/scant ¾ cup buttermilk

200 g/7 oz/8 squares dark/bittersweet chocolate

100 g/3½ oz/1 stick butter

300 ml/½ pint/1¼ cups double/heavy cream

Preheat the oven to 180°C/350°F/Gas Mark 4, 10 minutes before baking. Lightly oil and line a deep 23 cm/9 inch round cake tin/pan. Cream together the butter, vanilla extract and sugar until light and fluffy, then beat in the egg yolks, one at a time.

Sift together the flour and cocoa powder and fold into the egg mixture together with the buttermilk. Whisk the egg whites until soft peaks form and fold carefully into the chocolate mixture in two batches. Spoon the mixture into the prepared tin and bake in the preheated oven for 1 hour, or until firm. Cool slightly, then turn out onto a wire rack and leave until completely cold.

Place the chocolate and butter together in a heatproof bowl set over a saucepan of simmering water and heat until melted. Stir until smooth, then leave at room temperature until the chocolate is thick enough to spread.

Split the cake horizontally in half. Use some of the chocolate mixture to sandwich the two halves together. Spread and decorate the top of the cake with the remaining chocolate mixture. Finally, whip the cream until soft peaks form and use to spread around the sides of the cake. Chill in the refrigerator until required. Serve cut into slices. Store in the refrigerator.

## Difficulty Rating: 3 points

# Rich Devil's Food Cake

## Cuts into 12–16 slices

### Ingredients

450 g/1 lb/3½ cups plain/all-purpose flour

1 tbsp bicarbonate of soda/baking soda

½ tsp salt

75 g/3 oz/1 scant cup cocoa powder (unsweetened)

300 ml/½ pint/1¼ cups milk

150 g/5 oz/⅔ cup butter, softened

400 g/14 oz/2 cups soft dark brown sugar

2 tsp vanilla extract

4 large/extra-large eggs

### For the chocolate fudge icing:

275 g/10 oz/1⅓ cups caster/superfine sugar

½ tsp salt

125 g/4 oz dark/bittersweet chocolate, chopped

250 ml/8 fl oz/1 cup milk

2 tbsp golden/corn syrup

125 g/4 oz/1 stick plus 1 tbsp butter, diced

2 tsp vanilla extract

Preheat the oven to 180°C/350°F/Gas Mark 4, 10 minutes before baking. Lightly oil and line the bases of three 23 cm/9 inch cake tins/pans with greaseproof/waxed paper or baking parchment. Sift the flour, bicarbonate of soda/baking soda and salt into a bowl.

Sift the cocoa powder into another bowl and gradually whisk in a little of the milk to form a paste. Continue whisking in the milk until a smooth mixture results.

Beat the butter, sugar and vanilla extract until light and fluffy, then gradually beat in the eggs, beating well after each addition. Stir in the flour and cocoa mixtures alternately in three or four batches. Divide the mixture evenly among the three tins, smoothing the surfaces evenly. Bake in the preheated oven for 25–35 minutes until cooked and firm to the touch. Remove, cool and turn out onto a wire rack. Discard the lining paper.

To make the icing, put the sugar, salt and chocolate into a heavy-based saucepan and stir in the milk until blended. Add the golden/corn syrup and butter. Bring the mixture to the boil over a

medium–high heat, stirring to help dissolve the sugar. Boil for 1 minute, stirring constantly. Remove from the heat, stir in the vanilla extract and cool. When cool, whisk until thickened and slightly lightened in colour. Sandwich the three cake layers together with about a third of the icing, placing the third cake layer with the flat side up. Transfer the cake to a serving plate and, using a metal palette knife, spread the remaining icing over the top and sides. Swirl the top to create a decorative effect and serve.

## Difficulty Rating: 3 points

# Coffee & Walnut Gateau with Brandied Prunes

## Cuts into 10–12 slices

**Ingredients**

**For the prunes:**
225 g/8 oz/1¼ cups ready-to-eat pitted dried prunes
150 ml/¼ pint/⅔ cup cold tea
3 tbsp brandy

**For the cake:**
450 g/1 lb/4½ cups walnut pieces
50 g/2 oz/⅓ cup self-raising flour
½ tsp baking powder
1 tsp instant coffee powder (not granules)
5 large/extra-large eggs, separated
¼ tsp cream of tartar
150 g/5 oz/¾ cup caster/superfine sugar
2 tbsp sunflower/corn oil
8 walnut halves, to decorate

**For the filling:**
600 ml/1 pint/2½ cups double/heavy cream
4 tbsp icing/confectioners' sugar, sifted
2 tbsp coffee-flavoured liqueur

Preheat the oven to 180°C/350°F/Gas Mark 4, 10 minutes before baking. Put the prunes in a small bowl with the tea and brandy and allow to stand for 3–4 hours, or overnight. Oil and line the bases of two 23 cm/9 inch cake tins/pans. Chop the walnut pieces in a food processor. Reserve a quarter of the nuts. Add the flour, baking powder and coffee and blend until finely ground.

Whisk the egg whites with the cream of tartar until soft peaks form. Sprinkle in one third of the sugar, 2 tablespoons at a time, until stiff peaks form. In another bowl, beat the egg yolks, oil and the remaining sugar until thick. Using a metal spoon or rubber spatula, alternately fold in the nut mixture and egg whites until just blended. Divide the mixture evenly between the tins, smoothing the tops. Bake in the preheated oven for 30–35 minutes, or until the tops of the cakes spring back when

lightly pressed with a clean finger. Remove from the oven and cool. Remove from the tins and discard the lining paper.

Drain the prunes, reserving the soaking liquid. Dry on kitchen paper, then chop and reserve. Whisk the cream with the icing/confectioners' sugar and liqueur until soft peaks form. Spoon one eighth of the cream into a piping/decorating bag fitted with a star nozzle/tip.

Cut the cake layers in half horizontally. Sprinkle each cut side with 1 tablespoon of the reserved prune–soaking liquid. Sandwich the cakes together with half of the cream and all of the chopped prunes. Spread the remaining cream around the sides of the cake and press in the reserved chopped walnuts. Pipe rosettes around the edge of the cake. Decorate with walnut halves and serve.

## Difficulty Rating: 4 points

# French Chocolate Pecan Torte

## Cuts into 16 slices

### Ingredients

200 g/7 oz/8 squares dark/bittersweet chocolate, chopped

150 g/5 oz/1⅓ sticks butter, diced

4 large/extra-large eggs

100 g/3½ oz/½ cup caster/superfine sugar

2 tsp vanilla extract

125 g/4 oz/1¼ cups pecans, finely ground

2 tsp ground cinnamon

24 pecan halves, lightly toasted, to decorate

**For the chocolate glaze:**

125 g/4 oz/5 squares dark/bittersweet chocolate, chopped

65 g/2½ oz/½ stick butter, diced

2 tbsp clear honey

¼ tsp ground cinnamon

## Difficulty Rating: 4 points

Preheat the oven to 180°C/350°F/Gas Mark 4, 10 minutes before baking. Lightly butter and line a 20.5 x 5 cm/8 x 2 inch springform tin/pan with nonstick baking parchment. Wrap the tin in a large sheet of kitchen foil to prevent water seeping in.

Melt the chocolate and butter in a saucepan over a low heat and stir until smooth. Remove from the heat and cool.

Using an electric whisk, beat the eggs, sugar and vanilla extract until light and foamy. Gradually beat in the melted chocolate, ground nuts and cinnamon, then pour into the prepared tin. Set the foil-wrapped tin in a large roasting tin and pour in enough boiling water to come 2 cm/¾ inch up the sides of the tin. Bake in the preheated oven until the edge is set, but the centre is still soft when the tin is gently shaken. Remove from the oven and place on a wire rack to cool.

For the glaze, melt all the ingredients over a low heat until melted and smooth, then remove from the heat. Dip each pecan halfway into the glaze and set on a sheet of nonstick baking parchment until set. Allow the remaining glaze to thicken slightly.

Remove the cake from the tin and invert. Pour the glaze over the cake, smoothing the top and spreading the glaze around the sides. Arrange the glazed pecans around the edge of the torte. Allow to set and serve.

# Dark Chocolate Layered Torte

## Cuts into 10–12 slices

### Ingredients

175 g/6 oz/1½ sticks butter

1 tbsp instant coffee granules

150 g/5 oz/6 squares dark/bittersweet chocolate

350 g/12 oz/1¼ cups caster/superfine sugar

150 g/5 oz/1 heaped cup self-raising flour

125 g/4 oz/1 cup plain/all-purpose flour

2 tbsp cocoa powder (unsweetened)

2 medium/large eggs

1 tsp vanilla extract

215 g/7½ oz/9 squares dark/bittersweet chocolate, melted

125 g/4 oz/1 stick plus 1 tbsp butter, melted

40 g/1½ oz/scant ½ cup icing/confectioners' sugar, sifted

2 tsp raspberry jam/jelly

2½ tbsp chocolate liqueur

100 g/3½ oz/1 cup toasted flaked almonds

Preheat the oven to 150°C/300°F/Gas Mark 2, 10 minutes before baking. Lightly oil and line a 23 cm/9 inch square cake tin/pan. Melt the butter in a saucepan, remove from the heat and stir in the coffee granules and 250 ml/8 fl oz/1 cup hot water. Add the dark/bittersweet chocolate and sugar and stir until smooth, then pour into a bowl. In another bowl, sift together the flours and cocoa powder. Using an electric whisk, whisk the sifted mixture into the chocolate mixture until smooth. Beat in the eggs and vanilla extract. Pour into the tin and bake in the preheated oven for 1¼ hours, or until firm. Leave for at least 5 minutes before turning out onto a wire rack to cool.

Meanwhile, mix together all but 1 tablespoon of the melted dark chocolate with the butter and icing/confectioners' sugar and beat until smooth. Leave to cool, then beat again. Reserve 4–5 tablespoons of the chocolate filling. Cut the cooled cake in half to make two rectangles, then split each rectangle in three horizontally. Place one cake layer on a serving plate and spread thinly with the jam/jelly, then a thin layer of dark chocolate filling. Top with a second cake layer and sprinkle with a little liqueur, then spread thinly with filling. Repeat with the remaining cake layers, liqueur and filling. Chill in the refrigerator for 2–3 hours until firm. Cover the cake with the reserved chocolate filling and press the flaked almonds into the sides of the cake. Place the remaining melted chocolate in a nonstick baking parchment piping/decorating bag. Snip a small hole in the tip and pipe thin lines 2 cm/¾ inch apart crossways over the cake. Drag a cocktail stick lengthways through the icing in alternating directions to create a feathered effect on the top. Serve.

## Difficulty Rating: 4 points

# Double Marble Cake

## Cuts into 8–10 slices

### Ingredients

75 g/3 oz/3 squares white chocolate

75 g/3 oz/3 squares dark/bittersweet chocolate

175 g/6 oz/1 scant cup caster/superfine sugar

175 g/6 oz/1½ sticks butter; 4 medium/large eggs, separated

125 g/4 oz/1 cup plain/all-purpose flour, sifted

75 g/3 oz/¾ cup ground almonds

### For the topping:

100 g/3½ oz/4 squares white chocolate, chopped

100 g/3½ oz/4 squares dark/bittersweet chocolate, chopped

100 ml/3½ fl oz/⅓ cup double/heavy cream

200 g/7 oz/1¾ sticks unsalted butter

Preheat the oven to 180°C/350°F/Gas Mark 4, 10 minutes before baking. Lightly oil and line the base of a 20.5 cm/8 inch cake tin/pan. Break the white and dark/bittersweet chocolate into small pieces, then place in two separate bowls placed over two pans of simmering water. Heat the chocolate until melted and smooth.

In a large bowl, cream the sugar and butter together until light and fluffy. Beat in the egg yolks, one at a time, adding a spoonful of flour after each addition. Stir in the ground almonds. In another bowl, whisk the egg whites until stiff. Gently fold in the whites and the remaining flour alternately into the almond mixture until they have all been incorporated. Divide the mixture between two bowls. Gently stir the white chocolate into one bowl and the dark chocolate into the other. Place alternating spoonfuls of the mixtures in the cake tin. Using a skewer, swirl together to get a marbled effect. Tap the tin on the work surface to level. Bake in the oven for 40 minutes, or until cooked through, then leave to cool for 5 minutes in the tin before turning out onto a wire rack to cool completely.

For the topping, melt half of the cream and butter with the dark chocolate and the other half with the white chocolate and stir both until smooth. Cool, then whisk until thick and swirl both colours over the top of the cake to create a marbled effect.

## Difficulty Rating: 3 points

# Chocolate Mousse Sponge

## Cuts into 8–10 slices

**Ingredients**

3 medium/large eggs

75 g/3 oz/⅓ cup caster/superfine sugar

1 tsp vanilla extract

50 g/2 oz/⅓ cup self-raising flour, sifted

25 g/1 oz/¼ cup ground almonds

50 g/2 oz/2 squares dark/bittersweet chocolate, grated

icing/confectioners' sugar, for dusting

freshly sliced strawberries, to decorate

**For the mousse:**

2 sheets gelatine

50 ml/2 fl oz/¼ cup double/heavy cream

100 g/3½ oz/4 squares dark/bittersweet chocolate, chopped

1 tsp vanilla extract

4 medium egg whites

125 g/4 oz/⅔ cup caster/superfine sugar

Preheat the oven to 180°C/350°F/Gas Mark 4, 10 minutes before baking. Lightly oil and line a 23 cm/9 inch round cake tin/pan and lightly oil the sides of a 23 cm/9 inch springform tin. Whisk the eggs, caster/superfine sugar and vanilla extract until thick and creamy. Fold in the flour, ground almonds and dark chocolate. Spoon the mixture into the prepared round cake tin and bake in the preheated oven for 25 minutes, or until firm. Turn out onto a wire rack to cool.

For the mousse, soak the gelatine in 50 ml/2 fl oz of cold water for 5 minutes until softened. Meanwhile, heat the double/heavy cream in a small saucepan. When almost boiling, remove from the heat and stir in the chocolate and vanilla extract. Stir until the chocolate melts. Squeeze the excess water out of the gelatine and add to the chocolate mixture. Stir until dissolved, then pour into a large bowl.

Whisk the egg whites until stiff, then gradually add the caster sugar, whisking well between each addition. Fold the egg white mixture into the chocolate mixture in two batches.

Split the cake into two layers. Place one layer in the bottom of the springform tin. Pour in the chocolate mousse mixture, then top with the second layer of cake. Chill in the refrigerator for 4 hours, or until the mousse has set. Loosen the sides and remove the cake from the tin. Dust with icing/confectioners' sugar and decorate the top with a few freshly sliced strawberries. Serve cut into slices.

## Difficulty Rating: 3 points

# Chocolate Mousse Cake

## Cuts into 8–10 servings

### Ingredients

450 g/1 lb/18 squares dark/bittersweet chocolate, chopped

125 g/4 oz/1 stick plus 1 tbsp butter, softened

3 tbsp brandy

9 large/extra-large eggs, separated

150 g/5 oz/³⁄₄ cup caster/superfine sugar

### For the chocolate glaze:

250 ml/8 fl oz/1 cup double/heavy cream

225 g/8 oz/9 squares dark/bittersweet chocolate, chopped

2 tbsp brandy

1 tbsp single/light cream and white chocolate curls,
   to decorate

Preheat the oven to 180°C/350°F/Gas Mark 4, 10 minutes before baking. Lightly oil and line the bases of two 20.5 cm/8 inch springform tins/pans with baking parchment. Melt the chocolate and butter in a bowl set over a saucepan of simmering water. Stir until smooth. Remove from the heat and stir in the brandy.

Whisk the egg yolks and the sugar, reserving 2 tablespoons of the sugar, until thick and creamy. Slowly beat in the chocolate mixture until smooth and well blended.

Whisk the egg whites until soft peaks form, then sprinkle over the remaining sugar and continue whisking until stiff but not dry. Fold a large spoonful of the egg whites into the chocolate mixture. Gently fold in the remaining egg whites. Divide about two thirds of the mixture evenly between the tins, tapping to distribute the mixture evenly. Reserve the remaining one third of the chocolate mousse mixture for the filling. Bake in the preheated oven for about 20 minutes, or until the cakes are well risen and set. Remove and cool for at least 1 hour.

Loosen the edges of the cake layers with a knife. Using the fingertips, lightly press the crusty edges down. Pour the rest of the mousse over one layer, spreading until even. Carefully unclip the side, remove the other cake from the tin and gently invert onto the mousse, bottom side up to make a flat top layer. Discard lining paper and chill for 4–6 hours, or until set.

To make the glaze, melt the cream and chocolate with the brandy in a heavy-based saucepan and stir until smooth. Cool until thickened. Unclip the side of the mousse cake and place on a wire rack. Pour over half the glaze and spread to cover. Allow to set, then decorate with chocolate curls. To serve, heat the remaining glaze and pour round each slice, and dot with cream.

## Difficulty Rating: 4 points

# Chocolate Box Cake

## Cuts into 16 slices

**Ingredients**

175 g/6 oz/1⅓ cups self-raising flour
1 tsp baking powder
175 g/6 oz/1 scant cup caster/superfine sugar
175 g/6 oz/1½ sticks butter, softened
3 large/extra-large eggs
25 g/1 oz/¼ cup cocoa powder (unsweetened)
150 g/5 oz/½ cup apricot preserve
cocoa powder (unsweetened), to dust

**For the chocolate box:**
275 g/10 oz/11 squares dark/bittersweet chocolate

**For the chocolate whipped cream topping:**
450 ml/¾ pint/1¾ cups double/heavy cream
275 g/10 oz/11 squares dark/bittersweet chocolate, melted
2 tbsp brandy
1 tsp cocoa powder (unsweetened), to decorate

Preheat the oven to 180°C/350°F/Gas Mark 4, 10 minutes before baking. Lightly oil and flour a 20.5 cm/8 inch square cake tin/pan. Sift the flour and baking powder into a large bowl and stir in the sugar. Using an electric whisk, beat in the butter and eggs.

Blend the cocoa powder with 1 tablespoon water, then beat into the creamed mixture. Turn into the tin and bake in the preheated oven for about 25 minutes, or until well risen and cooked. Remove and cool before removing the cake from the tin.

To make the chocolate box, break the chocolate into small pieces, place in a heatproof bowl over a saucepan of gently simmering water and leave until soft. Stir occasionally until melted and smooth. Line a Swiss roll tin/jelly roll pan with nonstick baking parchment, then pour in the chocolate, tilting the tin to level. Leave to set. Once set, turn out onto a chopping board and carefully strip off the paper. Cut into four strips, the same length as the cooked sponge, using a large sharp knife that has been dipped into hot water. Gently heat the apricot preserve and sieve to remove lumps. Brush over the top and sides of the

cake. Carefully place the chocolate strips around the cake sides and press lightly. Leave to set for at least 10 minutes.

For the topping, whisk the cream to soft peaks and quickly fold into the melted chocolate with the brandy. Spoon the chocolate whipped cream into a pastry bag fitted with a star nozzle/tip and pipe a decorative design of rosettes or shells over the surface. Dust with cocoa powder and serve.

## Difficulty Rating: 4 points

# Chocolate Chiffon Cake

## Cuts into 10–12 slices

**Ingredients**

50 g/2 oz /²/₃ cup cocoa powder (unsweetened)

300 g/11 oz/2¹/₃ cups self-raising flour

550 g/1¹/₄ lb/2³/₄ cups caster/superfine sugar

7 medium/large eggs, separated

125 ml/4 fl oz/¹/₂ cup vegetable oil

1 tsp vanilla extract

75 g/3 oz/³/₄ cup walnuts

200 g/7 oz/8 squares dark/bittersweet chocolate, melted

**For the icing:**

175 g/6 oz/1¹/₂ sticks butter

275 g/10 oz/1¹/₃ cups icing/confectioners' sugar, sifted

2 tbsp cocoa powder, sifted

2 tbsp brandy

Preheat the oven to 170°C/325°F/Gas Mark 3, 10 minutes before baking. Lightly oil and line a 23 cm/9 inch round cake tin/pan. Lightly oil a baking sheet. Blend the cocoa powder with 175 ml/6 fl oz/scant ³/₄ cups boiling water and leave to cool. Place the flour and 350 g/12 oz/1³/₄ cups of the caster/superfine sugar in a large bowl and add the cocoa mixture, egg yolks, oil and vanilla extract. Whisk until smooth and lighter in colour.

Whisk the egg whites in a clean, grease-free bowl until soft peaks form, then fold into the cocoa mixture. Pour into the prepared tin and bake in the preheated oven for 1 hour, or until firm. Leave for 5 minutes before turning out onto a wire rack to cool.

To make the icing, cream together 125 g/4 oz/¹/₂ cup of the butter with the icing/confectioners' sugar, cocoa powder and brandy until smooth, then reserve. Melt the remaining butter and blend with three quarters of the melted dark chocolate. Stir until smooth and then leave until thickened.

Place the remaining caster sugar into a heavy-based saucepan over a low heat and heat until the sugar has melted and is a deep golden brown. Add the walnuts and the remaining melted chocolate to the melted sugar and pour onto the

prepared baking sheet. Leave until cold and brittle, then chop finely. Reserve.

Split the cake into three layers. Place one layer onto a serving plate and spread with half of the brandy butter icing. Top with a second layer and spread with the remaining brandy butter icing. Arrange the third cake layer on top. Cover the cake with the thickened chocolate glaze. Sprinkle with the walnut praline and serve.

## Difficulty Rating: 5 points

# Sachertorte

## Cuts into 10–12 slices

**Ingredients**

150 g/5 oz/6 squares dark/bittersweet chocolate

150 g/5 oz/1⅓ sticks unsalted butter, softened

125 g/4 oz/⅔ cup, plus 2 tbsp caster/superfine sugar

3 medium/large eggs, separated

150 g/5 oz/1 heaped cup plain/all-purpose flour, sifted

**To decorate:**

225 g/8 oz/¾ cup apricot jam/jelly

125 g/4 oz/5 squares dark/bittersweet chocolate, chopped

125 g/4 oz/1 stick plus 1 tbsp unsalted butter

25 g/1 oz/1 square milk/semisweet chocolate

Preheat the oven to 180°C/ 350°F/Gas Mark 4, 10 minutes before baking. Lightly oil and line a deep 23 cm/9 inch cake tin/pan. Melt the chocolate for the cake in a heatproof bowl set over a saucepan of simmering water. Stir in 1 tablespoon water and leave to cool. Beat the butter and 125 g/4 oz/⅔ cup of the sugar together until light and fluffy. Beat in the egg yolks, one at a time, beating well between each addition. Stir in the melted chocolate, then the flour. In a clean, grease-free bowl, whisk the egg whites until stiff peaks form, then whisk in the remaining sugar. Fold into the chocolate mixture and spoon into the prepared tin. Bake in the preheated oven for 30 minutes until firm. Leave for 5 minutes, then turn out onto a wire rack to cool. Leave the cake upside down.

To decorate, split the cake in two and place one half on a serving plate. Heat the jam/jelly and rub through a fine sieve. Brush half the jam onto the first cake half, then cover with the remaining cake layer and brush with the remaining jam. Leave at room temperature for 1 hour, or until the jam has set. Place the dark/bittersweet chocolate with the butter into a heatproof bowl set over a saucepan of simmering water and heat until melted. Stir occasionally until smooth, then leave until thickened. Use to cover the cake. Melt the milk/semisweet chocolate in a heatproof bowl set over simmering water. Place in a small greaseproof piping/decorating bag and snip a small hole at the tip. Pipe 'Sacher' with a large 'S' on the top. Leave to set at room temperature.

## Difficulty Rating: 4 points

# Toffee Walnut Swiss Roll

## Cuts into 10–12 slices

**Ingredients**

4 large/extra-large eggs, separated

¹/₂ tsp cream of tartar

125 g/4 oz/1¹/₄ cups icing/confectioners' sugar,
  plus extra for dusting

¹/₂ tsp vanilla extract

125 g/4 oz/1 cup self-raising flour

**For the toffee walnut filling:**

2 tbsp plain/all-purpose flour

150 ml/¹/₄ pint/²/₃ cup milk

5 tbsp golden/corn syrup or maple syrup

2 large/extra-large egg yolks, beaten

100 g/3¹/₂ oz/1 cup walnuts or pecans, toasted and chopped

300 ml/¹/₂ pint/1¹/₄ cups double/heavy cream, whipped

Preheat the oven to 190°C/375°F/Gas Mark 5, 10 minutes before baking. Lightly oil and line a Swiss roll tin/jelly roll pan with nonstick baking parchment. Beat the egg whites and cream of tartar until softly peaking. Gradually beat in 50 g/2 oz/¹/₂ cup of the icing/confectioners' sugar until stiff peaks form.

In another bowl, beat the egg yolks with the remaining icing sugar until thick. Beat in the vanilla extract. Gently fold in the flour and egg whites alternately, using a metal spoon or rubber spatula. Do not overmix. Spoon the batter into the tin and spread evenly. Bake in the preheated oven for 12 minutes, or until well risen and golden and the cake springs back when pressed with a clean finger.

Lay a clean dishtowel on a work surface and lay a piece of baking parchment about 33 cm/13 inches long on the towel. Dust with icing sugar. As soon as the cake is cooked, turn out onto the paper. Peel off the lining paper and cut off the crisp edges of the cake. Starting at one narrow end, roll the cake with the paper and towel. Transfer to a wire rack and cool completely.

For the filling, put the flour, milk and syrup into a small saucepan and place over a gentle heat. Bring to the boil, whisking until thick and smooth. Remove from the heat and

slowly beat into the beaten egg yolks. Pour the mixture back into the saucepan and cook over a low heat until it thickens and coats the back of a spoon. Strain the mixture into a bowl and stir in the chopped walnuts or pecans. Cool, stirring occasionally, then fold in about half of the whipped cream. Unroll the cooled cake and spread the filling over the cake. Re-roll and decorate with the remaining cream. Sprinkle with the icing sugar and serve.

## Difficulty Rating: 4 points

# Fruity Roulade

## Serves 4

**Ingredients**

3 eggs

75 g/3 oz/$^1/_3$ cup caster/superfine sugar, plus 1–2 tbsp,
   for sprinkling

75 g/3 oz/$^2/_3$ cup plain/all-purpose flour, sifted

**For the filling:**

125 g/4 oz/$^1/_2$ cup Quark

125 g/4 oz/$^1/_2$ cup low-fat plain Greek yogurt

2 tbsp caster/superfine sugar

1 tbsp orange liqueur (optional)

grated zest of 1 orange

125 g/4 oz/1 cup strawberries, hulled, cut into quarters

**To decorate:**

strawberries

sifted icing/confectioners' sugar

Preheat the oven to 220˚C/425˚F/Gas Mark 7. Lightly oil and
line a 33 x 23 cm/13 x 9 inch Swiss roll tin/jelly-roll pan with
greaseproof/waxed paper or baking parchment. Using an electric
whisk, whisk the eggs and the 75 g/3 oz/$^1/_3$ cup caster/superfine
sugar until the mixture has doubled in volume and leaves a trail
across the top. Fold in the flour with a metal spoon or rubber
spatula. Pour into the prepared tin and bake in the preheated
oven for 10–12 minutes, until well risen and golden.

Place a sheet of greaseproof/waxed paper or baking parchment
out on a flat work surface and sprinkle evenly with caster sugar.
Turn the cooked sponge out onto the paper, discard the paper,
trim the sponge and roll up, encasing the paper inside. Reserve
until cool.

To make the filling, mix together the Quark, yogurt, caster sugar,
liqueur (if using) and orange zest. Unroll the roulade and spread
the mixture over the sponge. Scatter over the strawberries
and roll up. Decorate the roulade with the strawberries. Dust
with the icing/confectioners' sugar and serve.

## Difficulty Rating: 3 points

# Chocolate Roulade

## Cuts into 8 slices

**Ingredients**

200 g/7 oz/8 squares dark/bittersweet chocolate
7 medium/large eggs, separated
200 g/7 oz/1 cup caster/superfine sugar
4 tbsp icing/confectioners' sugar, for dusting
300 ml/¹/₂ pint/1¹/₄ cups double/heavy cream
3 tbsp Cointreau or Grand Marnier

**To decorate:**
fresh raspberries
fresh mint sprigs

Preheat the oven to 180°C/350°F/Gas Mark 4, 10 minutes before baking. Lightly oil and line a 33 x 23 cm/13 x 9 inch Swiss roll tin/jelly roll pan with nonstick baking parchment. Break the chocolate into small pieces into a heatproof bowl set over a saucepan of simmering water. Leave until almost melted, stirring occasionally. Remove from the heat and leave to stand for 5 minutes. Whisk the egg yolks with the sugar until pale and creamy and the whisk leaves a trail in the mixture when lifted, then carefully fold in the melted chocolate.

In a clean, grease-free bowl, whisk the egg whites until stiff, then fold 1 large spoonful into the chocolate mixture. Mix lightly, then gently fold in the remaining egg whites. Pour the mixture into the prepared tin and level the surface. Bake in the preheated oven for 20–25 minutes until firm. Remove the cake from the oven, leave in the tin and cover with a wire rack and a damp dishtowel. Leave for 8 hours, or preferably overnight.

Dust a large sheet of nonstick baking parchment generously with 2 tablespoons of the icing sugar. Unwrap the cake and turn out onto the paper. Remove the lining paper. Whip the cream with the liqueur until soft peaks form. Spread over the cake, leaving a 2.5 cm/1 inch border all round. Using the paper to help, roll the cake up from a short end. Transfer to a serving plate, seam-side down, and dust with the remaining icing sugar. Decorate with fresh raspberries and mint. Serve.

## Difficulty Rating: 4 points

# Grated Chocolate Roulade

## Cuts into 8 slices

**Ingredients**

4 medium/large eggs, separated

125 g/4 oz/2/3 cup caster/superfine sugar

60 g/2½ oz/2½ squares dark/bittersweet chocolate, grated

75 g/3 oz/2/3 cup self-raising flour, sifted

2 tbsp caster/superfine sugar, plus extra for sprinkling

150 ml/¼ pint/2/3 cup double/heavy cream

2 tsp icing/confectioners' sugar

1 tsp vanilla extract

chocolate curls, to decorate

Preheat the oven to 180°C/350°F/Gas Mark 4, 10 minutes before baking. Lightly oil and line a 20.5 x 30.5 cm/8 x 12 inch Swiss roll tin/jelly roll pan. Beat the egg yolks and sugar with an electric mixer for 5 minutes, or until thick, then stir in 2 tablespoons hot water and the grated chocolate. Finally, fold in the sifted flour.

Whisk the egg whites until stiff, then fold 1–2 tablespoons of egg white into the chocolate mixture. Mix lightly, then gently fold in the remaining egg white. Pour into the prepared tin and bake in the preheated oven for about 12 minutes, or until firm.

Place a large sheet of nonstick baking parchment onto a work surface and sprinkle liberally with caster/superfine sugar. Turn the cake onto the baking parchment, discard the lining paper and trim away the crisp edges. Roll up as for a Swiss/jelly roll cake, leave for 2 minutes, then unroll and leave to cool.

Beat the double/heavy cream with the icing/confectioners' sugar and vanilla extract until thick. Reserve a little for decoration, then spread the remaining cream over the cake, leaving a 2.5 cm/1 inch border all round. Using the baking parchment, roll up from a short end. Carefully transfer the roulade to a large serving plate and use the reserved cream to decorate the top. Add the chocolate curls just before serving, then cut into slices and serve. Store in the refrigerator.

## Difficulty Rating: 4 points

# Christmas Cranberry Chocolate Roulade

## Cuts into 12–14 slices

**Ingredients**

**For the chocolate ganache frosting:**
300 ml/½ pint/1¼ cups double/heavy cream
350 g/12 oz/14 squares dark/bittersweet chocolate, chopped
2 tbsp brandy (optional)

**For the roulade:**
5 large/extra-large eggs, separated
3 tbsp cocoa powder (unsweetened), sifted,
    plus extra for dusting
125 g/4 oz/1¼ cups icing/confectioners' sugar, sifted,
    plus extra for dusting
¼ tsp cream of tartar

**For the filling:**
175 g/6 oz/⅔ cup cranberry sauce
1–2 tbsp brandy (optional)
450 ml/¾ pint/1¾ cups double/heavy cream,
    whipped to soft peaks

**To decorate:**
**caramelized orange strips**
**dried cranberries**

Preheat the oven to 200°C/400°F/Gas Mark 6. Bring the cream to the boil over a medium heat. Remove from the heat and add all of the chocolate, stirring until melted. Stir in the brandy, if using, and strain into a medium bowl. Cool, then refrigerate for 6–8 hours.

Lightly oil and line a 39 x 26 cm/15½ x 10½ inch Swiss roll tin/jelly roll pan with nonstick baking parchment. Using an electric whisk, beat the egg yolks until thick and creamy. Slowly beat in the cocoa powder and half the icing/confectioners' sugar and reserve. Whisk the egg whites and cream of tartar into soft peaks. Gradually whisk in the remaining sugar until the mixture is stiff and glossy. Gently fold the yolk mixture into the egg whites with a metal spoon or rubber spatula. Spread evenly into the tin. Bake in the preheated oven for 15 minutes.

Remove and invert onto a large sheet of greaseproof/waxed paper, dusted with cocoa powder. Cut off the crisp edges of the cake, then roll up. Leave on a wire rack until cold.

For the filling, heat the cranberry sauce with the brandy, if using, until warm and spreadable. Unroll the cooled cake and spread with the cranberry sauce. Allow to cool and set. Carefully spoon the whipped cream over the surface and spread to within 2.5 cm/1 inch of the edges. Re-roll the cake. Transfer to a cake plate or tray.

Allow the chocolate ganache to soften at room temperature, then beat until soft and of a spreadable consistency. Spread over the roulade and, using a fork, mark the roulade with ridges to resemble tree bark. Dust with icing sugar. Decorate with the caramelized orange strips and dried cranberries and serve.

## Difficulty Rating: 5 points

# Supreme Chocolate Gateau

## Cuts into 10–12 slices

### Ingredients

175 g/6 oz/1⅓ cups self-raising flour, sifted

1½ tsp baking powder, sifted

3 tbsp cocoa powder (unsweetened), sifted

175 g/6 oz/1½ sticks margarine or butter, softened

175 g/6 oz/1 scant cup caster/superfine sugar

3 large/extra-large eggs

### To decorate:

350 g/12 oz/14 squares dark/bittersweet chocolate

1 gelatine leaf

200 ml/7 fl oz/¾ cup double/heavy cream

75 g/3 oz/⅔ stick butter

cocoa powder (unsweetened), for dusting

Preheat the oven to 180°C/350°F/Gas Mark 4, 10 minutes before baking. Lightly oil and line three 20.5 cm/8 inch round cake tins/pans. Place all the cake ingredients into a bowl and whisk together until thick; add a little warm water if very thick. Divide the mixture evenly between the prepared tins. Bake in the preheated oven for 35–40 minutes until a skewer inserted in the centre comes out clean. Cool on wire racks.

Very gently heat 2 tablespoons hot water with 50 g/2 oz/2 squares of the chocolate and stir until combined. Remove from the heat and leave for 5 minutes. Place the gelatine into a shallow dish and add 2 tablespoons of cold water. Leave for 5 minutes, then squeeze out any excess water and add to the chocolate and water mixture. Stir until dissolved. Whip the double/heavy cream until just thickened. Add the chocolate mixture and continue whisking until soft peaks form. Leave until starting to set.

Place one of the cakes onto a serving plate and spread with half the cream mixture. Top with a second cake and the remaining cream, cover with the third cake and chill in the refrigerator until the cream has set.

Melt 175 g/6 oz of the chocolate with the butter and stir until smooth; leave until thickened. Melt the remaining chocolate. Cut twelve 10 cm/4 inch squares of kitchen foil. Spread the chocolate

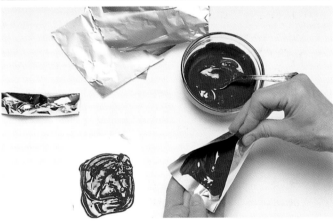

evenly over the squares to within 2.5 cm/1 inch of the edges. Refrigerate for 3–4 minutes until just set but not brittle. Gather up the corners and crimp together. Return to the refrigerator until firm.

Spread the chocolate and butter mixture over the top and sides of the cake. Remove the foil from the giant curls and use to decorate the top of the cake. Dust with cocoa powder and serve cut into wedges.

## Difficulty Rating: 3 points

# Chocolate Hazelnut Meringue Gateau

## Cuts into 8–10 slices

### Ingredients

5 medium/large egg whites

275 g/10 oz/1¹⁄₃ cups caster/superfine sugar

125 g/4 oz/1 cup hazelnuts, toasted and finely chopped

175 g/6 oz/7 squares dark/bittersweet chocolate

100 g/3¹⁄₂ oz/1 stick butter

3 medium/large eggs, separated, plus 1 medium egg white

25 g/1 oz/¹⁄₄ cup icing/confectioners' sugar

125 ml/4 fl oz/¹⁄₂ cup double/heavy cream

hazelnuts, toasted and chopped, to decorate

Preheat the oven to 150°C/300°F/Gas Mark 2, 5 minutes before baking. Cut three pieces of nonstick baking parchment into 30.5 x 12.5 cm/12 x 5 inch rectangles and then place onto two or three baking sheets.

Whisk the egg whites until stiff, add half the sugar and whisk until the mixture is stiff, smooth and glossy. Whisk in the remaining sugar, 1 tablespoon at a time, beating well between each addition. When all the sugar has been added, whisk for 1 minute. Stir in the hazelnuts.

Spoon the meringue inside the marked rectangles, spreading in a continuous backwards and forwards movement. Bake in the preheated oven for 1¹⁄₄ hours, remove and leave until cold. Trim the meringues until they measure 25.5 x 10 cm/10 x 4 inches. Reserve all the trimmings.

Melt the chocolate and the butter in a heatproof bowl set over a saucepan of gently simmering water and stir until smooth. Remove from the heat and beat in the egg yolks. Whisk the egg white until stiff, then whisk in the icing/confectioners' sugar a little at a time. Fold the egg whites into the chocolate mixture and chill in the refrigerator for 20–30 minutes until thick enough to spread. Whip the double cream until soft peaks form. Reserve.

Place one of the meringue layers onto a serving plate. Spread with about half of the mousse mixture, then top with a second

meringue layer. Spread the remaining mousse mixture over the top with the third meringue. Spread the cream over the top and sprinkle with the chopped hazelnuts. Chill in the refrigerator for at least 4 hours and up to 24 hours. Serve cut into slices.

## Difficulty Rating: 3 points

# Black Forest Gateau

## Cuts into 10–12 slices

**Ingredients**

250 g/9 oz/2¼ sticks butter

1 tbsp instant coffee granules

350 ml/12 fl oz/1½ cups hot water

200 g/7 oz/8 squares dark/bittersweet chocolate, chopped or broken

400 g/14 oz/2 cups caster/superfine sugar

225 g/8 oz/1¾ cups self-raising flour

150 g/5 oz/1 heaped cup plain/all-purpose flour

50 g/2 oz/²⁄₃ cup cocoa powder (unsweetened)

2 medium/large eggs

2 tsp vanilla extract

2 x 400 g/14 oz cans stoned cherries in juice

2 tsp arrowroot

600 ml/1 pint/2½ cups double/heavy cream

50 ml/2 fl oz/¼ cup kirsch

Preheat the oven to 150°C/300°F/Gas Mark 2, 5 minutes before baking. Lightly oil and line a deep 23 cm/9 inch cake tin/pan.

Melt the butter in a large saucepan. Blend the coffee with the hot water, add to the butter with the chocolate and sugar and heat gently, stirring until smooth. Pour into a large bowl and leave until just warm.

Sift together the flours and cocoa powder. Using an electric mixer, whisk the warm chocolate mixture on a low speed, then gradually whisk in the dry ingredients. Whisk in the eggs, one at a time, then the vanilla extract. Pour the mixture into the prepared tin and bake in the preheated oven for 1¾ hours, or until firm and a skewer inserted into the centre comes out clean. Leave in the tin for 5 minutes to cool slightly before turning out onto a wire rack.

Place the cherries and their juice in a small saucepan and heat gently. Blend the arrowroot with 2 teaspoons water until smooth, then stir into the cherries. Cook, stirring, until the liquid thickens. Simmer very gently for 2 minutes, then leave until cold.

Whisk the double/heavy cream until thick. Trim the top of the cake if necessary, then split the cake into three layers. Brush the

base of the cake with half the kirsch. Top with a layer of cream and one third of the cherries. Repeat the layering, then place the third layer on top. Reserve a little cream for decorating and use the remainder to cover the top and sides of the cake. Pipe a decorative edge around the cake, then arrange the remaining cherries in the centre and serve.

## Difficulty Rating: 4 points

# Whole Orange & Chocolate Cake with Marmalade Cream

## Cuts into 6–8 slices

### Ingredients

1 small orange, scrubbed

2 medium/large eggs, separated, plus 1 whole egg

150 g/5 oz/³⁄₄ cup caster/superfine sugar

125 g/4 oz/1¹⁄₃ cups ground almonds

75 g/3 oz/3 squares dark/bittersweet chocolate, melted

100 ml/3¹⁄₂ fl oz/¹⁄₃ cup double/heavy cream

200 g/7 oz/1 scant cup full fat soft cheese

25 g/1 oz/¹⁄₄ cup icing/confectioners' sugar

2 tbsp orange marmalade

orange zest, to decorate

Preheat the oven to 180°C/350°F/Gas Mark 4, 10 minutes before baking. Lightly oil and line the base of a 900 g/2 lb loaf tin/pan. Place the orange in a small saucepan, cover with cold water and bring to the boil. Simmer for 1 hour until completely soft. Drain and leave to cool.

Place 2 egg yolks, 1 whole egg and the caster/superfine sugar in a heatproof bowl set over a saucepan of simmering water and whisk until doubled in bulk. Remove from the heat and continue to whisk for 5 minutes until cooled.

Cut the whole orange in half and discard the seeds, then place into a food processor or blender and blend to a purée. Carefully fold the purée into the egg yolk mixture with the ground almonds and melted chocolate.

Whisk the egg whites until stiff peaks form. Fold a large spoonful of the egg whites into the chocolate mixture, then gently fold the remaining egg whites into the mixture. Pour into the prepared tin and bake in the preheated oven for 50 minutes, or until firm and a skewer inserted into the centre comes out clean. Cool in the tin before turning out of the tin and carefully discarding the lining paper.

Meanwhile, whip the double/heavy cream until just thickened. In another bowl, blend the soft cheese with the icing/confectioners' sugar and marmalade until smooth, then fold in the double cream. Chill the marmalade cream in the refrigerator until required. Decorate with orange zest and serve the cake cut into slices with the marmalade cream.

## Difficulty Rating: 4 points

# Chocolate Orange Fudge Cake

## Cuts into 8–10 slices

### Ingredients

65 g/2¹/₂ oz/³/₄ cup cocoa powder (unsweetened)

grated zest of 1 orange

350 g/12 oz/2³/₄ cups self-raising flour

2 tsp baking powder

1 tsp bicarbonate of soda/baking soda

¹/₂ tsp salt

225 g/8 oz/1 heaped cup soft light brown sugar

175 g/6 oz/1¹/₂ sticks butter, softened

3 medium/large eggs

1 tsp vanilla extract

250 ml/8 fl oz/1 cup sour cream

6 tbsp butter

6 tbsp milk

thinly pared rind of 1 orange

6 tbsp cocoa powder (unsweetened)

250 g/9 oz/2¹/₂ cups icing/confectioners' sugar, sifted

Preheat the oven to 180°C/350°F/Gas Mark 4, 10 minutes before baking. Lightly oil and line two 23 cm/9 inch round cake tins/pans with nonstick baking parchment. Blend the cocoa powder and 50 ml/2 fl oz/¹/₄ cup boiling water until smooth. Stir in the orange zest and reserve. Sift together the flour, baking powder, bicarbonate of soda/baking soda and salt, then reserve. Cream together the sugar and softened butter and beat in the eggs, one at a time, then the cocoa mixture and vanilla extract. Finally, stir in the flour mixture and the sour cream in alternate spoonfuls.

Divide the mixture between the prepared tins and bake in the preheated oven for 35 minutes, or until the edges of the cake pull away from the tin and the tops spring back when lightly pressed. Cool in the tins for 10 minutes, then turn out onto wire racks until cold.

Gently heat together the butter and milk with the pared orange rind. Simmer for 10 minutes, stirring occasionally. Remove from the heat and discard the orange rind. Pour the warm orange

and milk mixture into a large bowl and stir in the cocoa powder. Gradually beat in the sifted icing/confectioners' sugar and beat until the icing is smooth and spreadable. Place one cake onto a large serving plate. Top with about one quarter of the icing, place the second cake on top, then cover the cake completely with the remaining icing. Serve.

## Difficulty Rating: 3 points

# Biscuits & Cookies

**Whether you have been inspired while in Italy to make your own Biscotti to go with your coffee, or crave the cosy Oatmeal Raisin Cookies mum used to make, you'll find it here. Try the classic Chocolate Chip Cookies, the delectable Pecan Caramel Millionaire's Shortbread or the more fruity flavours of Fig & Chocolate Bars or Spiced Palmier Biscuits with Apple Pureé.**

# Italian Biscotti

## Makes 26–28

**Ingredients**

150 g/5 oz/1⅓ sticks butter

200 g/7 oz/1 cup caster/superfine sugar

¼ tsp vanilla extract

1 small egg, beaten

¼ tsp ground cinnamon

grated zest of 1 lemon

2⅓ tbsp ground almonds

150 g/5 oz/1 heaped cup plain/all-purpose flour

150 g/5 oz/6 squares dark/bittersweet chocolate

Preheat the oven to 190°C/375°F/Gas Mark 5, 10 minutes before baking. Lightly oil three or four baking sheets and reserve. Cream the butter and sugar together in a bowl and mix in the vanilla extract. When it is light and fluffy, beat in the egg with the cinnamon, lemon zest and the ground almonds. Stir in the flour to make a firm dough.

Knead lightly until smooth and free from cracks. Shape the dough into rectangular blocks about 4 cm/1½ inches in diameter, wrap in greaseproof/waxed paper and chill in the refrigerator for at least 2 hours.

Cut the chilled dough into 5 mm/¼ inch slices, place on the baking sheets and cook in the preheated oven for 12–15 minutes until firm. Remove from the oven, cool slightly, then transfer to wire racks to cool.

When completely cold, melt the chocolate in a heatproof bowl set over a saucepan of simmering water. Alternatively, melt the chocolate in the microwave according to the manufacturer's instructions. Spoon into a piping/decorating bag and pipe over the biscuits. Leave to dry on a sheet of nonstick baking parchment before serving.

## Difficulty Rating: 3 points

# Almond & Pistachio Biscotti

## Makes 12 biscuits

**Ingredients**

125 g/4 oz/1⅓ cups ground almonds

50 g/2 oz/⅓ cup shelled pistachios

50 g/2 oz/⅓ cup blanched almonds

2 medium/large eggs

1 medium/large egg yolk

125 g/4 oz/1¼ cups icing/confectioners' sugar

225 g/8 oz/1¾ cups plain/all-purpose flour

1 tsp baking powder

pinch salt

zest of ½ lemon

Preheat the oven to 180°C/350°F/Gas Mark 4, 10 minutes before baking. Line a large baking sheet with nonstick baking parchment. Toast the ground almonds and whole nuts lightly and reserve until cool.

Beat together the eggs, egg yolk and icing/confectioners' sugar until thick, then beat in the flour, baking powder and salt. Add the lemon zest, ground almonds and whole nuts and mix to form a slightly sticky dough.

Turn the dough onto a lightly floured surface and, using lightly floured hands, form into a log measuring approximately 30 cm/ 12 inches long. Place down the centre of the prepared baking sheet and transfer to the preheated oven. Bake for 20 minutes.

Remove from the oven and increase the oven temperature to 200°C/400°F/Gas Mark 6. Cut the log diagonally into 2.5 cm/1 inch slices. Return to the baking sheet, cut–side down, and bake for a further 10–15 minutes until golden, turning once. Leave to cool on a wire rack and store in an airtight container.

## Difficulty Rating: 2 points

# Cantuccini

## Makes 24 biscuits

### Ingredients

250 g/9 oz/2 cups plain/all-purpose flour

250 g/9 oz/2¹⁄₄ cups caster/superfine sugar

¹⁄₂ tsp baking powder

¹⁄₂ tsp vanilla extract

2 medium/large eggs

1 medium/large egg yolk

100 g/3¹⁄₂ oz/³⁄₄ cup mixed almonds and hazelnuts, toasted and
   roughly chopped

1 tsp whole aniseed

1 medium/large egg yolk mixed with 1 tbsp water, to glaze

Vin Santo dessert wine or coffee, to serve

## Difficulty Rating: 2 points

Preheat the oven to 180°C/350°F/Gas Mark 4. Line a large baking sheet with nonstick baking parchment. Place the flour, caster/superfine sugar, baking powder, vanilla extract, the whole eggs and one of the egg yolks into a food processor and blend until the mixture forms a ball, scraping down the sides once or twice. Turn the mixture out onto a lightly floured surface and knead in the chopped nuts and aniseed.

Divide the paste into three pieces and roll into logs about 4 cm/1¹⁄₂ inches wide. Place the logs onto the baking sheet at least 5 cm/2 inches apart. Brush lightly with the other egg yolk beaten with 1 tablespoon water and bake in the preheated oven for 30–35 minutes.

Remove from the oven and reduce the oven temperature to 150°C/300°F/Gas Mark 2. Cut the logs diagonally into 2.5 cm/1 inch slices and lay cut-side down on the baking sheet. Return to the oven for a further 30–40 minutes, or until dry and firm. Cool on a wire rack and store in an airtight container. Serve with Vin Santo or coffee.

# Oatmeal Raisin Cookies

## Makes 24

### Ingredients

175 g/6 oz/1½ cups plain/all-purpose flour

150 g/5 oz/2 cups rolled oats

1 tsp ground ginger

½ tsp baking powder

½ tsp bicarbonate of soda/baking soda

125 g/4 oz/⅔ cup demerara/turbinado sugar

50 g/2 oz/⅓ cup raisins

1 medium/large egg, lightly beaten

150 ml/¼ pint/⅔ cup vegetable or sunflower/corn oil

4 tbsp milk

## Difficulty Rating: 1 point

Preheat the oven to 200°C/400°F/Gas Mark 6, 15 minutes before baking. Lightly oil a baking sheet.

Mix together the flour, oats, ground ginger, baking powder, bicarbonate of soda/baking soda, sugar and the raisins in a large bowl.

In another bowl, mix the egg, oil and milk together. Make a well in the centre of the dry ingredients and pour in the egg mixture. Mix together well with either a fork or a wooden spoon to make a soft but not sticky dough.

Place spoonfuls of the dough well apart on the oiled baking sheet and flatten the tops down slightly with the tines of a fork. Transfer to the preheated oven and bake for 10–12 minutes until golden.

Remove from the oven, leave to cool for 2–3 minutes, then transfer the cookies to a wire rack to cool. Serve when cold, or otherwise store in an airtight container.

# Oatmeal Coconut Cookies

## Makes 30

### Ingredients

225 g/8 oz/2 sticks butter or margarine

125 g/4 oz/²⁄₃ cup demerara/turbinado sugar

125 g/4 oz/²⁄₃ cup caster/superfine sugar

1 large/extra-large egg, lightly beaten

1 tsp vanilla extract

225 g/8 oz/2 cups plain/all-purpose flour

1 tsp baking powder

¹⁄₂ tsp bicarbonate of soda/baking soda

125 g/4 oz/1¹⁄₄ cups rolled oats

75 g/3 oz/1 cup desiccated/shredded coconut

Preheat the oven to 180°C/350°F/Gas Mark 4, 10 minutes before baking. Lightly oil a baking sheet.

Cream together the butter or margarine and sugars until light and fluffy. Gradually stir in the egg and vanilla extract and beat until well blended.

Sift together the flour, baking powder and bicarbonate of soda/baking soda in another bowl. Add to the butter and sugar mixture and beat together until smooth. Fold in the rolled oats and coconut with a metal spoon or rubber spatula.

Roll heaped teaspoonfuls of the mixture into balls and place on the baking sheet about 5 cm/2 inches apart. Flatten each ball slightly with the heel of your hand. Transfer to the preheated oven and bake for 12–15 minutes until just golden. Remove from the oven and transfer the cookies to a wire rack to cool completely before serving.

## Difficulty Rating: 1 point

# Peanut Butter Truffle Cookies

## Makes 18

### Ingredients

125 g/4 oz/5 squares dark/bittersweet chocolate

150 ml/¼ pint/⅔ cup double/heavy cream

125 g/4 oz/1 stick plus 1 tbsp butter or margarine, softened

125 g/4 oz/⅔ cup caster/superfine sugar

125 g/4 oz/½ cup crunchy or smooth peanut butter

4 tbsp golden/corn syrup

1 tbsp milk

225 g/8 oz/1¾ cups plain/all-purpose flour

½ tsp bicarbonate of soda/baking soda

Preheat the oven to 180°C/350°F/Gas Mark 4, 10 minutes before baking. Make the chocolate filling by breaking the chocolate into small pieces and placing in a heatproof bowl.

Put the double/heavy cream into a saucepan and heat to boiling point. Immediately pour over the chocolate. Leave to stand for 1–2 minutes, then stir until smooth. Set aside to cool until firm enough to scoop. Do not refrigerate.

Lightly oil a baking sheet. Cream together the butter or margarine and the sugar until light and fluffy. Blend in the peanut butter, followed by the golden/corn syrup and milk.

Sift together the flour and bicarbonate of soda/baking soda. Add to the peanut butter mixture, mix well and knead until smooth. Flatten 1–2 tablespoons of the cookie mixture on a chopping board. Put a spoonful of the chocolate mixture into the centre of the cookie dough, then fold the dough around the chocolate to enclose completely. Repeat with the rest of the dough and filling. Put the balls onto the baking sheet and flatten slightly. Bake in the preheated oven for 10–12 minutes until golden. Remove from the oven and transfer to a wire rack to cool completely before serving.

## Difficulty Rating: 2 points

# Chocolate Chip Cookies

## Makes about 30

**Ingredients**

130 g/4¹/₂ oz/1¹/₄ sticks butter

50 g/2 oz/¹/₄ cup caster/superfine sugar

65 g/2¹/₂ oz/¹/₃ cup soft dark brown sugar

1 medium/large egg, beaten

¹/₂ tsp vanilla extract

125 g/4 oz/¹/₂ cup plain/all-purpose flour

¹/₂ tsp bicarbonate of soda/baking soda

150 g/5 oz/³/₄ cup dark/bittersweet or
    milk/semisweet chocolate chips

Preheat the oven to 180°C/350°F/Gas Mark 4, 10 minutes before baking. Lightly grease three or four large baking sheets with 1 tablespoon of the butter. Place the remaining butter and both sugars in a food processor and blend until smooth.

Add the egg and vanilla extract and blend briefly. Alternatively, cream the butter and sugars together in a bowl, then beat in the egg with the vanilla extract.

If using a food processor, scrape out the mixture with a spatula and place the mixture into a large bowl. Sift the flour and bicarbonate of soda together, then fold into the creamed mixture. When the mixture is blended thoroughly, stir in the chocolate chips.

Drop heaped teaspoons of the mixture onto the prepared baking sheets, spaced well apart, and bake the cookies in the preheated oven for 10–12 minutes, or until lightly golden.

Leave to cool for a few seconds, then, using a spatula, transfer to a wire rack and cool completely. The cookies are best eaten when just cooked, but can be stored in an airtight container for a few days.

## Difficulty Rating: 1 point

# Chewy Choc & Nut Cookies

## Makes 18

### Ingredients

15 g/¹/₂ oz/1 tbsp butter

4 egg whites

350 g/12 oz/3 cups icing/confectioners' sugar

75 g/3 oz/³/₄ cup cocoa powder (unsweetened)

2 tbsp plain/all-purpose flour

1 tsp instant coffee powder

125 g/4 oz/1 cup walnuts, finely chopped

Preheat the oven to 180°C/350°F/Gas Mark 4, 10 minutes before baking. Lightly grease several baking sheets with the butter. Line with a sheet of nonstick baking parchment. Place the egg whites in a large, grease–free bowl. Whisk with an electric mixer until very frothy.

Add the sugar, the cocoa powder, the flour and coffee powder. Whisk again until the ingredients are blended thoroughly. Add 1 tablespoon water and continue to whisk on the highest speed until the mixture is very thick. Fold in the chopped walnuts.

Place tablespoons of the mixture onto the prepared baking sheets, leaving plenty of space between to allow them to expand during cooking. Bake in the preheated oven for 12–15 minutes, or until the tops are firm, golden and quite cracked. Leave to cool for 30 seconds, then, using a spatula, transfer to a wire rack and leave to cool. Store in an airtight container.

## Difficulty Rating: 2 points

# White Chocolate Cookies

## Makes about 24

**Ingredients**

130 g/4¹/₂ oz/1¹/₄ sticks butter
3 tbsp caster/superfine sugar
65 g/2¹/₂ oz/¹/₃ cup muscovado/dark brown sugar
1 egg
100 g/4 oz/³/₄ cup plain/all-purpose flour
¹/₂ tsp bicarbonate of soda/baking soda
few drops vanilla extract
150 g/5 oz/6 squares white chocolate
50 g/2 oz/heaped ¹/₃ cup whole hazelnuts, shelled

Preheat the oven to 180°C/350°F/Gas Mark 4, 10 minutes before baking. Lightly butter several baking sheets with 15 g/¹/₂ oz/1 tbsp of the butter.

Place the remaining butter with both sugars into a large bowl and beat with a wooden spoon or an electric mixer until soft and fluffy.

Beat the egg, then gradually beat into the creamed mixture. Sift the flour and the bicarbonate of soda/baking soda together, then carefully fold into the creamed mixture with a few drops of vanilla extract.

Roughly chop the chocolate and hazelnuts into small pieces, add to the bowl and gently stir into the mixture. Mix together lightly to blend.

Spoon heaped teaspoons of the mixture onto the prepared baking sheets, making sure that there is plenty of space in between each one, as they will spread a lot during cooking.

Bake the cookies in the preheated oven for 10 minutes, or until golden, then remove from the oven and leave to cool for 1 minute. Using a spatula, carefully transfer to a wire rack and leave to cool completely. These cookies are best eaten on the day they are made.

## Difficulty Rating: 2 points

# Fudgy Chocolate Bars

## Makes 14

**Ingredients**

25 g/1 oz/²/₃ cup glacé/candied cherries
65 g/2¹/₂ oz/¹/₂ cup shelled hazelnuts
150 g/5 oz/5 squares dark/bittersweet chocolate
150 g/5 oz/1¹/₃ sticks unsalted butter
¹/₄ tsp salt
150 g/5 oz/1 cup digestive biscuits/Graham crackers, chopped
1 tbsp icing/confectioners' sugar, sifted (optional)

Preheat the oven to 180°C/350°F/Gas Mark 4, 10 minutes before baking. Lightly oil an 18 cm/7 inch square tin/pan and line the base with nonstick baking parchment. Rinse the glacé/candied cherries thoroughly, dry well on absorbent paper towels and reserve.

Place the nuts on a baking sheet and roast in the preheated oven for 10 minutes, or until light golden brown. Leave to cool slightly, then chop roughly and reserve.

Break the chocolate into small pieces, place with the butter and salt into the top of a double boiler, or in a bowl set over a saucepan of simmering water. Heat gently, stirring, until melted and smooth. Alternatively, melt the chocolate in the microwave, according to the manufacturer's instructions. Chop the biscuits/crackers into 5 mm/¹/₄ inch pieces and cut the cherries in half. Add to the chocolate mixture with the nuts and stir well. Spoon the mixture into the prepared tin and level the top.

Chill in the refrigerator for 30 minutes. Remove from the tin, discard the baking parchment and cut into 14 bars. Cover lightly, return to the refrigerator and keep chilled until ready to serve. To serve, lightly sprinkle the bars with sifted icing/confectioners' sugar, if using. Store covered in the refrigerator.

## Difficulty Rating: 1 point

# Miracle Bars

## Makes 12

### Ingredients

100 g/3½ oz/1 stick butter, melted,
   plus 1–2 tsp extra, for oiling
125 g/4 oz/1½ cups digestive biscuit/Graham cracker crumbs
   (about 7 biscuits/cookies)
175 g/6 oz/1 cup chocolate chips
75 g/3 oz/scant ½ cup desiccated (shredded) coconut
125 g/4 oz/1 cup chopped mixed nuts
400 g/14 oz can sweetened condensed milk

Preheat the oven to 180°C/350°F/Gas Mark 4, 10 minutes before baking. Generously butter a 23 cm/9 inch square cake tin/pan and line with nonstick baking paper.

Pour the butter into the prepared tin and sprinkle the biscuit crumbs over in an even layer. Add the chocolate chips, coconut and nuts in even layers and drizzle over the condensed milk.

Transfer the tin to the preheated oven and bake for 30 minutes, or until golden brown. Allow to cool in the tin, then cut into 12 squares and serve.

## Difficulty Rating: 1 point

# Whipped Shortbread

## Makes 36

**Ingredients**

225 g/8 oz/2 sticks butter, softened
125 g/4 oz/1 cup icing/confectioners' sugar
175 g/6 oz/1½ cups plain/all-purpose flour
hundreds and thousands/sprinkles
sugar strands
chocolate drops
silver balls
2–3 tsp lemon juice

Preheat the oven to 180°C/350°F/Gas Mark 4, 10 minutes before baking. Lightly oil a baking sheet. Cream the butter and 75 g/3 oz/⅔ cup icing/confectioners' sugar until fluffy. Gradually add the flour and continue beating for a further 2–3 minutes until it is smooth and light.

Roll into balls and place on a baking sheet. Cover half of the dough mixture with hundreds and thousands/sprinkles, sugar strands, chocolate drops or silver balls. Keep the other half plain.

Bake in the preheated oven for 6–8 minutes until the bottoms are lightly browned. Remove from the oven and transfer to a wire rack to cool.

Sift the remaining icing/confectioners' sugar into a small bowl. Add the lemon juice and blend until a smooth icing forms.

Using a small spoon, swirl the icing over the cooled plain cookies. Decorate with the extra hundreds and thousands, chocolate drops or silver balls and serve.

## Difficulty Rating: 1 point

# Marbled Toffee Shortbread

## Makes 12

### Ingredients

175 g/6 oz/1½ sticks butter

75 g/3 oz/⅓ cup caster/superfine sugar

175 g/6 oz/1½ cups plain/all-purpose flour

25 g/1 oz/¼ cup cocoa powder (unsweetened)

75 g/3 oz/½ cup fine semolina

**For the toffee filling:**

50 g/2 oz/½ stick butter

50 g/2 oz/¼ cup demerara/light brown sugar

397 g/14 oz can condensed milk

**For the chocolate topping:**

75 g/3 oz/3 squares dark/bittersweet chocolate

75 g/3 oz/3 squares milk/semisweet chocolate

75 g/3 oz/3 squares white chocolate

Preheat the oven to 180°C/350°F/Gas Mark 4, 10 minutes before baking. Oil and line a 20.5 cm/8 inch square cake tin/pan with nonstick baking parchment.

Cream the butter and sugar until light and fluffy. Sift in the flour and cocoa. Add the semolina. Mix together to form a soft dough. Press into the base of the tin. Prick all over with a fork. Bake in the preheated oven for 25 minutes. Leave to cool.

To make the toffee filling, gently heat the butter, sugar and condensed milk together until the sugar has dissolved. Bring to the boil, then simmer for 5 minutes, stirring constantly. Leave for 1 minute, then spread over the shortbread and leave to cool.

For the topping, place the different chocolates in separate heatproof bowls and melt one at a time, set over a saucepan of almost boiling water. Drop spoonfuls of each on top of the toffee and tilt the tin to cover evenly. Swirl with a knife for a marbled effect. Leave the chocolate to cool. When just set, mark into bars using a sharp knife. Leave for at least 1 hour to harden. Cut into bars.

**Difficulty Rating: 3 points**

# Pecan Caramel Millionaire's Shortbread

## Makes 20

**Ingredients**

125 g/4 oz/1 stick plus 1 tbsp butter, softened

2 tbsp smooth peanut butter

75 g/3 oz/¹⁄₃ cup caster/superfine sugar

75 g/3 oz/²⁄₃ cup cornflour/cornstarch

175 g/6 oz/1¹⁄₂ cups plain/all-purpose flour

**For the topping:**

200 g/7 oz/1 cup caster/superfine sugar

125 g/4 oz/1 stick plus 1 tbsp butter

2 tbsp golden syrup/corn syrup

75 g/3 oz/3 tbsp liquid glucose

85 ml/3 fl oz/6 tbsp water

397 g/14 oz can sweetened condensed milk

175 g/6 oz/1¹⁄₂ cups pecans, roughly chopped

75 g/3 oz/3 squares milk/semisweet chocolate

15 g/¹⁄₂ oz/1 tbsp butter

## Difficulty Rating: 3 points

Preheat the oven to 180°C/350°F/Gas Mark 4, 10 minutes before baking. Lightly oil and line an 18 x 28 cm/7 x 11 inch tin/pan with greaseproof/waxed paper or baking parchment.

Cream together the butter, peanut butter and sugar until light. Sift in the cornflour/cornstarch and flour together and mix in to make a smooth dough. Press the mixture into the prepared tin. Prick all over with a fork. Bake in the preheated oven for 20 minutes, or until just golden. Remove from the oven.

For the topping, combine the sugar, butter, golden/corn syrup, glucose, water and condensed milk in a heavy-based saucepan. Stir constantly over a low heat, without boiling, until the sugar has dissolved. Increase the heat and boil steadily. Stir constantly for about 10 minutes until the mixture turns a golden caramel colour. Remove the saucepan from the heat, add the pecans and pour over the shortbread base immediately. Allow to cool. Refrigerate for at least 1 hour.

Break the chocolate into small pieces and put into a heatproof bowl with the butter. Place over a saucepan of barely simmering water, ensuring that the bowl does not come into contact with the water. Leave until melted, then stir together well. Remove the shortbread from the refrigerator and pour the chocolate evenly over the top, spreading thinly to cover. Leave to set, cut into rectangles and serve.

# Fig & Chocolate Bars

## Makes 12

**Ingredients**

125 g/4 oz/1 stick plus 1 tbsp butter
150 g/5 oz/1 heaped cup plain/all-purpose flour
50 g/2 oz/¼ cup soft light brown sugar
225 g/8 oz/1½ cups ready-to-eat dried figs, halved
juice of ½ large lemon
1 tsp ground cinnamon
125 g/4 oz/5 squares dark/bittersweet chocolate

Preheat the oven to 180°C/350°F/Gas Mark 4, 10 minutes before baking. Lightly oil an 18 cm/7 inch square cake tin/pan. Place the butter and the flour in a large bowl and, using your fingertips, rub the butter into the flour until it resembles fine breadcrumbs.

Stir in the sugar, then, using your hands, bring the mixture together to form a dough. Knead until smooth, then press the dough into the prepared tin. Lightly prick the base with a fork and bake in the preheated oven for 20–30 minutes until golden. Remove from the oven and leave the shortbread to cool in the tin until completely cold.

Meanwhile, place the dried figs, lemon juice, 125 ml/4 fl oz/½ cup water and the ground cinnamon in a saucepan and bring to the boil. Cover and simmer for 20 minutes, or until soft, stirring occasionally during cooking. Cool slightly, then purée in a food processor until smooth. Cool, then spread over the cooked shortbread.

Melt the chocolate in a heatproof bowl set over a saucepan of simmering water. Alternatively, melt the chocolate in the microwave, according to the manufacturer's instructions. Stir until smooth, then spread over the top of the fig filling. Leave to become firm, then cut into 12 bars and serve.

## Difficulty Rating: 3 points

# Chocolate Shortcake

## Makes 30–32

**Ingredients**

225 g/8 oz/2 sticks unsalted butter, softened
150 g/5 oz/1½ cups icing/confectioners' sugar
1 tsp vanilla extract
250 g/9 oz/2 cups plain/all-purpose flour
25 g/1 oz/⅓ cup cocoa powder (unsweetened)
¼ tsp salt
extra icing/confectioners' sugar, to decorate

Preheat the oven to 170°C/325°F/Gas Mark 3, 10 minutes before baking. Lightly oil several baking sheets and line with nonstick baking parchment. Place the butter, icing/confectioners' sugar and vanilla extract together in a food processor and blend briefly until smooth. Alternatively, using a wooden spoon, cream the butter, icing sugar and vanilla extract in a large bowl.

Sift the flour, cocoa powder and salt together, then either add to the food processor bowl and blend quickly to form a dough, or add to the bowl and, using your hands, mix together until a smooth dough is formed.

Turn the dough out onto a clean board lined with clingfilm/plastic wrap. Place another sheet of clingfilm over the top and roll the dough out until it is 1 cm/½ inch thick. Transfer the whole board to the refrigerator and chill for 1½–2 hours.

Remove the top piece of clingfilm and use a 5 cm/2 inch cutter to cut the dough into 30–32 rounds. Place the rounds on the prepared baking sheets and bake in the preheated oven for about 15 minutes, or until firm.

Cool for 1 minute, then, using a spatula, carefully remove the shortcakes from the baking parchment and transfer to a wire rack. Leave to cool completely. Sprinkle the shortcakes with sifted icing sugar before serving. Store in an airtight container for a few days.

## Difficulty Rating: 2 points

# Shortbread Thumbs

## Makes 12

**Ingredients**

100 g/3½ oz/¾ cup self-raising flour
125 g/4 oz/1 stick plus 1 tbsp butter, softened
25 g/1 oz/2 tbsp white vegetable fat/shortening
50 g/2 oz/¼ cup caster/superfine sugar
3 tbsp cornflour/cornstarch, sifted
5 tbsp cocoa powder (unsweetened), sifted
100 g/3½ oz/1 cup icing/confectioners' sugar
6 assorted colour glacé/candied cherries,
    rinsed, dried and halved

Preheat the oven to 150°C/300°F/Gas Mark 2, 10 minutes before baking. Oil two baking sheets. Sift the flour into a large bowl, cut 75 g/3 oz/⅔ stick of the butter and the white vegetable fat/shortening into small cubes and add to the flour. Using your fingertips, rub in until the mixture resembles fine breadcrumbs.

Stir in the caster/superfine sugar, sifted cornflour/cornstarch and 4 tablespoons of the cocoa powder. Bring the mixture together with your hands to form a soft and pliable dough. Place on a lightly floured surface and shape into 12 small balls. Place onto the baking sheets at least 5 cm/2 inches apart, then press each one with a clean thumb to make a dent.

Bake in the preheated oven for 20–25 minutes, or until light golden brown. Remove from the oven and leave for 1–2 minutes to cool. Transfer to a wire rack and leave until cold.

Sift the icing/confectioners' sugar and the rest of the cocoa powder into a bowl and add the remaining softened butter. Blend to form a smooth and spreadable icing with 1–2 tablespoons hot water. Spread a little icing over the top of each biscuit and place half a cherry on each. Leave until set before serving.

## Difficulty Rating: 2 points

# Chocolate Macaroons

## Makes 20

**Ingredients**

65 g/2½ oz/2⅔ squares dark/bittersweet chocolate
125 g/4 oz/¾ cup ground almonds
125 g/4 oz/⅔ cup caster/superfine sugar
¼ tsp almond extract
1 tbsp cocoa powder (unsweetened)
2 medium/large egg whites
1 tbsp icing/confectioners' sugar

Preheat the oven to 180°C/350°F/Gas Mark 4, 10 minutes before baking. Lightly oil several baking sheets and line with sheets of nonstick baking parchment. Melt the chocolate in a heatproof bowl set over a saucepan of simmering water. Alternatively, melt in the microwave according to the manufacturer's instructions. Stir until smooth, then cool slightly.

Place the ground almonds in a food processor and add the sugar, almond extract, cocoa powder and one of the egg whites. Add the melted chocolate and a little of the other egg white and blend to make a soft, smooth paste. Alternatively, place the ground almonds with the sugar, almond extract and cocoa powder in a bowl and make a well in the centre. Add the melted chocolate with sufficient egg white and gradually blend together to form a smooth but not sticky paste.

Shape the dough into small balls the size of large walnuts and place them on the prepared baking sheets. Flatten them slightly, then brush with a little water. Sprinkle over a little icing/confectioners' sugar and bake in the preheated oven for 10–12 minutes, or until just firm.

Using a spatula, carefully lift the macaroons off the baking parchment and transfer to a wire rack to cool. These are best served immediately, but can be stored in an airtight container.

## Difficulty Rating: 2 points

# Almond Macaroons

## Makes 12

**Ingredients**

rice paper
125 g/4 oz/²/₃ cup caster/superfine sugar
50 g/2 oz/¹/₂ cup ground almonds
1 tsp ground rice
2–3 drops almond extract
1 medium/large egg white
8 blanched almonds, halved

Preheat the oven to 150˚C/300˚F/Gas Mark 2, 10 minutes before baking. Line a baking sheet with the rice paper.

Mix the caster/superfine sugar, ground almonds, ground rice and almond extract together and reserve.

Whisk the egg white until stiff, then gently fold in the caster sugar mixture with a metal spoon or rubber spatula. Mix to form a stiff but not sticky paste. (If the mixture is very sticky, add a little extra ground almonds.)

Place small spoonfuls of the mixture, about the size of an apricot, well apart on the rice paper. Place half a blanched almond in the centre of each. Bake in the preheated oven for 25 minutes, or until just pale golden.

Remove the macaroons from the oven and leave to cool for a few minutes on the baking sheet. Cut or tear the rice paper around the macaroons to release them. Once cold, serve or, otherwise, store them in an airtight container.

## Difficulty Rating: 2 points

# Coconut & Almond Munchies

## Makes 26–30

**Ingredients**

rice paper

5 medium/large egg whites

250 g/9 oz/2½ cups icing/confectioners' sugar,
 plus extra to sprinkle

225 g/8 oz/2⅓ cups ground almonds

200 g/7 oz/1 heaped cup desiccated/shredded coconut

grated zest of 1 lemon

125 g/4 oz/5 squares milk/semisweet chocolate

125 g/4 oz/5 squares white chocolate

Preheat the oven to 150°C/300°F/Gas Mark 2, 10 minutes before baking. Line several baking sheets with rice paper. Place the egg whites in a clean, grease-free bowl and whisk until stiff and standing in peaks. Sift the icing/confectioners' sugar, then carefully fold half of the sugar into the whisked egg whites together with the ground almonds. Add the coconut, the remaining icing sugar and the lemon zest and mix together to form a very sticky dough.

Place the mixture in a piping/decorating bag and pipe the mixture into walnut-sized mounds onto the rice paper, then sprinkle with a little extra icing sugar. Bake in the preheated oven for 20–25 minutes, or until set and golden on the outside. Remove from the oven and leave to cool slightly. Using a spatula, carefully transfer to a wire rack and leave until cold.

Break the milk/semisweet and white chocolate into pieces and place in two separate bowls. Melt both chocolates set over saucepans of gently simmering water. Alternatively, melt in the microwave, according to the manufacturer's instructions. Stir until smooth and free from lumps. Dip one edge of each munchie in the milk chocolate and leave to dry on nonstick baking parchment. When dry, dip the other side into the white chocolate. Leave to set, then serve as soon as possible.

## Difficulty Rating: 3 points

# Chocolate & Almond Biscuits

## Makes 18–20

**Ingredients**

130 g/4¹/₂ oz/1¹/₄ sticks butter

65 g/2¹/₂ oz/¹/₃ cup icing/confectioners' sugar

1 medium/large egg, beaten

1 tbsp milk

grated zest of 1 lemon

250 g/9 oz/2 cups plain/all-purpose flour

100 g/3¹/₂ oz/³/₄ cup blanched almonds, chopped

125 g/4 oz/5 squares dark/bittersweet chocolate

75 g/3 oz/³/₄ cup flaked almonds, toasted

## Difficulty Rating: 2 points

Preheat the oven to 200°C/400°F/Gas Mark 6, 15 minutes before baking. Lightly oil several baking sheets. Cream the butter and icing/confectioners' sugar together until light and fluffy, then gradually beat in the egg, beating well after each addition. When all the egg has been added, stir in the milk and lemon zest.

Sift the flour, then stir into the mixture together with the chopped almonds to form a smooth and pliable dough. Wrap in clingfilm/plastic wrap and chill in the refrigerator for 2 hours.

Roll the dough out on a lightly floured surface, in a large oblong about 5 mm/¹/₄ inch thick. Cut into strips, about 6.5 cm/2¹/₂ inches long and 4 cm/1¹/₂ inches wide and place on the prepared baking sheets

Bake in the preheated oven for 15 minutes, or until golden, then remove from the oven and leave to cool for a few minutes. Transfer to a wire rack and leave to cool completely.

Melt the chocolate in a heatproof bowl set over a saucepan of simmering water. Alternatively, melt the chocolate in the microwave according to the manufacturer's instructions until smooth. Spread the chocolate thickly over the biscuits, sprinkle over the toasted flaked almonds and leave to set before serving.

# Chocolate & Hazelnut Cookies

## Makes 12

### Ingredients

75 g/3 oz/½ cup blanched hazelnuts

100 g/3½ oz/½ cup caster/superfine sugar

50 g/2 oz/½ stick unsalted butter

pinch salt

5 tsp cocoa powder (unsweetened)

3 tbsp double/heavy cream

2 large/extra-large egg whites

40 g/1½ oz/⅓ cup plain/all-purpose flour

2 tbsp rum

75 g/3 oz/3 squares white chocolate

Preheat the oven to 180°C/350°F/Gas Mark 4, 10 minutes before baking. Lightly oil and flour two or three baking sheets. Chop 25 g/1 oz of the hazelnuts and reserve. Blend the remaining hazelnuts with the caster/superfine sugar in a food processor until finely ground. Add the butter to the processor bowl and blend until pale and creamy.

Add the salt, cocoa powder and the double/heavy cream and mix well. Scrape the mixture into a bowl, using a spatula, and stir in the egg whites. Sift the flour, then stir into the mixture together with the rum.

Spoon heaped tablespoons of the batter onto the baking sheets and sprinkle over a few of the reserved hazelnuts. Bake in the preheated oven for 5–7 minutes until firm. Remove the cookies from the oven and leave to cool for 1–2 minutes. Using a spatula, transfer to wire racks and leave to cool.

When the cookies are cold, melt the chocolate in a heatproof bowl set over a saucepan of simmering water. Stir until smooth, then drizzle a little of the chocolate over the top of each biscuit. Leave to dry on a wire rack before serving.

## Difficulty Rating: 2 points

# Ginger Snaps

## Makes 40

### Ingredients

300 g/11 oz/2²/₃ sticks butter or margarine, softened

225 g/8 oz/1 heaped cup demerara/turbinado sugar

3 tbsp black treacle/molasses

1 egg

400 g/14 oz/3 heaped cups plain/all-purpose flour

2 tsp bicarbonate of soda/baking soda

½ tsp salt

1 tsp ground ginger

1 tsp ground cloves

1 tsp ground cinnamon

50 g/2 oz/¼ cup caster/superfine sugar

Preheat the oven to 190°C/375°F/Gas Mark 5, 10 minutes before baking. Lightly oil a baking sheet. Cream together the butter or margarine and the sugar until light and fluffy. Warm the treacle/molasses in the microwave for 30–40 seconds, then add gradually to the butter mixture with the egg. Beat until combined well.

In a separate bowl, sift the flour, bicarbonate of soda/baking soda, salt, ground ginger, ground cloves and ground cinnamon. Add to the butter mixture and mix together to form a firm dough. Chill in the refrigerator for 1 hour. Shape the dough into small balls and roll in the caster/superfine sugar. Place well apart on the oiled baking sheet.

Sprinkle the baking sheet with a little water and transfer to the preheated oven. Bake for 12 minutes, or until golden and crisp. Transfer to a wire rack to cool and serve.

## Difficulty Rating: 1 point

# Chocolate & Ginger Florentines

## Makes 14–16

**Ingredients**

40 g/1½ oz/⅓ stick butter

5 tbsp double/heavy cream

50 g/2 oz/¼ cup caster/superfine sugar

65 g/2½ oz/½ cup chopped almonds

25 g/1 oz/¼ cup flaked almonds

40 g/1½ oz/¼ cup glacé/candied ginger, chopped

25 g/1 oz/scant ¼ cup plain/all-purpose flour

pinch salt

150 g/5 oz/6 squares dark/bittersweet chocolate

## Difficulty Rating: 2 points

Preheat the oven to 180°C/350°F/Gas Mark 4, 10 minutes before baking. Lightly oil several baking sheets. Melt the butter, cream and sugar together in a saucepan and bring slowly to the boil. Remove from the heat and stir in the almonds and the glacé/candied ginger.

Leave to cool slightly, then mix in the flour and the salt. Blend together, then place heaped teaspoons of the mixture on the baking sheets. Make sure they are spaced well apart, as they expand during cooking. Flatten them slightly with the back of a wet spoon.

Bake in the preheated oven for 10–12 minutes until just brown at the edges. Leave to cool slightly. Using a spatula, carefully transfer the Florentines to a wire rack and leave to cool.

Melt the chocolate in a heatproof bowl set over a saucepan of gently simmering water. Alternatively, melt the chocolate in the microwave according to the manufacturer's instructions until just liquid and smooth. Spread thickly over one side of the Florentines, then mark wavy lines through the chocolate using a fork and leave until firm.

# Chocolate Florentines

## Makes 20

### Ingredients

125 g/4 oz/1 stick plus 1 tbsp butter or margarine

125 g/4 oz/²⁄₃ cup soft light brown sugar

1 tbsp double/heavy cream

50 g/2 oz/¹⁄₃ cup blanched almonds, roughly chopped

50 g/2 oz/¹⁄₃ cup hazelnuts, roughly chopped

75 g/3 oz/¹⁄₂ cup sultanas/golden raisins

50 g/2 oz/¹⁄₄ cup glacé/candied cherries, roughly chopped

50 g/2 oz/2 squares dark/bittersweet chocolate,
   roughly chopped or broken

50 g/2 oz/2 squares milk/semisweet chocolate,
   roughly chopped or broken

50 g/2 oz/2 squares white chocolate,
   roughly chopped or broken

Preheat the oven to 180°C/350°F/Gas Mark 4, 10 minutes before baking. Lightly oil a baking sheet.

Melt the butter or margarine with the sugar and double/heavy cream in a small saucepan over a very low heat. Do not boil. Remove from the heat and stir in the almonds, hazelnuts, sultanas/golden raisins and cherries. Drop teaspoonfuls of the mixture onto the baking sheet. Transfer to the preheated oven and bake for 10 minutes, or until golden. Leave the biscuits to cool on the baking sheet for about 5 minutes, then carefully transfer to a wire rack to cool.

Melt the dark/bittersweet, milk/semisweet and white chocolates in separate bowls, either in the microwave according to the manufacturers' instructions or in a small bowl placed over a saucepan of gently simmering water. Spread one third of the biscuits with the dark chocolate, one third with the milk chocolate and one third with the white chocolate.

Mark out wavy lines on the chocolate when almost set with the tines of a fork, or dip some of the biscuits in chocolate to half coat and serve.

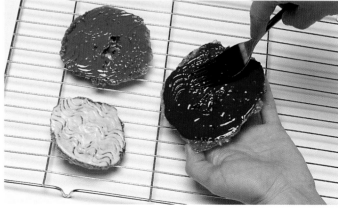

## Difficulty Rating: 3 points

# Chequered Biscuits

## Makes 20

**Ingredients**

150 g/5 oz/1⅓ sticks butter
75 g/3 oz/¾ cup icing/confectioners' sugar
pinch salt
200 g/7 oz/1½ cups plain/all-purpose flour
25 g/1 oz/¼ cup cocoa powder (unsweetened)
1 small egg white

Preheat the oven to 190°C/375°F/Gas Mark 5, 10 minutes before baking. Lightly oil three or four baking sheets. Place the butter and icing/confectioners' sugar in a bowl and cream together until light and fluffy.

Add the salt, then gradually add the flour, beating well after each addition. Mix well to form a firm dough. Cut the dough in half and knead the cocoa powder into one half. Wrap both portions of dough separately in clingfilm/plastic wrap and then leave to chill in the refrigerator for 2 hours.

Divide each piece of dough into three portions. Roll each portion of dough into a long roll and arrange these rolls on top of each other to form a chequerboard design, sealing them with egg white. Wrap in clingfilm and refrigerate for 1 hour.

Cut the dough into 5 mm/¼ inch thick slices, place on the baking sheets and bake in the preheated oven for 10–15 minutes. Remove from the oven and leave to cool for a few minutes. Transfer to a wire rack and leave until cold before serving. Store in an airtight container.

## Difficulty Rating: 3 points

# Honey & Chocolate Hearts

## Makes about 20

**Ingredients**

65 g/2½ oz/scant ⅓ cup caster/superfine sugar

1 tbsp butter

125 g/4 oz/⅓ cup thick honey

1 small egg, beaten

pinch salt

1 tbsp mixed/candied peel or chopped glacé/candied ginger

¼ tsp ground cinnamon

pinch ground cloves

225 g/8 oz/1¾ cups plain/all-purpose flour, sifted

½ tsp baking powder, sifted

75 g/3 oz/3 squares milk/semisweet chocolate

Preheat the oven to 220°C/425°F/Gas Mark 7, 15 minutes before baking. Lightly oil two baking sheets. Heat the sugar, butter and honey together in a small saucepan until everything has melted and the mixture is smooth.

Remove from the heat and stir until slightly cooled, then add the beaten egg with the salt and beat well. Stir in the mixed/candied peel or glacé/candied ginger, ground cinnamon, ground cloves, the flour and the baking powder and mix well until a dough is formed. Wrap in clingfilm/plastic wrap and chill in the refrigerator for 45 minutes.

Place the chilled dough on a lightly floured surface, roll out to about 5 mm/¼ inch thickness and cut out small heart shapes. Place onto the prepared baking sheets and bake in the preheated oven for 8–10 minutes. Remove from the oven and leave to cool slightly. Using a spatula, transfer to a wire rack until cold.

Melt the chocolate in a heatproof bowl set over a saucepan of simmering water. Alternatively, melt the chocolate in the microwave according to the manufacturer's instructions until smooth. Dip one half of each biscuit in the melted chocolate. Leave to set before serving.

## Difficulty Rating: 2 points

# Chocolate Orange Biscuits

## Makes 30

**Ingredients**

100 g/3½ oz/4 squares dark/bittersweet chocolate

125 g/4 oz/1 stick plus 1 tbsp butter

125 g/4 oz/⅔ cup caster/superfine sugar

pinch salt

1 egg, beaten

grated zest of 2 oranges

200 g/7 oz/1½ cups plain/all-purpose flour

1 tsp baking powder

100 g/4 oz/1 cup icing/confectioners' sugar

1–2 tbsp orange juice

Preheat the oven to 200°C/400°F/Gas Mark 6, 15 minutes before baking. Lightly oil several baking sheets. Coarsely grate the chocolate and reserve. Beat the butter and sugar together until creamy. Add the salt, beaten egg and half the orange zest and beat again.

Sift the flour and baking powder, add to the bowl with the grated chocolate and beat to form a dough. Shape into a ball, wrap in clingfilm/plastic wrap and chill in the refrigerator for 2 hours.

Roll the dough out on a lightly floured surface to 5 mm/¼ inch thickness. Cut into 5 cm/2 inch rounds. Place the rounds on the prepared baking sheets, allowing room for expansion. Bake in the preheated oven for 10–12 minutes until firm. Remove the biscuits from the oven and leave to cool slightly. Transfer to a wire rack and leave to cool.

Sift the icing/confectioners' sugar into a small bowl and stir in sufficient orange juice to make a smooth, spreadable icing. Spread or pipe the icing over the biscuits, leave until almost set, then sprinkle on the remaining grated orange zest before serving.

## Difficulty Rating: 2 points

# Rum & Chocolate Squares

## Makes 14–16

### Ingredients

125 g/4 oz/1 stick plus 1 tbsp butter
100 g/3½ oz/½ cup caster/superfine sugar
pinch salt
2 medium/large egg yolks
225 g/8 oz/1¾ cups plain/all-purpose flour
50 g/2 oz/scant ½ cup cornflour/cornstarch
¼ tsp baking powder
2 tbsp cocoa powder (unsweetened)
1 tbsp rum

Preheat the oven to 190°C/375°F/Gas Mark 5, 10 minutes before baking. Lightly oil several baking sheets. Cream the butter, sugar and salt together in a large bowl until light and fluffy. Add the egg yolks and beat well until smooth.

Sift together 175 g/6 oz of the flour, the cornflour/cornstarch and the baking powder and add to the mixture and mix well with a wooden spoon until a smooth and soft dough is formed.

Halve the dough and knead the cocoa powder into one half and the rum and the remaining flour into the other half. Place the two mixtures in two separate bowls, cover with clingfilm/plastic wrap and chill in the refrigerator for 1 hour.

Roll out both pieces of dough separately on a well-floured surface into two thin rectangles. Place one on top of the other, cut out squares approximately 5 cm/2 inches x 5 mm/¼ inch and place on the prepared baking sheets.

Bake in the preheated oven, half with the chocolate uppermost and the other half rum-side up for 10–12 minutes until firm. Remove from the oven and leave to cool slightly. Using a spatula, transfer to a wire rack and leave to cool, then serve.

## Difficulty Rating: 3 points

# Chocolate Whirls

## Makes 20

### Ingredients

125 g/4 oz/1 stick plus 1 tbsp soft margarine
75 g/3 oz/²/₃ stick unsalted butter, softened
75 g/3 oz/³/₄ cup icing/confectioners' sugar, sifted
75 g/3 oz/3 squares dark/bittersweet chocolate,
  melted and cooled
2 tbsp cornflour/cornstarch, sifted
125 g/4 oz/1 cup plain/all-purpose flour
125 g/4 oz/1 cup self-raising flour

**For the butter cream:**
125 g/4 oz/1 stick plus 1 tbsp unsalted butter, softened
¹/₂ tsp vanilla extract
225 g/8 oz/2¹/₄ cups icing/confectioners' sugar, sifted

Preheat the oven to 180°C/350°F/Gas Mark 4, 10 minutes before baking. Lightly oil two baking sheets. Cream the margarine, butter and icing/confectioners' sugar together until the mixture is light and fluffy.

Stir the chocolate until smooth, then beat into the creamed mixture. Stir in the cornflour/cornstarch. Sift the flours together, then gradually add to the creamed mixture, a little at a time, beating well between each addition. Beat until the consistency is smooth and stiff enough for piping. Put the mixture in a piping/decorating bag fitted with a large star nozzle/tip and pipe 40 small whirls onto the prepared baking sheets. Bake the whirls in the preheated oven for 12–15 minutes until firm to the touch. Remove from the oven and leave to cool for about 2 minutes. Using a spatula, transfer the whirls to wire racks and leave to cool.

Meanwhile, make the butter cream. Cream the butter with the vanilla extract until soft. Gradually beat in the icing sugar and add a little cooled boiled water, if necessary, to give a smooth consistency. When the whirls are cold, pipe or spread on the prepared butter cream, sandwich together and serve.

## Difficulty Rating: 3 points

# Pumpkin Cookies with Brown Butter Glaze

## Makes 48

### Ingredients

125 g/4 oz/1 stick plus 1 tbsp butter, softened

150 g/5 oz/1 heaped cup plain/all-purpose flour

175 g/6 oz/1 scant cup soft light brown sugar, lightly packed

225 g/8 oz/1 scant cup canned pumpkin or cooked pumpkin

1 medium/large egg, beaten

2 tsp ground cinnamon; 2½ tsp vanilla extract

½ tsp baking powder; ½ tsp bicarbonate of soda/baking soda

½ tsp freshly grated nutmeg

125 g/4 oz/1 heaped cup wholemeal/whole-wheat flour

75 g/3 oz/¾ cup pecans, roughly chopped

100 g/3½ oz/⅔ cup raisins

50 g/2 oz/½ stick unsalted butter

225 g/8 oz/2¼ cups icing/confectioners' sugar

2 tbsp milk

Preheat the oven to 190°C/375°F/Gas Mark 5, 10 minutes before baking. Lightly oil a baking sheet and reserve. Using an electric mixer, beat the butter until light and fluffy. Add the flour, sugar, pumpkin and beaten egg and beat with the mixer until mixed well. Stir in the ground cinnamon and 1 teaspoon of the vanilla extract and then sift in the baking powder, bicarbonate of soda/baking soda and grated nutmeg. Beat the mixture until combined well, scraping down the sides of the bowl.

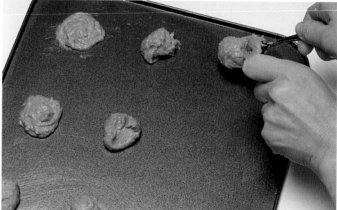

Add the wholemeal/whole-wheat flour, chopped nuts and raisins to the mixture and fold in with a metal spoon or rubber spatula until mixed thoroughly together. Place teaspoonfuls about 5 cm/ 2 inches apart onto the baking sheet. Bake in the preheated oven for 10–12 minutes until the cookie edges are firm. Remove the biscuits from the oven and leave to cool on a wire rack.

Meanwhile, melt the butter in a small saucepan over a medium heat until pale and just turning golden brown. Remove from the heat. Add the sugar, remaining vanilla extract and milk, stirring. Drizzle over the cooled cookies and serve.

## Difficulty Rating: 2 points

# Spiced Palmier Biscuits with Apple Purée

## Makes 20

### Ingredients

250 g/9 oz prepared puff pastry dough, thawed if frozen

40 g/1½ oz/scant ¼ cup caster/superfine sugar

25 g/1 oz/¼ cup icing/confectioners' sugar

1 tsp ground cinnamon

¼ tsp ground ginger

¼ tsp freshly grated nutmeg

450 g/1 lb/4 cups Bramley/tart cooking apples, roughly chopped

50 g/2 oz/¼ cup caster/superfine or granulated sugar

3 tbsp raisins

3 tbsp dried cherries

zest of 1 orange

double/heavy cream, lightly whipped, to serve

Preheat the oven to 200°C/400°F/Gas Mark 6, 15 minutes before baking. Roll out the pastry dough on a lightly floured surface to form a 25.5 x 30.5 cm/10 x 12 inch rectangle. Trim the edges with a small sharp knife.

Sift together the caster/superfine sugar, icing/confectioners' sugar, cinnamon, ginger and nutmeg into a bowl. Generously dust both sides of the pastry sheet with about a quarter of the sugar mixture. With a long edge facing the body, fold each side halfway towards the centre. Dust with a third of the remaining sugar mixture. Fold each side again so that they almost meet in the centre and dust again with about half the remaining sugar mixture. Fold the two sides together down the centre of the pastry to give six layers altogether. Wrap the pastry in clingfilm/plastic wrap and refrigerate for 1–2 hours until firm. Reserve the remaining spiced sugar.

Remove the pastry from the refrigerator, unwrap and roll in the remaining sugar to give a good coating all round. Using a sharp knife, cut the roll into about 20 thin slices and place their cut sides down onto a baking sheet. Bake in the preheated oven for 10 minutes, turn the biscuits and cook for a further 5–10 minutes, or until golden and crisp. Remove from the oven and transfer to a wire rack. Allow to cool completely.

Meanwhile, combine the remaining ingredients in a saucepan. Cover and cook gently for 15 minutes until the apple is completely soft. Stir well and allow to cool. Serve the palmiers with a spoonful of the apple purée and a little of the whipped double/heavy cream.

## Difficulty Rating: 4 points

# Fruit & Nut Flapjacks

## Makes 12

### Ingredients

75 g/3 oz/²/₃ stick butter or margarine
125 g/4 oz/²/₃ cup soft light brown sugar
3 tbsp golden/corn syrup
50 g/2 oz/¹/₃ cup raisins
50 g/2 oz/¹/₂ cup walnuts, roughly chopped
175 g/6 oz/2¹/₃ cups rolled oats
50 g/2 oz/¹/₂ cup icing/confectioners' sugar
1–1¹/₂ tbsp lemon juice

Preheat the oven to 180°C/350°F/Gas Mark 4, 10 minutes before baking. Lightly oil a 23 cm/9 inch square cake tin/pan.

Melt the butter or margarine with the sugar and syrup in a small saucepan over a low heat. Remove from the heat.

Stir the raisins, walnuts and oats into the syrup mixture and mix together well. Spoon evenly into the prepared tin and press down well. Transfer to the preheated oven and bake for 20–25 minutes. Remove from the oven and leave to cool in the tin. Cut into bars while still warm.

Sift the icing/confectioners' sugar into a small bowl, then gradually beat in the lemon juice a little at a time to form a thin icing. Place into an icing bag fitted with a writing nozzle/tip, then pipe thin lines over the flapjacks. Allow to cool and serve.

## Difficulty Rating: 2 points

# Chocolate-covered Flapjacks

## Makes 24

### Ingredients

215 g/7¹/₂ oz/1²/₃ cups plain/all-purpose flour

150 g/5 oz/2 cups rolled oats

225 g/8 oz/1 heaped cup light muscovado/golden brown sugar

1 tsp bicarbonate of soda/baking soda

pinch salt

150 g/5 oz/1¹/₃ sticks butter

2 tbsp golden/corn syrup

250 g/9 oz/10 squares dark/bittersweet chocolate

5 tbsp double/heavy cream

Preheat the oven to 180°C/350°F/Gas Mark 4, 10 minutes before baking. Lightly oil a 33 x 23 cm/13 x 9 inch Swiss roll tin/jelly roll pan and line with nonstick baking parchment. Place the flour, rolled oats, the light muscovado/golden brown sugar, bicarbonate of soda/baking soda and salt into a bowl and stir together well.

Melt the butter and golden/corn syrup together in a heavy-based saucepan and stir until smooth, then add to the oat mixture and mix together thoroughly. Spoon the mixture into the prepared tin, press down firmly and level the top. Bake in the preheated oven for 15–20 minutes until golden. Remove from the oven and leave to cool in the tin. Once cool, remove from the tin. Discard the parchment.

Melt the chocolate in a heatproof bowl set over a saucepan of gently simmering water. Alternatively, melt the chocolate in the microwave according to the manufacturer's instructions. Once the chocolate has melted, quickly beat in the cream, then pour over the flapjack. Mark patterns over the chocolate with a fork when almost set.

Chill in the refrigerator for at least 30 minutes before cutting into bars. When the chocolate has set, serve. Store in an airtight container for a few days.

## Difficulty Rating: 2 points

# Sweet Pastry, Tarts & Pies

**You do not have to be a pastry whizz to make these delicious tarts and pies – a lot of the recipes can be made using bought ready-made pastry. Create melt-in-the-mouth confections ranging from the fresh flavours of Goats' Cheese and Lemon Tart to the sugary goodness of Lattice Treacle Tart. Rejoice in the heartiness of Rich Double-crust Plum Pie and indulge in Triple Chocolate Cheesecake.**

# Almond & Pine Nut Tart

## Serves 6

**Ingredients**

250 g/9 oz/1¼ cups ready-made sweet shortcrust pastry dough
   (*see* page 22)
75 g/3 oz/¾ cup blanched almonds
75 g/3 oz/⅓ cup caster/superfine sugar
pinch salt
2 eggs
1 tsp vanilla extract
2–3 drops almond extract
125 g/4 oz/1 stick plus 1 tbsp unsalted butter, softened
2 tbsp plain/all-purpose flour
½ tsp baking powder
3–4 tbsp raspberry jam/jelly
50 g/2 oz/½ cup pine nuts
icing/confectioners' sugar, to decorate
whipped/whipping cream, to serve

Preheat the oven to 200°C/400°F/Gas Mark 6, 15 minutes
before baking. Roll out the pastry/dough and use to line a
23 cm/9 inch fluted flan tin/tart pan. Chill in the refrigerator for
10 minutes, then line with greaseproof/waxed paper and baking
beans/pie weights. Bake blind in the preheated oven for
10 minutes. Remove the paper and beans. Bake for a further
10–12 minutes until cooked. Leave to cool. Reduce the
temperature to 190°C/375°F/Gas Mark 5.

Grind the almonds in a food processor until fine. Add the sugar,
salt, eggs, vanilla and almond extracts and blend. Add the
butter, flour and baking powder and blend until smooth.

Spread a thick layer of the raspberry jam/jelly over the cooled
pastry case/pie crust, then pour in the almond filling. Sprinkle the
pine nuts evenly over the top and bake for 30 minutes, or until firm
and browned. Remove the tart from the oven and leave to cool.

Dust generously with icing/confectioners' sugar and serve cut
into wedges with whipped cream.

## Difficulty Rating: 2 points

# Raspberry & Almond Tart

## Serves 6–8

**Ingredients**

**For the pastry:**
225 g/8 oz/2 cups plain/all-purpose flour
pinch salt
125 g/4 oz/1 stick plus 1 tbsp butter, cut into pieces
50 g/2 oz/$^1/_4$ cup caster/superfine sugar
grated zest of $^1/_2$ lemon
1 egg yolk

**For the filling:**
75 g/3 oz/$^2/_3$ stick butter
75 g/3 oz/$^1/_3$ cup caster/superfine sugar
75 g/3 oz/$^3/_4$ cup ground almonds
2 eggs
225 g/8 oz/2 cups raspberries, thawed if frozen
2 tbsp flaked/slivered almonds
icing/confectioners' sugar, for dusting

Preheat the oven to 200˚C/400˚F/Gas Mark 6, 15 minutes before baking. Blend the flour, salt and butter in a food processor until the mixture resembles breadcrumbs. Add the sugar and lemon zest and blend again for 1 minute. Mix the egg yolk with 2 tablespoons cold water and add to the mixture. Blend until the mixture starts to come together, adding a little more water if necessary, then tip out onto a lightly floured surface. Knead until smooth, wrap in clingfilm/plastic wrap and chill in the refrigerator for 30 minutes.

Roll the dough out thinly on a lightly floured surface and use to line a 23 cm/9 inch fluted tart tin/pan. Chill in the refrigerator for 10 minutes. Line the pastry case/shell with greaseproof/waxed paper and baking beans/pie weights. Bake for 10 minutes, then remove the paper and beans and return to the oven for a further 10–12 minutes until cooked. Allow to cool slightly, then reduce the oven temperature to 190˚C/375˚F/Gas Mark 5.

Blend together the butter, sugar, ground almonds and eggs until smooth. Spread the raspberries over the base of the pastry, then cover with the almond mixture. Bake for 15 minutes. Remove from the oven. Sprinkle with the flaked/

slivered almonds and dust generously with icing/confectioners' sugar. Bake for a further 15–20 minutes until firm and golden brown. Leave to cool, then serve.

## Difficulty Rating: 3 points

# Goats' Cheese & Lemon Tart

## Serves 4

### Ingredients

**For the pastry:**
125 g/4 oz/1 stick plus 1 tbsp butter, cut into small pieces
225 g/8 oz/2 cups plain/all-purpose flour
pinch salt
50 g/2 oz/¼ cup sugar
1 egg yolk

**For the filling:**
350 g/12 oz/1½ cups mild fresh goats' cheese
3 eggs, beaten
150 g/5 oz/¾ cup sugar
grated zest and juice of 3 lemons
450 ml/¾ pint/1¾ cups double/heavy cream
fresh raspberries, to decorate

## Difficulty Rating: 3 points

Preheat the oven to 200°C/400°F/Gas Mark 6, 15 minutes before baking. Rub the butter into the plain/all-purpose flour and salt until the mixture resembles breadcrumbs, then stir in the sugar. Beat the egg yolk with 2 tablespoons cold water and add to the mixture. Mix together until a dough is formed, then turn the dough out onto a lightly floured surface and knead until smooth. Chill in the refrigerator for 30 minutes.

Roll the dough out thinly on a lightly floured surface and use to line a 4 cm/1½ inch deep 23 cm/9 inch fluted flan tin/tart pan. Chill in the refrigerator for 10 minutes. Line the pastry case/pie crust with greaseproof/waxed paper and baking beans/pie weights or kitchen foil and bake blind in the preheated oven for 10 minutes. Remove the paper and beans or foil. Return to the oven for a further 12–15 minutes until cooked. Leave to cool slightly, then reduce the oven temperature to 150°C/300°F/Gas Mark 2.

Beat the goats' cheese until smooth. Whisk in the eggs, sugar, lemon zest and juice. Add the cream and mix well. Carefully pour the cheese mixture into the pastry case and return to the oven. Bake in the oven for 35–40 minutes, or until just set. If it begins to brown or swell, open the oven door for 2 minutes. Reduce the temperature to 120°C/250°F/Gas Mark ½ and leave the tart to cool in the oven. Chill in the refrigerator until cold. Decorate and serve with fresh raspberries.

# Passion Fruit & Pomegranate Citrus Tart

## Serves 4

**Ingredients**

**For the pastry:**
175 g/6 oz/1⅓ cups plain/all-purpose flour
pinch salt
125 g/4 oz/1 stick plus 1 tbsp butter
4 tsp caster/superfine sugar
1 small egg, separated

**For the filling:**
2 passion fruit
175 g/6 oz/1 scant cup caster/superfine sugar
4 large/extra-large eggs
175 ml/6 fl oz/scant ¾ cup double/heavy cream
3 tbsp lime juice
1 pomegranate
icing/confectioners' sugar, for dusting

Preheat the oven to 200°C/400°F/Gas Mark 6, 15 minutes before baking. Sift the flour and salt into a large bowl and rub in the butter until the mixture resembles fine breadcrumbs. Stir in the sugar.

Whisk the egg yolk and add to the dry ingredients. Mix well to form a smooth, pliable dough. Knead gently on a lightly floured surface until smooth. Wrap the pastry in clingfilm/plastic wrap and leave to rest in the refrigerator for 30 minutes.

Roll out the pastry on a lightly floured surface and use to line a 25.5 cm/10 inch loose-based flan tin/tart pan. Line the pastry case/pie crust with greaseproof/waxed paper and baking beans/pie weights. Brush the edges of the pastry with the egg white and bake blind in the preheated oven for 15 minutes. Remove the paper and beans and bake for 5 minutes. Remove and reduce the temperature to 180°C/350°F/Gas Mark 4.

Halve the passion fruit and spoon the flesh into a bowl. Whisk the sugar and eggs together in a bowl. When mixed thoroughly, stir in the double/heavy cream with the passion fruit juice and

flesh and the lime juice. Pour the mixture into the pastry case and bake for 30–40 minutes until the filling is just set. Remove and cool slightly, then chill in the refrigerator for 1 hour. Cut the pomegranate in half and scoop the seeds into a sieve. Spoon the drained seeds over the top and, just before serving, dust with icing/confectioners' sugar.

## Difficulty Rating: 3 points

# Iced Bakewell Tart

## Cuts into 8 slices

### Ingredients

**For the pastry:**
175 g/6 oz/1½ cups plain/all-purpose flour
pinch salt
65 g/2½ oz/5 tbsp butter, cut into small pieces
50 g/2 oz/4 tbsp white vegetable fat/shortening,
    cut into small pieces
2 small egg yolks, beaten

**For the filling:**
125 g/4 oz/1 stick plus 1 tbsp butter, melted
125 g/4 oz/⅔ cup caster/superfine sugar
125 g/4 oz/1⅓ cups ground almonds
2 large/extra-large eggs, beaten
few drops almond extract
2 tbsp seedless raspberry jam/jelly

**For the icing:**
125 g/4 oz/1 cup icing/confectioners' sugar, sifted
6–8 tsp fresh lemon juice
25 g/1 oz/¼ cup toasted flaked/slivered almonds

Preheat the oven to 200°C/400°F/Gas Mark 6, 15 minutes before baking. Place the flour and salt in a bowl and rub in the butter and vegetable fat/shortening until the mixture resembles breadcrumbs. Alternatively, blend in short bursts in a food processor. Add the eggs with sufficient water to make a soft, pliable dough. Knead lightly on a floured board, then chill in the refrigerator for about 30 minutes. Roll out the dough and use to line a 23 cm/9 inch loose-bottomed flan tin/tart pan.

For the filling, mix together the melted butter, sugar, almonds and beaten eggs and add a few drops of almond extract. Spread the base of the pastry case/pie crust with the raspberry jam/jelly and spoon over the egg mixture. Bake in the preheated oven for about 30 minutes, or until the filling is firm and golden brown. Remove from the oven and allow to cool completely.

When the tart is cold, make the icing by mixing together the icing/confectioners' sugar and lemon juice, a little at a time,

until the icing is smooth and of a spreadable consistency. Spread the icing over the tart, leave to set for 2–3 minutes and sprinkle with the almonds. Chill in the refrigerator for about 10 minutes and then serve.

## Difficulty Rating: 3 points

# Strawberry Flan

## Serves 6

### Ingredients

**For the sweet pastry:**
175 g/6 oz/1⅓ cups plain/all-purpose flour
50 g/2 oz/½ stick butter
50 g/2 oz/¼ cup white vegetable fat/shortening
2 tsp caster/superfine sugar
1 medium/large egg yolk, beaten

**For the filling:**
1 medium/large egg, plus 1 extra egg yolk
50 g/2 oz/¼ cup caster/superfine sugar
25 g/1 oz/3 heaped tbsp plain/all-purpose flour
300 ml/½ pint/1¼ cups milk
few drops vanilla extract
450 g/1 lb/3 heaped cups strawberries, cleaned and hulled
mint leaves, to decorate

Preheat the oven to 200°C/400°F/Gas Mark 6, 15 minutes before baking. Place the flour, butter and vegetable fat in a food processor and blend until the mixture resembles fine breadcrumbs. Stir in the sugar, then, with the machine running, add the egg yolk and enough water to make a fairly stiff dough. Knead lightly, cover and chill in the refrigerator for 30 minutes. Roll out the pastry dough and use to line a 23 cm/9 inch loose-bottomed flan tin/tart pan. Place a piece of greaseproof/waxed paper in the pastry case/pie crust and cover with baking beans/pie weights or rice. Bake in the preheated oven for 15–20 minutes until just firm. Reserve until cool.

Make the filling by whisking the eggs and sugar together until thick and pale. Gradually stir in the flour and then the milk. Pour into a small saucepan and simmer for 3–4 minutes, stirring throughout. Add the vanilla extract to taste, then pour into a bowl and leave to cool. Cover with greaseproof paper to prevent a skin from forming.

When the filling is cold, whisk until smooth, then pour onto the cooked flan case. Slice the strawberries and arrange on the top of the filling. Allow to set. Decorate with the mint leaves and serve.

## Difficulty Rating: 3 points

# Rich Double-crust Plum Pie

## Serves 6

### Ingredients

**For the pastry:**
75 g/3 oz/²/₃ stick butter
75 g/3 oz/¹/₃ cup white vegetable fat/shortening
225 g/8 oz/2 cups plain/all-purpose flour
2 egg yolks

**For the filling:**
450 g/1 lb/3 cups fresh plums
50 g/2 oz/¹/₄ cup caster/superfine sugar
1 tbsp milk
a little extra caster/superfine sugar

Preheat the oven to 200°C/400°F/Gas Mark 6, 15 minutes before baking. Make the pastry dough by rubbing the butter and white vegetable fat/shortening into the flour until it resembles fine breadcrumbs or blend in a food processor. Add the egg yolks and enough water to make a soft dough. Knead lightly, then wrap and leave in the refrigerator for about 30 minutes.

Meanwhile, prepare the fruit. Rinse and dry the plums, then cut in half and remove the stones. Slice the plums into chunks and cook in a saucepan with 25 g/1 oz/2 tablespoons of the sugar and 2 tablespoons water for 5–7 minutes, or until slightly softened. Remove from the heat and add the remaining sugar to taste and allow to cool.

Roll out half the chilled pastry dough on a lightly floured surface and use to line the base and sides of a 1.2 litre/2 pint/1¹/₄ quart pie dish. Allow the dough to hang over the edge of the dish. Spoon in the prepared plums.

Roll out the remaining dough to use as the lid and brush the edge with a little water. Wrap the dough around the rolling pin and place over the plums. Press the edges together to seal and mark a decorative edge around the rim by pinching with the thumb and forefinger or using the back of a fork. Brush the lid with milk and make a few slits in the top. Use any trimmings to decorate the top of the pie with dough leaves. Place on a baking sheet and bake in the preheated oven for 30 minutes, or until golden brown. Sprinkle with a little caster/superfine sugar. Serve hot or cold.

## Difficulty Rating: 3 points

# Egg Custard Tart

## Serves 6

**Ingredients**

**For the sweet pastry:**
50 g/2 oz/½ stick butter
50 g/2 oz/¼ cup white vegetable fat/shortening
175 g/6 oz/1⅓ cups plain/all-purpose flour
1 egg yolk, beaten
2 tsp caster/superfine sugar

**For the filling:**
300 ml/½ pint/1¼ cups milk
2 eggs, plus 1 egg yolk
2 tbsp caster/superfine sugar
½ tsp freshly grated nutmeg

Preheat the oven to 200°C/400°F/Gas Mark 6, 15 minutes before baking. Oil a 20.5 cm/8 inch flan tin/tart pan. Make the pastry by cutting the butter and vegetable fat/shortening into small cubes. Add to the flour in a large bowl and rub in until the mixture resembles fine breadcrumbs. Add the egg yolk, sugar and enough water to form a soft and pliable dough. Turn onto a lightly floured surface and knead. Wrap and chill in the refrigerator for 30 minutes.

Roll the dough out onto a lightly floured surface and use to line the oiled flan tin. Place in the refrigerator to chill.

Warm the milk in a small saucepan. Briskly whisk together the eggs, egg yolk and sugar. Pour the milk into the egg mixture and whisk until blended. Strain through a sieve into the pastry case/pie crust. Place the flan tin on a baking sheet.

Sprinkle the top of the tart with nutmeg and bake in the preheated oven for about 15 minutes. Turn the oven down to 170°C/325°F/Gas Mark 3 and bake for a further 30 minutes, or until the custard has set. Serve hot or cold.

## Difficulty Rating: 3 points

# Lattice Treacle Tart

## Serves 6–8

**Ingredients**

**For the pastry:**
175 g/6 oz/1⅓ cups plain/all-purpose flour
40 g/1½ oz/⅓ stick butter
40 g/1½ oz/3 tbsp white vegetable fat/shortening
1 small egg, beaten, for brushing

**For the filling:**
225 g/8 oz/¾ cup golden/light corn syrup
finely grated zest and juice of 1 lemon
75 g/3 oz/1½ cups fresh white breadcrumbs

Preheat the oven to 190°C/375°F/Gas Mark 5, 15 minutes before baking. Make the pastry by placing the flour, butter and white vegetable fat/shortening in a food processor. Blend in short, sharp bursts until the mixture resembles fine breadcrumbs.

Remove from the processor and place on a pastry board or in a large bowl. Stir in enough cold water to make a dough and knead in a large bowl or on a floured surface until smooth and pliable.

Roll out the dough and use to line a 20.5 cm/8 inch loose-bottomed fluted flan dish or tin/tart pan. Reserve the dough trimmings for decoration. Chill for 30 minutes.

Meanwhile, to make the filling, place the golden/corn syrup in a saucepan and warm gently with the lemon zest and juice. Tip the breadcrumbs into the pastry case/pie crust and pour the syrup mixture over the top.

Roll the dough trimmings out on a lightly floured surface and cut into 6–8 thin strips. Lightly dampen the edge of the tart, then place the strips across the filling in a lattice pattern. Brush the ends of the strips with water and seal to the edge of the tart. Brush a little beaten egg over the pastry and bake in the preheated oven for 25 minutes, or until the filling is just set. Serve hot or cold.

## Difficulty Rating: 2 points

# Chocolate, Orange & Pine Nut Tart

## Cuts into 8–10 slices

### Ingredients

**For the sweet shortcrust pastry:**

150 g/5 oz/1 heaped cup plain/all-purpose flour

1/2 tsp salt

3–4 tbsp icing/confectioners' sugar

125 g/4 oz/1 stick plus 1 tbsp unsalted butter, diced

2 medium/large egg yolks, beaten

1/2 tsp vanilla extract

**For the filling:**

125 g/4 oz/5 squares dark/bittersweet chocolate, chopped

65 g/2 1/2 oz/scant 1/2 cup pine nuts, lightly toasted

2 large/extra-large eggs

grated zest of 1 orange

1 tbsp Cointreau

250 ml/8 fl oz/1 cup whipping cream

2 tbsp orange marmalade

Preheat the oven to 200°C/400°F/Gas Mark 6, 15 minutes before baking. Place the flour, salt and sugar in a food processor with the butter and blend briefly. Add the egg yolks, 2 tablespoons of iced water and the vanilla extract and blend until a soft dough is formed. Remove and knead until smooth, wrap in clingfilm/plastic wrap and chill in the refrigerator for 1 hour.

Lightly oil a 23 cm/9 inch loose-based flan tin/tart pan. Roll the dough out on a lightly floured surface to a 28 cm/11 inch round and use to line the tin. Press into the sides of the flan tin, crimp the edges, prick the base with a fork and chill in the refrigerator for 1 hour. Bake blind in the preheated oven for 10 minutes. Remove and place on a baking sheet. Reduce the oven temperature to 190°C/375°F/Gas Mark 5.

To make the filling, sprinkle the chocolate and the pine nuts evenly over the base of the pastry case/pie crust. Beat the eggs, orange zest, Cointreau and cream in a bowl until well blended, then pour over the chocolate and pine nuts. Bake in the oven for 30 minutes, or until the pastry is golden and the custard mixture is just set. Transfer to a wire rack to cool slightly. Heat the marmalade with 1 tablespoon water and brush over the tart. Serve warm or at room temperature.

## Difficulty Rating: 3 points

# Chocolate Pecan Pie

## Cuts into 8–10 slices

### Ingredients

225 g/8 oz prepared sweet shortcrust pastry dough
   (see page 22)
200 g/7 oz/2 cups pecan halves
125 g/4 oz/5 squares dark/bittersweet chocolate, chopped
25 g/1 oz/¼ stick butter, diced
3 eggs
125 g/4 oz/⅔ cup light brown sugar
175 ml/6 fl oz/scant ¾ cup golden/corn syrup
2 tsp vanilla extract
vanilla ice cream, to serve

Preheat the oven to 180°C/350°F/Gas Mark 4, 10 minutes before baking. Roll the prepared pastry dough out on a lightly floured surface and use to line a 25.5 cm/10 inch pie tin/plate. Roll the trimmings out and use to make a decorative edge around the pie, then chill in the refrigerator for 1 hour.

Reserve about 60 perfect pecan halves, or enough to cover the top of the pie, then coarsely chop the remainder and reserve. Melt the chocolate and butter in a small saucepan over a low heat or in the microwave and reserve.

Beat the eggs and brush the base and sides of the pastry with a little of the beaten egg. Beat the sugar, golden/corn syrup and vanilla extract into the beaten eggs. Add the pecans, then beat in the chocolate mixture.

Pour the filling into the pastry case/pie crust and arrange the reserved pecan halves in concentric circles over the top. Bake in the preheated oven for 45–55 minutes, or until the filling is well risen and just set. If the edge begins to brown too quickly, cover with strips of kitchen foil. Remove from the oven. Serve with ice cream.

## Difficulty Rating: 2 points

# Pear & Chocolate Custard Tart

## Cuts into 6–8 slices

**Ingredients**

**For the chocolate pastry:**
125 g/4 oz/1 stick plus 1 tbsp unsalted butter, softened
65 g/2½ oz/⅓ cup caster/superfine sugar
2 tsp vanilla extract
175 g/6 oz/1⅓ cups plain/all-purpose flour, sifted
40 g/1½ oz/½ cup cocoa powder (unsweetened)
whipped cream, to serve

**For the filling:**
125 g/4 oz/5 squares dark/bittersweet chocolate, chopped
250 ml/8 fl oz/1 cup whipping cream
50 g/2 oz/¼ cup caster/superfine sugar
1 large/extra-large egg; 1 large/extra-large egg yolk
1 tbsp crème de cacao (chocolate crème liqueur)
3 ripe pears

Preheat the oven to 190°C/375°F/Gas Mark 5, 10 minutes before baking. To make the pastry, put the butter, sugar and vanilla extract into a food processor and blend until creamy. Add the flour and cocoa powder and process until a soft dough forms. Remove the dough, wrap in clingfilm/plastic wrap and chill in the refrigerator for at least 1 hour. Roll out the dough between two sheets of clingfilm to a 28 cm/11 inch round. Peel off the top sheet of clingfilm and invert the pastry round into a lightly oiled 23 cm/9 inch loose-based flan tin/tart pan, easing the dough into the base and sides. Prick the base with a fork, then chill in the refrigerator for 1 hour. Place a sheet of nonstick baking parchment and baking beans/pie weights in the case and bake blind in the preheated oven for 10 minutes. Remove the parchment and beans and bake for a further 5 minutes. Remove and cool.

To make the filling, heat the chocolate, cream and half the sugar in a medium saucepan over a low heat, stirring until melted and smooth. Remove from the heat and cool slightly before beating in the egg, egg yolk and crème de cacao. Spread evenly over the pastry case/pie crust base.

Peel the pears, then cut each in half and remove the core. Cut into thin slices and arrange over the custard, gently fanning them towards the centre and pressing into the custard. Bake in the oven for 10 minutes. Reduce the temperature to 180°C/350°F/Gas Mark 4 and sprinkle the surface evenly with the remaining sugar. Bake for 20–25 minutes, or until the custard is set and the pears are tender and glazed. Remove from the oven and leave to cool slightly. Cut into slices, then serve with whipped cream.

## Difficulty Rating: 4 points

# Double Chocolate Truffle Slice

## Cuts into 12–14 slices

**Ingredients**

1 quantity chocolate pastry dough
(*see* page 185)
300 ml/¹/₂ pint/1¹/₄ cups double/heavy cream
300 g/11 oz/12 squares dark/bittersweet chocolate, chopped
25–40 g/1–1¹/₂ oz/¹/₄–¹/₃ stick unsalted butter, diced
50 ml/2 fl oz/¹/₄ cup brandy or liqueur
icing/confectioners' sugar or cocoa powder (unsweetened),
   for dusting

Preheat the oven to 200°C/400°F/Gas Mark 6, 15 minutes before baking. Prepare the chocolate pastry dough and chill in the refrigerator, according to instructions.

Roll the dough out to a rectangle about 38 x 15 cm/15 x 6 inches and use to line a rectangular loose-based flan tin/tart pan, trim, then chill in the refrigerator for 1 hour.

Place a sheet of nonstick baking parchment and baking beans/pie weights in the pastry case, then bake blind in the preheated oven for 20 minutes. Remove the baking parchment and beans and bake for 10 minutes more. Leave to cool completely.

Bring the cream to the boil. Remove from the heat and add the chocolate all at once, stirring until melted and smooth. Beat in the butter, then stir in the brandy or liqueur. Leave to cool slightly, then pour into the cooked pastry case/pie crust. Refrigerate until set.

Cut out 2.5 cm/1 inch strips of nonstick baking parchment. Place over the tart in a crisscross pattern and dust with icing/confectioners' sugar or cocoa powder. Arrange chocolate leaves, caraques or curls around the edges of the tart. Refrigerate until ready to serve. Leave to soften at room temperature for 15 minutes before serving.

## Difficulty Rating: 3 points

# Double Chocolate Banoffee Tart

## Cuts into 8 slices

### Ingredients

2 x 400 g/14 oz cans sweetened condensed milk

175 g/6 oz/7 squares dark/bittersweet chocolate, chopped

600 ml/1 pint/2$^1$/$_2$ cups whipping cream

1 tbsp golden/corn syrup

25 g/1 oz/$^1$/$_4$ stick butter, diced

150 g/5 oz/6 squares white chocolate,
    grated or finely chopped

1 tsp vanilla extract

2–3 ripe bananas

cocoa powder (unsweetened), for dusting

### For the ginger crumb crust:

24–26 gingernut biscuits/ginger snap cookies,
    roughly crushed

100 g/3$^1$/$_2$ oz/1 stick butter, melted

1–2 tbsp sugar, or to taste

$^1$/$_2$ tsp ground ginger

Preheat the oven to 190°C/375°F/Gas Mark 5, 10 minutes before baking. Place the condensed milk in a heavy-based saucepan and place over a gentle heat. Bring to the boil, stirring constantly. Boil gently for about 3–5 minutes until golden. Remove from the heat and leave to cool.

To make the crust, place the biscuits/cookies with the melted butter, sugar and ground ginger in a food processor and blend together. Press into the sides and base of a 23 cm/9 inch loose-based flan tin/tart pan with the back of a spoon. Chill in the refrigerator for 15–20 minutes, then bake in the preheated oven for 5–6 minutes. Remove from the oven and leave to cool.

Melt the dark chocolate in a medium-sized saucepan with 150 ml/$^1$/$_4$ pint/$^2$/$_3$ cup of the whipping cream, the golden/corn syrup and the butter over a low heat. Stir until smooth. Carefully pour into the crumb crust, tilting the tin to distribute the chocolate layer evenly. Chill in the refrigerator for at least 1 hour, or until set.

Heat 150 ml/$^1$/$_4$ pint/$^2$/$_3$ cup of the remaining cream until hot, then add all the white chocolate and stir until melted and smooth. Stir in the vanilla extract and strain into a bowl. Leave to cool to room temperature.

Scrape the cooked condensed milk into a bowl and whisk until smooth, adding a little of the remaining cream if too thick. Spread over the chocolate layer, then slice the bananas and arrange evenly over the top.

Whisk the remaining cream until soft peaks form. Stir a spoonful of the cream into the white chocolate mixture, then fold in the remaining cream. Spread over the bananas, swirling to the edge. Dust with cocoa powder and chill in the refrigerator until ready to serve.

## Difficulty Rating: 3 points

# Chocolate Apricot Linzer Torte

## Cuts into 10–12 slices

### Ingredients

**For the chocolate almond pastry:**

75 g/3 oz/½ cup whole blanched almonds

125 g/4 oz/⅔ cup caster/superfine sugar

215 g/7½ oz/1⅔ cups plain/all-purpose flour

2 tbsp cocoa powder (unsweetened)

1 tsp ground cinnamon

½ tsp salt

grated zest of 1 orange

225 g/8 oz/2 sticks unsalted butter, diced

2–3 tbsp iced water

**For the filling:**

350 g/12 oz apricot jam/jelly

75 g/3 oz/3 squares milk/semisweet chocolate, chopped

icing/confectioners' sugar, for dusting

Preheat the oven to 190°C/375°F/Gas Mark 5, 10 minutes before baking. Lightly oil a 28 cm/11 inch flan tin/tart pan. Place the almonds and half the sugar into a food processor and blend until finely ground. Add the remaining sugar, flour, cocoa powder, cinnamon, salt and orange zest and blend again. Add the diced butter and blend in short bursts to form coarse crumbs. Add the water one tablespoon at a time until the mixture starts to come together.

Turn onto a lightly floured surface and knead lightly, roll out, then, using your fingertips, press half the dough into the base and sides of the tin. Prick the base with a fork and chill in the refrigerator. Roll out the remaining dough between two pieces of clingfilm/plastic wrap to a 28–30.5 cm/11–12 inch round. Slide the round onto a baking sheet and chill in the refrigerator for 30 minutes.

For the filling, spread the apricot jam/jelly evenly over the chilled pastry base and sprinkle with the chopped chocolate.

Slide the dough round onto a lightly floured surface and peel off the top layer of clingfilm. Using a straight edge, cut the

round into 1 cm/½ inch strips; allow to soften until slightly flexible. Place the strips across the torte, about 1 cm/½ inch apart, to create a lattice pattern. Press down on each side of each crossing to accentuate the effect. Press the ends of the strips to the edge, cutting off any excess. Bake in the preheated oven for 35 minutes, or until cooked. Leave to cool before dusting with icing/confectioners' sugar and serve cut into slices.

## Difficulty Rating: 2 points

# Mini Pistachio & Chocolate Strudels

## Makes 24

### Ingredients

5 large sheets ready-made filo/phyllo pastry

50 g/2 oz/½ stick butter, melted

1–2 tbsp caster/superfine sugar, for sprinkling

50 g/2 oz/2 squares white chocolate, melted, to decorate

### For the filling:

125 g/4 oz/1 cup unsalted pistachios, finely chopped

3 tbsp caster/superfine sugar

50 g/2 oz/2 squares dark/bittersweet chocolate, finely chopped

1–2 tsp rosewater

1 tbsp icing/confectioners' sugar, for dusting

Preheat the oven to 170°C/325°F/Gas Mark 3, 10 minutes before baking. Lightly oil two large baking sheets. For the filling, mix the finely chopped pistachio nuts, the sugar and dark/bittersweet chocolate in a bowl. Sprinkle with the rosewater and stir lightly together and reserve.

Cut each filo/phyllo pastry sheet into four to make 23 x 18 cm/9 x 7 inch rectangles. Place one rectangle on the work surface and brush with a little melted butter. Place another rectangle on top and brush with a little more butter. Sprinkle with a little caster/superfine sugar and spread about 1 dessertspoon of the filling along one short end. Fold the short end over the filling, then fold in the long edges and roll up. Place on the baking sheet seam-side down. Continue with the remaining pastry sheets and filling until both are used.

Brush each strudel with the remaining melted butter and sprinkle with a little caster sugar. Bake in the preheated oven for 20 minutes, or until golden brown and the pastry is crisp. Remove from the oven and leave on the baking sheet for 2 minutes, then transfer to a wire rack. Dust with icing/confectioners' sugar. Place the melted white chocolate in a small piping/decorating bag fitted with a plain writing nozzle/tip and pipe squiggles over the strudels. Leave to set before serving.

## Difficulty Rating: 1 point

# 'Mars' Bar Mousse in Filo Cups

## Serves 6

### Ingredients

6 large sheets ready-made filo/phyllo pastry,
   thawed if frozen
40 g/1½ oz/⅓ stick unsalted butter, melted
1 tbsp caster/superfine sugar
3 x 58 g/2 oz 'Mars' bars/caramel nougat chocolate bars, coarsely
   chopped
1½ tbsp milk
300 ml/½ pint/1¼ cups double/heavy cream
1 large/extra-large egg white
1 tsp cocoa powder (unsweetened)
1 tbsp dark/bittersweet chocolate, grated
chocolate sauce (see page 220), to serve (optional)

### For the topping:
300 ml/½ pint/1¼ cups whipping cream
125 g/4 oz/5 squares white chocolate, grated
1 tsp vanilla extract

Preheat the oven to 180°C/350°F/Gas Mark 4, 10 minutes before baking. Lightly oil six 150 ml/¼ pint ramekins. Cut the filo/phyllo pastry into 15 cm/6 inch squares, place one square on the work surface, then brush with a little of the melted butter; sprinkle with a little caster/superfine sugar. Butter a second square and lay it over the first at an angle, sprinkle with a little more caster sugar and repeat with two more pastry squares.

Press the assembled filo pastry into the oiled ramekin, pressing into the base to make a flat bottom and keeping the edges pointing up. Continue making the cups in this way, then place on a baking sheet and bake in the preheated oven for 10–15 minutes until crisp and golden. Remove and leave to cool before removing the filo cups from the ramekins. Leave until cold.

Melt the 'Mars' bars/caramel nougat chocolate bars and milk in a small saucepan, stirring constantly, until melted and smooth. Leave to cool for 10 minutes, stirring occasionally.

Whisk the cream until thick and stir a spoonful into the melted 'Mars' bar mixture, then fold in the remaining cream. Whisk the egg white until stiff and fold into the 'Mars' bar mixture together with the cocoa powder. Chill the mousse in the refrigerator for 2–3 hours.

For the topping, boil 125 ml/4 fl oz/½ cup of the whipping cream, add the grated white chocolate and vanilla extract and stir until smooth, then strain into a bowl and leave to cool. Whisk the remaining cream until thick, then fold into the white chocolate cream mixture.

Spoon the mousse into the filo cups, cover with the cream mixture and sprinkle with grated chocolate. Chill in the refrigerator before serving with chocolate sauce, if liked.

## Difficulty Rating: 3 points

# Raspberry Chocolate Ganache & Berry Tartlets

## Serves 8

### Ingredients

1 quantity chocolate pastry dough (*see* page 185)

600 ml/1 pint/2¹/₂ cups whipping cream

275 g/10 oz/1 cup seedless raspberry jam/jelly

225 g/8 oz/9 squares dark/bittersweet chocolate, chopped

700 g/1¹/₂ lb/5³/₄ cups raspberries or other summer berries

50 ml/2 fl oz/¹/₄ cup framboise liqueur

1 tbsp caster/superfine sugar

crème fraîche/sour cream, to serve

Preheat the oven to 200°C/400°F/Gas Mark 6, 15 minutes before baking. Make the chocolate pastry dough and use to line eight 7.5 cm/3 inch tartlet tins/pans. Bake blind in the preheated oven for 12 minutes.

Place 400 ml/14 fl oz/1²/₃ cups of the whipping cream and half of the raspberry jam/jelly in a saucepan and bring to the boil, whisking constantly to dissolve the jam. Remove from the heat and add the chocolate all at once, stirring until the chocolate has melted. Pour into the pastry-lined tartlet tins, shaking gently to distribute the ganache evenly. Chill in the refrigerator for 1 hour, or until set.

Place the berries in a large shallow bowl. Heat the remaining raspberry jam with half the framboise liqueur over a medium heat until melted and bubbling. Drizzle over the berries and toss gently to coat. Divide the berries among the tartlets, piling them up if necessary. Chill in the refrigerator until ready to serve.

Remove the tartlets from the refrigerator at least 30 minutes before serving. Using an electric whisk, whisk the remaining cream with the caster/superfine sugar and the remaining framboise liqueur until it is thick and softly peaking. Serve with the tartlets and crème fraîche.

## Difficulty Rating: 4 points

# White Chocolate & Macadamia Tartlets

Makes 10 (Pictured page 172)

**Ingredients**

1 quantity sweet shortcrust pastry (*see page 22*)
2 medium/large eggs
50 g/2 oz/$\frac{1}{4}$ cup caster/superfine sugar
250 ml/8 fl oz/1 cup golden/corn syrup
40 g/1$\frac{1}{2}$ oz/$\frac{1}{3}$ stick butter, melted
50 ml/2 fl oz/$\frac{1}{4}$ cup whipping cream
1 tsp vanilla or almond extract
225 g/8 oz/1$\frac{2}{3}$ cups unsalted macadamia nuts, coarsely chopped
150 g/5 oz/6 squares white chocolate, coarsely chopped

Preheat the oven to 200°C/400°F/Gas Mark 6, 15 minutes before baking. Roll the pastry out on a lightly floured surface and use to line ten 7.5–9 cm/3–3$\frac{1}{2}$ inch tartlet tins/pans. Line each tin with a small piece of kitchen foil and fill with baking beans/pie weights. Arrange on a baking sheet and bake blind in the preheated oven for 10 minutes. Remove the foil and baking beans and leave to cool.

Beat the eggs with the sugar until light and creamy, then beat in the golden syrup, the butter, cream and vanilla or almond extract. Stir in the macadamia nuts. Sprinkle 100 g/3$\frac{1}{2}$ oz/$\frac{3}{4}$ cup of the chopped white chocolate equally over the bases of the tartlet cases and divide the mixture evenly among them.

Reduce the oven temperature to 180°C/350°F/Gas Mark 4 and bake the tartlets for 20 minutes, or until the tops are puffy and golden and the filling is set. Remove from the oven and leave to cool on a wire rack.

Carefully remove the tartlets from their tins and arrange close together on a wire rack. Melt the remaining white chocolate and, using a teaspoon or a small paper piping/decorating bag, drizzle the melted chocolate over the surface of the tartlets in a zigzag pattern. Serve slightly warm or at room temperature.

**Difficulty Rating: 3 points**

# Caramelized Chocolate Tartlets

Serves 6

**Ingredients**

350 g/12 oz/1$\frac{1}{2}$ cups ready-made shortcrust pastry dough, thawed if frozen
150 ml/$\frac{1}{4}$ pint/$\frac{2}{3}$ cup coconut milk
3 tbsp demerara/turbinado sugar
50 g/2 oz/2 squares dark/bittersweet chocolate, melted
1 egg, beaten
few drops vanilla extract
1 small mango, peeled, stoned and sliced
1 small papaya, peeled, deseeded and chopped
1 star fruit, sliced
1 kiwi, peeled and sliced, or use fruits of your choice

Preheat the oven to 200°C/400°F/Gas Mark 6, 15 minutes before baking. Lightly oil six individual tartlet tins/pans. Roll out the ready-made pastry dough on a lightly floured surface and use to line the oiled tins. Prick the bases and sides with a fork and line with nonstick baking parchment and baking beans/pie weights. Bake blind for 10 minutes in the preheated oven, then remove from the oven and discard the baking beans and the baking parchment.

Reduce the oven temperature to 180°C/350°F/Gas Mark 4. Heat the coconut milk and a heaped tablespoon of the sugar in a heavy-based saucepan, stirring constantly, until the sugar has dissolved. Remove the saucepan from the heat and leave to cool. Stir the melted chocolate, the beaten egg and the vanilla extract into the cooled coconut milk. Stir until well mixed, then strain into the cooked pastry cases/pie crusts. Place on a baking sheet and bake in the oven for 25 minutes, or until set. Remove and leave to cool, then chill in the refrigerator.

Preheat the grill/broiler, then arrange the fruits decoratively on the top of each tartlet. Sprinkle with the remaining sugar and grill the tartlets for 2 minutes, or until the sugar bubbles and browns. Turn the tartlets if necessary and take care not to burn the sugar. Remove from the grill and leave to cool before serving.

**Difficulty Rating: 2 points**

# Chocolate Raspberry Mille Feuille

## Serves 6

**Ingredients**

450 g/1 lb puff pastry dough, thawed if frozen
1 quantity chocolate raspberry ganache (*see* page 191), chilled
700 g/11/2 lbs/53/4 cups fresh raspberries, plus extra for decorating
icing/confectioners' sugar, for dusting

**For the raspberry sauce:**
225 g/8 oz/2 scant cups fresh raspberries
2 tbsp seedless raspberry jam/jelly
1–2 tbsp caster/superfine sugar, or to taste
2 tbsp lemon juice or framboise liqueur

Preheat the oven to 200°C/400°F/Gas Mark 6, 15 minutes before baking. Lightly oil a large baking sheet and sprinkle with a little water. Roll out the pastry dough on a lightly floured surface to a rectangle about 43 x 28 cm/17 x 11 inches. Cut into three long strips. Mark each strip crossways at 6.5 cm/2½ inch intervals using a sharp knife; this will make cutting the baked pastry easier and neater. Carefully transfer to the baking sheet, keeping the edges as straight as possible. Bake in the preheated oven for 20 minutes, or until well risen and golden brown. Place on a wire rack and leave to cool. Carefully transfer each rectangle to a work surface and, using a sharp knife, trim the long edges straight. Cut along the knife marks to make 18 rectangles.

Place all the ingredients for the raspberry sauce in a food processor and blend until smooth. If the purée is too thick, add a little water. Taste and adjust the sweetness if necessary. Strain into a bowl, cover and chill in the refrigerator.

Place one pastry rectangle on the work surface flat–side down, spread with a little chocolate ganache and sprinkle with a few fresh raspberries. Spread a second rectangle with a little ganache, place over the first, pressing gently, then sprinkle with a few raspberries. Place a third rectangle on top, flat–side up, and spread with a little chocolate ganache. Arrange some raspberries

on top and dust lightly with a little icing/confectioners' sugar. Repeat with the remaining pastry rectangles, chocolate ganache and fresh raspberries. Chill in the refrigerator until required and serve with the raspberry sauce and any remaining fresh raspberries.

## Difficulty Rating: 4 points

# Rice Pudding & Chocolate Tart

## Serves 8

### Ingredients

1 quantity chocolate pastry dough (*see* page 185)
1 tsp cocoa powder (unsweetened), for dusting

**For the chocolate ganache:**
200 ml/7 fl oz/³⁄₄ cup double/heavy cream
1 tbsp golden/corn syrup
175 g/6 oz/7 squares dark/bittersweet chocolate, chopped
1 tbsp butter; 1 tsp vanilla extract

**For the rice pudding:**
1 litre/1³⁄₄ pints/1 quart milk
¹⁄₂ tsp salt; 1 vanilla pod
100 g/3¹⁄₂ oz/¹⁄₂ cup long-grain white rice
1 tbsp cornflour/cornstarch; 2 tbsp sugar

**To decorate:**
**few fresh blueberries**
**fresh mint sprigs**

Preheat the oven to 200˚C/400˚F/Gas Mark 6, 15 minutes before baking. Roll the chocolate pastry dough out and use to line a 23 cm/9 inch flan tin/tart pan. Place a sheet of nonstick baking parchment and baking beans/pie weights in the tin and bake blind in the preheated oven for 15 minutes.

For the ganache, place the cream and golden/corn syrup in a heavy-based saucepan and bring to the boil. Remove from the heat and add the chocolate all at once, stirring until smooth. Beat in the butter and vanilla extract, pour into the baked pastry case/pie crust and reserve.

For the rice pudding, bring the milk and salt to the boil in a medium-sized saucepan. Split the vanilla pod and scrape the seeds into the milk and add the vanilla pod. Sprinkle in the rice, then bring to the boil. Reduce the heat and simmer until the rice is tender and the milk is creamy. Remove from the heat. Blend the cornflour/cornstarch and sugar together, then stir in

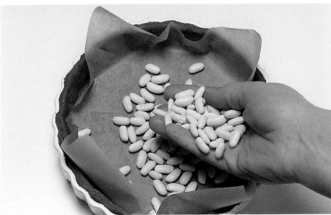

2 tablespoons water to make a paste. Stir a little of the hot rice mixture into the cornflour mixture, then stir the cornflour mixture into the rice. Bring to the boil and cook, stirring constantly, until thickened. Set the base of the saucepan into a bowl of iced water and stir until cooled and thickened. Spoon the rice pudding into the tart, smoothing the surface. Leave to set. Dust with cocoa powder and decorate with a few blueberries and fresh mint to serve.

## Difficulty Rating: 4 points

# Chocolate Fruit Pizza

## Serves 8

**Ingredients**

1 quantity sweet shortcrust pastry dough (*see page 22*)

2 tbsp chocolate spread

1 small peach, very thinly sliced

1 small nectarine, very thinly sliced

150 g/5 oz/1 cup strawberries, halved or quartered

75 g/3 oz/²/₃ cup raspberries

75 g/3 oz blueberries

75 g/3 oz/3 squares dark/bittersweet chocolate,
   coarsely chopped

1 tbsp butter, melted

2 tbsp sugar

75 g/3 oz/3 squares white chocolate, chopped

1 tbsp hazelnuts, toasted and chopped

fresh mint sprigs, to decorate

Preheat the oven to 200°C/400°F/Gas Mark 6, 15 minutes before baking. Lightly oil a large baking sheet. Roll the prepared pastry out to a 23 cm/9 inch round, place the pastry round onto the baking sheet and crimp the edges. Using a fork, prick the base all over and chill in the refrigerator for 30 minutes.

Line the pastry with kitchen foil and weigh down with an ovenproof flat dinner plate or base of a large flan tin/tart pan and bake blind in the preheated oven until the edges begin to colour. Remove from the oven and discard the weight and foil.

Carefully spread the chocolate spread over the pizza base and arrange the peach and nectarine slices around the outside edge in overlapping circles. Toss the berries with the dark/bittersweet chocolate and arrange in the centre. Drizzle with the melted butter and sprinkle with the sugar. Bake in the preheated oven for 10–12 minutes, or until the fruit begins to soften. Transfer the pizza to a wire rack. Sprinkle the white chocolate and hazelnuts over the surface and return to the oven for 1 minute, or until the chocolate begins to soften. If the pastry starts to darken too much, cover the edge with strips of foil. Remove to a wire rack and leave to cool. Decorate with sprigs of fresh mint and serve warm.

## Difficulty Rating: 2 points

# Chocolate Lemon Tartlets

## Makes 10

### Ingredients

1 quantity sweet shortcrust pastry dough (*see* page 22)

175 ml/6 fl oz/scant ³/₄ cup double/heavy cream

175 g/6 oz/7 squares dark/bittersweet chocolate, chopped

25 g/1 oz/¹/₄ stick butter, diced

1 tsp vanilla extract

350 g/12 oz/1 cup lemon curd

250 ml/8 fl oz/1 cup prepared custard

250 ml/8 fl oz/1 cup single/light cream

¹/₂–1 tsp almond extract

### To decorate:

grated chocolate

toasted flaked/slivered almonds

Preheat the oven to 200°C/400°F/Gas Mark 6, 15 minutes before baking. Roll the prepared pastry dough out on a lightly floured surface and use to line ten 7.5 cm/3 inch tartlet tins/pans. Place a small piece of crumpled kitchen foil in each and bake blind in the preheated oven for 12 minutes. Remove from the oven and leave to cool.

Bring the cream to the boil, then remove from the heat and add the chocolate. Stir until smooth and melted. Beat in the butter and vanilla extract, pour into the tartlets and leave to cool.

Beat the lemon curd until soft and spoon a thick layer over the chocolate in each tartlet, spreading gently to the edges. Do not chill in the refrigerator or the chocolate will be too firm.

Place the prepared custard into a large bowl and gradually whisk in the cream and almond extract until smooth and runny. To serve, spoon a little custard sauce onto a plate and place a tartlet in the centre. Sprinkle with grated chocolate and almonds, then serve.

## Difficulty Rating: 2 points

# Fudgy Mocha Pie with Espresso Custard Sauce

## Cuts into 10 slices

### Ingredients

125 g/4 oz/5 squares dark/bittersweet chocolate, chopped

125 g/4 oz/1 stick plus 1 tbsp butter, diced

1 tbsp instant espresso powder

4 large/extra-large eggs

1 tbsp golden/corn syrup

125 g/4 oz/²/₃ cup sugar

1 tsp ground cinnamon

3 tbsp milk

icing/confectioners' sugar, for dusting

few fresh strawberries, to serve

For the espresso custard sauce:

2–3 tbsp instant espresso powder, or to taste

250 ml/8 fl oz/1 cup prepared custard

250 ml/8 fl oz/1 cup single/light cream

2 tbsp coffee-flavoured liqueur (optional)

Preheat the oven to 180˚C/350˚F/Gas Mark 4, 10 minutes before serving. Line with kitchen foil or lightly oil a deep 23 cm/9 inch pie plate. Melt the chocolate and butter in a small saucepan over a low heat and stir until smooth, then reserve. Dissolve the instant espresso powder in 1–2 tablespoons of hot water and reserve.

Beat the eggs with the golden/corn syrup, the sugar, the dissolved espresso powder, the cinnamon and milk until blended. Add the melted chocolate mixture and whisk until blended. Pour into the pie plate. Bake in the preheated oven for about 20–25 minutes, or until the edge has set but the centre is still very soft. Leave to cool, remove from the plate, then dust lightly with icing/confectioners' sugar.

To make the custard sauce, dissolve the instant espresso powder with 2–3 tablespoons of hot water, then whisk into the prepared custard. Slowly add the single/light cream, whisking constantly, then stir in the coffee-flavoured liqueur, if using. Serve slices of the pie in a pool of espresso custard with strawberries.

## Difficulty Rating: 1 point

# Chocolate Pecan Angel Pie

## Cuts into 8–10 slices

### Ingredients

4 large/extra-large egg whites

$^1/_4$ tsp cream of tartar

225 g/8 oz/1 heaped cup caster/superfine sugar

3 tsp vanilla extract

100 g/3$^1/_2$ oz/1 cup pecans, lightly toasted and chopped

75 g/3 oz/$^1/_2$ cup dark/bittersweet chocolate chips

150 ml/$^1/_4$ pint/$^2/_3$ cup double/heavy cream

150 g/5 oz/6 squares white chocolate, grated

### To decorate:

fresh raspberries

dark chocolate curls

few fresh mint sprigs

Preheat the oven to 110 C/225 F/Gas Mark $^1/_4$, 5 minutes before baking. Lightly oil a 23 cm/9 inch pie plate.

Using an electric mixer, whisk the egg whites and cream of tartar on a low speed until foamy, then increase the speed and beat until soft peaks form. Gradually beat in the sugar, one tablespoon at a time, beating well after each addition, until stiff glossy peaks form and the sugar is completely dissolved. (Test by rubbing a bit of meringue between your fingers – if gritty, continue beating.) This will take about 15 minutes. Beat in 2 teaspoons of the vanilla extract, then fold in the nuts and the chocolate chips.

Spread the meringue evenly in the pie plate, making a shallow well in the centre and slightly building up the sides. Bake in the preheated oven for 1–1$^1/_4$ hours until a golden creamy colour. Lower the oven temperature if the meringue colours too quickly. Turn the oven off, but do not remove the meringue. Leave the oven door ajar (about 5 cm/2 inches) for about 1 hour. Transfer to a wire rack until cold.

Pour the double/heavy cream into a small saucepan and bring to the boil. Remove from the heat, add the grated white

chocolate and stir until melted. Add the remaining vanilla extract and leave to cool, then whip until thick. Spoon the white chocolate whipped cream into the meringue shell, piling it high and swirling decoratively. Decorate with fresh raspberries and chocolate curls. Chill in the refrigerator for 2 hours before serving. When ready to serve, add sprigs of mint on the top and cut into slices.

## Difficulty Rating: 2 points

# White Chocolate Mousse & Strawberry Tart

## Cuts into 10 slices

### Ingredients

1 quantity sweet shortcrust pastry dough (*see page 22*)

65 g/2½ oz/¼ cup strawberry jam/jelly

1–2 tbsp kirsch or framboise liqueur

450–700 g/1–1½ lb/4–6 cups ripe strawberries, sliced lengthways

**For the white chocolate mousse:**

250 g/9 oz/10 squares white chocolate, chopped

350 ml/12 fl oz/1½ cups double/heavy cream

1–2 large/extra-large egg whites (optional)

3 tbsp kirsch or framboise liqueur

Preheat the oven to 200°C/400°F/Gas Mark 6, 15 minutes before baking. Roll the prepared pastry dough out on a lightly floured surface and use to line a 25 cm/10 inch flan tin/tart pan. Line with either kitchen foil or nonstick baking parchment and baking beans/pie weights, then bake blind in the preheated oven for 15–20 minutes. Remove the kitchen foil or baking parchment and beans and return to the oven for a further 5 minutes.

To make the mousse, place the white chocolate with 2 tablespoons water and 125 ml/4 fl oz/½ cup of the cream in a saucepan and heat gently, stirring, until the chocolate has melted and is smooth. Remove from the heat, stir in the kirsch or framboise liqueur and cool.

Whip the remaining cream until soft peaks form. Fold a spoonful of the cream into the cooled white chocolate mixture, then fold in the remaining cream. If using, whisk the egg whites until stiff and gently fold into the white chocolate cream mixture to make a softer, lighter mousse. Chill in the refrigerator for 15–20 minutes.

Heat the strawberry jam/jelly with the kirsch or framboise liqueur and brush or spread half the mixture onto the pastry base. Leave to cool. Spread the chilled chocolate mousse over the jam and arrange the sliced strawberries in concentric circles

over the mousse. Reheat the remaining jam, if necessary, and glaze the strawberries lightly. Chill the tart in the refrigerator for about 3–4 hours, or until the chocolate mousse has set. Cut into slices and serve.

## Difficulty Rating: 3 points

# White Chocolate Cheesecake

## Cuts into 16 slices

### Ingredients

**For the base:**
150 g/5 oz/1²/₃ cups digestive biscuits/Graham crackers
50 g/2 oz/¹/₂ cup whole almonds, lightly toasted
50 g/2 oz/¹/₂ stick butter, melted
¹/₂ tsp almond extract

**For the filling:**
350 g/12 oz/14 squares good-quality white chocolate, chopped
125 ml/4 fl oz/¹/₂ cup double/heavy cream
700 g/1¹/₂ lb/3 cups cream cheese, softened
50 g/2 oz/¹/₄ cup caster/superfine sugar
4 large/extra-large eggs
2 tbsp amaretto or almond-flavoured liqueur

**For the topping:**
450 ml/³/₄ pint/2 cups sour cream
50 g/2 oz/¹/₄ cup caster/superfine sugar
¹/₂ tsp almond or vanilla extract
white chocolate curls

Preheat the oven to 180°C/350°F/Gas Mark 4, 10 minutes before baking. Lightly oil a 23 x 7.5 cm/9 x 3 inch springform tin/pan. Crush the biscuits/crackers and almonds in a food processor to form fine crumbs. Pour in the butter and almond extract and blend. Pour the crumbs into the tin. Using the back of a spoon, press onto the bottom and up the sides to within 1 cm/¹/₂ inch of the top of the tin edge. Bake in the preheated oven for 5 minutes to set. Remove and transfer to a wire rack. Reduce the oven temperature to 150°C/300°F/Gas Mark 2.

Heat the white chocolate and cream in a saucepan over a low heat, stirring constantly, until melted. Remove and cool.

Beat the cream cheese and sugar until smooth. Add the eggs, one at a time, beating well after each addition. Slowly beat in the cooled white chocolate cream and the amaretto. Pour into the baked crust. Place on a baking sheet and bake for 45–55 minutes until the edge of the cake is firm but the centre slightly soft. Reduce the temperature of the oven if the top begins to brown. Remove to a wire rack and increase the temperature to 200°C/400°F/Gas Mark 6.

To make the topping, beat the sour cream, sugar and almond or vanilla extract until smooth. Pour gently over the cheesecake, tilting the pan to distribute the topping evenly. Alternatively, spread with a metal palette knife. Bake for another 5 minutes to set. Turn off the oven and leave the door halfway open for about 1 hour. Transfer to a wire rack and run a sharp knife around the edge of the crust to separate from the tin. Cool and refrigerate until chilled. Remove from the tin, decorate with white chocolate curls and serve.

## Difficulty Rating: 3 points

# Triple Chocolate Cheesecake

Serves 6

**Ingredients**

**For the base:**
150 g/5 oz/2 cups digestive biscuits/Graham crackers, crushed
50 g/2 oz/½ stick butter, melted

**For the cheesecake:**
75 g/3 oz/3 squares white chocolate, roughly chopped
300 ml/½ pint/1¼ cups double/heavy cream
50 g/2 oz/¼ cup caster/superfine sugar
3 eggs, beaten
400 g/14 oz/1¾ cups full-fat soft cream cheese
2 tbsp cornflour/cornstarch
75 g/3 oz/3 squares each dark/bittersweet chocolate
    and milk/semisweet chocolate, roughly chopped
fromage frais/sour cream, to serve

Preheat the oven to 180°C/350°F/Gas Mark 4, 10 minutes before baking. Lightly oil a 23 x 7.5 cm/9 x 3 inch springform tin/pan. To make the base, mix together the crushed biscuits/crackers and the melted butter. Press into the base of the tin and leave to set. Chill in the refrigerator. Place the white chocolate and cream in a small, heavy-based saucepan and heat gently until the chocolate has melted. Stir until smooth and reserve.

Beat the sugar and eggs together until light and creamy in colour, add the cream cheese and beat until the mixture is smooth and free from lumps. Stir the reserved white chocolate cream together with the cornflour/cornstarch into the cream cheese mixture. Add the dark/bittersweet chocolate and milk/semisweet chocolate to the cream cheese mixture. Mix lightly together until blended. Spoon over the chilled base. Place on a baking sheet and bake in the preheated oven for 1 hour. Switch off the heat, open the oven door and leave the cheesecake to cool in the oven. Chill in the refrigerator for at least 6 hours before removing from the tin. Cut into slices, transfer to serving plates and serve with fromage frais/sour cream.

**Difficulty Rating: 1 point**

# Ricotta Cheesecake with Strawberry Coulis

## Serves 6–8

**Ingredients**

8 digestive biscuits/Graham crackers

100 g/3¹/₂ oz/²/₃ cup mixed/candied peel, chopped

65 g/2¹/₂ oz/¹/₂ stick butter, melted

150 ml/¹/₄ pint/²/₃ cup crème fraîche/sour cream

575 g/1¹/₄ lb/2¹/₃ cups ricotta cheese

100 g/3¹/₂ oz/¹/₂ cup caster/superfine sugar

1 vanilla pod, seeds only

2 large/extra-large eggs

225 g/8 oz/1¹/₂ cups strawberries, hulled

2–4 tbsp caster/superfine sugar, to taste

zest and juice of 1 orange

Preheat the oven to 170°C/325°F/Gas Mark 3. Line a 20.5 cm/8 inch springform tin/pan with baking parchment. Put the biscuits/crackers in a food processor together with the peel. Blend until the biscuits are crushed and the peel is chopped. Add 50 g/2 oz/¹/₂ cup of the melted butter and process until mixed. Tip into the tin and spread firmly and evenly over the bottom.

Blend together the crème fraîche/sour cream, ricotta cheese, sugar, vanilla seeds and eggs in a food processor. With the motor running, add the remaining melted butter and blend for a few seconds. Pour the mixture onto the base. Transfer to the preheated oven and cook for about 1 hour, or until set and risen round the edges, but slightly wobbly in the centre. Switch off the oven and allow to cool there. Chill in the refrigerator for at least 8 hours, or preferably overnight.

Wash and drain the strawberries. Put into the food processor along with 2 tablespoons of the sugar, the orange zest and juice. Blend until smooth. Add any remaining sugar, to taste. Pass through a sieve to remove seeds and chill in the refrigerator until needed. Cut the cheesecake into wedges, spoon over some of the strawberry coulis and serve.

## Difficulty Rating: 1 point

# Baked Lemon & Sultana Cheesecake

Cuts into 10 slices

**Ingredients**

275 g/9½ oz/1⅓ cups caster/superfine sugar

50 g/2 oz/½ stick butter

50 g/2 oz/½ cup self-raising flour

½ level tsp baking powder

5 large/extra-large eggs

450 g/1 lb/2 cups cream cheese

40 g/1½ oz/⅓ cup plain/all-purpose flour

grated zest of 1 lemon

3 tbsp fresh lemon juice

150 ml/¼ pint/½ cup crème fraîche/sour cream

75 g/3 oz/½ cup sultanas/golden raisins

**To decorate:**

1 tbsp icing/confectioners' sugar

fresh blackcurrants or blueberries

mint leaves

Preheat the oven to 170°C/325°F/Gas Mark 3. Oil a 20.5 cm/8 inch loose-bottomed round cake tin/pan with nonstick baking parchment.

Beat 50 g/2 oz/¼ cup of the sugar and the butter together until light and creamy, then stir in the self-raising flour, baking powder and 1 egg. Mix together lightly until well blended. Spoon into the prepared tin and spread the mixture over the base. Separate the 4 remaining eggs and reserve.

Blend the cheese in a food processor until soft. Gradually add the egg yolks and sugar and blend until smooth. Turn into a bowl and stir in the plain/all-purpose flour, lemon zest and juice. Mix lightly before adding the crème fraîche/sour cream and sultanas/golden raisins, stirring well.

Whisk the egg whites until stiff, fold into the cheese mixture and pour into the tin. Tap lightly on the work surface to remove any air bubbles. Bake in the preheated oven for about 1 hour, or until golden and firm. Cover lightly if browning too much. Switch the

oven off and leave in the oven to cool for 2–3 hours. Remove the cheesecake from the oven. When completely cold, remove from the tin. Sprinkle with icing/confectioners' sugar, decorate with the blackcurrants or blueberries and mint and serve.

**Difficulty Rating: 2 points**

# Chocolate & Saffron Cheesecake

## Serves 6

### Ingredients

¹/₄ tsp saffron threads

175 g/6 oz/1¹/₃ cups plain/all-purpose flour

pinch salt

75 g/3 oz/²/₃ stick butter

1 tbsp caster/superfine sugar

1 medium/large egg yolk

350 g/12 oz/1¹/₂ cups curd cheese/sieved cottage cheese

75 g/3 oz/¹/₃ cup golden/unrefined granulated sugar

125 g/4 oz/5 squares dark/bittersweet chocolate, melted and cooled

6 tbsp milk

3 medium/large eggs

1 tbsp icing/confectioners' sugar, sifted, to decorate

Preheat the oven to 200°C/400°F/Gas Mark 6, 15 minutes before baking. Lightly oil a 20.5 cm/8 inch fluted flan tin/tart pan. Soak the saffron threads in 1 tablespoon of hot water for 20 minutes. Sift the flour and salt into a bowl. Cut the butter into small dice, then add to the flour and, using your fingertips, rub in the butter until the mixture resembles breadcrumbs. Stir in the sugar.

Beat the egg yolk with 1 tablespoon cold water, add to the mixture and mix together until a smooth and pliable dough is formed. Add a little extra water if necessary. Knead on a lightly floured surface until free from cracks, then wrap in clingfilm/plastic wrap and chill in the refrigerator for 30 minutes.

Roll the pastry dough out on a lightly floured surface and use to line the flan tin. Prick the pastry base and sides with a fork and line with nonstick baking parchment and baking beans/pie weights. Bake blind in the preheated oven for 12 minutes. Remove the beans and baking parchment and continue to bake blind for 5 minutes.

Beat together the curd cheese/sieved cottage cheese and granulated sugar, then beat in the melted chocolate, saffron liquid, the milk and eggs; mix until blended thoroughly. Pour the mixture into the cooked pastry case/pie crust and place on a

baking sheet. Reduce the oven temperature to 190°C/375°F/Gas Mark 5 and bake for 15 minutes, then reduce the oven temperature to 180°C/350°F/Gas Mark 4 and continue to bake for 20–30 minutes until set. Remove the cheesecake from the oven and leave for 10 minutes before removing from the flan tin, if serving warm. If serving cold, leave in the flan tin to cool before removing and placing on a serving platter. Sprinkle with icing/confectioners' sugar before serving.

## Difficulty Rating: 3 points

# Baked Puddings & Desserts

**Traditional puddings will always be firm favourites – this selection includes the classics Jam Roly Poly, Rice Pudding and Golden Castle Pudding. Try something a little different with Baked Stuffed Amaretti Peaches or delight your dinner guests with Raspberry & Hazelnut Meringue Cake – you cannot go wrong with cream, raspberries and meringue!**

# Rice Pudding

## Serves 4

### Ingredients

65 g/2¹/₂ oz/¹/₃ cup pudding rice
50 g/2 oz/¹/₄ cup granulated sugar
410 g/14 oz can light evaporated milk
300 ml/¹/₂ pint/1¹/₄ cups semi-skimmed/low-fat milk
pinch freshly grated nutmeg
25 g/1 oz/¹/₄ stick butter
jam/jelly, to decorate

Preheat the oven to 150°C/300°F/Gas Mark 2, 10 minutes before baking. Lightly oil a large ovenproof dish. Sprinkle the rice and the sugar into the dish and mix.

Bring the evaporated milk and milk to the boil in a small pan, stirring occasionally. Stir the milks into the rice and mix well until the rice is coated thoroughly.

Sprinkle over the nutmeg, cover with kitchen foil and bake in the preheated oven for 30 minutes.

Remove the pudding from the oven and stir well, breaking up any lumps. Cover with the same kitchen foil. Bake in the preheated oven for a further 30 minutes. Remove from the oven and stir well again.

Dot the pudding with butter and bake for a further 45–60 minutes until the rice is tender and the skin is browned.

Divide the pudding into four individual serving bowls. Top with a large spoonful of the jam/jelly. Serve immediately.

## Difficulty Rating: 2 points

# Chocolate Rice Pudding

## Serves 6–8

**Ingredients**

65 g/2¹/₂ oz/¹/₃ cup pudding rice

75 g/3 oz/¹/₃ cup caster/superfine sugar

410 g/14 oz can evaporated milk

600 ml/1 pint/2¹/₂ cups milk

pinch freshly grated nutmeg

¹/₄ tsp ground cinnamon, optional

50 g/2 oz/²/₃ cup dark/bittersweet chocolate chips

25 g/1 oz/¹/₄ stick butter

freshly sliced strawberries, to decorate

crème fraîche/sour cream, to serve

Preheat the oven to 170°C/325°F/Gas Mark 3, 10 minutes before baking. Lightly butter a large ovenproof dish. Rinse the pudding rice, then place in the base of the buttered dish and sprinkle over the caster/superfine sugar.

Pour the evaporated milk and milk into a heavy–based saucepan and bring slowly to the boil over a low heat, stirring occasionally to avoid sticking. Pour the milk over the rice and sugar and stir well until well mixed and the sugar has dissolved.

Grate a little nutmeg over the top, then sprinkle with the ground cinnamon, if using. Cover tightly with kitchen foil and bake in the preheated oven for 30 minutes.

Remove the pudding from the oven and stir well to break up any lumps that may have formed. Cover with kitchen foil and return to the oven for a further 30 minutes.

Remove the pudding from the oven once again and stir to break up any more lumps. Stir the chocolate chips into the rice pudding and then dot with the butter. Continue to bake, uncovered, in the oven for a further 45 minutes–1 hour, or until the rice is tender and the skin is golden brown. Serve warm, with or without the skin, according to personal preference. Serve with a few sliced strawberries and a spoonful of crème fraîche/sour cream.

## Difficulty Rating: 2 points

# Chocolate Rice Pudding Brûlée

## Serves 6

**Ingredients**

2 tbsp cocoa powder (unsweetened)

75 g/3 oz/⅓ cup short-grain rice

600 ml/1 pint/2½ cups milk

1 bay leaf

grated zest of 1 orange

50 g/2 oz/2 squares white chocolate, roughly chopped

1 tbsp golden caster/unrefined superfine sugar

4 medium/large egg yolks

250 ml/8 fl oz/1 cup double/heavy cream

½ tsp vanilla extract

4 tbsp demerara/turbinado sugar

Preheat the oven to 150°C/300°F/Gas Mark 2, 10 minutes before baking. Preheat the grill/broiler on high when ready to use. Gradually blend the cocoa powder with 3 tablespoons boiling water to form a soft, smooth paste. Place the rice and milk, bay leaf, orange zest and the cocoa powder paste in a saucepan. Bring to the boil, stirring constantly. Reduce the heat and simmer for 20 minutes, or until the rice is tender. Remove from the heat and discard the bay leaf, then add the white chocolate and stir until melted.

Whisk together the caster/superfine sugar and egg yolks until thick, then stir in the cream. Stir in the rice mixture together with the vanilla extract. Pour into a buttered shallow dish. Stand the dish in a baking tin/pan with sufficient hot water to come halfway up the sides of the dish. Cook in the preheated oven for 1½ hours, or until set. Stir occasionally during cooking, either removing the skin from the top or stirring the skin into the pudding. Remove from the tin and leave until cool.

Sprinkle the demerara/turbinado sugar over the surface of the pudding. Place under the preheated grill and cook until the sugar melts and caramelizes, turning the dish occasionally. Serve immediately or chill in the refrigerator for 1 hour before serving.

## Difficulty Rating: 3 points

# Crème Brûlée with Sugared Raspberries

## Serves 6

**Ingredients**

600 ml/1 pint/2¹/₂ cups fresh whipping cream
4 egg yolks
75 g/3 oz/¹/₃ cup caster/superfine sugar
¹/₂ tsp vanilla extract
25 g/1 oz/2 tbsp demerara/turbinado sugar
175 g/6 oz/1 heaped cup fresh raspberries

Preheat the oven to 150°C/300°F/Gas Mark 2. Pour the cream into a bowl and place over a saucepan of gently simmering water. Heat gently but do not allow to boil.

Meanwhile, whisk together the egg yolks, 50 g/2 oz/4 tablespoons of the caster/superfine sugar and the vanilla extract. When the cream is warm, pour it over the egg mixture, whisking briskly until it is completely mixed. Pour into six individual ramekin dishes and place in a roasting tin/pan. Fill the tin with enough water to come halfway up the sides of the dishes. Bake in the preheated oven for about 1 hour, or until the puddings are set. (To test if set, carefully insert a round–bladed knife into the centre. If the knife comes out clean, they are set.) Remove the puddings from the roasting tin and allow to cool. Chill in the refrigerator, preferably overnight.

Sprinkle the demerara/turbinado sugar over the top of each dish and place the puddings under a preheated hot grill/broiler. When the sugar has caramelized and turned deep brown, remove from the heat and cool. Chill the puddings in the refrigerator for 2–3 hours before serving.

Toss the raspberries in the remaining caster sugar and sprinkle over the top of each dish. Serve with a little extra cream, if liked.

## Difficulty Rating: 4 points

# Lemon Surprise

## Serves 4

### Ingredients

75 g/3 oz/¹/₂ stick low-fat margarine/spread
175 g/6 oz/³/₄ cup caster/superfine sugar
3 eggs, separated
75 g/3 oz/²/₃ cup self-raising flour
450 ml/³/₄ pint/2 cups semi-skimmed/low-fat milk
juice of 2 lemons
juice of 1 orange
2 tsp icing/confectioners' sugar
lemon zest, to decorate
sliced strawberries, to serve

Preheat the oven to 190°C/375°F/Gas Mark 5. Lightly oil a deep ovenproof dish.

Beat together the margarine/spread and sugar until pale and fluffy. Add the egg yolks, one at a time, with 1 tablespoon of the flour and beat well after each addition. Once added, stir in the remaining flour. Stir in the milk, 4 tablespoons of the lemon juice and 3 tablespoons of the orange juice.

Whisk the egg whites until stiff and fold into the pudding mixture with a metal spoon or rubber spatula until well combined. Pour into the prepared dish.

Stand the dish in a roasting tin/pan and pour in just enough boiling water to come halfway up the sides of the dish. Bake in the preheated oven for 45 minutes, or until well risen and spongy to the touch.

Remove the pudding from the oven and sprinkle with the icing/confectioners' sugar. Decorate with the lemon zest and serve immediately with the strawberries.

## Difficulty Rating: 2 points

# Orange Curd & Plum Pie

## Serves 4

### Ingredients

700 g/1¹/₂ lb/4¹/₄ cups stoned plums, quartered
2 tbsp light brown sugar
grated zest of ¹/₂ lemon
25 g/1 oz/¹/₄ stick butter, melted
1 tbsp olive oil
6 sheets filo/phyllo pastry dough, plus 1 for decoration
¹/₂ x 411 g/14 oz jar luxury orange (or lemon) curd
50 g/2 oz/¹/₃ cup sultanas/golden raisins
icing/confectioners' sugar, to decorate
Greek yogurt, to serve

Preheat the oven to 200°C/400°F/Gas Mark 6. Lightly oil a 20.5 cm/8 inch round cake tin/pan. Cook the plums with the light brown sugar for 8–10 minutes to soften them. Remove from the heat and reserve.

Mix together the lemon zest, butter and oil. Lay one of the sheets of filo/phyllo pastry in the prepared cake tin and brush with the lemon zest mixture. Cut four of the remaining pastry sheets in half and then place one half sheet in the cake tin and brush again. Top with the remaining halved sheets, brushing each time with the lemon zest mixture. Fold each sheet in half lengthways so that part of them line the sides of the tin at the same time as the bottom to make a filo case.

Mix together the plums, orange curd and sultanas/golden raisins. Spoon into the pastry case/pie crust. Draw the pastry edges up over the filling to enclose. Brush the extra remaining pastry sheet with the lemon zest mixture. Cut into thick strips. Scrunch each strip of pastry and arrange on top of the pie. Bake in the preheated oven for 25 minutes, or until golden. Sprinkle with icing/confectioners' sugar and serve with the Greek yogurt.

## Difficulty Rating: 3 points

# Topsy Turvy Pudding

## Serves 6

**Ingredients**

**For the topping:**
175 g/6 oz demerara/turbinado sugar
2 oranges

**For the sponge:**
175 g/6 oz/1½ sticks butter, softened
175 g/6 oz/1 scant cup caster/superfine sugar
3 medium/large eggs, beaten
175 g/6 oz/1⅓ cups self-raising flour, sifted
50 g/2 oz/2 squares dark/bittersweet chocolate, melted
grated zest of 1 orange
25 g/1 oz/¼ cup cocoa powder (unsweetened), sifted
custard or sour cream, to serve

Preheat the oven to 180°C/350°F/Gas Mark 4, 10 minutes before baking. Lightly oil a 20.5 cm/8 inch deep round loose-based cake tin/pan. Place the demerara/turbinado sugar and 3 tablespoons water in a small heavy-based saucepan and heat gently until the sugar has dissolved. Stir with a clean wooden spoon to ensure the sugar has dissolved, then boil rapidly until a golden caramel is formed. Pour into the base of the tin and leave to cool.

Cream the butter and sugar together until light and fluffy. Beat in the eggs gradually, beating well after each addition. Add a spoonful of flour after each addition to prevent curdling. Add the melted chocolate and then stir well. Fold in the orange zest, self-raising flour and sifted cocoa powder and mix well.

Remove the peel from both oranges, taking care to remove as much of the pith as possible. Thinly slice the peel into strips and then slice the oranges. Arrange the peel and then the orange slices over the caramel. Top with the sponge mixture and level the top. Place the tin on a baking sheet and bake in the preheated oven for 40–45 minutes until well risen, golden brown and an inserted skewer comes out clean. Remove from the oven, leave for about 5 minutes, invert onto a serving plate and sprinkle with cocoa powder. Serve with either custard or sour cream.

## Difficulty Rating: 4 points

# Chocolate & Almond Daquoise with Summer Berries

## Cuts into 8 servings

**Ingredients**

**For the almond meringues:**
6 large/extra-large egg whites
¼ tsp cream of tartar
275 g/10 oz/1⅓ cups caster/superfine sugar
½ tsp almond extract
50 g/2 oz/½ cup blanched or flaked almonds,
   lightly toasted and finely ground

**For the chocolate buttercream:**
75 g/3 oz/⅔ stick butter, softened
450 g/1 lb/4½ cups icing/confectioners' sugar, sifted
50 g/2 oz/½ cup cocoa powder (unsweetened), sifted
3–4 tbsp milk or single/light cream
550 g/1¼ lb/4½ cups mixed summer berries,
   such as raspberries, strawberries and blackberries

**To decorate:**
toasted flaked almonds
icing/confectioners' sugar

Preheat the oven to 140°C/275°F/Gas Mark 1, 10 minutes before baking. Line three baking sheets with nonstick baking parchment and draw a 20.5 cm/8 inch round on each one.

Whisk the egg whites and cream of tartar until soft peaks form. Gradually beat in the sugar, 2 tablespoons at a time, beating well after each addition, until the whites are stiff and glossy. Beat in the almond extract, then, using a metal spoon or rubber spatula, gently fold in the ground almonds. Divide the mixture evenly between the three circles of baking paper, spreading neatly into the rounds and smoothing the tops evenly. Bake in the preheated oven for about 1¼ hours, or until crisp, rotating the baking sheets halfway through cooking. Turn off the oven, allow to cool for about 1 hour, then remove and cool completely before discarding the lining paper.

Beat the butter, icing/confectioners' sugar and cocoa until smooth and creamy, adding the milk or cream to form a soft consistency.

Reserve about a quarter of the berries to decorate. Spread one meringue with a third of the buttercream and top with a third of the remaining berries. Repeat with the other meringue rounds, buttercream and berries. Scatter with the toasted flaked almonds and the reserved berries and sprinkle with icing sugar and serve.

## Difficulty Rating: 3 points

# Raspberry & Hazelnut Meringue Cake

## Cuts into 8 slices

### Ingredients

**For the meringue:**

4 large/extra-large egg whites

¼ tsp cream of tartar

225 g/8 oz/1 heaped cup caster/superfine sugar

75 g/3 oz/¾ cup hazelnuts, skinned, toasted and finely ground

**For the filling:**

300 ml/½ pint/1¼ cups double/heavy cream

1 tbsp icing/confectioners' sugar

1–2 tbsp raspberry-flavoured liqueur (optional)

350 g/12 oz/3 scant cups fresh raspberries

## Difficulty Rating: 2 points

Preheat the oven to 140°C/275°F/Gas Mark 1. Line two baking sheets with nonstick baking parchment and draw a 20.5 cm/8 inch circle on each. Whisk the egg whites and cream of tartar until soft peaks form, then gradually beat in the sugar, 2 tablespoons at a time. Beat well after each addition, beating until the whites are stiff and glossy. Using a metal spoon or rubber spatula, gently fold in the ground hazelnuts.

Divide the mixture evenly between the two circles and spread neatly. Swirl one of the circles to make a decorative top layer. Bake in the preheated oven for about 1½ hours, until crisp and dry. Turn off the oven and allow the meringues to cool for 1 hour. Transfer to a wire rack to cool completely. Carefully peel off the papers.

For the filling, whip the cream, icing/confectioners' sugar and liqueur, if using, together until soft peaks form. Place the flat round on a serving plate. Spread over most of the cream, reserving some for decorating, and arrange the raspberries in concentric circles over the cream. Place the swirly meringue on top of the cream and raspberries, pressing down gently. Pipe the remaining cream onto the meringue and decorate with a few raspberries and serve.

# Hazelnut, Chocolate & Chestnut Meringue Torte

## Serves 8–10

### Ingredients

**For the chocolate meringue:**

1 medium/large egg white

50 g/2 oz/¹⁄₄ cup caster/superfine sugar

2 tbsp cocoa powder (unsweetened)

**For the hazelnut meringue:**

75 g/3 oz/³⁄₄ cup hazelnuts, toasted

2 medium/large egg whites

125 g/4 oz/²⁄₃ cup caster/superfine sugar

**For the filling:**

300 ml/¹⁄₂ pint/1¹⁄₄ cups double/heavy cream

250 g/9 oz can sweetened chestnut purée

50 g/2 oz dark/bittersweet chocolate, melted

25 g/1 oz dark/bittersweet chocolate, grated

Preheat the oven to 130˚C/250˚F/Gas Mark ¹⁄₂. Line three baking sheets with nonstick baking parchment and draw a 20.5 cm/8 inch circle on each. Beat 1 egg white until stiff peaks form. Add 25 g/1 oz/¹⁄₈ cup of the sugar and beat until shiny. Mix the cocoa powder with the remaining 25 g/1 oz/¹⁄₈ cup of sugar, adding 1 tablespoon at a time, beating well after each addition, until all the sugar is added and the mixture is stiff and glossy. Spread on to one of the baking sheets within the circle drawn on the underside.

Put the hazelnuts in a food processor and blend until chopped. In a clean bowl, beat the 2 egg whites until stiff. Add 50 g/2 oz/¹⁄₄ cup of the sugar and beat. Add the remaining sugar about 1 tablespoon at a time, beating after each addition, until all the sugar is added and the mixture is stiff and glossy.

Reserve 2 tablespoons of the nuts, then fold in the remainder and divide between the two remaining baking sheets. Sprinkle one of the hazelnut meringues with the reserved hazelnuts and transfer all the baking sheets to the oven. Bake in the preheated oven for 1¹⁄₂ hours. Turn the oven off and leave in the oven until cold.

Whip the cream until thick. Beat the chestnut purée in another bowl until soft. Add a spoonful of the cream and fold together before adding the remaining cream and melted chocolate and folding together. Place the plain hazelnut meringue on a serving plate. Top with half the cream and chestnut mixture. Add the chocolate meringue and top with the remaining cream. Add the final meringue. Sprinkle over the grated chocolate and serve.

## Difficulty Rating: 3 points

# Hazelnut Meringues with Chocolate Sauce

## Serves 6

### Ingredients

4 medium/large egg whites

225 g/8 oz/1 heaped cup caster/superfine sugar

125 g/4 oz/1²/₃ cups ground hazelnuts

50 g/2 oz/¹/₃ cup toasted hazelnuts

sliced fresh berries, such as raspberries, strawberries and
blueberries, to serve

### For the chocolate sauce:

225 g/8 oz/5 squares dark/bittersweet chocolate,
broken into pieces

50 g/2 oz/¹/₂ stick butter

300 ml/¹/₂ pint/1¹/₄ cups double/heavy cream

1 tbsp golden/corn syrup

## Difficulty Rating: 2 points

Preheat the oven to 150°C/300°F/Gas Mark 2, 10 minutes before baking. Line two baking sheets with nonstick baking parchment. Whisk the egg whites in a large grease–free bowl until stiff, then add the caster/superfine sugar, 1 teaspoonful at a time, whisking well after each addition. Continue to whisk until the mixture is stiff and dry, then, using a metal spoon, fold in the ground hazelnuts.

Using two dessertspoons, spoon the mixture into 12 quenelle shapes onto the baking parchment. Sprinkle over the toasted hazelnuts and bake in the preheated oven for 1¹/₂–2 hours until dry and crisp. Switch the oven off and leave to cool in the oven.

To make the chocolate sauce, place the chocolate with the butter and 4 tablespoons of the cream and the golden/corn syrup in a heavy–based saucepan and heat, stirring occasionally, until the chocolate has melted and the mixture is blended. Do not boil. Whip the remaining cream until soft peaks form.

Sandwich the meringues together with the whipped cream and place on serving plates. Spoon over the sauce and serve with a few fresh berries.

# Chocolate Meringue Nests with Fruity Filling

## Serves 8

### Ingredients

125 g/4 oz/1²/₃ cups hazelnuts, toasted

125 g/4 oz/²/₃ cup golden caster/unrefined superfine sugar

75 g/3 oz/3 squares dark/bittersweet chocolate, broken into pieces

2 medium/large egg whites

pinch salt

1 tsp cornflour/cornstarch

¹/₂ tsp white wine vinegar

chocolate curls, to decorate

### For the filling:

150 ml/¹/₄ pint/²/₃ cup double/heavy cream

150 g/5 oz/²/₃ cup mascarpone cheese

prepared summer fruits, such as strawberries, raspberries
  and redcurrants

## Difficulty Rating: 2 points

Preheat the oven to 110°C/225°F/Gas Mark ¹/₄, 5 minutes before baking and line a baking sheet with nonstick baking parchment. Place the hazelnuts and 2 tablespoons of the caster/superfine sugar in a food processor and blend to a powder. Add the chocolate and blend again until the chocolate is roughly chopped.

In a clean, grease-free bowl, whisk the egg whites and salt until soft peaks form. Gradually whisk in the remaining sugar a teaspoonful at a time and continue to whisk until the meringue is stiff and shiny. Fold in the cornflour/cornstarch and the white wine vinegar with the chocolate and hazelnut mixture.

Spoon the mixture into eight mounds, about 10 cm/4 inches in diameter, on the baking parchment. Do not worry if not perfect shapes. Make a hollow in each mound, then place in the preheated oven. Cook for 1¹/₂ hours, then switch the oven off and leave in the oven until cool.

To make the filling, whip the cream until soft peaks form. In another bowl, beat the mascarpone cheese until it is softened, then mix with the cream. Spoon the mixture into the meringue nests and top with the fresh fruits. Decorate with a few chocolate curls and serve.

# Chocolaty Puffs

## Makes 12 large puffs

**Ingredients**

**For the choux pastry:**
150 g/5 oz/1 heaped cup plain/all-purpose flour
2 tbsp cocoa powder (unsweetened)
1/2 tsp salt
1 tbsp sugar
125 g/4 oz/1 stick plus 1 tbsp butter, cut into pieces
5 large/extra-large eggs

**For the chocolate cream filling:**
225 g/8 oz/9 squares dark/bittersweet chocolate, chopped
600 ml/1 pint/2 1/2 cups double/heavy cream
1 tbsp caster/superfine sugar (optional)
2 tbsp crème de cacao/chocolate crème liqueur (optional)

**For the chocolate sauce:**
225 g/8 oz/9 squares dark/bittersweet chocolate
300 ml/1/2 pint/1 1/4 cups whipping cream
50 g/2 oz/1/2 stick butter, diced
1–2 tbsp golden/corn syrup
1 tsp vanilla extract

Preheat the oven to 220°C/425°F/Gas Mark 7, 15 minutes before baking. Lightly oil a large baking sheet.

To make the choux pastry, sift the flour and cocoa powder together. Place 250 ml/8 fl oz/1 cup water, the salt, sugar and butter in a saucepan and bring to the boil. Remove from the heat and add the flour mixture all at once, beating vigorously with a wooden spoon until the mixture forms a ball in the centre of the saucepan. Return to the heat and cook for 1 minute, stirring, then cool slightly.

Using an electric mixer, beat in 4 of the eggs, one at a time, beating well after each addition. Beat the last egg and add a little at a time until the dough is thick and shiny and just falls from a spoon when tapped lightly on the side of the saucepan.

Pipe or spoon 12 large puffs onto the prepared baking sheet, leaving space between them. Cook in the preheated oven for

30–35 minutes, or until puffy and golden. Remove from the oven, slice off the top third of each bun and return to the oven for 5 minutes to dry out. Remove and leave to cool.

For the filling, heat the chocolate with 125 ml/4 fl oz/1/2 cup of the double/heavy cream and the 1 tablespoon caster sugar, if using, stirring until smooth, then leave to cool. Whisk the remaining cream until soft peaks form and stir in the crème de cacao, if using. Quickly fold the cream into the chocolate, then spoon or pipe into the choux buns and place the lids on top.

Place all the ingredients for the sauce in a small saucepan and heat gently, stirring until smooth. Remove from the heat and leave to cool, stirring occasionally, until thickened. Pour over the puffs and serve immediately.

## Difficulty Rating: 4 points

# Baked Stuffed Amaretti Peaches

## Serves 4

**Ingredients**

4 ripe peaches
juice and grated zest of 1 lemon
8 amaretti biscuits/cookies
50 g/2 oz/$^1/_2$ cup chopped blanched almonds, toasted
50 g/2 oz/$^1/_3$ cup pine nuts, toasted
3 tbsp light muscovado/golden brown sugar
50 g/2 oz/$^1/_2$ stick butter
1 egg yolk
2 tsp clear honey
crème fraîche/sour cream or Greek yogurt, to serve

Preheat the oven to 180°C/350°F/Gas Mark 4. Halve the peaches and remove the stones. Take a very thin slice from the bottom of each peach half so that it will sit flat in a baking tray. Dip the peach halves in lemon juice and arrange in a baking tray.

Crush the amaretti biscuits/cookies lightly and put into a large bowl. Add the almonds, pine nuts, sugar, lemon zest and butter. Work with the fingertips until the mixture resembles coarse breadcrumbs. Add the egg yolk and mix well until the mixture is just binding.

Divide the amaretti and nut mixture between the peach halves, pressing down lightly. Bake in the preheated oven for 15 minutes, or until the peaches are tender and the filling is golden. Remove from the oven and drizzle with the honey.

Place two peach halves on each serving plate and spoon over a little crème fraîche/sour cream or Greek yogurt, then serve.

## Difficulty Rating: 1 point

# Chocolate Brioche Bake

## Serves 6

**Ingredients**

200 g/7 oz/8 squares dark/bittersweet chocolate,
  broken into pieces
75 g/3 oz/²/₃ stick unsalted butter
225 g/8 oz/1 large brioche, sliced
1 tsp pure orange oil or 1 tbsp grated orange zest
¹/₂ tsp freshly grated nutmeg
3 eggs, beaten
2 tbsp golden caster/unrefined superfine sugar
600 ml/1 pint/2¹/₂ cups milk
cocoa powder (unsweetened) and icing/confectioners' sugar,
  for dusting

Preheat the oven to 180°C/350°F/Gas Mark 4, 10 minutes before baking. Lightly oil or butter a 1.7 litre/3 pint/1³/₄ quart ovenproof dish. Melt the chocolate with 25 g/1 oz/2 tbsp of the butter in a heatproof bowl set over a saucepan of simmering water. Stir until smooth.

Arrange half of the sliced brioche in the ovenproof dish, overlapping the slices slightly, then pour over half of the melted chocolate. Repeat the layers, finishing with a layer of chocolate.

Melt the remaining butter in a saucepan. Remove from the heat and stir in the orange oil or zest, the nutmeg and the beaten eggs. Continuing to stir, add the sugar and finally the milk. Beat thoroughly and pour over the brioche. Leave to stand for 30 minutes before baking. Bake on the centre shelf in the preheated oven for 45 minutes, or until the custard is set and the topping is golden brown. Leave to stand for 5 minutes, then dust with cocoa powder and icing/confectioners' sugar. Serve warm.

## Difficulty Rating: 1 point

# Individual Steamed Chocolate Puddings

## Serves 8

**Ingredients**

150 g/5 oz/1⅓ sticks unsalted butter, softened

175 g/6 oz/1 scant cup light muscovado/golden brown sugar

½ tsp freshly grated nutmeg

3 tbsp plain/all-purpose white flour, sifted

4 tbsp cocoa powder (unsweetened), sifted

5 eggs, separated

125 g/4 oz/1⅓ cups ground almonds

50 g/2 oz/1 cup fresh white breadcrumbs

**To serve:**

Greek yogurt

orange-flavoured chocolate curls

Preheat the oven to 180°C/350°F/Gas Mark 4, 10 minutes before baking. Lightly oil and line the bases of eight individual 175 ml/6 fl oz/⅔ cup pudding basins/ovenproof bowls with small circles of nonstick baking parchment. Cream the butter with 50 g/2 oz/¼ cup of the sugar and the nutmeg until light and fluffy.

Sift the flour and cocoa powder together, then stir into the creamed mixture. Beat in the egg yolks and mix well, then fold in the ground almonds and the breadcrumbs.

Whisk the egg whites in a clean, grease-free bowl until stiff and standing in peaks, then gradually whisk in the remaining sugar. Using a metal spoon, fold a quarter of the egg whites into the chocolate mixture and mix well, then fold in the remaining egg whites. Spoon the mixture into the prepared basins, filling them two-thirds full to allow for expansion. Cover with a double sheet of kitchen foil and secure tightly with string. Stand the pudding basins in a roasting tin and pour in sufficient water to come halfway up the sides of the basins. Bake in the centre of the preheated oven for 30 minutes, or until the puddings are firm to the touch. Remove from the oven, loosen around the edges and invert onto warmed plates. Serve with Greek yogurt and chocolate curls.

## Difficulty Rating: 2 points

# Peach & Chocolate Bake

Serves 6 (Pictured page 206)

**Ingredients**

200 g/7 oz/8 squares dark/bittersweet chocolate
125 g/4 oz/1 stick plus 1 tbsp unsalted butter
4 medium/large eggs, separated
125 g/4 oz/²⁄₃ cup caster/superfine sugar
425 g/15 oz can peach slices, drained
¹⁄₂ tsp ground cinnamon
1 tbsp icing/confectioners' sugar, sifted, to decorate
crème fraîche/sour cream, to serve

Preheat the oven to 170°C/325°F/Gas Mark 3, 10 minutes before baking. Lightly oil a 1.7 litre/3 pint ovenproof dish.

Break the chocolate and butter into small pieces and place in a small heatproof bowl set over a saucepan of gently simmering water. Ensure the water is not touching the base of the bowl and leave to melt. Remove the bowl from the heat and stir until smooth.

Whisk the egg yolks with the sugar until very thick and creamy, then stir the melted chocolate and butter into the whisked egg yolk mixture and mix together lightly.

Place the egg whites in a clean, grease-free bowl and whisk until stiff, then fold 2 tablespoons of the whisked egg whites into the chocolate mixture. Mix well, then add the remaining egg white and fold in very lightly.

Fold the peach slices and the cinnamon into the mixture, then spoon into the prepared dish. Do not level the mixture, leave a little uneven. Bake in the preheated oven for 35–40 minutes, or until well risen and just firm to the touch. Sprinkle the bake with the icing/confectioners' sugar and serve immediately with spoonfuls of crème fraîche/sour cream.

## Difficulty Rating: 2 points

# Chocolate Pear Pudding

Serves 6

**Ingredients**

140 g/4¹⁄₂ oz/1¹⁄₄ sticks butter, softened
2 tbsp soft brown sugar
400 g/14 oz can pear halves, drained and juice reserved
25 g/1 oz/¹⁄₄ cup walnut halves
125 g/4 oz/²⁄₃ cup golden caster/unrefined superfine sugar
2 medium/large eggs, beaten
75 g/3 oz/¹⁄₂ cup self-raising flour, sifted
50 g/2 oz/¹⁄₂ cup cocoa powder (unsweetened)
1 tsp baking powder
prepared chocolate custard, to serve

Preheat the oven to 190°C/375°F/Gas Mark 5, 10 minutes before baking. Butter a 20.5 cm/8 inch sandwich tin with 1 tablespoon of the butter and sprinkle the base with the soft brown sugar. Arrange the drained pear halves on top of the sugar, cut-side down. Fill the spaces between the pears with the walnut halves, flat-side upwards.

Cream the remaining butter with the caster/superfine sugar, then gradually beat in the beaten eggs, adding 1 tablespoon of the flour after each addition. When all the eggs have been added, stir in the remaining flour.

Sift the cocoa powder and baking powder together, then stir into the creamed mixture with 1–2 tablespoons of the reserved pear juice to give a smooth dropping consistency. Spoon the mixture over the pear halves, smoothing the surface. Bake in the preheated oven for 20–25 minutes, or until well risen and the surface springs back when lightly pressed.

Remove from the oven and leave to cool for 5 minutes. Using a palette knife, loosen the sides and invert onto a serving plate. Serve with custard.

## Difficulty Rating: 2 points

# Cherry Batter Pudding

## Serves 4

### Ingredients

450 g/1 lb/3 cups fresh cherries (or 425 g/15 oz can
   pitted cherries)

50 g/2 oz/scant ½ cup plain/all-purpose flour

pinch salt

3 tbsp caster/superfine sugar

2 eggs

300 ml/½ pint/1¼ cups milk

40 g/1½ oz/3 tbsp butter

1 tbsp rum

extra caster/superfine sugar, to decorate

double/heavy cream, to serve

## Difficulty Rating: 3 points

Preheat the oven to 220°C/425°F/Gas Mark 7. Lightly oil a shallow casserole dish. Rinse the cherries, drain well and remove the stones (using a cherry stoner/pitter, if possible). If using canned cherries, drain well, discard the juice and place in the prepared dish.

Sift the flour and salt into a large bowl. Stir in 2 tablespoons of the caster/superfine sugar and make a well in the centre. Beat the eggs, then pour into the well.

Warm the milk and slowly pour into the well, beating throughout and gradually drawing in the flour from the sides of the bowl. Continue until a smooth batter has formed.

Melt the butter in a small saucepan over a low heat, then stir into the batter with the rum. Reserve for 15 minutes, then beat again until smooth and easy to pour. Pour into the prepared baking dish and bake in the preheated oven for 30–35 minutes, or until golden brown and set.

Remove the pudding from the oven, sprinkle with the remaining sugar and serve hot with plenty of double/heavy cream.

# Osborne Pudding

## Serves 4

**Ingredients**

8 slices white bread

50 g/2 oz/¹/₂ stick butter

2 tbsp marmalade

50 g/2 oz/¹/₃ cup mixed dried fruit

2 tbsp fresh orange juice

3 tbsp caster/superfine sugar

2 large/extra-large eggs

450 ml/³/₄ pint/1¹/₄ cups milk

150 ml/¹/₄ pint/²/₃ cup whipping cream

**For the marmalade sauce:**

zest and juice of 1 orange

2 tbsp thick-cut orange marmalade

1 tbsp brandy (optional)

2 tsp cornflour/cornstarch

Preheat the oven to 170°C/325°F/Gas Mark 3. Lightly oil a 1.2 litre/2 pint/1¹/₄ quart baking dish. Remove the crusts from the bread and spread thickly with butter and marmalade. Cut the bread into small triangles. Place half the bread in the base of the dish and sprinkle over the dried mixed fruit, 1 tablespoon of the orange juice and half the caster/superfine sugar. Top with the remaining bread and marmalade, buttered side up, and pour over the remaining orange juice. Sprinkle over the remaining sugar.

Whisk the eggs with the milk and cream and pour over the pudding. Reserve for about 30 minutes to allow the bread to absorb the liquid, then place in a roasting tin/pan and pour in enough boiling water to come halfway up the sides of the dish. Bake in the preheated oven for 50–60 minutes, or until the pudding is set and the top is crisp and golden.

Meanwhile, make the sauce. Heat the orange zest and juice with the marmalade and brandy, if using. Mix 1 tablespoon water with the cornflour/cornstarch and mix together well. Add to the saucepan and cook on a low heat, stirring until warmed through and thickened. Serve the pudding hot with the sauce.

## Difficulty Rating: 1 point

# Fruity Chocolate Bread Pudding

## Serves 4

### Ingredients

175 g/6 oz/7 squares dark/bittersweet chocolate
1 small fruit loaf
125 g/4 oz/1 cup ready-to-eat dried apricots, roughly chopped
450 ml/³/₄ pint/1³/₄ cups single/light cream
300 ml/¹/₂ pint/1¹/₄ cups milk
1 tbsp caster/superfine sugar
3 medium/large eggs
3 tbsp demerara/turbinado sugar, for sprinkling

Preheat the oven to 180°C/350°F/Gas Mark 4, 10 minutes before baking. Lightly butter a shallow ovenproof dish. Break the chocolate into small pieces, then place in a heatproof bowl set over a saucepan of gently simmering water. Heat gently, stirring frequently, until the chocolate has melted and is smooth. Remove from the heat and leave for about 10 minutes, or until the chocolate begins to thicken slightly.

Cut the fruit loaf into medium to thick slices, then spread with the melted chocolate. Leave until almost set, then cut each slice in half to form triangles. Layer the chocolate–coated bread slices and the chopped apricots in the buttered ovenproof dish.

Stir the cream and the milk together, then stir in the caster/superfine sugar.

Beat the eggs, then gradually beat in the cream and milk mixture. Beat thoroughly until well blended. Carefully pour over the bread slices and apricots and leave to stand for 30 minutes.

Sprinkle with the demerara/turbinado sugar and place in a roasting tin/pan half filled with boiling water. Cook in the preheated oven for 45 minutes, or until golden and the custard is lightly set. Serve immediately.

## Difficulty Rating: 1 point

# Sticky Chocolate Surprise Pudding

## Serves 6–8

### Ingredients

150 g/5 oz/1 heaped cup self-raising flour
25 g/1 oz/¼ cup cocoa powder (unsweetened)
200 g/7 oz/1 cup caster/superfine sugar
75 g/3 oz/3 squares mint-flavoured chocolate, chopped
175 ml/6 fl oz/scant ¾ cup whole milk
2 tsp vanilla extract
50 g/2 oz/½ stick unsalted butter, melted
1 egg
fresh mint sprig, to decorate

### For the sauce:
175 g/6 oz/¾ cup muscovado/dark brown sugar
125 g/4 oz/1⅓ cups cocoa powder (unsweetened)
600 ml/1 pint/2½ cups hot water

Preheat the oven to 180°C/350°F/Gas Mark 4, 10 minutes before baking. Lightly oil a 1.5 litre/2½ pint/1½ quart ovenproof soufflé dish. Sift the flour and cocoa powder into a large bowl and stir in the caster/superfine sugar and the chocolate and make a well in the centre.

Whisk the milk, vanilla extract and the melted butter together, then beat in the egg. Pour into the well in the dry ingredients and gradually mix together, drawing the dry ingredients in from the sides of the bowl. Beat well until mixed thoroughly. Spoon into the prepared soufflé dish.

To make the sauce, blend the muscovado/dark brown sugar and the cocoa powder together and mix with the hot water until the sugar and cocoa have dissolved. Carefully pour over the top of the pudding, but do not stir in. Bake in the preheated oven for 35–40 minutes, or until firm to the touch and the mixture has formed a sauce underneath. Decorate with mint and serve immediately.

## Difficulty Rating: 2 points

# White Chocolate Eclairs

## Serves 4–6

### Ingredients

50 g/2 oz/¹/₂ stick unsalted butter

65 g/2¹/₂ oz/¹/₂ cup plain/all-purpose flour, sifted

2 medium/large eggs, lightly beaten

6 ripe passion fruit

300 ml/¹/₂ pint/1¹/₄ cups double/heavy cream

3 tbsp kirsch

1 tbsp icing/confectioners' sugar

125 g/4 oz white chocolate, broken into pieces

Preheat the oven to 190°C/375°F/Gas Mark 5, 10 minutes before baking. Lightly oil a baking sheet. Place the butter and 150 ml/¹/₄ pint water in a saucepan and heat until the butter has melted, then bring to the boil. Remove the saucepan from the heat and immediately add the flour all at once, beating with a wooden spoon until the mixture forms a ball in the centre of the saucepan. Leave to cool for 3 minutes. Add the eggs a little at a time, beating well after each addition, until the paste is smooth, shiny and of a piping consistency. Spoon the mixture into a piping/decorating bag fitted with a plain nozzle/tip. Sprinkle the oiled baking sheet with water. Pipe the mixture onto the baking sheet in 7.5 cm/3 inch lengths, using a knife to cut each pastry length neatly. Bake in the preheated oven for 18–20 minutes, or until well risen and golden. Make a slit along the side of each eclair to let the steam escape. Return the eclairs to the oven for a further 2 minutes to dry out. Transfer to a wire rack and leave to cool.

Halve the passion fruit and, using a small spoon, scoop the pulp of 4 of the fruits into a bowl. Add the cream, kirsch and icing/confectioners' sugar and whip until the cream holds its shape. Carefully spoon or pipe into the eclairs.

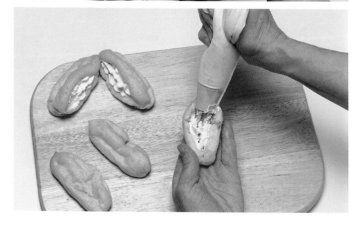

Melt the chocolate in a small heatproof bowl set over a saucepan of simmering water and stir until smooth. Leave the chocolate to cool slightly, then spread over the tops of the eclairs. Scoop the seeds and pulp out of the remaining passion fruit. Sieve. Use the juice to drizzle around the eclairs when serving.

## Difficulty Rating: 3 points

# Oaty Fruit Puddings

## Serves 4

**Ingredients**

125 g/4 oz/1²/₃ cups rolled oats
50 g/2 oz/¹/₄ cup low-fat margarine/spread, melted
2 tbsp chopped almonds
1 tbsp clear honey
pinch ground cinnamon
2 pears, peeled, cored and finely chopped
1 tbsp marmalade
orange zest, to decorate
low-fat custard or fruit-flavoured low-fat yogurt, to serve

Preheat the oven to 200°C/400°F/Gas Mark 6. Lightly oil and line the bases of four individual pudding bowls or muffin tins/pans with a small circle of greaseproof/waxed paper.

Mix together the oats, low-fat margarine/spread, nuts, honey and cinnamon in a small bowl. Using a spoon, spread two thirds of the oaty mixture over the bases and around the sides of the pudding bowls or muffin tins.

Toss together the pears and marmalade and spoon into the oaty cases. Scatter over the remaining oaty mixture to cover the pears and marmalade. Bake in the preheated oven for 15–20 minutes until cooked and the tops of the puddings are golden and crisp.

Leave for 5 minutes before removing the pudding bowls or the muffin tins. Decorate with orange zest and serve hot with low–fat custard or low–fat fruit–flavoured yogurt.

**Difficulty Rating: 1 point**

# Crunchy Rhubarb Crumble

## Serves 4

### Ingredients

100 g/3½ oz/1 scant cup plain/all-purpose flour
50 g/2 oz/½ stick softened butter
50 g/2 oz/⅔ cup rolled oats
50 g/2 oz/¼ cup demerara/turbinado sugar
1 tbsp sesame seeds
½ tsp ground cinnamon
450 g/1 lb/3¾ cups (prepared as below) fresh rhubarb
50 g/2 oz/¼ cup caster/superfine sugar, plus extra, for sprinkling
custard or cream, to serve

Preheat the oven to 180°C/350°F/Gas Mark 4. Place the flour in a large bowl and cut the butter into cubes. Add to the flour and rub in with the fingertips until the mixture looks like fine breadcrumbs, or blend for a few seconds in a food processor. Stir in the oats, demerara/turbinado sugar, sesame seeds and cinnamon. Mix well and reserve.

Prepare the rhubarb by removing the thick ends of the stalks and cut diagonally into 2.5 cm/1 inch chunks. Wash thoroughly and pat dry with a clean dishtowel. Place the rhubarb in a 1.1 litre/2 pint/1¼ quart pie dish.

Sprinkle the caster/superfine sugar over the rhubarb and top with the reserved crumble/crisp mixture. Level the top of the crumble so that all the fruit is well covered and press down firmly. If liked, sprinkle the top with a little extra caster sugar.

Place on a baking sheet and bake in the preheated oven for 40–50 minutes, or until the fruit is soft and the topping is golden brown. Sprinkle the pudding with some more caster sugar and serve hot with custard or cream.

## Difficulty Rating: 1 point

# Chocolate & Fruit Crumble

## Serves 4

### Ingredients

**For the crumble/crisp:**
125 g/4 oz/1 cup plain/all-purpose flour
130 g/4½ oz/1 stick plus 1 tbsp butter
75 g/3 oz/⅓ cup soft light brown sugar
50 g/2 oz/⅔ cup rolled oats
50 g/2 oz/½ cup hazelnuts, chopped

**For the filling:**
450 g/1 lb Bramley/tart cooking apples
1 tbsp lemon juice
50 g/2 oz/⅓ cup sultanas/golden raisins
50 g/2 oz/⅓ cup seedless raisins
50 g/2 oz/¼ cup soft light brown sugar
350 g/12 oz/¾ cup pears, peeled, cored and chopped
1 tsp ground cinnamon
125 g/4 oz/5 squares dark/bittersweet chocolate,
   very roughly chopped
2 tsp caster/superfine sugar, for sprinkling

Preheat the oven to 190°C/375°F/Gas Mark 5, 10 minutes before baking. Lightly oil an ovenproof dish.

For the crumble/crisp, sift the flour into a large bowl. Cut the butter into small cubes and add to the flour. Rub the butter into the flour until the mixture resembles fine breadcrumbs. Stir the sugar, oats and the chopped hazelnuts into the mixture and reserve.

For the filling, peel the apples, core and slice thickly. Place in a large heavy-based saucepan with the lemon juice and 3 tablespoons water. Add the sultanas/golden raisins, raisins and the soft brown sugar. Bring slowly to the boil, cover and simmer over a gentle heat for 8–10 minutes, stirring occasionally, or until the apples are slightly softened.

Remove the saucepan from the heat and leave to cool slightly before stirring in the pears, ground cinnamon and the chopped

chocolate. Spoon into the prepared ovenproof dish. Sprinkle the crumble evenly over the top, then bake in the preheated oven for 35–40 minutes until the top is golden. Remove from the oven, sprinkle with the caster/superfine sugar and serve immediately.

## Difficulty Rating: 2 points

# Apple & Cinnamon Crumble-top Cake

## Cuts into 8 slices

### Ingredients

**For the topping:**
350 g/12 oz/³/₄ lb eating apples, peeled
1 tbsp lemon juice
125 g/4 oz/1 cup self-raising flour
1 tsp ground cinnamon
75 g/3 oz/²/₃ stick butter or margarine
75 g/3 oz/¹/₃ cup demerara/turbinado sugar
1 tbsp milk

**For the base:**
125 g/4 oz/1 stick plus 1 tbsp butter or margarine
125 g/4 oz/²/₃ cup caster/superfine sugar
2 eggs
150 g/5 oz/1 heaped cup self-raising flour
cream or freshly made custard, to serve (*see* page 235)

Preheat the oven to 180°C/350°F/Gas Mark 4, 10 minutes before baking. Lightly oil and line the base of a 20.5 cm/8 inch deep round cake tin/pan with greaseproof/waxed paper or baking parchment.

Finely chop the apples and mix with the lemon juice. Reserve while making the cake.

For the crumble topping, sift the flour and cinnamon together into a large bowl. Rub the butter or margarine into the flour and cinnamon until the mixture resembles coarse breadcrumbs. Stir the sugar into the breadcrumbs and reserve.

For the base, cream the butter or margarine and sugar together until light and fluffy. Gradually beat the eggs into the sugar and butter mixture a little at a time until all the egg has been added. Sift the flour and gently fold in with a metal spoon or rubber spatula. Spoon into the base of the prepared cake tin. Arrange the apple pieces on top.

Lightly stir the milk into the crumble mixture. Scatter the crumble mixture over the apples and bake in the preheated oven for 1½ hours. Serve cold with cream or custard.

## Difficulty Rating: 3 points

# Apple & Cinnamon Brown Betty

## Serves 2

### Ingredients

450 g/1 lb cooking apples, peeled, cored and sliced

50 g/2 oz/¼ cup caster/superfine sugar

finely grated zest of 1 lemon

125 g/4 oz/2¾ cups fresh white breadcrumbs

125 g/4 oz/⅔ cup Demerara/turbinado sugar

½ tsp ground cinnamon

25 g/1 oz/¼ stick butter

### For the custard:

3 egg yolks

1 tbsp caster/superfine sugar

500 ml/18 fl oz/2½ cups milk

1 tbsp cornflour/cornstarch

few drops vanilla extract

Preheat the oven to 180°C/350°F/Gas Mark 4. Lightly oil a 900 ml/1½ pint/1 scant quart ovenproof dish. Place the apples in a saucepan with the caster/superfine sugar, lemon zest and 2 tablespoons water. Simmer for 10–15 minutes until soft.

Mix the breadcrumbs with the sugar and the cinnamon. Place half the sweetened apples in the base of the prepared dish and spoon over half of the crumb mixture. Place the remaining apples on top and cover with the rest of the crumb mixture. Melt the butter and pour over the surface of the dessert. Cover the dish with nonstick baking parchment and bake in the preheated oven for 20 minutes. Remove the paper and bake for a further 10–15 minutes, or until golden.

Meanwhile, make the custard by whisking the egg yolks and sugar together until creamy. Mix 1 tablespoon of the milk with the cornflour/cornstarch until a paste forms and reserve. Warm the rest of the milk until nearly boiling and pour over the egg mixture with the paste and vanilla extract. Place the bowl over a saucepan of gently simmering water. Stir over the heat until the custard is thickened and can coat the back of a spoon. Strain into a jug and serve hot, poured over the dessert.

## Difficulty Rating: 4 points

# Eve's Pudding

## Serves 6

**Ingredients**

450 g/1 lb cooking apples
175 g/6 oz/1½ cups blackberries
75 g/3 oz/⅓ cup demerara/turbinado sugar
grated zest of 1 lemon
125 g/4 oz/⅔ cup caster/superfine sugar
125 g/4 oz/1 stick plus 1 tbsp butter
few drops vanilla extract
2 eggs, beaten
125 g/4 oz/1 cup self-raising flour
1 tbsp icing/confectioners' sugar
ready-made custard, to serve

Preheat the oven to 180°C/350°F/Gas Mark 4. Oil a 1.2 litre/2 pint/1¼ quart baking dish. Peel, core and slice the apples and place a layer in the base of the prepared dish. Sprinkle over some of the blackberries, a little demerara/turbinado sugar and lemon zest. Continue to layer the apple and blackberries in this way until all the ingredients have been used.

Cream the sugar and butter together until light and fluffy. Beat in the vanilla extract and then the eggs, a little at a time, adding a spoonful of flour after each addition. Fold in the extra flour with a metal spoon or rubber spatula and mix well.

Spread the sponge mixture over the top of the fruit and level with the back of a spoon. Place the dish on a baking sheet and bake in the preheated oven for 35–40 minutes, or until well risen and golden brown. To test if the pudding is cooked, press the cooked sponge lightly with a clean finger – if it springs back, the sponge is cooked. Dust the pudding with a little icing/confectioners' sugar and serve immediately with custard.

## Difficulty Rating: 1 point

# Apricot & Almond Slice

## Cuts into 10 slices

### Ingredients

2 tbsp demerara/turbinado sugar

25 g/1 oz/¼ cup flaked/slivered almonds

400 g/14 oz can apricot halves, drained

225 g/8 oz/2 sticks butter, softened

225 g/8 oz/1 heaped cup caster/superfine sugar

4 eggs

200 g/7 oz/1½ cups self-raising flour

25 g/1 oz/¼ cup ground almonds

½ tsp almond extract

50 g/2 oz/⅓ cup ready-to-eat dried apricots, chopped

3 tbsp clear honey

3 tbsp chopped almonds, toasted

Preheat the oven to 180°C/350°F/Gas Mark 4. Oil a 20.5 cm/ 8 inch square cake tin/pan and line with nonstick baking parchment. Sprinkle the sugar and the flaked/slivered almonds over the paper, then arrange the apricot halves cut–side down on top.

Cream the butter and sugar together in a large bowl until light and fluffy. Gradually beat the eggs into the butter mixture, adding a spoonful of flour after each addition of egg. When all the eggs have been added, stir in the remaining flour and the ground almonds and mix thoroughly. Add the almond extract and the dried apricots and stir well. Spoon the mixture into the prepared tin, taking care not to dislodge the apricot halves. Bake in the preheated oven for 1 hour, or until golden and firm to touch.

Remove from the oven and allow to cool slightly for 15–20 minutes. Turn out carefully, discard the lining paper and transfer to a serving dish. Pour the honey over the top of the cake, sprinkle on the toasted almonds and serve.

## Difficulty Rating: 1 point

# Lemon & Apricot Pudding

## Serves 4

**Ingredients**

125 g/4 oz/1 cup dried apricots

3 tbsp orange juice, warmed

50 g/2 oz/½ stick butter

125 g/4 oz/⅔ cup caster/superfine sugar

juice and grated zest of 2 lemons

2 eggs, separated

100 g/3½ oz/1 scant cup self-raising flour

300 ml/½ pint/1¼ cups milk

custard or fresh cream, to serve

Preheat the oven to 180°C/350°F/Gas Mark 4. Oil a 1.2 litre/2 pint/1¼ quart pie dish. Soak the apricots in the orange juice for 10–15 minutes, or until most of the juice has been absorbed, then place in the base of the pie dish.

Cream the butter and sugar together with the lemon zest until light and fluffy. Beat the egg yolks into the creamed mixture with a spoonful of flour after each addition. Add the remaining flour and beat well until smooth. Stir the milk and lemon juice into the creamed mixture.

Whisk the egg whites in a grease–free mixing bowl until stiff and standing in peaks. Fold into the mixture using a metal spoon or rubber spatula. Pour into the prepared dish and place in a baking tray filled with enough cold water to come halfway up the sides of the dish.

Bake in the preheated oven for about 45 minutes, or until the sponge is firm and golden brown. Remove from the oven. Serve immediately with the custard or fresh cream.

## Difficulty Rating: 2 points

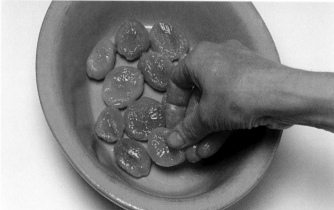

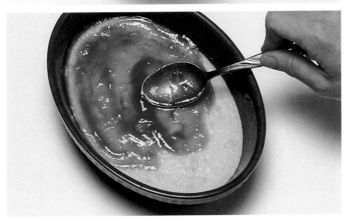

# Queen of Puddings

## Serves 4

**Ingredients**

75 g/3 oz/1²/₃ cups fresh white breadcrumbs

2 tbsp granulated sugar

450 ml/³/₄ pt/1³/₄ cups whole milk

25 g/1 oz/¹/₄ stick butter

grated zest of 1 small lemon

2 medium/large eggs, separated

2 tbsp seedless raspberry jam/jelly

50 g/2 oz/¹/₄ cup caster/superfine sugar

Preheat the oven to 170°C/325°F/Gas Mark 3. Oil a 900 ml/1¹/₂ pint/1 scant quart ovenproof baking dish and reserve. Mix the breadcrumbs and sugar together in a bowl.

Pour the milk into a small saucepan and heat gently with the butter and lemon zest until the butter has melted. Allow the mixture to cool a little, then pour over the breadcrumbs. Stir well and leave to soak for 30 minutes.

Whisk the egg yolks into the cooled breadcrumb mixture and pour into the prepared dish. Place the dish on a baking sheet and bake in the preheated oven for about 30 minutes, or until firm and set. Remove from the oven. Allow to cool slightly, then spread the jam/jelly over the pudding.

Whisk the egg whites until stiff and standing in peaks. Gently fold in the caster/superfine sugar with a metal spoon or rubber spatula. Pile the meringue over the top of the pudding. Return the dish to the oven for a further 25–30 minutes, or until the meringue is crisp and just slightly coloured. Serve hot or cold.

## Difficulty Rating: 3 points

# Baked Apple Dumplings

## Serves 4

**Ingredients**

225 g/8 oz/1¾ cups self-raising flour
¼ tsp salt
125 g/4 oz/1 cup shredded suet
4 medium cooking apples
4–6 tsp luxury mincemeat/mince pie filling
1 medium/large egg white, beaten
2 tsp caster/superfine sugar
custard or vanilla sauce, to serve

Preheat the oven to 200°C/400°F/Gas Mark 6. Lightly oil a baking tray. Place the flour and salt in a bowl and stir in the suet. Add just enough water to the mixture to mix to a soft but not sticky dough, using the fingertips.

Turn the dough onto a lightly floured board and knead lightly into a ball. Divide the dough into four pieces and roll out each piece into a thin square, large enough to encase the apples.

Peel and core the apples and place an apple in the centre of each square of dough. Fill the centre of each apple with mincemeat/mince pie filling, brush the edges of the pastry squares with water and draw the corners up to meet over each apple. Press the edges of the dough firmly together and decorate with leaves and shapes made from the extra dough trimmings.

Place the apples on the prepared baking tray, brush with the egg white and sprinkle with the sugar. Bake in the preheated oven for 30 minutes, or until golden and the pastry and apples are cooked. Serve the dumplings hot with the custard or vanilla sauce.

## Difficulty Rating: 2 points

# Jam Roly Poly

## Serves 4

### Ingredients

225 g/8 oz/1³⁄₄ cups self-raising flour

¹⁄₄ tsp salt

125 g/4 oz/1 cup shredded suet

about 150 ml/¹⁄₄ pint/²⁄₃ cup water

3 tbsp strawberry jam/jelly

1 tbsp milk, to glaze

1 tsp caster/superfine sugar

ready-made jam/jelly sauce, to serve

Preheat the oven to 200°C/400°F/Gas Mark 6. Make the pastry by sifting the flour and salt into a large bowl. Add the suet and mix lightly, then add the water a little at a time and mix to form a soft and pliable dough. (Take care not to make the dough too wet.)

Turn the dough out onto a lightly floured board and knead gently until smooth. Roll the dough out into a 23 x 28 cm/9 x 11 inch rectangle.

Spread the jam/jelly over the dough, leaving a border of 1 cm/¹⁄₂ inch all round. Fold the border over the jam and brush the edges with water. Lightly roll the rectangle up from one of the short sides, seal the top edge and press the ends together. (Do not roll the pudding up too tightly.)

Turn the pudding upside down onto a large piece of greaseproof/ waxed paper large enough to come halfway up the sides. (If not using nonstick paper, then oil lightly.) Tie the ends of the paper to make a boat-shaped paper case for the pudding to sit in, leaving plenty of room for the roly poly to expand.

Brush the pudding lightly with milk and sprinkle with the sugar. Bake in the preheated oven for 30–40 minutes, or until well risen and golden. Serve immediately with the jam sauce.

## Difficulty Rating: 2 points

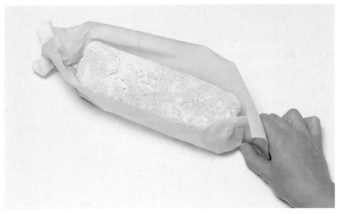

# Chocolate Sponge Pudding with Fudge Sauce

## Serves 4

### Ingredients

75 g/3 oz/²⁄₃ stick butter

75 g/3 oz/¹⁄₃ cup caster/superfine sugar

50 g/2 oz/2 squares dark/bittersweet chocolate, melted

50 g/2 oz/¹⁄₃ cup self-raising flour

25 g/1 oz/¹⁄₃ cup drinking chocolate/sweetened cocoa powder

1 large/extra-large egg

1 tbsp icing/confectioners' sugar, for dusting

crème fraîche/sour cream, to serve

### For the fudge sauce:

50 g/2 oz/¹⁄₄ cup soft light brown sugar

1 tbsp cocoa powder (unsweetened)

40 g/1¹⁄₂ oz/¹⁄₃ cup pecan nuts, roughly chopped

2 tbsp caster/superfine sugar

300 ml/¹⁄₂ pint/1¹⁄₄ cups hot, strong black coffee

Preheat the oven to 170°C/325°F/Gas Mark 3. Oil a 900 ml/1¹⁄₂ pint/1 quart pie dish. Cream the butter and sugar together in a large bowl until light and fluffy. Stir in the melted chocolate, flour, drinking chocolate and egg and mix together. Turn the mixture into the prepared dish and level the surface.

To make the fudge sauce, blend the brown sugar, cocoa powder and pecan nuts together and sprinkle evenly over the top of the pudding.

Stir the caster/superfine sugar into the hot black coffee until it has dissolved. Carefully pour the coffee over the top of the pudding. Bake in the preheated oven for 50–60 minutes until the top is firm to the touch.

There will now be a rich sauce underneath the sponge. Remove from the oven, dust with icing/confectioners' sugar and serve hot with crème fraîche/sour cream.

## Difficulty Rating: 2 points

# Golden Castle Pudding

## Serves 4–6

**Ingredients**

125 g/4 oz/1 stick plus 1 tbsp butter
125 g/4 oz/²/₃ cup caster/superfine sugar
few drops vanilla extract
2 medium/large eggs, beaten
125 g/4 oz/1 cup self-raising flour
4 tbsp golden/corn syrup
crème fraîche/sour cream or ready-made custard, to serve

Preheat the oven to 180°C/350°F/Gas Mark 4. Lightly oil four to six individual pudding bowls and place a small circle of lightly oiled greaseproof/waxed paper or baking parchment in the base of each one.

Place the butter and caster/superfine sugar in a large bowl, then beat together until the mixture is pale and creamy. Stir in the vanilla extract and gradually add the beaten eggs, a little at a time. Add a tablespoon of flour after each addition of egg and beat well.

When the mixture is smooth, add the remaining flour and fold in gently. Add a tablespoon of water and mix to form a soft mixture that will drop easily off a spoon.

Spoon enough mixture into each basin to come halfway up, allowing enough space for the puddings to rise. Place on a baking sheet and bake in the preheated oven for about 25 minutes until firm and golden brown.

Allow the puddings to stand for 5 minutes. Discard the paper circle and turn out onto individual serving plates.

Warm the golden/corn syrup in a small saucepan and pour a little over each pudding. Serve hot with the crème fraîche/sour cream or custard.

## Difficulty Rating: 1 point

# College Pudding

## Serves 4

**Ingredients**

125 g/4 oz/1 cup shredded suet
125 g/4 oz/2¾ cups fresh white breadcrumbs
50 g/2 oz/⅓ cup sultanas/golden raisins
50 g/2 oz/⅓ cup seedless raisins
½ tsp ground cinnamon
¼ tsp freshly grated nutmeg
¼ tsp mixed/pumpkin pie spice
50 g/2 oz/¼ cup caster/superfine sugar
½ tsp baking powder
2 medium/large eggs, beaten
orange zest, to decorate

Preheat the oven to 180°C/350°F/Gas Mark 4. Lightly oil an ovenproof 900 ml/1½ pint/1 scant quart ovenproof pudding basin and place a small circle of greaseproof/waxed paper in the base.

Mix the shredded suet and breadcrumbs together and rub lightly together with the fingertips to remove any lumps. Stir in the dried fruit, spices, sugar and baking powder. Add the eggs and beat lightly together until the mixture is well blended and the fruit is evenly distributed.

Spoon the mixture into the prepared pudding basin and level the surface. Place on a baking sheet and cover lightly with some greaseproof/waxed paper. Bake in the preheated oven for 20 minutes, then remove the paper and continue to bake for a further 10–15 minutes, or until the top is firm.

When the pudding is cooked, remove from the oven and carefully turn out onto a warmed serving dish. Decorate with the orange zest and serve immediately.

## Difficulty Rating: 1 point

# Chocolate Profiteroles

## Serves 4

### Ingredients

**For the pastry:**
150 ml/¼ pint/⅔ cup water
50 g/2 oz/½ stick butter
65 g/2½ oz/½ cup plain/all-purpose flour, sifted
2 eggs, lightly beaten

**For the custard:**
300 ml/½ pint/1¼ cups milk
pinch freshly grated nutmeg
3 egg yolks
50 g/2 oz/¼ cup caster/superfine sugar
2 tbsp plain/all-purpose flour, sifted
2 tbsp cornflour/cornstarch, sifted

**For the sauce:**
175 g/6 oz/1 scant cup soft brown sugar
150 ml/¼ pint/⅔ cup boiling water
1 tsp instant coffee
1 tbsp cocoa powder (unsweetened)
1 tbsp brandy
75 g/3 oz/⅔ stick butter
1 tbsp golden/corn syrup

Preheat the oven to 220°C/425°F/Gas Mark 7, 15 minutes before baking. Lightly oil two baking sheets. For the pastry, place the water and the butter in a heavy-based saucepan and bring to the boil. Remove from the heat and beat in the flour. Return to the heat and cook for 1 minute, or until the mixture forms a ball in the centre of the saucepan. Remove from the heat and leave to cool slightly, then gradually beat in the eggs a little at a time, beating well after each addition. Once all the eggs have been added, beat until the paste is smooth and glossy.

Pipe or spoon the dough in 20 small balls onto the baking sheets, allowing plenty of room for expansion. Bake in the preheated oven for 25 minutes, or until well risen and golden brown. Reduce the oven temperature to 180°C/350°F/Gas Mark 4. Make a hole in each ball and continue to bake for a further 5 minutes. Remove from the oven and leave to cool.

For the custard, place the milk and nutmeg in a heavy-based saucepan and bring to the boil. In another saucepan, whisk together the egg yolks, sugar and flours, then beat in the hot milk. Bring to the boil and simmer, whisking constantly, for 2 minutes. Cover and leave to cool. Spoon the custard into the profiteroles and arrange on a serving dish. Place all the sauce ingredients in a small saucepan and bring to the boil, then simmer for 10 minutes. Cool slightly before serving with the profiteroles.

## Difficulty Rating: 4 points

# Savoury Pastry & Pizzas

Let's not forget the wonderfully tasty savoury dishes that can be made using dough and pastry, from moreish Smoked Mackerel Vol-au-Vents and rich Luxury Fish Pasties to hearty Beef & Red Wine Pie and fragrant Tomato & Courgette Herb Tart. Making pizza from scratch can be very rewarding – try Roquefort, Parma & Rocket Pizza.

# Smoked Mackerel Vol-au-vents

## Serves 1–2

**Ingredients**

350 g/12 oz prepared puff pastry dough

1 small egg, beaten

2 tsp sesame seeds

225 g/8 oz peppered smoked mackerel, skinned and chopped

5 cm/2 inch piece cucumber

4 tbsp soft cream cheese

2 tbsp cranberry sauce

1 tbsp freshly chopped dill

1 tbsp finely grated lemon zest

dill sprigs, to garnish

mixed salad leaves, to serve

Preheat the oven to 230°C/450°F/Gas Mark 8, 15 minutes before baking. Roll the pastry dough out on a lightly floured surface and, using a 9 cm/3½ inch fluted cutter, cut out 12 rounds.

Using a 1 cm/½ inch cutter, mark a lid in the centre of each round. Place on a damp baking sheet and brush the rounds with a little beaten egg. Sprinkle the dough with the sesame seeds and bake in the preheated oven for 10–12 minutes, or until golden brown and well risen.

Transfer the vol-au-vents to a chopping board and, when cool enough to touch, carefully remove the lids with a small sharp knife. Scoop out any uncooked pastry from the inside of each vol-au-vent, then return to the oven for 5–8 minutes to dry out. Remove and allow to cool.

Flake the mackerel into small pieces and reserve. Peel the cucumber, if desired, cut into very small cubes and add to the mackerel. Beat the soft cream cheese with the cranberry sauce, dill and lemon zest. Stir in the mackerel and cucumber and use to fill the vol-au-vents. Place the lids on top, garnish with dill sprigs and serve with mixed salad leaves.

## Difficulty Rating: 1 point

# Smoked Haddock Tart

## Serves 6

### Ingredients

**For the shortcrust pastry:**

150 g/5 oz/1 heaped cup plain/all-purpose flour

pinch salt

25 g/1 oz/2 tbsp lard or white vegetable fat/shortening,
  cut into small cubes

40 g/1½ oz/⅓ stick butter or hard margarine,
  cut into small cubes

**For the filling:**

225 g/8 oz/½ lb smoked haddock, skinned and cubed

2 large/extra-large eggs, beaten

300 ml/½ pint/1¼ cups double/heavy cream

1 tsp Dijon mustard

freshly ground black pepper

125 g/4 oz/1 heaped cup Gruyère/hard Swiss cheese, grated

1 tbsp freshly snipped chives

**To serve:**

lemon wedges

tomato wedges

fresh green salad leaves

Preheat the oven to 190°C/375°F/Gas Mark 5, 10 minutes before baking. Sift the flour and salt into a large bowl. Add the fats and mix lightly. With the fingertips, rub into the flour until the mixture resembles breadcrumbs. Sprinkle 1 tablespoon cold water into the mixture. With a knife, start bringing the dough together, using your hands if necessary. If the dough does not form a ball instantly, add a little more water.

Put the dough in a polythene/plastic bag and chill for at least 30 minutes. On a lightly floured surface, roll out the dough and use to line an 18 cm/7 inch lightly oiled quiche or flan tin/tart pan. Prick the base all over with a fork and bake blind in the preheated oven for 15 minutes. Carefully remove the pastry from the oven and brush with a little of the beaten egg. Return to the oven for a further 5 minutes, then place the fish in the pastry case/pie crust. For the filling, beat together the eggs and cream. Add the mustard, black pepper and cheese and pour

over the fish. Sprinkle with the chives and bake for 35–40 minutes until the filling is golden brown and set in the centre. Serve hot or cold with the lemon and tomato wedges and salad leaves.

## Difficulty Rating: 2 points

# Russian Fish Pie

## Serves 4–6

### Ingredients

450 g/1 lb orange roughy or haddock fillet

150 ml/¼ pint/⅔ cup dry white wine

salt and freshly ground black pepper

75 g/3 oz/¾ stick butter or margarine

1 large onion, peeled and finely chopped

75 g/3 oz/½ cup long-grain rice

1 tbsp freshly chopped dill

125 g/4 oz/1⅓ cups button/white mushrooms, quartered

125 g/4 oz/¾ cup peeled prawns/shrimp, thawed if frozen

3 eggs, hard-boiled and chopped

550 g/1¼ lb ready-prepared puff pastry dough, thawed if frozen

1 small egg, beaten with a little salt

assorted bitter salad leaves, to serve

Preheat the oven to 200°C/400°F/Gas Mark 6, 15 minutes before baking. Place the fish in a shallow frying pan with the wine, 150 ml/¼ pint/⅔ cup water and salt and pepper. Simmer for 8–10 minutes. Strain the fish, reserving the liquid, and, when cool enough to handle, flake into a bowl.

Melt the butter or margarine in a saucepan and cook the onion for 2–3 minutes, then add the rice, reserved fish liquid and dill. Season lightly. Cover and simmer for 10 minutes, then stir in the mushrooms and cook for a further 10 minutes, or until all the liquid is absorbed. Mix the rice with the cooked fish, prawns/shrimp and eggs. Leave to cool.

Roll half the pastry dough out on a lightly floured surface into a 23 x 30 cm/9 x 12 inch rectangle. Place on a dampened baking sheet and arrange the fish mixture on top, leaving a 1 cm/½ inch border. Brush the border with a little water. Roll out the remaining dough to a rectangle and use to cover the fish. Brush the edges lightly with a little of the beaten egg and press to seal. Roll out the dough trimmings and use to decorate the top. Chill in the refrigerator for 30 minutes. Brush with the beaten egg and bake for 30 minutes, or until golden. Serve immediately with salad leaves.

## Difficulty Rating: 2 points

# Salmon & Filo Parcels

## Serves 4

### Ingredients

1 tbsp sunflower/corn oil

1 bunch spring onions/scallions, trimmed and finely chopped

1 tsp paprika

175 g/6 oz/1 cup long-grain white rice

300 ml/¹/₂ pint/1¹/₄ cups fish stock

salt and freshly ground black pepper

450 g/1 lb salmon fillet, cubed

1 tbsp freshly chopped parsley

grated zest and juice of 1 lemon

150 g/5 oz/1¹/₄ cups rocket/arugula

150 g/5 oz/¹/₄ lb spinach

12 sheets filo/phyllo pastry dough

50 g/2 oz/¹/₂ stick butter, melted

Preheat the oven to 200°C/400°F/Gas Mark 6, 15 minutes before baking. Heat the oil in a small frying pan. Gently cook the spring onions/scallions for 2 minutes. Stir in the paprika, cook for 1 minute. Remove from the heat and reserve.

Put the rice in a sieve, rinse under cold running water until the water runs clear and drain. Put the rice and stock in a saucepan, bring to the boil, then cover and simmer for 10 minutes, or until the liquid is absorbed and the rice is tender. Add the spring onion mixture and fork through. Season to taste with salt and pepper, then leave to cool.

In a nonmetallic bowl, mix together the salmon, parsley, lemon zest and juice and salt and pepper. Mix well and reserve. Blanch the rocket/arugula and spinach for 30 seconds in a large saucepan of boiling water until just wilted. Drain well in a colander and refresh in plenty of cold water, then squeeze out as much moisture as possible.

Brush three sheets of filo/phyllo pastry dough with melted butter and lay them on top of one another. Take a quarter of the rice mixture and arrange it in an oblong in the centre. On top of this, place a quarter of the salmon followed by a quarter of the rocket and spinach. Draw up the dough around the filling and twist at the top to create a parcel. Repeat with the

remaining dough and filling until you have four parcels. Brush with the remaining butter. Place the parcels on a lightly oiled baking sheet and cook in the preheated oven for 20 minutes, or until golden brown and cooked. Serve immediately.

## Difficulty Rating: 3 points

# Smoked Salmon Quiche

## Serves 6 (Pictured page 246)

**Ingredients**

225 g/8 oz/2 cups plain/all-purpose flour

50 g/2 oz/½ stick butter

50 g/2 oz/4 tbsp white vegetable fat/shortening or lard

2 tsp sunflower/corn oil

2 potatoes, peeled and diced

125 g/4 oz/1¼ cups Gruyère/hard Swiss cheese, grated

75 g/3 oz smoked salmon trimmings

5 eggs, beaten

300 ml/½ pint/⅔ cup single/light cream

salt and freshly ground black pepper

1 tbsp freshly chopped flat-leaf/Italian parsley

**To serve:**
mixed salad
baby new potatoes

Preheat the oven to 200°C/400°F/Gas Mark 6, 15 minutes beofre baking. Blend the flour, butter and white vegetable fat/shortening or lard together until it resembles fine breadcrumbs. Blend again, adding sufficient water to make a firm but pliable dough. Use the pastry dough to line a 23 cm/9 inch flan dish or tin/tart pan, then chill the pastry case/pie crust in the refrigerator for 30 minutes. Bake blind with baking beans/pie weights for 10 minutes.

Heat the oil in a small frying pan, add the diced potato and cook for 3–4 minutes until lightly browned. Reduce the heat and cook for 2–3 minutes, or until tender. Leave to cool.

Scatter the grated cheese evenly over the base of the pastry case, then arrange the cooled potato on top. Add the smoked salmon in an even layer.

Beat the eggs with the cream and season to taste with salt and pepper. Whisk in the parsley and pour the mixture carefully into the dish. Reduce the oven to 180°C/350°F/Gas Mark 4 and bake for about 30–40 minutes, or until the filling is set and golden. Serve hot or cold with a mixed salad and baby new potatoes.

## Difficulty Rating: 3 points

# Luxury Fish Pasties

## Makes 6

**Ingredients**

125 g/4 oz/1 stick plus 1 tbsp butter

125 g/4 oz/1 cup plain/all-purpose flour

300 ml/½ pint/1¼ cups milk

225 g/8 oz salmon fillet, skinned and cut into chunks

1 tbsp freshly chopped parsley

1 tbsp freshly chopped dill

grated zest and juice of 1 lime

225 g/8 oz (about 35–40 medium-sized) peeled prawns/shrimp

salt and freshly ground black pepper

2 quantities quick flaky pastry dough (see page 268), chilled

1 small egg, beaten

1 tsp sea salt

fresh green salad leaves, to serve

Preheat the oven to 200°C/400°F/Gas Mark 6, 15 minutes before baking. Place the butter in a saucepan and slowly heat until melted. Add the flour and cook, stirring, for 1 minute.

Remove from the heat and gradually add the milk a little at a time, stirring between each addition. Return to the heat and simmer, stirring continuously, until thickened.

Remove from the heat and add the salmon, parsley, dill, lime zest, lime juice, prawns/shrimp and seasoning.

Roll out the pastry dough on a lightly floured surface and cut out six 12.5 cm/5 inch circles and six 15 cm/6 inch circles. Brush the edges of the smallest circles with the beaten egg and place two tablespoons of filling in the centre of each one. Place the larger circles over the filling and press the edges together to seal. Pinch the edge of the pastry between the forefinger and thumb to ensure a firm seal and decorative edge.

Cut a slit in each parcel, brush with the beaten egg and sprinkle with sea salt. Transfer to a baking sheet and cook in the preheated oven for 20 minutes, or until golden brown. Serve immediately with some fresh green salad leaves.

## Difficulty Rating: 3 points

# Cornish Pasties

## Makes 8

### Ingredients

**For the pastry:**
350 g/12 oz/2³⁄₄ cups self-raising flour
75 g/3 oz/²⁄₃ stick butter or margarine
75 g/3 oz/¹⁄₃ cup lard or white vegetable fat/shortening
salt and freshly ground black pepper

**For the filling:**
550 g/1¹⁄₄ lb braising steak, very finely chopped
1 large onion, peeled and finely chopped
1 large potato, peeled and diced
200 g/7 oz/¹⁄₂ cup swede/rutabaga, peeled and diced
3 tbsp Worcestershire sauce
1 small egg, beaten, to glaze
salt and pepper

**To garnish:**
tomato slices or wedges
fresh parsley sprigs

Preheat the oven to 180°C/350°F/Gas Mark 4, about 15 minutes before baking. To make the pastry, sift the flour into a large bowl and add the fats, chopped into little pieces. Rub the fats and flour together until the mixture resembles coarse breadcrumbs. Season to taste with salt and pepper and mix again. Add about 2 tablespoons cold water, a little at a time, and mix until the mixture comes together to form a firm but pliable dough. Turn onto a lightly floured surface, knead until smooth, then wrap and chill in the refrigerator.

To make the filling, put the braising steak in a large bowl with the onion. Add the potato and swede/rutabaga to the bowl together with the Worcestershire sauce and salt and pepper. Mix well.

Divide the dough into eight balls and roll each ball into a circle about 25.5 cm/10 inches across. Divide the filling between the circles of pastry. Wet the edges of the pastry, then fold over the filling. Pinch the edges to seal. Transfer the pasties to a lightly oiled baking sheet. Make a couple of small holes in each pasty and brush with beaten egg. Cook in the preheated oven for 15 minutes, remove and brush again with the egg. Return to the oven for a further 15–20 minutes until golden. Cool slightly, garnish with tomato and parsley and serve.

## Difficulty Rating: 2 points

# Chilli Beef Calzone

## Serves 4

**Ingredients**

1 tbsp sunflower/corn oil
1 onion, peeled and finely chopped
1 green pepper, deseeded and chopped
225 g/8 oz/1 cup minced/ground beef steak
420 g/15 oz can chilli beans
225 g/8 oz can chopped tomatoes
1 quantity pizza dough (*see* page 275)
mixed salad leaves, to serve

Preheat the oven to 220°C/425°F/Gas Mark 7, 15 minutes before baking. Heat the oil in a large saucepan and gently cook the onion and pepper for 5 minutes. Add the beef to the saucepan and cook for 10 minutes, or until browned.

Add the chilli beans and tomatoes and simmer gently for 30 minutes, or until the beef is tender. Place a baking sheet into the preheated oven to heat up.

Divide the pizza dough into four equal pieces. Cover three pieces of the dough with clingfilm/plastic wrap and roll out the other piece on a lightly floured board to a 20.5 cm/8 inch round.

Spoon a quarter of the chilli mixture onto half of the dough round and dampen the edges with a little water. Fold over the empty half of the dough and press the edges together well to seal.

Repeat this process with the remaining dough. Place on the hot baking sheet and bake for 15 minutes. Serve with the salad leaves.

## Difficulty Rating: 2 points

# Caribbean Empanadas

## Serves 4–6

**Ingredients**

175 g/6 oz/³/₄ cup lean fresh minced/ground beef
175 g/6 oz/³/₄ cup lean fresh minced/ground pork
1 onion, peeled and finely chopped
1 Scotch bonnet chilli, deseeded and finely chopped
1 small red pepper, deseeded and finely chopped
¹/₂ tsp ground cloves
1 tsp ground cinnamon
¹/₂ tsp ground allspice
1 tsp sugar
1 tbsp tomato purée/paste
6 tbsp water
700 g/1¹/₂ lb prepared shortcrust pastry dough
melted butter, for brushing, or vegetable oil, for deep-frying
fresh herbs, to garnish
ready-made mango relish, to serve

Preheat the oven to 200°C/400°F/Gas Mark 6, 15 minutes before baking. Place the beef and pork in a nonstick frying pan and cook, stirring, for 5–8 minutes, or until sealed. Break up any lumps with a wooden spoon. Add the onion, chilli and red pepper together with the spices and cook, stirring, for 10 minutes, or until the onion has softened. Sprinkle in the sugar.

Blend the tomato purée/paste with the water and stir into the meat. Bring to the boil, then reduce the heat and simmer for 10 minutes. Allow to cool.

Roll the pastry dough out on a lightly floured surface and cut into 10 cm/4 inch rounds. Place a spoonful of the meat mixture onto the centre of each pastry round and brush the edges with water. Fold over, encasing the filling to form small pasties. Brush with melted butter and bake in the preheated oven for 20 minutes.

Alternatively, heat the oil to 180°C/350°F and deep–fry the empanadas in batches, about three or four at a time, for 3–4 minutes, or until golden. Drain on absorbent paper towels. Garnish with herbs and serve with the mango relish.

## Difficulty Rating: 1 point

# Beef & Red Wine Pie

## Serves 4

### Ingredients

700 g/1½ lb stewing beef (chuck or round meat), cubed

4 tbsp seasoned plain/all-purpose flour

2 tbsp sunflower/corn oil

2 onions, peeled and chopped

2 garlic cloves, peeled and crushed

1 tbsp freshly chopped thyme

300 ml/½ pint/1¼ cups red wine

150 ml/¼ pint/⅔ cup beef stock

1–2 tsp Worcestershire sauce

2 tbsp tomato ketchup

2 bay leaves

knob butter

225 g/8 oz/2¼ cups button/white mushrooms

beaten egg or milk, to glaze

parsley sprig, to garnish

### For the quick flaky pastry:

125 g/4 oz/1 stick plus 1 tbsp butter

175 g/6 oz/1⅓ cups plain/all-purpose flour

pinch salt

Place the butter in the freezer for 30 minutes. Sift the flour and salt into a large bowl. Remove the butter from the freezer and grate using the coarse side of a grater, dipping the butter in the flour every now and again to make it easier to grate. Mix the butter into the flour using a palette knife, making sure all the butter is thoroughly coated with flour. Add 2 tablespoons cold water and continue to mix, bringing the mixture together. Use your hands to complete the mixing. Add a little more water if needed to leave a clean bowl. Place the dough in a plastic bag and chill in the refrigerator for 30 minutes.

Toss the beef cubes in the seasoned flour. Heat the oil in a large heavy-based frying pan. Fry the beef in batches for about 5 minutes until golden brown. Return all of the beef to the pan and add the onions, garlic and thyme. Fry for about 10 minutes, stirring occasionally. If the beef begins to stick, add a little water. Add the red wine and stock and bring to the boil. Stir in the Worcestershire sauce, tomato ketchup and bay leaves.

Cover and simmer on a very low heat for about 1 hour, or until the beef is tender.

Preheat the oven to 200°C/400°F/Gas Mark 6, 15 minutes before baking. Heat the butter and gently fry the mushrooms until golden brown. Add to the stew. Simmer, uncovered, for a further 15 minutes. Remove the bay leaves, spoon the beef into a 1.2 litre/2 pint/1¼ quart pie dish and reserve.

Roll out the dough on a lightly floured surface. Cut out the lid to 5 mm/¼ inch wider than the dish. Brush the rim with the beaten egg and lay the dough lid on top. Press to seal, then knock the edges with the back of a knife. Cut a slit in the lid and brush with the beaten egg or milk to glaze. Bake the pie in the preheated oven for 30 minutes, or until it turns golden brown. Garnish with the parsley sprig and serve immediately.

## Difficulty Rating: 3 points

# Lamb & Pasta Pie

Serves 8

**Ingredients**

400 g/14 oz/3 heaped cups plain white/all-purpose flour

100 g/3½ oz/½ stick/scant ½ cup margarine

100 g/3½ oz/scant ½ cup white vegetable fat/shortening

pinch salt

1 small egg, separated

50 g/2 oz/½ stick butter

50 g/2 oz/1 scant cup flour

450 ml/¾ pint/1¾ cups milk

salt and freshly ground black pepper

225 g/8 oz/2 heaped cups macaroni

50 g/2 oz/½ cup Cheddar cheese, grated

1 tbsp vegetable oil

1 onion, peeled and chopped

1 garlic clove, peeled and crushed

2 celery stalks, trimmed and chopped

450 g/1 lb/2 cups minced/ground lamb

1 tbsp tomato purée/paste

400 g/14 oz can chopped tomatoes

Preheat the oven to 190°C/375°F/Gas Mark 5, 10 minutes before baking. Lightly oil a 20.5 cm/8 inch springform cake tin/pan. Blend the flour, salt, margarine and white vegetable fat in a food processor and add sufficient cold water to make a smooth, pliable dough. Knead on a lightly floured surface, then roll out two thirds to line the base and sides of the tin. Brush the pastry with egg white and reserve.

Melt the butter in a heavy-based pan, stir in the flour and cook for 2 minutes. Stir in the milk and cook, stirring, until a smooth, thick sauce is formed. Season to taste with salt and pepper and reserve.

Bring a large pan of lightly salted water to a rolling boil. Add the macaroni and cook according to the packet instructions, or until *al dente*. Drain, then stir into the white sauce with the grated cheese.

Heat the oil in a frying pan, add the onion, garlic, celery and lamb and cook, stirring, for 5–6 minutes. Stir in the tomato paste and tomatoes and cook for 10 minutes. Cool slightly.

Place half the pasta mixture, then all the mince, in the pastry-lined tin. Top with a layer of pasta. Roll out the remaining pastry dough and cut out a lid. Brush the edge with water, place over the filling and pinch the edges together. Use trimmings to decorate the top of the pie. Brush the pie with beaten egg yolk and bake in the preheated oven for 50–60 minutes, covering the top with kitchen foil if browning too quickly. Stand for 15 minutes before turning out. Serve immediately.

## Difficulty Rating: 4 points

# Moroccan Lamb with Apricots

## Serves 6

### Ingredients

5 cm/2 inch piece root ginger, peeled and grated

3 garlic cloves, peeled and crushed

1 tsp ground cardamom

1 tsp ground cumin

2 tbsp olive oil

450 g/1 lb lamb neck fillet, cubed

1 large red onion, peeled and chopped

400 g/14 oz can chopped tomatoes

125 g/4 oz/1 cup ready-to-eat dried apricots

400 g/14 oz can chickpeas, drained

7 large sheets filo/phyllo pastry dough

50 g/2 oz/¹⁄₂ stick butter, melted

pinch nutmeg

dill sprigs, to garnish

Preheat the oven to 190°C/375°F/Gas Mark 5, 10 minutes before baking. Pound the ginger, garlic, cardamom and cumin to a paste with a pestle and mortar. Heat 1 tablespoon of the oil in a large frying pan and fry the spice paste for 3 minutes. Remove and reserve.

Add the remaining oil and fry the lamb in batches for about 5 minutes, or until golden brown. Return all the lamb to the pan and add the onions and spice paste. Fry for 10 minutes, stirring occasionally. Add the chopped tomatoes, cover and simmer for 15 minutes. Add the apricots and chickpeas and simmer for a further 15 minutes.

Lightly oil a round 18 cm/7 inch springform cake tin/pan. Lay one sheet of filo/phyllo pastry dough in the base of the tin, allowing the excess to fall over the sides. Brush with melted butter, then layer five more sheets in the tin and brush each one with butter. Spoon in the filling and level the surface. Layer half the remaining filo sheets on top, again brushing each with butter. Fold the overhanging pastry over the top of the filling. Brush the remaining sheet with butter and scrunch up and place on top of the pie so that the whole pie is completely covered.

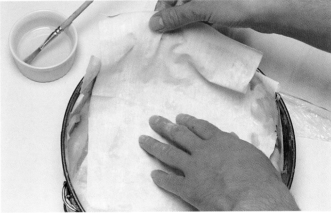

Brush with melted butter once more. Bake in the preheated oven for 45 minutes, then reserve for 10 minutes. Unclip the tin and remove the pie. Sprinkle with the nutmeg, garnish with the dill sprigs and serve.

## Difficulty Rating: 2 points

# Bacon, Mushroom & Cheese Puffs

## Serves 4

### Ingredients

1 tbsp olive oil

225 g/8 oz/2½ cups field mushrooms,
    wiped and roughly chopped

225 g/8 oz/½ lb rindless streaky bacon, roughly chopped

2 tbsp freshly chopped parsley

salt and freshly ground black pepper

350 g/12 oz/¾ lb ready-rolled puff pastry dough sheet,
    thawed if frozen

25 g/1 oz/¼ cup Emmenthal/Swiss cheese, grated

1 egg, beaten

rocket/arugula or watercress, to garnish

tomatoes, to serve

Preheat the oven to 200°C/400°F/Gas Mark 6, 15 minutes before baking. Heat the olive oil in a large frying pan. Add the mushrooms and bacon and fry for 6–8 minutes until golden in colour. Stir in the parsley, season to taste with salt and pepper and allow to cool.

Roll the sheet of pastry dough a little thinner on a lightly floured surface until you have a 30.5 cm/12 inch square. Cut the dough into four equal squares.

Stir the grated cheese into the mushroom mixture. Spoon a quarter of the mixture onto one half of each square. Brush the edges of each square with a little of the beaten egg. Fold over the dough to form triangular parcels. Seal the edges well and place on a lightly oiled baking sheet. Make shallow slashes in the tops of the parcels with a knife and brush with the remaining beaten egg. Cook in the preheated oven for 20 minutes, or until puffy and golden brown.

Serve warm or cold, garnished with the rocket/arugula or watercress and served with tomatoes.

## Difficulty Rating: 1 point

# Sauvignon Chicken & Mushroom Filo Pie

## Serves 4

### Ingredients

1 onion, peeled and chopped

1 leek, trimmed and chopped

250 ml/8 fl oz/1 cup chicken stock

3 skinless chicken breast fillets/halves, 175 g/6 oz each

150 ml/¼ pint/⅔ cup dry white wine

1 bay leaf

175 g/6 oz/2½ cups button/white mushrooms

2 tbsp plain/all-purpose flour

1 tbsp freshly chopped tarragon

salt and freshly ground black pepper

fresh parsley sprig, to garnish

seasonal vegetables, to serve

### For the topping:

5–6 sheets filo/phyllo pastry dough

1 tbsp sunflower/corn oil

1 tsp sesame seeds

Preheat the oven to 190°C/375°F/Gas Mark 5, 10 minutes before baking. Put the onion and leek in a heavy-based saucepan with 125 ml/4 fl oz/½ cup of the stock. Bring to the boil, cover and simmer for 5 minutes, then uncover and cook until all the stock has evaporated and the vegetables are tender.

Cut the chicken into bite-size cubes. Add to the pan with the remaining stock, the wine and bay leaf. Cover and gently simmer for 5 minutes. Add the mushrooms and simmer for a further 5 minutes.

Blend the flour with 3 tablespoons cold water. Stir into the pan and cook, stirring all the time, until the sauce has thickened. Stir the tarragon into the sauce and season with salt and pepper. Spoon the mixture into a 1.2 litre/2 pint/1¼ quart pie dish, discarding the bay leaf.

Lightly brush a sheet of filo/phyllo pastry dough with a little of the oil. Crumple the pastry slightly. Arrange on top of the filling. Repeat with the remaining pastry sheets and oil. Sprinkle the top of the pie with sesame seeds. Bake the pie on the centre shelf of the preheated oven for 20 minutes until the pastry topping is golden and crisp. Garnish with a sprig of parsley. Serve the pie with the seasonal vegetables.

## Difficulty Rating: 2 points

# Chicken & Ham Pie

## Serves 6

### Ingredients

1 tbsp olive oil

1 leek, trimmed and sliced

175 g/6 oz piece bacon, cut into small cubes

225 g/8 oz/2½ cups cooked boneless chicken meat

2 avocados, peeled, pitted and chopped

1 tbsp lemon juice

salt and freshly ground black pepper

2 quantities shortcrust pastry dough (see page 22)

2 large/extra-large eggs, beaten

150 ml/¼ pint/⅔ cup natural/plain yogurt

4 tbsp chicken stock

1 tbsp poppy seeds

**To serve:**

sliced red onion

mixed salad leaves

Preheat the oven to 200°C/400°F/Gas Mark 6, 15 minutes before baking. Heat the oil in a frying pan and fry the leek and bacon for 4 minutes until soft but not coloured. Transfer to a bowl and reserve. Cut the chicken into bite-size pieces and add to the leek and bacon. Toss the avocados in the lemon juice, add to the chicken and season to taste with salt and pepper.

Roll out half the dough on a lightly floured surface and use to line an 18 cm/7 inch loose-bottomed deep flan tin/tart pan. Scoop the chicken mixture into the pastry case/pie crust. Mix together 1 egg, the yogurt and the chicken stock. Pour over the chicken.

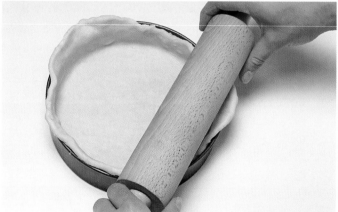

Roll out the remaining dough on a lightly floured surface and cut out the lid to 5 mm/¼ inch wider than the dish. Brush the pie edge with the remaining beaten egg and lay the dough lid on top, pressing to seal. Knock the edges with the back of a knife to seal further. Cut a slit in the lid and brush with the egg. Sprinkle with the poppy seeds and bake in the preheated oven for about 30 minutes, or until the pastry is golden brown. Serve with the sliced onion and mixed salad leaves.

## Difficulty Rating: 3 points

# Leek & Potato Tart

## Serves 6

**Ingredients**

225 g/8 oz/1³/₄ cups plain/all-purpose flour
pinch salt
150 g/5 oz/1¹/₃ sticks butter, cubed
50 g/2 oz/¹/₂ cup walnuts, very finely chopped
1 large/extra-large egg yolk

**For the filling:**
450 g/1 lb leeks, trimmed and thinly sliced
40 g/1¹/₂ oz/¹/₃ stick butter
450 g/1 lb large new potatoes, scrubbed
300 ml/¹/₂ pint/1¹/₄ cups sour cream; 3 eggs, lightly beaten
175 g/6 oz/1¹/₂ cups grated Gruyère/hard Swiss cheese
freshly grated nutmeg; salt and freshly ground black pepper
fresh chives, to garnish

Preheat the oven to 200°C/400°F/Gas Mark 6, about 15 minutes before baking. Sift the flour and salt into a bowl. Rub in the butter until the mixture resembles breadcrumbs. Stir in the nuts. Mix together the egg yolk and 3 tablespoons cold water. Sprinkle over the dry ingredients and mix to form a dough. Knead on a lightly floured surface for a few seconds, then wrap in clingfilm/plastic wrap and chill in the refrigerator for 20 minutes. Roll out and use to line a 20.5 cm/8 inch springform tin/pan or a very deep flan tin/tart pan. Chill for a further 30 minutes.

Cook the leeks in the butter over a high heat for 2–3 minutes, stirring constantly. Lower the heat, cover and cook for 25 minutes until soft, stirring occasionally. Remove the leeks from the heat.

Cook the potatoes in boiling salted water for 15 minutes, or until almost tender. Drain, slice thickly and add to the leeks. Stir the sour cream into the leeks and potatoes, followed by the eggs, cheese, nutmeg and salt and pepper. Pour into the pastry case/pie crust and bake on the centre shelf in the preheated oven for 20 minutes. Reduce the oven temperature to 190°C/375°F/Gas Mark 5 and cook for a further 30–35 minutes until the filling is set. Garnish with chives and serve immediately.

## Difficulty Rating: 4 points

# Tomato & Courgette Herb Tart

## Serves 4

**Ingredients**

4 tbsp olive oil

1 onion, peeled and finely chopped

3 garlic cloves, peeled and crushed

400 g/14 oz prepared puff pastry dough, thawed if frozen

1 small egg, beaten

2 tbsp freshly chopped rosemary

2 tbsp freshly chopped parsley

175 g/6 oz rindless fresh soft goats' cheese

4 ripe plum tomatoes, sliced

1 courgette/zucchini, trimmed and sliced

thyme sprigs, to garnish

Preheat the oven to 230°C/450°F/Gas Mark 8, 15 minutes before baking. Heat 2 tablespoons of the oil in a large frying pan. Fry the onion and garlic for about 4 minutes until softened and reserve.

Roll out the pastry dough on a lightly floured surface and cut out a 30.5 cm/12 inch circle. Brush with a little beaten egg, then prick all over with a fork. Transfer onto a dampened baking sheet and bake in the preheated oven for 10 minutes.

Turn the pastry over and brush with a little more egg. Bake for 5 more minutes, then remove from the oven. Mix together the onion, garlic and herbs with the goats' cheese and spread over the pastry. Arrange the tomatoes and courgette/zucchini over the goats' cheese and drizzle with the remaining oil. Bake for 20–25 minutes, or until the pastry is golden brown and the topping is bubbling. Garnish with the thyme sprigs and serve immediately.

## Difficulty Rating: 1 point

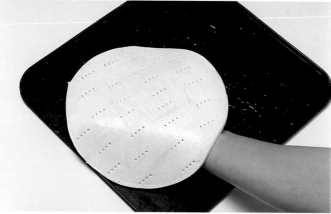

# Stilton, Tomato & Courgette Quiche

## Serves 4

### Ingredients

**For the shortcrust pastry:**
225 g/8 oz/2 cups plain/all-purpose flour
pinch salt
50 g/2 oz/scant ¼ cup white vegetable fat/shortening or lard
50 g/2 oz/½ stick butter or block margarine

**For the filling:**
25 g/1 oz/¼ stick butter
1 onion, peeled and finely chopped
1 courgette/zucchini, trimmed and sliced
125 g/4 oz/1 cup Stilton/blue cheese, crumbled
6 cherry tomatoes, halved
2 large/extra-large eggs, beaten
200 ml/7 fl oz/¾ cup crème fraîche/sour cream
salt and freshly ground black pepper

## Difficulty Rating: 3 points

Preheat the oven to 190°C/375°F/Gas Mark 5, 10 minutes before baking. Sift the flour and salt into a mixing bowl. Cut the fats into small pieces and add to the bowl. Rub the fats into the flour using your fingertips until the mixture resembles fine breadcrumbs. Add 1–2 tablespoons cold water and mix to form a soft, pliable dough. Knead gently on a lightly floured surface until smooth and free from cracks, then wrap and chill for 30 minutes.

On a lightly floured surface, roll out the dough and use to line an 18 cm/7 inch lightly oiled flan tin/tart pan, trimming any excess dough with a knife. Prick the base all over with a fork and bake blind in the preheated oven for 15 minutes. Remove the pastry from the oven and brush with a little of the beaten egg. Return to the oven for a further 5 minutes.

Heat the butter in a frying pan and fry the onion and courgette/zucchini for about 4 minutes until soft and starting to brown. Transfer into the pastry case/pie crust. Sprinkle the Stilton/blue cheese over evenly and top with the halved cherry tomatoes.

Beat together the eggs and crème fraîche/sour cream and season to taste with salt and pepper. Pour into the pastry case and bake in the oven for 35–40 minutes, or until the filling is golden brown and set in the centre. Serve the quiche hot or cold.

# Olive & Feta Parcels

## Makes 6

### Ingredients

1 small red and 1 small yellow pepper
125 g/4 oz/²⁄₃ cup assorted marinated green and black olives
125 g/4 oz/1 scant cup feta cheese, chopped into small cubes
2 tbsp pine nuts, lightly toasted
6 sheets filo/phyllo pastry dough
3 tbsp olive oil
sour cream and chive dip, to serve

Preheat the oven to 180°C/350°F/Gas Mark 4, 10 minutes before baking. Preheat the grill/broiler, then line the rack with kitchen foil.

Cut the peppers into quarters and remove the seeds. Place skin-side up on the foil-lined rack and cook under the preheated grill for 10 minutes, turning occasionally, until the skins begin to blacken. Place the peppers in a polythene/plastic bag and leave until cool enough to handle, then skin and thinly slice.

Chop the olives into small cubes. Mix together the olives, feta, sliced peppers and pine nuts.

Cut a sheet of filo/phyllo pastry dough in half, then brush with a little of the oil. Place a spoonful of the olive and feta mix about one third of the way up the dough. Fold over the dough and wrap to form a square package, encasing the filling completely. Place this package in the centre of the second half of the dough sheet. Brush the edges lightly with a little oil, bring up the corners to meet in the centre and twist them loosely to form a parcel. Brush with a little more oil and repeat with the remaining dough and filling.

Place the parcels on a lightly oiled baking sheet and bake in the preheated oven for 10–15 minutes, or until crisp and golden brown. Serve with the dip.

## Difficulty Rating: 2 points

# Potato & Goats' Cheese Tart

## Serves 6

### Ingredients

275 g/10 oz prepared shortcrust pastry dough, thawed if frozen

550 g/1¼ lb small waxy potatoes

salt and freshly ground black pepper

beaten egg, for brushing

2 tbsp sun-dried tomato paste

¼ tsp chilli powder, or to taste

1 large/extra-large egg

150 ml/¼ pint/⅔ cup sour cream

150 ml/¼ pint/⅔ cup milk

2 tbsp freshly snipped chives

300 g/11 oz goats' cheese, sliced

salad and warm crusty bread, to serve

Preheat the oven to 190°C/375°F/Gas Mark 5, about 10 minutes before cooking. Roll the pastry dough out on a lightly floured surface and use to line a 23 cm/9 inch fluted flan tin/tart pan. Chill in the refrigerator for 30 minutes. Scrub the potatoes, place in a large saucepan of lightly salted water and bring to the boil. Simmer for 10–15 minutes, or until the potatoes are tender. Drain and reserve until cool enough to handle.

Line the pastry case/pie crust with baking parchment and baking beans/pie weights and bake blind in the preheated oven for 15 minutes. Remove from the oven and discard the paper and beans. Brush the base with a little beaten egg, then return to the oven and cook for a further 5 minutes. Remove from the oven.

Cut the potatoes into 1 cm/½ inch thick slices and reserve. Spread the sun-dried tomato paste over the base of the pastry case, sprinkle with the chilli powder, then arrange the potato slices on top in a decorative pattern. Beat together the egg, sour cream, milk and chives, then season to taste with salt and pepper. Pour over the potatoes. Arrange the goats' cheese on top of the potatoes. Bake in the preheated oven for 30 minutes until golden brown and set. Serve immediately with a salad and some warm bread.

## Difficulty Rating: 2 points

# French Onion Tart

## Serves 4

**Ingredients**

**For the quick flaky pastry:**
125 g/4 oz/1 stick plus 1 tbsp butter
175 g/6 oz/1½ cups plain/all-purpose flour
pinch salt

**For the filling:**
2 tbsp olive oil
4 large onions, peeled and thinly sliced
3 tbsp white wine vinegar
2 tbsp muscovado/dark brown sugar
175 g/6 oz/1½ cups grated Cheddar cheese
a little beaten egg or milk
salt and freshly ground black pepper

Preheat the oven to 200°C/400°F/Gas Mark 6, 15 minutes before baking. Place the butter in the freezer for 30 minutes. Sift the flour and salt into a large bowl. Remove the butter from the freezer and grate using the coarse side of a grater, dipping the butter in the flour every now and again to make it easier to grate.

Mix the butter into the flour using a palette knife, making sure all the butter is thoroughly coated with flour. Add 2 tablespoons cold water and continue to mix, bringing the mixture together. Use your hands to complete the mixing. Add a little more water if needed to leave a clean bowl. Place the pastry dough in a polythene/plastic bag and chill in the refrigerator for 30 minutes.

Heat the oil in a large frying pan, then fry the onions for 10 minutes, stirring occasionally, until softened. Stir in the white wine vinegar and muscovado/dark brown sugar. Increase the heat and stir frequently for another 4–5 minutes until the onions turn a deep caramel colour. Cook for another 5 minutes, then reserve to cool.

On a lightly floured surface, roll out the pastry dough to a 35 cm/14 inch round. Wrap over a rolling pin and lift the round onto a baking sheet. Sprinkle half the cheese over the dough, leaving a 5 cm/2 inch border around the edge, then spoon the

caramelized onions over the cheese. Fold the uncovered dough edges over the edge of the filling to form a rim. Brush the rim with beaten egg or milk. Season to taste with salt and pepper. Sprinkle over the remaining cheese and bake for 20–25 minutes. Transfer to a large plate and serve immediately.

## Difficulty Rating: 3 points

# Parsnip Tatin

## Serves 4

**Ingredients**

**1 quantity shortcrust pastry dough (*see page 249*)**

**For the filling:**
**50 g/2 oz/¹/₂ stick butter**
**8 small parsnips, peeled and halved**
**1 tbsp brown sugar**
**75 ml/3 fl oz apple juice**

Preheat the oven to 200°C/400°F/Gas Mark 6, 15 minutes before baking. Heat the butter in a 20.5 cm/8 inch frying pan. Add the parsnips, arranging them cut sides down, with the narrow ends towards the centre. Sprinkle the parsnips with sugar and cook for 15 minutes, turning halfway through, until golden.

Add the apple juice and bring to the boil. Remove the pan from the heat.

On a lightly floured surface, roll the pastry dough out to a size slightly larger than the frying pan. Position the dough over the parsnips and press down slightly to enclose the parsnips.

Bake in the preheated oven for 20–25 minutes until the pastry is golden.

Invert a warm serving plate over the pan and carefully turn the pan over to flip the tart onto the plate. Serve immediately.

## Difficulty Rating: 3 points

# Red Pepper & Basil Tart

## Serves 4–6

### Ingredients

**For the olive dough:**

225 g/8 oz/2 cups plain/all-purpose flour

pinch salt

1 egg, lightly beaten, plus 1 egg yolk

3 tbsp olive oil

50 g/2 oz/⅓ cup pitted black olives, finely chopped

**For the filling:**

2 large red peppers, quartered and deseeded

175 g/6 oz/¾ cup mascarpone cheese

4 tbsp milk

2 eggs

3 tbsp freshly chopped basil

salt and freshly ground black pepper

fresh basil sprig, to garnish

mixed salad, to serve

## Difficulty Rating: 3 points

Preheat the oven to 200°C/400°F/Gas Mark 6, 15 minutes before baking. Sift the flour and salt into a bowl and make a well in the centre. Stir together the egg, oil and 1 tablespoon tepid water. Add to the dry ingredients, drop in the olives and mix to a dough. Knead on a lightly floured surface for a few seconds until smooth, then wrap in clingfilm/plastic wrap and chill in the refrigerator for 30 minutes.

Roll out the pastry dough and use to line a 23 cm/9 inch loose-bottomed fluted flan tin/tart pan. Lightly prick the base with a fork. Cover and chill in the refrigerator for 20 minutes.

Cook the peppers under a hot grill/broiler for 10 minutes, or until the skins are blackened and blistered. Put the peppers in a polythene/plastic bag, cool for 10 minutes, then remove the skins and slice. Line the pastry case/pie crust with kitchen foil or baking parchment weighed down with baking beans/pie weights. Bake in the preheated oven for 10 minutes. Remove the foil or paper and beans. Bake for a further 5 minutes. Reduce the oven temperature to 180°C/350°F/Gas Mark 4.

Beat the mascarpone cheese until smooth. Gradually add the milk and eggs. Stir in the peppers and basil and season to taste with salt and pepper. Spoon into the pastry case and bake for 25–30 minutes, or until lightly set. Garnish with a sprig of fresh basil and serve immediately with a mixed salad.

# Fennel & Caramelized Shallot Tartlets

## Serves 6

### Ingredients

**For the cheese pastry:**
175 g/6 oz/1½ cups plain/all-purpose flour
75 g/3 oz/¾ stick slightly salted butter
50 g/2 oz/½ cup grated Gruyère cheese
1 small/medium egg yolk

**For the filling:**
2 tbsp olive oil
225 g/8 oz/½ lb shallots, peeled and halved
1 fennel bulb, trimmed and sliced
1 tsp soft brown sugar
1 egg
150 ml/¼ pint/⅔ cup double/heavy cream
salt and freshly ground black pepper
25 g/1 oz/¼ cup grated Gruyère/hard Swiss cheese
½ tsp ground cinnamon
mixed salad leaves, to serve

Preheat the oven to 200°C/400°F/Gas Mark 6, 15 minutes before baking. Sift the flour into a bowl, then rub in the butter with your fingertips. Stir in the cheese.

Add the egg yolk and about 2 tablespoons cold water. Mix to a firm dough, then knead lightly. Wrap in clingfilm/plastic wrap. Chill in the refrigerator for 30 minutes.

Roll out the pastry dough on a lightly floured surface and use to line six 10 cm/4 inch individual flan tins/tartlet pans (of about 2 cm/¾ inch depth). Line the pastry cases/pie crusts with greaseproof/waxed paper. Fill with baking beans/pie weights or rice. Bake blind in the preheated oven for about 10 minutes, then remove the paper and beans.

Heat the oil in a frying pan, add the shallots and fennel. Fry gently for 5 minutes. Sprinkle with sugar. Cook for a further 10 minutes, stirring occasionally, until lightly caramelized. Reserve until cooled.

Beat together the egg and cream and season to taste with salt and pepper. Divide the shallot mixture between the pastry cases. Pour over the egg mixture and sprinkle with the cheese and cinnamon. Bake for 20 minutes, or until golden and set. Serve with salad leaves.

## Difficulty Rating: 3 points

# Garlic Wild Mushroom Galettes

## Serves 6

### Ingredients

1 quantity quick flaky pastry dough (see page 268), chilled

1 onion, peeled and thinly sliced

275 g/10 oz/2½ cups mixed mushrooms, e.g. oyster, chestnut/crimini, morels, chanterelles

25 g/1 oz/¼ stick butter

1 red chilli, deseeded and thinly sliced

2 garlic cloves, peeled and very thinly sliced

2 tbsp freshly chopped parsley

125 g/4 oz mozzarella cheese, sliced

**To serve:**

cherry tomatoes

mixed green salad leaves

Preheat the oven to 220°C/425°F/Gas Mark 7, 15 minutes before baking. On a lightly floured surface, roll out the chilled pastry dough very thinly. Cut out six 15 cm/6 inch circles and place on a lightly oiled baking sheet.

Divide the onion into rings and reserve. Wipe or lightly rinse the mushrooms. Halve or quarter any large mushrooms and keep the small ones whole.

Heat the butter in a frying pan and sauté the onion, chilli and garlic gently for about 3 minutes. Add the mushrooms and cook for about 5 minutes, or until beginning to soften. Stir the parsley into the mushroom mixture and drain off any excess liquid.

Pile the mushroom mixture onto the pastry circles within 5 mm/¼ inch of the edges. Arrange the sliced mozzarella cheese on top. Bake in the preheated oven for 12–15 minutes until golden brown, and serve with the tomatoes and salad.

## Difficulty Rating: 2 points

# Roasted Vegetable Pie

## Serves 4

### Ingredients

225 g/8 oz/2 cups plain/all-purpose flour

pinch salt

50 g/2 oz/4 tbsp white vegetable fat/shortening or lard,
 cut into cubes

50 g/2 oz/½ stick butter, cut into cubes

2 tsp herbes de Provence

1 red pepper, deseeded and halved

1 green pepper, deseeded and halved

1 yellow pepper, deseeded and halved

3 tbsp extra virgin olive oil

1 aubergine/eggplant, trimmed and sliced

1 courgette/zucchini, trimmed and halved lengthways

1 leek, trimmed and cut into chunks

1 egg, beaten

125 g/4 oz mozzarella cheese, sliced

salt and freshly ground black pepper

mixed herb sprigs, to garnish

Preheat the oven to 220°C/425°F/Gas Mark 7, 15 minutes before baking. Sift the flour and salt into a large bowl, add the fats and mix lightly. Using the fingertips, rub into the flour until the mixture resembles breadcrumbs. Stir in the herbes de Provence. Sprinkle over a tablespoon of cold water. With a knife, start bringing the dough together – use your hands for the final stage, if necessary. If the dough does not form a ball instantly, add a little more water. Place in a polythene/plastic bag and chill for 30 minutes.

Place the peppers in a baking tray and sprinkle with 1 tablespoon oil. Roast in the preheated oven for 20 minutes, or until the skins start to blacken. Brush the aubergine/eggplant, courgette/zucchini and leeks with oil and place in another baking tray. Roast in the oven with the peppers for 20 minutes. Place the blackened peppers in a polythene bag and leave the skins to loosen for 10 minutes. When cool enough to handle, peel the skins off the peppers.

Roll out half the dough on a lightly floured surface and use to line a 20.5 cm/8 inch round pie dish. Line with greaseproof/waxed paper and fill with baking beans/pie weights and bake blind for about 10 minutes. Remove the beans and the paper, then brush the base with a little beaten egg. Return to the oven for 5 minutes. Layer the cooked vegetables and the cheese in the base, seasoning each layer. Roll out the remaining pastry and cut out the lid 5 mm/¼ inch wider than the dish. Brush the rim with the beaten egg, lay the lid on top and press to seal. Knock the edges with the back of a knife, then cut a slit in the lid and brush with the beaten egg. Bake for 30 minutes. Transfer to a large serving dish, garnish with herb sprigs and serve immediately.

## Difficulty Rating: 3 points

# Three-Tomato Pizzas

## Serves 4

**Ingredients**

**For the basic pizza dough:**
225 g/8 oz/2 cups strong white/bread flour
½ tsp salt; ¼ tsp quick-acting dried yeast
150 ml/¼ pint/⅔ cup warm water
1 tbsp extra virgin olive oil

**For the topping:**
3 plum tomatoes
8 cherry tomatoes
6 sun-dried tomatoes
pinch sea salt
1 tbsp freshly chopped basil
2 tbsp extra virgin olive oil
125 g/4 oz buffalo mozzarella cheese, sliced
freshly ground black pepper
fresh basil leaves, to garnish

Preheat the oven to 220°C/425°F/Gas Mark 7 and place a baking sheet in the oven to heat up. Sift the flour and salt into a bowl and stir in the yeast. Make a well in the centre and gradually add the water and oil to form a soft dough. Knead on a floured surface for about 5 minutes until smooth and elastic. Place in a lightly oiled bowl and cover with clingfilm/plastic wrap. Leave to rise in a warm place for 1 hour. Knock the dough with your fist a few times, then divide into four equal pieces. Roll out one piece on a lightly floured board to form a 20.5 cm/8 inch round. Roll out the other three pieces into rounds, one at a time. While rolling out any piece, keep the others lightly covered with clingfilm.

Slice the plum tomatoes, halve the cherry tomatoes and chop the sun-dried tomatoes into small pieces. Place a few pieces of each type of tomato on each pizza base, then season to taste with the salt. Sprinkle with the chopped basil and drizzle with the olive oil. Place a few slices of mozzarella on each pizza and season with black pepper. Transfer the pizzas onto the heated baking sheet and cook for 15–20 minutes, or until the cheese is golden brown and bubbling. Garnish with the basil and serve immediately.

## Difficulty Rating: 2 points

# Chargrilled Vegetable & Goats' Cheese Pizza

## Serves 4

### Ingredients

1 small (125 g/4 oz) baking potato

1 tbsp olive oil

225 g/8 oz strong white/bread flour

1/2 tsp salt

1 tsp easy-blend dried yeast

### For the topping:

1 medium aubergine/eggplant, thinly sliced

2 small courgettes/zucchini, trimmed and sliced lengthways

1 yellow pepper, quartered and deseeded

1 red onion, peeled and sliced into very thin wedges

5 tbsp olive oil

175 g/6 oz/1 heaped cup cooked new potatoes, halved

400 g/14 oz can chopped tomatoes, drained

2 tsp freshly chopped oregano

125 g/4 oz/1 heaped cup mozzarella cheese,
    cut into small cubes

125 g/4 oz/1/2 cup goats' cheese, crumbled

Preheat the oven to 220°C/425°F/Gas Mark 7, 15 minutes before baking. Put a baking sheet in the oven to heat up. Cook the potato in lightly salted boiling water until tender. Peel and mash with the olive oil until smooth.

Sift the flour and salt into a bowl. Stir in the yeast. Add the mashed potato and 150 ml/1/4 pint/2/3 cup warm water and mix to a soft dough. Knead for 5–6 minutes until smooth. Put the dough in a bowl, cover with clingfilm/plastic wrap and leave to rise in a warm place for 30 minutes.

To make the topping, arrange the aubergine/eggplant, courgettes/zucchini, pepper and onion, skin-side up, on a grill/boiler rack and brush with 4 tablespoons of the oil. Grill/broil for 4–5 minutes. Turn the vegetables and brush with the remaining oil. Grill for 3–4 minutes. Cool, skin and slice the pepper. Put all of the vegetables in a bowl, add the halved new potatoes and toss gently together. Set aside.

Briefly re-knead the dough, then roll out to a 30.5–35.5 cm/12–14 inch round, according to preferred thickness. Mix the tomatoes and oregano together and spread over the pizza base. Scatter over the mozzarella cheese. Put the pizza on the preheated baking sheet and bake for 8 minutes. Arrange the vegetables and goats' cheese on top and bake for 8–10 minutes. Serve.

## Difficulty Rating: 3 points

# Spinach, Pine Nut & Mascarpone Pizza

## Serves 2–4

**Ingredients**

1 quantity pizza dough (*see page 274*)

**For the topping:**
3 tbsp olive oil
1 large red onion, peeled and chopped
2 garlic cloves, peeled and finely sliced
450 g/1 lb/3 cups frozen spinach, thawed, drained
salt and freshly ground black pepper
3 tbsp passata (or use tomata sauce)
125 g/4¹⁄₂ oz/heaped ¹⁄₂ cup mascarpone cheese
1 tbsp toasted pine nuts

Preheat the oven to 220°C/425°F/Gas Mark 7. Shape and thinly roll out the pizza dough on a lightly floured board. Place on a lightly floured baking sheet and lift the edge to make a little rim. Place another baking sheet into the preheated oven to heat up.

Heat half the oil in a frying pan. Gently fry the onion and garlic until soft and starting to change colour.

Squeeze out any excess water from the spinach and finely chop. Add to the onion and garlic with the remaining olive oil. Season to taste with salt and pepper.

Spread the passata on the pizza dough and top with the spinach mixture. Mix the mascarpone with the pine nuts and dot over the pizza. Slide the pizza on to the hot baking sheet and bake for 15–20 minutes. Transfer to a large plate and serve immediately.

## **Difficulty Rating: 2 points**

# Roquefort, Parma & Rocket Pizza

## Serves 2–4

### Ingredients

1 quantity pizza dough (see page 274)

**For the basic tomato sauce:**
400 g/14 oz can/2 cups canned chopped tomatoes
2 garlic cloves, peeled and crushed
grated zest of ½ lime
2 tbsp extra virgin olive oil
2 tbsp freshly chopped basil
½ tsp sugar
salt and freshly ground black pepper

**For the topping:**
125 g/4 oz/1 cup Roquefort cheese, cut into chunks
6 slices Parma ham/prosciutto
50 g/2 oz/1 bunch rocket/arugula leaves, rinsed
1 tbsp extra virgin olive oil
50 g/2 oz/8 tbsp Parmesan cheese, freshly shaved

Preheat the oven to 220°C/425°F/Gas Mark 7. Roll the pizza dough out on a lightly floured board to form a 25.5 cm/10 inch round. Lightly cover the dough and reserve while making the sauce. Place a baking sheet in the preheated oven to heat up.

Place all of the tomato sauce ingredients in a large heavy-based saucepan and slowly bring to the boil. Cover and simmer for 15 minutes, uncover and cook for a further 10 minutes until the sauce has thickened and reduced by half.

Spoon the tomato sauce over the shaped pizza dough. Place on the hot baking sheet and bake for 10 minutes. Remove the pizza from the oven and top with the Roquefort and Parma ham/prosciutto, then bake for a further 10 minutes.

Toss the rocket/arugula in the olive oil and pile onto the pizza. Sprinkle with the Parmesan cheese and serve immediately.

## Difficulty Rating: 2 points

# Baked Fish & Seafood

**Baking fish can be one of the healthiest and easiest ways to cook it, not to mention one of the tastiest. This section provides all sorts of variations, from Zesty Whole-baked Fish to Saucy Cod & Pasta Bake.**

# Baked Cod with Saffron Aïoli

## Serves 4

**Ingredients**

**For the saffron aïoli:**
2 garlic cloves, peeled
¼ tsp saffron strands
sea salt, to taste
1 medium/large egg yolk
200 ml/7 fl oz/¾ cup extra virgin olive oil
2 tbsp lemon juice

**For the marinade:**
2 tbsp olive oil
4 garlic cloves, peeled and finely chopped
1 red onion, peeled and finely chopped
1 tbsp freshly chopped rosemary; 2 tbsp freshly chopped thyme
4–6 fresh rosemary sprigs; 1 lemon, sliced

4 x 175 g/6 oz thick cod fillets with skin
freshly cooked vegetables, to serve

Preheat oven to 180°C/350°F/Gas Mark 4, 10 minutes before baking. Crush the garlic, saffron and pinch of salt in a pestle and mortar to form a paste. Place in a blender with the egg yolk and blend for 30 seconds. With the motor running, slowly add the olive oil in a thin, steady stream until the mayonnaise is smooth and thick. Spoon into a small bowl and stir in the lemon juice. Cover and leave in the refrigerator until required.

Combine the olive oil, garlic, red onion, rosemary and thyme for the marinade and leave to infuse for about 10 minutes. Place the rosemary sprigs and slices of lemon in the bottom of a lightly oiled roasting tin/pan. Add the cod, skinned-side up. Pour over the prepared marinade and leave to marinate in the refrigerator for 15–20 minutes. Bake in the preheated oven for 15–20 minutes, or until the cod is cooked and the flesh flakes easily with a fork. Leave the cod to rest for 1 minute before serving with the saffron aïoli and vegetables.

## Difficulty Rating: 3 points

# Saucy Cod & Pasta Bake

## Serves 4

**Ingredients**

450 g/1 lb cod fillets, skinned

2 tbsp sunflower/corn oil

1 onion, peeled and chopped

4 rashers smoked streaky bacon, rind removed, chopped

150 g/5 oz/1½ cups baby button/white mushrooms, wiped

2 celery stalks, trimmed and thinly sliced

2 small courgettes/zucchini, halved lengthways, sliced

400 g/14 oz can chopped tomatoes

100 ml/3½ fl oz/7 tbsp fish stock or dry white wine

1 tbsp freshly chopped tarragon

salt and freshly ground black pepper

**For the pasta topping:**

225–275 g/8–10 oz/2–2½ cups pasta shells

25 g/1 oz/¼ stick butter

4 tbsp plain/all-purpose flour

450 ml/¾ pint/1¾ cups milk

Preheat the oven to 200°C/400°F/Gas Mark 6, 15 minutes before cooking. Cut the cod into bite-size pieces and reserve.

Heat the sunflower/corn oil in a large saucepan, add the onion and bacon and cook for 7–8 minutes. Add the mushrooms and celery and cook for 5 minutes, or until fairly soft. Add the courgettes/zucchini and tomatoes to the bacon mixture and pour in the fish stock or wine. Bring to the boil, then simmer uncovered for 5 minutes, or until the sauce has thickened slightly.

Remove from the heat and stir in the cod and the tarragon. Season to taste with salt and pepper, then spoon into a large oiled baking dish.

Meanwhile, bring a large pan of lightly salted water to a rolling boil. Add the pasta shells and cook according to the packet instructions, or until *al dente*.

For the topping, place the butter and flour in a saucepan and pour in the milk. Bring to the boil slowly, whisking until thickened and smooth.

Drain the pasta thoroughly and stir into the sauce. Spoon carefully over the fish and vegetables. Place in the preheated oven and bake for 20–25 minutes, or until the top is lightly browned and bubbling.

## Difficulty Rating: 3 points

# Supreme Baked Potatoes

## Serves 4

**Ingredients**

**4 large baking potatoes**
**40 g/1½ oz/3 tbsp butter**
**1 tbsp sunflower/corn oil**
**1 carrot, peeled and chopped**
**2 celery stalks, trimmed and finely chopped**
**200 g/7 oz can white crab meat**
**2 spring onions/scallions, trimmed and finely chopped**
**salt and freshly ground black pepper**
**50 g/2 oz/½ cup grated Cheddar cheese**
**tomato salad, to serve**

Preheat the oven to 200°C/400°F/Gas Mark 6, 15 minutes before baking. Scrub the potatoes and prick all over with a fork, or thread onto two long metal skewers. Place in the preheated oven for 1–1½ hours, or until soft to the touch. Allow to cool a little, then cut in half.

Scoop out the cooked potato and turn into a bowl, leaving a reasonably firm potato shell. Mash the cooked potato flesh, then mix in the butter and mash until the butter has melted.

While the potatoes are cooking, heat the oil in a frying pan and cook the carrot and celery for 2 minutes. Cover the pan tightly and continue to cook for another 5 minutes, or until the vegetables are tender.

Add the cooked vegetables to the bowl of mashed potato and mix well. Fold in the crab meat and the spring onions/scallions, then season to taste with salt and pepper. Pile the mixture back into the potato shells and press in firmly. Sprinkle the grated cheese over the top and return the potato halves to the oven for 12–15 minutes until hot, golden and bubbling. Serve immediately with a tomato salad.

## Difficulty Rating: 1 point

# Haddock with an Olive Crust

## Serves 4

**Ingredients**

**12 pitted black olives, finely chopped**
**75 g/3 oz/1¼ cups fresh white breadcrumbs**
**1 tbsp freshly chopped tarragon**
**1 garlic clove, peeled and crushed**
**3 spring onions/scallions, trimmed and finely chopped**
**1 tbsp olive oil**
**4 thick skinless haddock fillets, 175 g/6 oz each**

**To serve:**
**freshly cooked carrots**
**freshly cooked beans**

Preheat the oven to 190°C/375°F/Gas Mark 5, 10 minutes before baking. Place the black olives in a small bowl with the breadcrumbs and add the chopped tarragon. Add the garlic to the olives with the chopped spring onions/scallions and the olive oil. Mix together lightly.

Wipe the fillets with either a clean damp cloth or damp paper towels, then place on a lightly oiled baking sheet. Place spoonfuls of the olive and breadcrumb mixture on top of each fillet and press the mixture down lightly and evenly over the top of the fish.

Bake the fish in the preheated oven for 20–25 minutes until the fish is cooked thoroughly and the topping is golden brown. Serve immediately with the freshly cooked carrots and beans.

## Difficulty Rating: 1 point

# Foil-baked Fish

## Serves 4

**Ingredients**

**For the tomato sauce:**

125 ml/4 fl oz/½ cup olive oil

4 garlic cloves, peeled and finely chopped

4 shallots, peeled and finely chopped

400 g/14 oz can chopped Italian tomatoes

2 tbsp freshly chopped flat-leaf/Italian parsley

3 tbsp basil leaves

salt and freshly ground black pepper

700 g/1½ lb red mullet, bass or haddock fillets

450 g/1 lb live mussels

4 squid

8 large raw prawns/shrimp

2 tbsp olive oil

3 tbsp dry white wine

3 tbsp freshly chopped basil leaves

lemon wedges, to garnish

Preheat oven to 180°C/350°F/Gas Mark 4, 10 minutes before baking. Heat the olive oil and gently fry the garlic and shallots for 2 minutes. Stir in the tomatoes and simmer for 10 minutes, breaking the tomatoes down with the wooden spoon. Add the parsley and basil, season to taste with salt and pepper and cook for a further 2 minutes. Reserve and keep warm.

Lightly rinse the fish fillets and cut into four portions. Scrub the mussels thoroughly, removing the beard and any barnacles from the shells. Discard any mussels that are open. Clean the squid and cut into rings. Peel the prawns/shrimp and remove the thin black intestinal vein that runs down the back.

Cut four large pieces of kitchen foil, then place them on a large baking sheet and brush with olive oil. Place one fish portion in the centre of each piece of foil. Close the foil to form parcels and bake in the preheated oven for 10 minutes, then remove. Carefully open up the parcels and add the mussels, squid and prawns. Pour in the wine and spoon over a little of the tomato sauce. Sprinkle with the basil leaves and return to the oven and bake for 5 minutes, or until cooked thoroughly. Discard any unopened mussels, then garnish with lemon wedges and serve with the extra tomato sauce.

## Difficulty Rating: 3 points

# Fish Lasagne

## Serves 4

### Ingredients

75 g/3 oz/³⁄₄ cup mushrooms

1 tsp sunflower/corn oil

1 small onion, peeled and finely chopped

1 tbsp freshly chopped oregano

400 g/14 oz can chopped tomatoes

1 tbsp tomato purée/paste

salt and freshly ground black pepper

450 g/1 lb cod or haddock fillets, skinned

9–12 sheets precooked lasagne verde

### For the topping:

1 egg, beaten

125 g/4 oz/¹⁄₂ cup cottage cheese

150 ml/¹⁄₄ pint/²⁄₃ cup natural/low-fat plain yogurt

50 g/2 oz/¹⁄₂ cup grated Cheddar cheese

### To serve:

mixed salad leaves

cherry tomatoes

Preheat the oven to 190°C/375°F/Gas Mark 5, 10 minutes before baking. Wipe the mushrooms, trim the stalks and chop. Heat the oil in a large heavy-based pan, add the onion and cook gently for 3–5 minutes until soft. Stir in the mushrooms, oregano and chopped tomatoes.

Blend the tomato purée/paste with 1 tablespoon water. Stir into the pan and season to taste with salt and pepper. Bring the sauce to the boil, then simmer, uncovered, for 5–10 minutes.

Remove as many of the tiny pin bones as possible from the fish and cut into cubes. Add to the tomato sauce mixture and stir gently, then remove the pan from the heat.

Cover the base of an ovenproof dish with 2–3 sheets of the lasagne verde. Top with half of the fish mixture. Repeat the layers, finishing with the lasagne sheets.

To make the topping, mix together the beaten egg, cottage cheese and yogurt. Pour over the lasagne and sprinkle with the cheese. Cook the lasagne in the preheated oven for 35–40 minutes, or until the topping is golden brown and bubbling. Serve the lasagne immediately with the mixed salad leaves and cherry tomatoes.

## Difficulty Rating: 2 points

# Zesty Whole-baked Fish

## Serves 8

### Ingredients

1.8 kg/4 lb whole salmon, cleaned

sea salt and freshly ground black pepper

50 g/2 oz/¹/₂ stick butter

1 garlic clove, peeled and finely sliced

zest and juice of 1 lemon

zest of 1 orange

1 tsp freshly grated nutmeg

3 tbsp Dijon mustard

2 tbsp fresh white breadcrumbs

2 bunches fresh dill

1 bunch fresh tarragon

a little butter, for rubbing (optional)

1 lime, sliced

150 ml/¹/₄ pint/²/₃ cup crème fraîche/sour cream

450 ml/³/₄ pint/1³/₄ cups fromage frais/reduced-fat sour cream

dill sprigs, to garnish

Preheat the oven to 220°C/425°F/Gas Mark 7, 15 minutes before baking. Lightly rinse the fish and pat dry with absorbent paper towels. Season the cavity with a little salt and pepper. Make several diagonal cuts across the flesh of the fish and season.

Mix together the butter, garlic, lemon and orange zest and lemon juice, nutmeg, mustard and fresh breadcrumbs. Spoon the breadcrumb mixture into the slits with a small sprig of dill. Place the remaining herbs inside the fish cavity. Weigh the fish and calculate the cooking time. Allow 10 minutes per 450 g/1 lb.

Lay the fish on a double thickness of kitchen foil. If liked, smear the fish with a little butter. Top with the lime slices and fold the foil into a parcel. Chill in the refrigerator for about 15 minutes.

Place in a roasting tin/pan and cook in the preheated oven for the calculated cooking time. Fifteen minutes before the end of cooking, open the foil and return to the oven until the skin begins to crisp. Remove the fish from the oven and stand for 10 minutes.

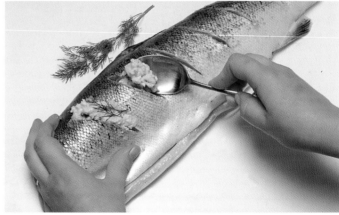

Pour the juices from the roasting tin into a saucepan. Bring to the boil and stir in the crème fraîche/sour cream and fromage frais/reduced-fat sour cream. Simmer for 3 minutes, or until hot. Garnish with dill sprigs and serve immediately alongside the fish.

## Difficulty Rating: 1 point

# Salmon Parcels

## Serves 4–6

**Ingredients**

4 salmon fillets, each about 150 g/5 oz in weight

5 cm/2 inch piece fresh root ginger, peeled and grated

1 red chilli, deseeded and sliced

1 green chilli, deseeded and sliced

2–3 garlic cloves, peeled and crushed

1 tbsp curry paste

4 tbsp sweet chilli sauce

few fresh coriander/cilantro sprigs

**To serve:**

lime wedges

new potatoes

steamed vegetables

Preheat the oven to 180˚C/350˚F/Gas Mark 4, 10 minutes before baking. Cut out four 20.5 cm/8 inch squares of nonstick baking parchment or foil. Lightly rinse the salmon and pat dry with absorbent paper towels. Place a salmon fillet on each square of paper.

Sprinkle the fillets equally with the ginger, chillies and garlic. Blend the curry paste with the sweet chilli sauce and pour 1 tablespoon of the mixture over each salmon fillet. Top with fresh coriander/cilantro sprigs.

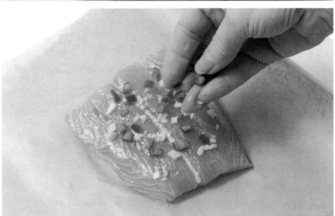

Fold the paper to completely encase the fillets and all the flavourings. Place in a roasting tin/pan or on a baking tray and cook in the preheated oven for 20 minutes.

Place a parcel on each warmed dinner plate and let each person open up the parcels, so they can enjoy the pleasure of the spicy aroma. Serve with lime wedges, new potatoes and steamed vegetables.

## Difficulty Rating: 1 point

# Salmon with Herbed Potatoes

## Serves 4

### Ingredients

450 g/1 lb (about 20) baby new potatoes
salt and freshly ground black pepper
4 salmon steaks, each about 175 g/6 oz
1 carrot, peeled and cut into fine strips
175 g/6 oz (about 12) asparagus spears, trimmed
175 g/6 oz/1 cup sugar snap peas, trimmed
finely grated zest and juice of 1 lemon
25 g/1 oz/¼ stick butter
4 large fresh parsley sprigs

Preheat the oven to 190°C/375°F/Gas Mark 5, about 10 minutes before baking. Parboil the potatoes in lightly salted boiling water for 5–8 minutes until they are barely tender. Drain and reserve.

Cut out four pieces of baking parchment, measuring 20.5 cm/8 inches square, and place on the work surface. Arrange the parboiled potatoes on top. Wipe the salmon steaks and place on top of the potatoes.

Place the carrot strips in a bowl with the asparagus spears, sugar snap peas and grated lemon zest and juice. Season to taste with salt and pepper. Toss lightly together. Divide the vegetables evenly among the salmon steaks. Dot the top of each parcel with butter and a sprig of parsley.

To create a parcel, lift up two opposite sides of the paper and fold the edges together. Twist the paper at the other two ends to seal the parcel well. Repeat with the remaining parcels.

Place the parcels on a baking sheet and bake in the preheated oven for 15 minutes. Place an unopened parcel on each plate and open just before eating.

## Difficulty Rating: 1 point

# Traditional Fish Pie

## Serves 4

### Ingredients

450 g/1 lb cod or coley/white fish fillets, skinned

450 ml/³/₄ pint/1³/₄ cups milk

1 small onion, peeled and quartered

salt and freshly ground black pepper

6–8 potatoes, peeled and cut into chunks

100 g/3¹/₂ oz/1 stick butter

125 g/4 oz large prawns/shrimp, peeled

2 large/extra-large eggs, hard-boiled and quartered

198 g/7 oz can sweetcorn, drained

2 tbsp freshly chopped parsley

3 tbsp plain/all-purpose flour

50 g/2 oz/¹/₂ cup grated Cheddar cheese

## Difficulty Rating: 3 points

Preheat the oven to 200°C/400°F/Gas Mark 6, about 15 minutes before baking. Place the fish in a shallow frying pan, pour over 300 ml/¹/₂ pint/1¹/₄ cups of the milk and add the onion. Season to taste with salt and pepper. Bring to the boil and simmer for 8–10 minutes until the fish is cooked. Remove the fish with a slotted spoon and place in a 1.5 litre/2¹/₂ pint/1¹/₂ quart baking dish. Strain the cooking liquid and reserve.

Boil the potatoes until soft, then mash with 40 g/1¹/₂ oz/3 tbsp of the butter and 2–3 tablespoons of the remaining milk. Reserve.

Arrange the prawns/shrimp and quartered eggs on top of the fish, then scatter the sweetcorn over and sprinkle with the parsley.

Melt the remaining butter in a saucepan, stir in the flour and cook gently for 1 minute, stirring. Whisk in the reserved cooking liquid and remaining milk. Cook for 2 minutes, or until thickened, then pour over the fish mixture and cool slightly.

Spread the mashed potato over the top of the pie and sprinkle the grated cheese over. Bake in the preheated over for 30 minutes until golden. Serve immediately.

# Fish Crumble

## Serves 6

### Ingredients

450 g/1 lb whiting or halibut fillets

300 ml/$^1$/$_2$ pint/1$^1$/$_4$ cups milk

salt and freshly ground black pepper

1 tbsp sunflower/corn oil

75 g/3 oz/$^3$/$_4$ stick butter or margarine

1 onion, peeled and finely chopped

2 leeks, trimmed and sliced

1 carrot, peeled and cut into small cubes

2 medium potatoes, peeled and cut into small pieces

75 g/3 oz/$^2$/$_3$ cup plain/all-purpose flour

300 ml/$^1$/$_2$ pint/1$^1$/$_4$ cups fish or vegetable stock

2 tbsp whipping cream

1 tsp freshly chopped dill

runner/string beans, to serve

**For the crumble/crisp topping:**

75 g/3 oz/$^3$/$_4$ stick butter or margarine

175 g/6 oz/1$^1$/$_2$ cups plain/all-purpose flour

75 g/3 oz/3 cups grated Parmesan cheese

$^3$/$_4$ tsp cayenne pepper

Preheat the oven to 200°C/400°F/Gas Mark 6, 15 minutes before baking. Oil a 1.5 litre/2$^1$/$_2$ pint/1$^1$/$_2$ quart pie dish. Place the fish in a saucepan with the milk, salt and pepper. Bring to the boil, cover and simmer for 8–10 minutes until the fish is cooked. Remove with a slotted spoon, reserving the cooking liquid. Flake the fish into the prepared dish.

Heat the oil and 15 g/$^1$/$_2$ oz/1 tbsp of the butter or margarine in a small frying pan and gently fry the onion, leeks, carrot and potatoes for 1–2 minutes. Cover tightly and cook over a gentle heat for a further 10 minutes until softened. Spoon the vegetables over the fish.

Melt the remaining butter or margarine in a saucepan, add the flour and cook for 1 minute, stirring. Whisk in the reserved cooking liquid and the stock. Cook until thickened, then stir in the cream. Remove from the heat and stir in the dill. Pour over the fish.

To make the crumble/crisp, rub the butter or margarine into the flour until it resembles breadcrumbs, then stir in the cheese and cayenne pepper. Sprinkle over the dish and bake in the preheated oven for 20 minutes until piping hot. Serve with runner/string beans.

## Difficulty Rating: 3 points

# Potato Boulangere with Sea Bass

## Serves 2

### Ingredients

450 g/1 lb (about 2 medium) potatoes, peeled and thinly sliced
1 large onion, peeled and thinly sliced
salt and freshly ground black pepper
300 ml/$\frac{1}{2}$ pint/1$\frac{1}{4}$ cups fish or vegetable stock
75 g/3 oz/$\frac{2}{3}$ stick butter or margarine
350 g/12 oz sea bass fillets
fresh flat-leaf/Italian parsley sprigs, to garnish

Preheat the oven to 200°C/400°F/Gas Mark 6, 15 minutes before baking. Lightly grease a shallow 1.5 litre/2$\frac{1}{2}$ pint/1$\frac{1}{2}$ quart baking dish with oil or butter. Layer the potato slices and onions alternately in the prepared dish, seasoning each layer with salt and pepper.

Pour the stock over the top, then cut 50 g/2 oz/$\frac{1}{4}$ cup of the butter or margarine into small pieces and dot over the top layer. Bake in the preheated oven for 50–60 minutes. Do not cover the dish at this stage.

Lightly rinse the sea bass fillets and pat dry on absorbent paper towels. Cook in a griddle pan, or heat the remaining butter or margarine in a frying pan and shallow fry the fish fillets for 3–4 minutes per side, flesh side first. Remove from the pan with a slotted spatula and drain on paper towels.

Remove the partly cooked potato and onion mixture from the oven and place the fish on the top. Cover with foil and return to the oven for 10 minutes until heated through. Garnish with sprigs of parsley and serve immediately.

## Difficulty Rating: 2 points

# Tuna Cannelloni

## Serves 4

### Ingredients

1 tbsp olive oil

6 spring onions/scallions, trimmed and finely sliced

1 sweet red pepper, deseeded and finely chopped

200 g/7 oz can tuna in brine

250 g/9 oz tub ricotta or quark cheese

zest and juice of 1 lemon

1 tbsp freshly snipped chives

salt and freshly ground black pepper

8 dried cannelloni tubes

1 medium/large egg, beaten

125 g/4 oz/¼ cup cottage cheese

150 ml/¼ pt/½ cup natural/plain yogurt

pinch freshly grated nutmeg

50 g/2 oz/¼ cup mozzarella cheese, grated

tossed green salad, to serve

Preheat oven to 180°C/375°F/Gas Mark 5, 10 minutes before baking. Heat the olive oil in a frying pan and cook the spring onions/scallions and pepper until soft. Remove from the pan with a slotted draining spoon and place in a large bowl.

Drain the tuna, then stir into the spring onions and pepper. Beat the ricotta cheese with the lemon zest and juice and the snipped chives and season to taste with salt and pepper until soft and blended. Add to the tuna and mix together. If the mixture is still a little stiff, add a little extra lemon juice.

With a teaspoon, carefully spoon the mixture into the cannelloni tubes, then lay the filled tubes in a lightly oiled shallow ovenproof dish. Beat the egg, cottage cheese, yogurt and nutmeg together and pour over the cannelloni. Sprinkle with the grated mozzarella cheese and bake in the preheated oven for 15–20 minutes, or until the topping is golden brown and bubbling. Serve immediately with a tossed green salad.

## Difficulty Rating: 2 points

# Plaice with Parmesan & Anchovies

## Serves 4

### Ingredients

4 plaice/flounder fillets

4 anchovy fillets, finely chopped

450 g/1 lb/2½ cups spinach

3 firm tomatoes, sliced

200 ml/7 fl oz/¾ cup double/heavy cream

5 slices olive ciabatta bread

50 g/2 oz/2 cups wild rocket/arugula

8 tbsp grated Parmesan cheese

freshly cooked pasta, to serve

Preheat the oven to 220°C/425°F/Gas Mark 7, 15 minutes before baking. Put the plaice/flounder on a chopping board and, holding the tail, strip off the skin from both sides. With a filleting knife, fillet the fish, then wipe with a clean, damp cloth or dampened paper towels.

Place the fillets on a large chopping board, skinned-side up, and halve lengthways along the centre. Dot each one with some of the chopped anchovies, then roll up from the thickest end and reserve.

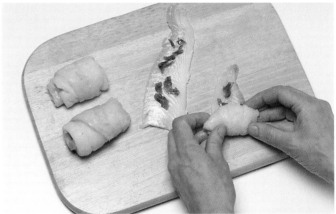

Pour boiling water over the spinach, leave for 2 minutes, then drain, squeezing out as much moisture as possible. Place in the base of an ovenproof dish and arrange the tomatoes on top of the spinach. Arrange the rolled-up fillets standing up in the dish and pour over the cream.

Place the ciabatta and rocket/arugula in a food processor and blend until finely chopped, then stir in the grated Parmesan cheese.

Sprinkle the topping over the fish and bake in the preheated oven for 8–10 minutes until the fish is cooked and has lost its translucency and the topping is golden brown. Serve with freshly cooked pasta.

## Difficulty Rating: 3 points

# Cheesy Vegetable & Prawn Bake

## Serves 4

**Ingredients**

175 g/6 oz/1 cup long-grain rice
salt and freshly ground black pepper
1 garlic clove, peeled and crushed
1 large/extra-large egg, beaten
3 tbsp freshly shredded basil
4 tbsp grated Parmesan cheese
125 g/4 oz (about 10) baby asparagus spears, trimmed
150 g/5 oz/1 cup baby carrots, trimmed
150 g/5 oz/1¼ cups fine green beans, trimmed
150 g/5 oz cherry tomatoes, quartered or halved
175 g/6 oz/1 cup peeled prawns/shrimp,
   thawed if frozen
125 g/4 oz/¾ cup thinly sliced mozzarella cheese

Preheat the oven to 200°C/400°F/Gas Mark 6, about 10 minutes before baking. Cook the rice in lightly salted boiling water for 12–15 minutes, or until tender, and drain. Stir in the garlic, beaten egg, shredded basil and half the Parmesan cheese and season to taste with salt and pepper. Press this mixture into a greased 23 cm/9 inch square ovenproof dish and reserve.

Bring a large saucepan of water to the boil, then drop in the asparagus, carrots and green beans. Return to the boil and cook for 3–4 minutes. Drain and leave to cool.

Mix the cherry tomatoes into the cooled vegetables. Spread the prepared vegetables over the rice and top with the prawns/shrimp. Season to taste with salt and pepper.

Cover the prawns with the mozzarella. Sprinkle the remaining Parmesan cheese over and bake in the preheated oven for 20–25 minutes until piping hot and golden brown in places. Serve immediately.

## Difficulty Rating: 2 points

# Stuffed Squid with Romesco Sauce

## Serves 4

### Ingredients

8 small squid, about 350 g/12 oz

5 tbsp olive oil

50 g/2 oz/⅓ cup pancetta/unsmoked streaky bacon, diced

1 onion, peeled and chopped

3 garlic cloves, peeled and finely chopped

2 tsp freshly chopped thyme

50 g/2 oz/½ cup sun-dried tomatoes in oil,
    drained and chopped

75 g/3 oz/1⅔ cups fresh white breadcrumbs

2 tbsp freshly chopped basil

juice of ½ lime

salt and freshly ground black pepper

2 vine-ripened tomatoes, peeled and finely chopped

pinch dried chilli flakes

1 tsp dried oregano

1 large red pepper, skinned and chopped

assorted salad leaves, to serve

Preheat oven to 230°C/450°F/Gas Mark 8, 15 minutes before baking. Clean the squid if necessary, rinse lightly, pat dry with absorbent paper towels and finely chop the tentacles.

Heat 2 tablespoons of the olive oil in a large nonstick frying pan and fry the pancetta/bacon for 5 minutes, or until crisp. Remove the pancetta and reserve. Add the tentacles, onion, 2 garlic cloves, thyme and sun–dried tomatoes to the oil remaining in the pan and cook gently for 5 minutes, or until softened.

Remove the pan from the heat and stir in the diced pancetta. Blend in a food processor if a smoother stuffing is preferred, then stir in the breadcrumbs, basil and lime juice. Season to taste with salt and pepper. Spoon the stuffing into the cavity of the squid and secure the tops with cocktail sticks.

Place the squid in a large roasting tin/pan and sprinkle over 2 tablespoons each of oil and water. Place in the preheated oven and cook for 20 minutes.

Heat the remaining oil in a saucepan and cook the remaining garlic for 3 minutes. Add the tomatoes, chilli flakes and oregano and simmer gently for 15 minutes before stirring in the red pepper. Cook gently for a further 5 minutes. Blend in a food processor to make a smooth sauce and season to taste. Pour the sauce over the squid and serve immediately with some assorted salad leaves.

## Difficulty Rating: 3 points

# Parmesan & Garlic Lobster

## Serves 2

**Ingredients**

1 large cooked lobster

25 g/1 oz/¼ stick unsalted butter

4 garlic cloves, peeled and crushed

1 tbsp plain/all-purpose flour

300 ml/½ pint/1¼ cups milk

125 g/4 oz/1¼ cups Parmesan cheese, grated

sea salt and freshly ground black pepper

assorted salad leaves, to serve

Preheat oven to 180°C/350°F/Gas Mark 4, 10 minutes before baking. Halve the lobster and crack the claws. Remove the gills, green sac behind the head and the black vein running down the body. Place the two lobster halves in a shallow ovenproof dish.

Melt the butter in a small saucepan and gently cook the garlic for 3 minutes until softened. Add the flour and stir over a medium heat for 1 minute. Draw the saucepan off the heat, then gradually stir in the milk, stirring until the sauce thickens. Return to the heat and cook for 2 minutes, stirring throughout, until smooth and thickened. Stir in half the cheese and continue to cook for 1 minute, then season to taste with salt and pepper.

Pour the cheese sauce over the lobster halves and sprinkle with the remaining Parmesan cheese. Bake in the preheated oven for 20 minutes, or until heated through and the cheese sauce is golden brown. Serve with assorted salad leaves.

## Difficulty Rating: 4 points

# Baked Monkfish with Parma Ham

## Serves 4

### Ingredients

700 g/1½ lb monkfish tail

sea salt and freshly ground black pepper

4 slices Fontina/Emmenthal cheese, rind removed

4 bay leaves

8 slices Parma ham/prosciutto

225 g/8 oz angel hair pasta

50 g/2 oz/½ stick butter

zest and juice of 1 lemon

fresh coriander/cilantro sprigs, to garnish

**To serve:**
chargrilled courgettes/zucchini

chargrilled tomatoes

Preheat oven to 200°C/400°F/Gas Mark 6, 15 minutes before baking. Discard any skin from the monkfish and cut away and discard the central bone. Cut the fish into four equal-sized pieces, season to taste with salt and pepper and lay a slice of cheese and a bay leaf on each fillet. Wrap each fillet with 2 slices of the Parma ham/prosciutto, so that the fish is covered completely. Tuck the ends of the ham in and secure with a cocktail stick.

Lightly oil a baking sheet and place in the preheated oven for a few minutes. Place the fish on the preheated baking sheet, then place in the oven and cook for 12–15 minutes.

Bring a large saucepan of lightly salted water to the boil, then slowly add the pasta and cook for 5 minutes until *al dente*, or according to packet instructions. Drain, reserving 2 tablespoons of the pasta cooking liquor. Return the pasta to the saucepan and add the reserved pasta liquor, butter, lemon zest and juice. Toss until the pasta is well coated and glistening. Twirl the pasta into small nests on four warmed serving plates and top with the monkfish parcels. Garnish with coriander/cilantro sprigs and serve with chargrilled courgettes/zucchini and tomatoes.

## Difficulty Rating: 3 points

# Special Seafood Lasagne

## Serves 4–6

### Ingredients

450 g/1 lb fresh haddock fillet, skinned

150 ml/¼ pint/⅔ cup dry white wine

150 ml/¼ pint/⅔ cup fish stock

½ onion, peeled and thickly sliced

1 bay leaf

75 g/3 oz/⅔ stick butter

350 g/12 oz/3 cups leeks, trimmed and
   thickly sliced

1 garlic clove, peeled and crushed

3 tbsp plain/all-purpose flour

150 ml/¼ pint/⅔ cup single/light cream

2 tbsp freshly chopped dill

salt and freshly ground black pepper

8–12 sheets dried lasagne verde, cooked

225 g/8 oz ready-cooked seafood cocktail/mix

50 g/2 oz/½ cup Gruyère/hard Swiss cheese, grated

## Difficulty Rating: 3 points

Preheat the oven to 200°C/400°F/Gas Mark 6, 15 minutes before cooking. Place the haddock in a pan with the wine, fish stock, onion and bay leaf. Bring to the boil slowly, cover and simmer gently for 5 minutes, or until the fish is opaque. Remove and flake the fish, discarding any bones. Strain the cooking juices and reserve.

Melt 50 g/2 oz/¼ cup of the butter in a large saucepan. Add the leeks and garlic and cook gently for 10 minutes. Remove from the pan, using a slotted draining spoon, and reserve.

Melt the remaining butter in a small saucepan. Stir in the flour, then gradually whisk in the cream, off the heat, followed by the reserved cooking juices. Bring to the boil slowly, whisking until thickened. Stir in the dill and season to taste with salt and pepper.

Spoon a little of the sauce into the base of a buttered 2.8 litre/5 pint/3 quart shallow ovenproof dish. Top with a layer of lasagne, followed by the haddock, seafood cocktail/mix and leeks. Spoon over enough sauce to cover. Continue layering up, finishing with sheets of lasagne topped with sauce. Sprinkle over the grated Gruyère/hard Swiss cheese and bake in the preheated oven for 40–45 minutes, or until golden brown and bubbling. Serve immediately.

# Seafood Parcels with Pappardelle & Coriander Pesto

## Serves 4

### Ingredients

300 g/11 oz pappardelle or tagliatelle

8 raw tiger prawns/jumbo shrimp, shelled

12 raw queen/bay scallops

225 g/8 oz baby squid, cleaned and cut into rings

4 tbsp dry white wine

4 thin slices lemon

### For the pesto:

50 g/2 oz/1 cup fresh coriander/cilantro leaves

1 garlic clove, peeled

25 g/1 oz/¼ cup pine nuts, toasted

1 tsp lemon juice; 5 tbsp olive oil

1 tbsp grated Parmesan cheese

salt and freshly ground black pepper

Preheat the oven to 180°C/350°F/Gas Mark 4, 10 minutes before baking. To make the pesto, blend the coriander/cilantro leaves, garlic, pine nuts and lemon juice with 1 tablespoon of the olive oil to a smooth paste in a food processor. With the motor running slowly, add the remaining oil. Stir the Parmesan cheese into the pesto and season to taste with salt and pepper.

Bring a pan of lightly salted water to a rolling boil. Add the pasta and cook for 3 minutes only. Drain thoroughly, return to the pan and spoon over two thirds of the pesto. Toss to coat.

Cut out four circles about 30 cm/12 inches in diameter from nonstick baking parchment. Spoon the pasta onto one half of each circle. Top each pile of pasta with 2 prawns/shrimp, 3 scallops and a few squid rings. Spoon 1 tablespoon wine over each serving, then drizzle with the remaining coriander pesto and top with a slice of lemon. Close the parcels by folding over the other half of the paper to make a semicircle, then turn and twist the edges of the paper to secure.

Place the parcels on a baking sheet and bake in the preheated oven for 15 minutes, or until cooked. Serve immediately, allowing each person to open their own parcel.

## Difficulty Rating: 2 points

# Scallop & Potato Gratin

## Serves 4

### Ingredients

8 fresh scallops in their shells, cleaned

4 tbsp white wine

salt and freshly ground black pepper

50 g/2 oz/¹/₂ stick butter

3 tbsp plain/all-purpose flour

2 tbsp single/light cream

50 g/2 oz/¹/₂ cup Cheddar cheese, grated

450 g/1 lb (2–3 medium) potatoes, peeled and cut into chunks

1 tbsp milk

Preheat the oven to 220°C/425°F/Gas Mark 7, 15 minutes before baking. Clean four scallop shells to use as serving dishes and reserve. Place the scallops in a small saucepan with the wine, 150 ml/¹/₄ pint/²/₃ cup water and salt and pepper. Cover and simmer very gently for 5 minutes, or until just tender. Remove with a slotted spoon and cut each scallop into three pieces. Reserve the cooking juices.

Melt 25 g/1 oz/¹/₄ stick of the butter in a saucepan, stir in the flour and cook for 1 minute, stirring, then gradually whisk in the reserved cooking juices. Simmer, stirring, for 3–4 minutes until the sauce has thickened. Season to taste with salt and pepper. Remove from the heat and stir in the cream and 25 g/1 oz/¹/₄ cup of the grated cheese. Fold in the scallops.

Boil the potatoes in lightly salted water until tender, then mash with the remaining butter and the milk. Spoon or pipe the mashed potato around the edges of the cleaned scallop shells.

Divide the scallop mixture between the four shells, placing the mixture neatly in the centre. Sprinkle with the remaining grated cheese and bake in the preheated oven for about 10–15 minutes until golden brown and bubbling. Serve immediately.

## Difficulty Rating: 3 points

# Conchiglioni with Crab au Gratin

## Serves 4

### Ingredients

175 g/6 oz large pasta shells

50 g/2 oz/½ stick butter

1 shallot, peeled and finely chopped

1 bird's-eye chilli, deseeded and finely chopped

2 x 200 g/7 oz cans crab meat, drained

3 tbsp plain/all-purpose flour

50 ml/2 fl oz/¼ cup white wine

50 ml/2 fl oz/¼ cup milk

3 tbsp crème fraîche/sour cream

15 g/½ oz/1½ tbsp Cheddar cheese, grated

salt and freshly ground black pepper

50 g/2 oz/1 cup fresh white breadcrumbs

1 tbsp oil or melted butter

### To serve:

cheese or tomato sauce

tossed green salad or freshly cooked baby vegetables

Preheat the oven to 200°C/400°F/Gas Mark 6, 15 minutes before baking. Bring a large pan of lightly salted water to a rolling boil. Add the pasta shells and cook according to the packet instructions, or until *al dente*. Drain thoroughly and allow to dry completely.

Melt half the butter in a heavy–based pan, add the shallot and chilli and cook for 2 minutes, then stir in the crab meat. Stuff the cooled shells with the crab mixture and reserve. Melt the remaining butter in a small pan and stir in the flour. Cook for 1 minute, then whisk in the wine and milk and cook, stirring, until thickened. Stir in the crème fraîche/sour cream and grated cheese and season the sauce to taste with salt and pepper.

Place the crab–filled shells in a lightly oiled, large shallow baking dish or tray and spoon a little of the sauce over. Toss the breadcrumbs in the melted butter or oil, then sprinkle over the pasta shells. Bake in the preheated oven for 10 minutes.

Serve immediately with a cheese or tomato sauce and a tossed green salad or cooked baby vegetables.

## Difficulty Rating: 3 points

# Baked Meat & Poultry

**This section is packed with mouthwatering recipes for beef, lamb, pork, chicken and turkey – there is even one for Duck Lasagne. Fill your belly with that family favourite, Shepherd's Pie, or try a fruity twist with Sausage & Redcurrant Bake.**

# Traditional Lasagne

## Serves 4

### Ingredients

450 g/1 lb lean minced/ground beef

175 g/6 oz/³/₄ cup pancetta or unsmoked streaky bacon, chopped

1 large onion, peeled and chopped

2 celery stalks, trimmed and chopped

125 g/4 oz/1 cup button/white mushrooms, wiped and chopped

2 garlic cloves, peeled and chopped

100 g/3¹/₂ oz/1 cup plain/all-purpose flour

300 ml/¹/₂ pint/1¹/₄ cups beef stock

1 tbsp freeze-dried mixed herbs

5 tbsp tomato purée/paste

salt and freshly ground black pepper

8–12 precooked lasagne sheets

### For the sauce:

75 g/3 oz/²/₃ stick butter

1 tsp English mustard powder

pinch freshly grated nutmeg

900 ml/1¹/₂ pints/1 scant quart milk

125 g/4 oz/1¹/₄ cups Parmesan cheese, grated

125 g/4 oz/1 cup Cheddar cheese, grated

### To serve:

crusty bread

fresh green salad leaves

Preheat oven to 200˚C/400˚F/Gas Mark 6, 15 minutes before baking. Cook the beef and pancetta in a large saucepan for 10 minutes, stirring to break up any lumps. Add the onion, celery and mushrooms and cook for 4 minutes, or until softened slightly. Stir in the garlic and 1 tablespoon of the flour, then cook for 1 minute. Stir in the stock, herbs and tomato purée/paste. Season to taste with salt and pepper. Bring to the boil, then cover, reduce the heat and simmer for 45 minutes.

Meanwhile, to make the sauce, melt the butter in a small saucepan and stir in the remaining flour, mustard powder and nutmeg until well blended. Cook for 2 minutes. Remove from the heat and gradually blend in the milk until smooth. Return to the heat and bring to the boil, stirring, until thickened. Gradually stir in half the Parmesan and Cheddar cheeses until melted. Season to taste.

Spoon half the meat into the base of a large ovenproof dish. Top with a layer of pasta. Top with half the sauce and half the cheese. Repeat layers, finishing with cheese. Bake for 30 minutes, or until the pasta is cooked and the top is golden brown and bubbly. Serve immediately with crusty bread and salad.

## Difficulty Rating: 3 points

# Gnocchi with Tuscan Beef Ragù

## Serves 4

### Ingredients

25 g/1 oz/²⁄₃ cup dried porcini

3 tbsp olive oil

1 small onion, peeled and finely chopped

1 carrot, peeled and finely chopped

1 celery stalk, trimmed and finely chopped

1 fennel bulb, trimmed and sliced

2 garlic cloves, peeled and crushed

450 g/1 lb fresh minced/ground beef

4 tbsp red wine

50 g/2 oz/½ cup pine nuts

1 tbsp freshly chopped rosemary

2 tbsp tomato purée/paste

400 g/14 oz can chopped tomatoes

225 g/8 oz fresh gnocchi

salt and freshly ground black pepper

100 g/3½ oz mozzarella cheese, cubed

Preheat the oven to 200°C/400°F/Gas Mark 6, 15 minutes before baking. Place the porcini in a small bowl and cover with almost boiling water. Leave to soak for 30 minutes. Drain, reserving the soaking liquid and straining it through a muslin/cheesecloth-lined sieve/strainer. Chop the porcini.

Heat the olive oil in a large heavy-based pan. Add the onion, carrot, celery, fennel and garlic and cook for 8 minutes, stirring, or until soft. Add the minced/ground steak and cook, stirring, for 5–8 minutes, or until sealed and any lumps are broken up.

Pour in the wine, then add the porcini with half the pine nuts, the rosemary and tomato purée/paste. Stir in the porcini soaking liquid, then simmer for 5 minutes. Add the chopped tomatoes and simmer gently for about 40 minutes, stirring occasionally.

Meanwhile, bring 1.7 litres/3 pints/1¾ quarts of lightly salted water to a rolling boil in a large pan. Add the gnocchi and cook for 1–2 minutes until they rise to the surface.

Drain the gnocchi and place in an ovenproof dish. Stir in three quarters of the mozzarella cheese with the beef sauce. Top with the remaining mozzarella and pine nuts, then bake in the preheated oven for 20 minutes until golden brown. Serve immediately.

## Difficulty Rating: 2 points

# Chilli Con Carne with Crispy-skinned Potatoes

## Serves 4

### Ingredients

2 tbsp vegetable oil, plus extra for brushing
1 large onion, peeled and finely chopped
1 garlic clove, peeled and finely chopped
1 red chilli, deseeded and finely chopped
450 g/1 lb chuck steak, finely chopped,
    or lean minced/ground beef
1 tbsp chilli powder
400 g/14 oz can chopped tomatoes
2 tbsp tomato purée/paste
4 large baking potatoes
400 g/14 oz can red kidney beans, drained and rinsed
coarse salt and freshly ground black pepper

**To serve:**
ready-made guacamole
sour cream

Preheat the oven to 150°C/300°F/Gas Mark 2, 10 minutes before baking. Heat the oil in a large flameproof casserole dish and add the onion. Cook gently for 10 minutes until soft and lightly browned. Add the garlic and chilli and cook briefly. Increase the heat. Add the beef and cook for a further 10 minutes, stirring occasionally, until browned. Add the chilli powder and stir well. Cook for about 2 minutes, then add the chopped tomatoes and tomato purée/paste. Bring slowly to the boil. Cover and cook in the preheated oven for 1½ hours.

Meanwhile, brush a little oil all over the potatoes and rub on some coarse salt. Put the potatoes in the oven alongside the chilli.

Remove the chilli from the oven and stir in the kidney beans. Return to the oven for a further 15 minutes. Remove the chilli and potatoes from the oven. Cut a cross in each potato, squeeze to open slightly and season to taste with salt and pepper. Serve with the chilli, guacamole and sour cream.

## Difficulty Rating: 1 point

# Shepherd's Pie

## Serves 4

### Ingredients

2 tbsp vegetable or olive oil

1 onion, peeled and finely chopped

1 carrot, peeled and finely chopped

1 celery stalk, trimmed and finely chopped

1 tbsp fresh thyme leaves

450 g/1 lb leftover roast lamb, finely chopped, or fresh lean minced/ground lamb

150 ml/¼ pint/⅔ cup red wine

150 ml/¼ pint/⅔ cup lamb or vegetable stock, or leftover gravy

2 tbsp tomato purée/paste

salt and freshly ground black pepper

700 g/1½ lb (3–4 medium) potatoes, peeled and cut into chunks

25 g/1 oz/¼ stick butter

6 tbsp milk

1 tbsp freshly chopped parsley

fresh herbs, to garnish

Preheat the oven to 200°C/400°F/Gas Mark 6, about 15 minutes before baking. If using fresh lamb, dry–fry the meat in a nonstick frying pan over a high heat until well browned, and reserve. Heat the oil in a large saucepan and add the onion, carrot and celery. Cook over a medium heat for 8–10 minutes until softened and starting to brown. Add the thyme and cook briefly, then add the cooked lamb, wine, stock and tomato purée/paste. Season to taste with salt and pepper and simmer gently for 25–30 minutes until reduced and thickened. Remove from the heat to cool slightly and season again.

Meanwhile, boil the potatoes in plenty of salted water for 12–15 minutes until tender. Drain and return to the saucepan over a low heat to dry out. Remove from the heat and add the butter, milk and parsley. Mash until creamy, adding a little more milk if necessary. Adjust the seasoning.

Transfer the lamb mixture to a shallow ovenproof dish. Spoon the mash over the filling and spread evenly to cover completely. Fork the surface, place on a baking sheet, then cook in the preheated oven for 25–30 minutes until the potato topping is browned and the filling is piping hot. Garnish and serve.

## Difficulty Rating: 1 point

# Lamb & Potato Moussaka

## Serves 4

### Ingredients

700 g/1½ lb (3–4 medium) potatoes, peeled

125 g/4 oz/1 stick plus 1 tbsp butter

1 large onion, peeled and chopped

2–4 garlic cloves, peeled and crushed

700 g/1½ lb cooked roast lamb, trimmed and cubed

3 tbsp tomato purée/paste

1 tbsp freshly chopped parsley

salt and freshly ground black pepper

3–4 tbsp olive oil

2 aubergines/eggplants, trimmed and sliced

4 tomatoes, sliced

2 eggs

300 ml/½ pint/1¼ cups Greek yogurt

2–3 tbsp grated Parmesan cheese

## Difficulty Rating: 2 points

Preheat the oven to 200°C/400°F/Gas Mark 6, about 15 minutes before baking. Thinly slice the potatoes and rinse thoroughly in cold water, then pat dry with a clean dishtowel.

Melt 50 g/2 oz/½ stick of the butter in a frying pan and fry the potatoes, in batches, until crisp and golden. Using a slotted spoon, remove from the pan and reserve. Use one third of the potatoes to line the base of an ovenproof dish.

Add the onion and garlic to the butter remaining in the pan and cook for 5 minutes. Add the lamb and fry for 1 minute. Blend the tomato purée/paste with 3 tablespoons water and stir into the pan with the parsley and salt and pepper. Spoon over the layer of potatoes, then top with the remaining potato slices.

Heat the oil and the remaining butter in the pan and brown the aubergine/eggplant slices for 5–6 minutes. Arrange the tomatoes on top of the potatoes, then the aubergines on top of the tomatoes. Beat the eggs with the yogurt and Parmesan cheese. Pour over the aubergine and tomatoes. Bake in the preheated oven for 25 minutes, or until golden and piping hot. Serve.

# Cassoulet

## Serves 4

**Ingredients**

1 tbsp olive oil

1 onion, peeled and chopped

2 celery stalks, trimmed and chopped

175 g/6 oz/1⅓ cups carrots, peeled and sliced

2–3 garlic cloves, peeled and crushed

350 g/12 oz pork belly (optional)

8 spicy thick sausages, such as Toulouse

few fresh thyme sprigs

salt and freshly ground black pepper

2 x 400 g/14 oz cans cannellini beans, drained and rinsed

600 ml/1 pint/2½ cups vegetable stock

75 g/3 oz/1⅔ cups fresh breadcrumbs

2 tbsp freshly chopped thyme

Preheat the oven to 180°C/350°F/Gas Mark 4, 10 minutes before baking. Heat the oil in a large saucepan or ovenproof casserole dish, add the onion, celery, carrot and garlic and sauté for 5 minutes.

Cut the pork, if using, into small pieces and cut the sausages into chunks. Add the meat to the vegetables and cook, stirring, until lightly browned.

Add the thyme sprigs and season to taste with salt and pepper. If a saucepan was used, transfer everything to an ovenproof casserole dish.

Spoon the beans on top, then pour in the stock. Mix the breadcrumbs with 1 tablespoon of the chopped thyme in a small bowl and sprinkle on top of the beans. Cover with a lid and bake in the oven for 40 minutes.

Remove the lid and cook for a further 15 minutes, or until the breadcrumbs are crisp. Sprinkle with the remaining chopped thyme and serve.

## Difficulty Rating: 1 point

# Roast Cured Pork Loin with Baked Sliced Potatoes

## Serves 4

**Ingredients**

2 tbsp wholegrain mustard

2 tbsp clear honey

1 tsp coarsely crushed black pepper

900 g/2 lb piece smoked cured pork loin

900 g/2 lb (4–5 medium) potatoes, peeled and thinly sliced

75 g/3 oz/²⁄₃ stick butter, diced

1 large onion, peeled and finely chopped

25 g/1 oz/3 tbsp plain/all-purpose flour

salt and freshly ground black pepper

600 ml/1 pint/2¹⁄₂ cups milk

fresh green salad, to serve

Preheat the oven to 190°C/375°F/Gas Mark 5, 10 minutes before baking. Mix together the mustard, honey and black pepper. Spread evenly over the pork loin. Place in the centre of a large square of kitchen foil and wrap loosely. Cook in the preheated oven for 15 minutes per 450 g/1 lb, plus an extra 15 minutes (45 minutes), unwrapping the joint for the last 30 minutes of cooking time.

Meanwhile, layer one third of the potatoes, one third of the butter, half the onion and half the flour in a large gratin dish. Add half the remaining potatoes and butter and the remaining onion and flour. Finally, cover with the remaining potatoes. Season well with salt and pepper between layers. Pour in the milk and dot with the remaining butter. Cover the dish loosely with foil and put in the oven below the pork. Cook for 1¹⁄₂ hours.

Remove the foil from the potatoes and cook for a further 20 minutes until tender and golden. Remove the pork loin from the oven and leave to rest for 10 minutes before carving thinly. Serve with the potatoes and a fresh green salad.

## Difficulty Rating: 2 points

# Hot Salami & Vegetable Gratin

## Serves 4

### Ingredients

350 g/12 oz (about 6 medium) carrots

175 g/6 oz/$^1$/$_3$ cup fine green beans

250 g/9 oz/2 scant cups asparagus tips

175 g/6 oz/1$^1$/$_4$ cups frozen peas

225 g/8 oz Italian salami

1 tbsp olive oil

1 tbsp freshly chopped mint

25 g/1 oz/$^1$/$_4$ cup butter

150 g/5 oz/5 cups baby spinach leaves

150 ml/$^1$/$_4$ pint/$^2$/$_3$ cup double/heavy cream

salt and freshly ground black pepper

1 small, or $^1$/$_2$ olive ciabatta loaf

75 g/3 oz/$^3$/$_4$ cup Parmesan cheese, grated

green salad, to serve

Preheat oven to 200°C/400°F/Gas Mark 6, 15 minutes before baking. Peel and slice the carrots, trim the beans and asparagus and reserve. Cook the carrots in a saucepan of lightly salted boiling water for 5 minutes. Add the remaining vegetables, except the spinach, and cook for about a further 5 minutes, or until tender. Drain and place in an ovenproof dish.

Discard any skin from the outside of the salami, if necessary, then chop roughly. Heat the oil in a frying pan and fry the salami for 4–5 minutes, stirring occasionally, until golden. Transfer the salami to the ovenproof dish and scatter over the mint.

Add the butter to the pan and cook the spinach for 1–2 minutes, or until just wilted. Stir in the double/heavy cream and season well with salt and pepper. Spoon the mixture over the vegetables.

Whizz the ciabatta loaf in a food processor to make breadcrumbs. Stir in the Parmesan cheese and sprinkle over the vegetables. Bake in the preheated oven for 20 minutes, or until golden and heated through. Serve with a green salad.

## Difficulty Rating: 2 points

# Oven-baked Pork Balls with Peppers

## Serves 4

### Ingredients

**For the garlic bread:**
2–4 garlic cloves, peeled
50 g/2 oz/¹⁄₂ stick butter, softened
1 tbsp freshly chopped parsley
2–3 tsp lemon juice
1 focaccia loaf

**For the pork balls:**
450 g/1 lb fresh minced/ground pork
4 tbsp freshly chopped basil
2 garlic cloves, peeled and chopped
3 sun-dried tomatoes, chopped
salt and freshly ground black pepper
3 tbsp olive oil
1 medium red pepper, deseeded and cut into chunks
1 medium green pepper, deseeded and cut into chunks
1 medium yellow pepper, deseeded and cut into chunks
225 g/8 oz/1¹⁄₂ cups cherry tomatoes
2 tbsp balsamic vinegar

Preheat oven to 200˚C/400˚F/Gas Mark 6, 15 minutes before baking. Crush the garlic, then blend with the softened butter, the parsley and enough lemon juice to give a soft consistency. Shape into a roll, wrap in baking parchment and chill in the refrigerator for at least 30 minutes.

Mix together the pork, basil, 1 chopped garlic clove, sun-dried tomatoes and seasoning until well combined. With damp hands, divide the mixture into 16, roll into balls and reserve.

Spoon the olive oil in a large roasting tin/pan and place in the preheated oven for about 3 minutes until very hot. Remove from the oven and stir in the pork balls, the remaining chopped garlic and peppers. Bake for about 15 minutes. Remove from the oven and stir in the cherry tomatoes and season to taste with plenty of salt and pepper. Bake for about a further 20 minutes.

Just before the pork balls are ready, slice the bread, toast lightly and spread with the prepared garlic butter. Remove the pork balls from the oven, stir in the vinegar and serve immediately with garlic bread.

**Difficulty Rating: 1 point**

# Crispy Baked Potatoes with Serrano Ham

## Serves 4

**Ingredients**

**4 large baking potatoes**
**4 tsp half-fat crème fraîche/sour cream**
**salt and freshly ground black pepper**
**50 g/2 oz/2 slices lean serrano ham or prosciutto,**
  **fat removed**
**50 g/2 oz/1 cup cooked baby broad/fava beans**
**50 g/2 oz/¼ cup cooked carrots, diced**
**50 g/2 oz/1 cup cooked peas**
**50 g/2 oz/½ cup grated reduced-fat hard cheese**
**fresh green salad, to serve**

Preheat the oven to 200°C/400°F/Gas Mark 6, 15 minutes before baking. Scrub the potatoes dry. Prick with a fork and place on a baking sheet. Bake for 1–1½ hours until tender when squeezed. (Use oven gloves/mitts to pick up the potatoes, as they will be very hot.)

Cut the potatoes in half horizontally and scoop out all the flesh into a bowl. Spoon the crème fraîche/sour cream into the bowl and mix thoroughly with the potatoes. Season to taste with a little salt and pepper. Cut the ham into strips and carefully stir into the potato mixture with the broad/fava beans, carrots and peas.

Pile the mixture back into the eight potato shells and sprinkle a little grated cheese on top. Place under a hot grill/broiler and cook until golden and heated through. Serve with a fresh green salad.

## Difficulty Rating: 1 point

# Cannelloni

## Serves 4

### Ingredients

2 tbsp olive oil

175 g/6 oz/³/₄ cup fresh minced/ground pork

75 g/3 oz/²/₃ cup chicken livers, chopped

1 small onion, peeled and chopped

1 garlic clove, peeled and chopped

175 g/6 oz/1 cup frozen spinach, thawed and chopped

1 tbsp freeze-dried oregano

pinch freshly grated nutmeg

salt and freshly ground black pepper

175 g/6 oz/³/₄ cup ricotta or quark cheese

25 g/1 oz/¹/₄ stick butter

25 g/1 oz/¹/₄ cup plain/all-purpose flour

600 ml/1 pt/2¹/₂ cups milk

600 ml/1 pt/2¹/₂ cups ready-made tomato sauce

16 precooked cannelloni tubes

50 g/2 oz/¹/₂ cup Parmesan cheese, grated

green salad, to serve

Preheat oven to 190°C/375°F/Gas Mark 5, 10 minutes before baking. Heat the olive oil in a frying pan and cook the pork and chicken livers for about 5 minutes, stirring occasionally, until browned all over. Break up any lumps, if necessary, with a wooden spoon. Add the onion and garlic and cook for 4 minutes until softened. Add the spinach, oregano and nutmeg and season to taste with salt and pepper. Cook until all the liquid has evaporated, then remove the pan from the heat and allow to cool. Stir in the ricotta or quark cheese.

Meanwhile, melt the butter in a small saucepan and stir in the plain/all-purpose flour to form a roux. Cook for 2 minutes, stirring occasionally. Remove from the heat and blend in the milk until smooth. Return to the heat and bring to the boil, stirring until the sauce has thickened. Reserve.

Spoon a thin layer of the tomato sauce on the base of a large ovenproof dish. Divide the pork filling between the cannelloni tubes. Arrange on top of the tomato sauce. Spoon over the remaining tomato sauce. Pour over the white sauce and sprinkle with the Parmesan cheese. Bake in the preheated oven for

30–35 minutes, or until the cannelloni is tender and the top is golden brown. Serve immediately with a green salad.

## Difficulty Rating: 3 points

# Sausage & Redcurrant Pasta Bake

## Serves 4

### Ingredients

450 g/1 lb (about 7–8) good-quality thick pork sausages

2 tsp sunflower/corn oil

25 g/1 oz/¹⁄₄ stick butter

1 onion, peeled and sliced

2 tbsp plain/all-purpose flour

450 ml/³⁄₄ pint/1³⁄₄ cups chicken stock

150 ml/¹⁄₄ pint/²⁄₃ cup port or good-quality red wine

1 tbsp freshly chopped thyme leaves, plus sprigs to garnish

1 bay leaf

4 tbsp redcurrant jelly

salt and freshly ground black pepper

350 g/12 oz/2¹⁄₄ cups fresh penne

75 g/3 oz/³⁄₄ cup Gruyère/hard Swiss cheese, grated

Preheat the oven to 220°C/425°F/Gas Mark 7, 15 minutes before baking. Prick the sausages, place in a shallow ovenproof dish and toss in the sunflower/corn oil. Cook in the oven for 25–30 minutes, or until golden brown.

Meanwhile, melt the butter in a frying pan, add the sliced onion and fry for 5 minutes, or until golden brown. Stir in the flour and cook for 2 minutes. Remove the pan from the heat and gradually stir in the chicken stock with the port or red wine. Return the pan to the heat and bring to the boil, stirring continuously, until the sauce starts to thicken. Add the thyme, bay leaf and redcurrant jelly and season well with salt and pepper. Simmer the sauce for 5 minutes.

Bring a large pan of salted water to a rolling boil, add the pasta and cook for about 4 minutes, or until *al dente*. Drain thoroughly and reserve.

Lower the oven temperature to 200°C/400°F/Gas Mark 6. Remove the sausages from the oven, drain off any excess fat and return the sausages to the dish. Add the pasta. Pour over the sauce, removing the bay leaf, and toss together. Sprinkle with the Gruyère/hard Swiss cheese and return to the oven for

15–20 minutes, or until bubbling and golden brown. Serve immediately, garnished with thyme sprigs.

## Difficulty Rating: 2 points

# Tagliatelle with Spicy Sausage Ragù

## Serves 4

### Ingredients

3 tbsp olive oil

6 spicy sausages

1 small onion, peeled and finely chopped

1 tsp fennel seeds

175 g/6 oz/³⁄₄ cup fresh minced/ground pork

225 g/8 oz can chopped tomatoes with garlic

1 tbsp sun-dried tomato purée/paste

2 tbsp red wine or port

salt and freshly ground black pepper

350 g/12 oz tagliatelle

300 ml/¹⁄₂ pint/1¹⁄₄ cups prepared white sauce

50 g/2 oz/¹⁄₂ cup freshly grated Parmesan cheese

## Difficulty Rating: 3 points

Preheat the oven to 200°C/400°F/Gas Mark 6, 15 minutes before cooking. Heat 1 tablespoon of the olive oil in a large frying pan. Prick the sausages, add to the pan and cook for 8–10 minutes, or until browned and cooked through. Remove and cut into thin diagonal slices. Reserve.

Return the pan to the heat and pour in the remaining olive oil. Add the onion and cook for 8 minutes, or until softened. Add the fennel seeds and minced/ground pork and cook, stirring, for 5–8 minutes, or until the meat is sealed and browned. Stir in the tomatoes, tomato purée/paste and the wine or port. Season to taste with salt and pepper. Bring to the boil, cover and simmer for 30 minutes, stirring occasionally. Remove the lid and simmer for 10 minutes.

Bring a large pan of lightly salted water to a rolling boil. Add the pasta and cook according to the packet instructions, or until al dente. Drain thoroughly and toss with the meat sauce. Place half the pasta in an ovenproof dish and cover with 4 tablespoons of the white sauce. Top with half the sausages and grated Parmesan cheese. Repeat the layering, finishing with white sauce and Parmesan cheese. Bake in the preheated oven for 20 minutes, or until golden brown. Serve immediately.

# Gnocchi & Parma Ham Bake

## Serves 4

**Ingredients**

3 tbsp olive oil

1 red onion, peeled and sliced

2 garlic cloves, peeled

175 g/6 oz (about 3) plum tomatoes, skinned and quartered

2 tbsp sun-dried tomato purée/paste

250 g/9 oz tub mascarpone cheese

salt and freshly ground black pepper

1 tbsp freshly chopped tarragon

300 g/11 oz fresh gnocchi

125 g/4 oz/1 cup grated Cheddar or Parmesan cheese

50 g/2 oz/1 cup fresh white breadcrumbs

50 g/2 oz Parma ham/prosciutto, sliced

10 pitted green olives, halved

flat-leaf/Italian parsley sprigs, to garnish

Preheat the oven to 180°C/350°F/Gas Mark 4, 10 minutes before baking. Heat 2 tablespoons of the olive oil in a large frying pan and cook the onion and garlic for 5 minutes, or until softened. Stir in the tomatoes, sun-dried tomato purée/paste and mascarpone cheese. Season to taste with salt and pepper. Add half the tarragon. Bring to the boil, then lower the heat immediately and simmer for 5 minutes.

Meanwhile, bring 1.7 litres/3 pints/1¼ quarts water to the boil in a large pan. Add the remaining olive oil and a good pinch of salt. Add the gnocchi and cook for 1–2 minutes, or until they rise to the surface. Drain the gnocchi thoroughly and transfer to a large ovenproof dish. Add the tomato sauce and toss gently to coat the gnocchi.

Combine the Cheddar or Parmesan cheese with the breadcrumbs and remaining tarragon and scatter over the gnocchi mixture. Top with the Parma ham/prosciutto and olives and season again. Cook in the preheated oven for 20–25 minutes, or until golden and bubbling. Serve immediately, garnished with parsley sprigs.

## Difficulty Rating: 1 point

# Chicken Baked in a Salt Crust

## Serves 4

**Ingredients**

1.8 kg/4 lb oven-ready chicken
salt and freshly ground black pepper
1 onion, peeled
1 fresh rosemary sprig
1 fresh thyme sprig
1 bay leaf
1 tbsp butter, softened
1 garlic clove, peeled and crushed
pinch ground paprika
finely grated zest of ½ lemon

**For the salt crust:**
900 g/2 lb/8 cups plain/all-purpose flour
450 g/1 lb/3²/₃ cups fine cooking salt
450 g/1 lb/3²/₃ cups coarse sea salt
2 tbsp oil

**To garnish:**
fresh herbs
lemon slices

Preheat the oven to 170°C/325°F/Gas Mark 3, 10 minutes before baking. Remove the giblets, if necessary, and rinse the chicken with cold water. Sprinkle the inside with salt and pepper. Put the onion inside with the rosemary, thyme and bay leaf. Mix the butter, garlic, paprika and lemon zest together. Starting at the neck end, gently ease the skin from the chicken and push the mixture under.

To make the salt crust, put the flour and salts in a large mixing bowl and stir together. Make a well in the centre. Pour in 600 ml/1 pint/2½ cups cold water and the oil. Mix to a stiff dough, then knead on a lightly floured surface for 2–3 minutes. Roll out the dough to a circle with a diameter of about 51 cm/20 inches. Place the chicken breast-side down in the centre. Lightly brush the edges with water, then fold over to enclose. Pinch the joins together to seal. Put the chicken

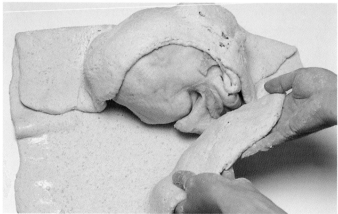

join-side down in a roasting tin/pan and cook in the preheated oven for 2¾ hours. Remove from the oven and stand for 20 minutes. Break open the hard crust and remove the chicken. Discard the crust and remove the skin from the chicken. Garnish with the fresh herbs and lemon slices and serve immediately.

## Difficulty Rating: 3 points

# Chicken Pie with Sweet Potato Topping

## Serves 4

**Ingredients**

700 g/1½ lb/5¼ cups sweet potatoes, peeled and cut into chunks

salt and freshly ground black pepper

150 ml/¼ pint/⅔ cup milk

25 g/1 oz/¼ stick butter

2 tsp brown sugar

grated zest of 1 orange

4 skinless chicken breast fillets, diced

1 medium onion, peeled and coarsely chopped

125 g/4 oz/1¼ cups baby mushrooms, stems trimmed

2 leeks, trimmed and thickly sliced

150 ml/¼ pint/⅔ cup dry white wine

1 chicken stock cube

1 tbsp freshly chopped parsley

50 ml/2 fl oz/¼ cup crème fraîche or thick double/heavy cream

green vegetables, to serve

Preheat the oven to 190°C/375°F/Gas Mark 5, 10 minutes before baking. Cook the potatoes in lightly salted boiling water until tender. Drain well, then return to the saucepan and mash until smooth and creamy, gradually adding the milk, then the butter, sugar and orange zest. Season to taste and reserve.

Place the chicken in a saucepan with the onion, mushrooms, leeks, wine and stock cube and season to taste. Simmer, covered, until the chicken and vegetables are tender. Using a slotted spoon, transfer the chicken and vegetables to a 1.1 litre/2 pint/1.2 quart pie dish. Add the parsley and crème fraîche or cream to the liquid in the pan and bring to the boil. Simmer until thickened and smooth, stirring constantly. Pour over the chicken, mix and cool. Spread the mashed potato over the chicken filling and swirl the surface into decorative peaks. Bake in the preheated oven for 35 minutes, or until the top is golden and the chicken filling is heated through. Serve immediately with fresh green vegetables.

## Difficulty Rating: 2 points

# Lemon Chicken with Potatoes, Rosemary & Olives

## Serves 6

### Ingredients

12 skinless, boneless chicken thighs
1 large lemon
125 ml/4 fl oz/¹⁄₂ cup extra virgin olive oil
6 garlic cloves, peeled and sliced
2 onions, peeled and thinly sliced
bunch fresh rosemary
1.1 kg/2¹⁄₂ lb (about 5 medium) potatoes,
    peeled and cut into 4 cm/1¹⁄₂ inch pieces
salt and freshly ground black pepper
18–24 black olives, pitted

### To serve:
steamed carrots
steamed courgettes/zucchini

Preheat oven to 200°C/400°F/Gas Mark 6, 15 minutes before baking. Trim the chicken thighs and place in a shallow baking dish large enough to hold them in a single layer.

Remove the zest from the lemon with a zester or, if using a peeler, cut into thin julienne strips. Reserve half and add the remainder to the chicken. Squeeze the lemon juice over the chicken, toss to coat well and leave to stand for 10 minutes. Add the remaining lemon zest or julienne strips, olive oil, garlic, onions and half of the rosemary sprigs. Toss gently and leave for about 20 minutes.

Cover the potatoes with lightly salted water and bring to the boil. Cook for 2 minutes, then drain well and add to the chicken. Season to taste with salt and pepper. Roast the chicken in the preheated oven for 50 minutes, turning frequently and basting, or until the chicken is cooked. Just before the end of cooking time, discard the rosemary and add fresh rosemary sprigs. Add the olives and stir. Serve immediately with steamed carrots and courgettes/zucchini.

## Difficulty Rating: 2 points

# Creamy Chicken Cannelloni

## Serves 6

### Ingredients

50 g/2 oz/¹/₂ stick butter

2 garlic cloves, peeled and finely crushed

225 g/8 oz/2¹/₄ cups button/white mushrooms, thinly sliced

2 tbsp freshly chopped basil

450 g/1 lb/10 cups fresh spinach, blanched

salt and freshly ground black pepper

2 tbsp plain/all-purpose flour

300 ml/¹/₂ pint/1¹/₄ cups chicken stock

150 ml/¹/₄ pint/²/₃ cup dry white wine

150 ml/¹/₄ pint/²/₃ cup double/heavy cream

350 g/12 oz/3³/₄ cups skinless, boneless and cooked chicken, chopped

175 g/6 oz/³/₄ cup Parma ham/prosciutto, finely chopped

¹/₂ tsp dried thyme

225 g/8 oz (about 16) precooked cannelloni tubes

175 g/6 oz/1¹/₂ cups Gruyère/hard Swiss cheese, grated

40 g/1¹/₂ oz/¹/₂ cup Parmesan cheese, grated

fresh basil sprig, to garnish

Preheat the oven to 190°C/375°F/Gas Mark 5, 10 minutes before baking. Lightly butter a 28 x 23 cm/11 x 9 inch ovenproof baking dish. Heat half the butter in a large heavy–based frying pan, then add the garlic and mushrooms and cook gently for 5 minutes. Stir in the basil and the spinach and cook, covered, until the spinach is wilted and just tender, stirring frequently. Season to taste with salt and pepper, then spoon into the dish and reserve.

Melt the remaining butter in a small saucepan, then stir in the flour and cook for about 2 minutes, stirring constantly. Remove from the heat, stir in the stock, then the wine and the cream. Return to the heat, bring to the boil and simmer until the sauce is thick and smooth, then season to taste. Measure 125 ml/4 fl oz/¹/₂ cup of the cream sauce into a bowl. Add the chopped chicken, Parma ham/prosciutto and the dried thyme. Season to taste, then spoon the chicken mixture into the cannelloni tubes, arranging them in two long rows on top of the spinach layer. Add half the Gruyère/hard Swiss cheese to the cream sauce and heat, stirring, until the cheese melts. Pour over the sauce and

top with the remaining Gruyère and the Parmesan cheeses. Bake in the preheated oven for 35 minutes, or until golden and bubbling. Garnish with a sprig of fresh basil and serve immediately.

## Difficulty Rating: 3 points

# Chicken Parcels with Courgettes & Pasta

## Serves 4

### Ingredients

2 tbsp olive oil

125 g/4 oz/2¼ cups farfalle pasta

1 onion, peeled and thinly sliced

1 garlic clove, peeled and finely chopped

2 medium courgettes/zucchini, trimmed and thinly sliced

salt and freshly ground black pepper

2 tbsp freshly chopped oregano

4 plum tomatoes, deseeded and coarsely chopped

4 x 175 g/6 oz boneless, skinless chicken breasts

150 ml/¼ pint/⅔ cup Italian white wine

Preheat oven to 200°C/400°F/Gas Mark 6, 15 minutes before baking. Lightly brush four large sheets of nonstick baking parchment with half the oil. Bring a saucepan of lightly salted water to the boil and cook the pasta for 10 minutes, or until *al dente*. Drain and reserve.

Heat the remaining oil in a frying pan and cook the onion for 2–3 minutes. Add the garlic and cook for 1 minute. Add the courgettes/zucchini and cook for 1 minute, then remove from the heat, season to taste with salt and pepper and add half the oregano.

Divide the cooked pasta equally between the four sheets of baking parchment, positioning the pasta in the centre. Top the pasta with equal amounts of the vegetable mixture and sprinkle a quarter of the chopped tomatoes over each.

Score the surface of each chicken breast about 1 cm/½ inch deep. Place a chicken breast on top of the pasta and sprinkle each with the remaining oregano and the white wine. Fold the edges of the paper along the top, then along each side, creating a sealed envelope. Bake in the preheated oven for 30–35 minutes, or until cooked. Serve immediately.

## Difficulty Rating: 2 points

# Herb–baked Chicken with Tagliatelle

## Serves 4

### Ingredients

75 g/3 oz/1½ cups fresh white breadcrumbs

3 tbsp olive oil

1 tsp dried oregano

2 tbsp sun-dried tomato purée/paste

salt and freshly ground black pepper

4 boneless, skinless chicken breast fillets,
  each about 150 g/5 oz

2 x 400 g/14 oz cans plum tomatoes

4 tbsp freshly chopped basil

2 tbsp dry white wine

350 g/12 oz tagliatelle

fresh basil sprigs, to garnish

Preheat the oven to 200°C/400°F/Gas Mark 6, 15 minutes before baking. Mix together the breadcrumbs, 1 tablespoon of the olive oil, the oregano and tomato purée/paste. Season to taste with salt and pepper. Place the chicken breasts well apart in a roasting tin/pan and coat with the breadcrumb mixture.

Mix the plum tomatoes with the chopped basil and white wine. Season to taste, then spoon evenly round the chicken.

Drizzle the remaining olive oil over the chicken breasts and cook in the preheated oven for 20–30 minutes, or until the chicken is golden and the juices run clear when a skewer is inserted into the flesh.

Meanwhile, bring a large pan of lightly salted water to a rolling boil. Add the pasta and cook according to the packet instructions, or until *al dente*.

Drain the pasta thoroughly and transfer to warmed serving plates. Arrange the chicken breasts on top of the pasta and spoon over the sauce. Garnish with sprigs of basil and serve immediately.

## Difficulty Rating: 1 point

# Pasta Ring with Chicken & Sun-dried Tomatoes

## Serves 6

### Ingredients

125 g/4 oz/1 stick plus 1 tbsp butter, plus extra for brushing
2 tbsp white breadcrumbs
40 g/1½ oz/⅓ cup plain/all-purpose flour
450 ml/¾ pint/1¾ cups milk
1 small onion, peeled and very finely chopped
salt and freshly ground black pepper
225 g/8 oz fresh tagliatelle
450 g/1 lb chicken breast fillets, skinned and cut into strips
200 ml/7 fl oz/¾ cup white wine
1 tsp cornflour/cornstarch
2 tbsp freshly chopped tarragon
2 tbsp chopped sun-dried tomatoes

Preheat the oven to 190°C/375°F/Gas Mark 5, 10 minutes before baking. Lightly brush a 20.5 cm/8 inch ring mould with a little melted butter and dust with the breadcrumbs. Melt 50 g/2 oz/¼ cup of the butter in a heavy-based pan. Add the flour and cook for 1 minute. Whisk in the milk and cook, stirring, until thickened. Add the chopped onion, season to taste with salt and pepper and reserve.

Bring a large pan of lightly salted water to a rolling boil. Add the tagliatelle and cook according to the packet instructions, about 3–4 minutes until *al dente*. Drain thoroughly and stir into the white sauce. Pour the pasta mixture into the prepared mould and bake in the preheated oven for 25–30 minutes.

Melt the remaining butter in a pan, add the chicken and cook for 4–5 minutes until cooked. Pour in the wine and cook over a high heat for 30 seconds. Blend the cornflour/cornstarch with 1 teaspoon water and stir into the pan. Add half the chopped tarragon and the tomatoes. Season well, then cook for a few minutes until thickened. Allow the pasta to cool for 5 minutes, then unmould onto a large serving plate. Fill the centre with the chicken sauce. Garnish with the remaining tarragon and serve.

## Difficulty Rating: 3 points

# Turkey & Mixed Mushroom Lasagne

## Serves 4

### Ingredients

1 tbsp olive oil

225 g/8 oz/2¼ cups mixed mushrooms
   e.g. button/white, chestnut and portabello, wiped and sliced

1 tbsp butter

3 tbsp plain/all-purpose flour

300 ml/½ pint/1¼ cups skimmed milk

1 bay leaf

225 g/8 oz/1½ cups cooked turkey, cubed

¼ tsp freshly grated nutmeg

salt and freshly ground black pepper

400 g/14 oz can plum tomatoes, drained and chopped

1 tsp dried mixed herbs

9 lasagne sheets (about 150 g/5 oz)

### For the topping:

200 ml/7 fl oz/¾ cup low-fat Greek yogurt

1 medium/large egg, lightly beaten

1 tbsp finely grated Parmesan cheese

mixed salad leaves, to serve

Preheat the oven to 180°C/350°F/Gas Mark 4. Heat the oil and cook the mushrooms until tender and all the juices have evaporated. Remove and reserve.

Put the butter, flour, milk and bay leaf in the pan. Slowly bring to the boil, stirring until thickened. Simmer for 2–3 minutes. Remove the bay leaf and stir in the mushrooms, turkey, nutmeg, salt and pepper.

Mix together the tomatoes and mixed herbs and season with salt and pepper. Spoon half into the base of a 1.7 litre/3 pint/1¾ quart ovenproof dish. Top with three sheets of lasagne, then with half the turkey mixture. Repeat the layers, then arrange the remaining three sheets of pasta on top.

Mix together the yogurt and egg. Spoon over the lasagne, spreading the mixture into the corners. Sprinkle with the

Parmesan and bake in the preheated oven for 45 minutes. Serve with the mixed salad.

## Difficulty Rating: 2 points

# Turkey Tetrazzini

## Serves 4

**Ingredients**

275 g/10 oz/3¼ cups green and white tagliatelle

50 g/2 oz/½ stick butter

4 slices streaky/fatty bacon, diced

1 onion, peeled and finely chopped

175 g/6 oz/1¾ cups mushrooms, thinly sliced

40 g/1½ oz/⅓ cup plain/all-purpose flour

450 ml/¾ pint/1¾ cups chicken stock

150 ml/¼ pint/⅓ cup double/heavy cream

2 tbsp sherry

450 g/1 lb/3 cups cooked turkey meat, cut into bite-size pieces

1 tbsp freshly chopped parsley; freshly grated nutmeg, to taste

salt and freshly ground black pepper

25 g/1 oz/¼ cup grated Parmesan cheese

**To garnish:**

freshly chopped parsley

grated Parmesan cheese

Preheat the oven to 180°C/350°F/Gas Mark 4, 10 minutes before baking. Lightly oil a large ovenproof dish. Bring a large saucepan of lightly salted water to the boil. Add the tagliatelle and cook for 7–9 minutes, or until *al dente*. Drain well and reserve.

In a heavy-based saucepan, heat the butter and add the bacon. Cook for 2–3 minutes until crisp and golden. Add the onion and mushrooms and cook for 3–4 minutes until tender. Stir in the flour and cook for 2 minutes. Remove from the heat and slowly stir in the stock. Return to the heat and cook, stirring, until a smooth, thick sauce has formed. Add the tagliatelle, then pour in the cream and sherry. Add the turkey and parsley. Season to taste with the nutmeg and salt and pepper. Toss well to coat.

Turn the mixture into the prepared dish, spreading evenly. Sprinkle the top with the Parmesan cheese and bake in the preheated oven for 30–35 minutes, or until crisp, golden and bubbling. Garnish with chopped parsley and Parmesan cheese and serve straight from the dish.

## Difficulty Rating: 1 point

# Duck Lasagne with Porcini & Basil

## Serves 6

**Ingredients**

1.4–1.8 kg/3–4 lb duck, quartered

1 onion, unpeeled and quartered

2 carrots, peeled and cut into pieces

1 celery stalk, cut into pieces

1 leek, trimmed and cut into pieces

2 garlic cloves, unpeeled and smashed

1 tbsp black peppercorns

2 bay leaves

6–8 fresh thyme sprigs

50 g/2 oz/$\frac{1}{2}$ cup dried porcini mushrooms

125 ml/4 fl oz/$\frac{1}{2}$ cup dry sherry

75 g/3 oz/$\frac{3}{4}$ stick butter, diced

1 bunch fresh basil leaves, stripped from stems

24 precooked lasagne sheets

75 g/3 oz/1 cup grated Parmesan cheese

parsley sprig, to garnish

mixed salad, to serve

Preheat the oven to 180°C/350°F/Gas Mark 4, 10 minutes before baking. Put the duck with the vegetables, garlic, peppercorns, bay leaves and thyme into a large stock pot and cover with cold water. Bring to the boil, skimming off any fat, then reduce the heat and simmer for 1 hour. Transfer the duck to a bowl and cool slightly. When cool enough to handle, remove the meat from the duck and dice. Add all the bones and trimmings to the simmering stock and continue to simmer for 1 hour. Strain the stock into a large bowl and leave until cold. Remove and discard the fat that has risen to the top of the stock.

Put the porcini in a colander and rinse under cold running water. Leave for 1 minute to dry off, then turn out onto a chopping board and chop finely. Place in a small bowl, then pour over the sherry and leave for about 1 hour, or until the porcini are plump and all the sherry is absorbed. Heat 25 g/1 oz/$\frac{1}{4}$ stick of the butter in a frying pan. Shred the basil leaves and add to the hot butter, stirring until wilted. Add the soaked porcini and any liquid, mix well and reserve.

Oil a 30 x 23 cm/12 x 9 inch deep baking dish and pour a little stock into the base. Cover with 6–8 lasagne sheets, making sure that the sheets overlap slightly. Continue to layer the pasta with a little stock, duck meat, the mushroom–basil mixture and Parmesan. Add a little butter every other layer. Cover with kitchen foil and bake in the preheated oven for 40–45 minutes, or until cooked. Leave to stand for 10 minutes before serving. Garnish with a sprig of parsley and serve with salad.

## Difficulty Rating: 4 points

# Baked Vegetable Dishes

**You will not miss meat with these hearty dishes, such as Vegetable Cassoulet with a crispy topping or Courgette Lasagne. Cheese fans can try Cheese & Onion Oat Pie and Baked Macaroni Cheese – yum!**

# Boston-style Baked Beans

### Serves 8

**Ingredients**

350 g/12 oz/2 cups mixed dried pulses, e.g. haricot/kidney beans, flageolet/lima beans, chickpeas or pinto beans

1 large onion, peeled and finely chopped

5 tbsp black treacle/molasses

2 tbsp Dijon mustard

2 tbsp soft light brown sugar

125 g/4 oz/1 cup plain/all-purpose flour

150 g/5 oz/1 cup fine cornmeal

2 tbsp caster/superfine sugar

2¹⁄₂ tsp baking powder

¹⁄₂ tsp salt

2 tbsp freshly chopped thyme

2 eggs

200 ml/7 fl oz/1 cup milk

25 g/1 oz/¹⁄₄ stick butter, melted

salt and freshly ground black pepper

fresh parsley sprigs, to garnish

Preheat the oven to 130°C/250°F/Gas Mark ¹⁄₂, 10 minutes before baking. Put the pulses into a large saucepan and cover with at least twice their volume of water. Bring to the boil and simmer for 2 minutes. Leave to stand for 1 hour. Return to the boil and boil rapidly for about 10 minutes. Drain and reserve.

Mix together the onion, treacle/molasses, mustard and sugar in a large mixing bowl. Add the drained beans and 300 ml/¹⁄₂ pint/1¹⁄₄ cups fresh water. Stir well, bring to the boil, cover and transfer to the preheated oven for 4 hours in an ovenproof dish, stirring once every hour and adding more water if necessary.

When the beans are cooked, remove from the oven and keep warm. Increase the oven temperature to 200°C/400°F/Gas Mark 6. Mix together the flour, cornmeal, sugar, baking powder, salt and most of the thyme, reserving about one third for garnish. In a separate bowl, beat the eggs, then stir in the milk and butter. Pour the wet ingredients onto the dry ones and stir just enough to combine. Pour into a buttered 18 cm/7 inch square

cake tin/pan. Sprinkle over the remaining thyme. Bake for 30 minutes until golden and risen, or until a cocktail stick/toothpick inserted into the centre comes out clean. Cut into squares, then reheat the beans. Season to taste with salt and pepper and serve immediately, garnished with parsley sprigs.

## Difficulty Rating: 3 points

# Vegetable Cassoulet

## Serves 6

**Ingredients**

125 g/4 oz/²⁄₃ cup dried haricot/navy beans, soaked overnight

2 tbsp olive oil

2 garlic cloves, peeled and chopped

225 g/8 oz (about 9) baby onions, peeled and halved

2 carrots, peeled and diced

2 celery stalks, trimmed and finely chopped

1 red pepper, deseeded and chopped

175 g/6 oz/1¹⁄₂ cups mixed mushrooms, sliced

1 tbsp each freshly chopped rosemary, thyme and sage

150 ml/¹⁄₄ pint/²⁄₃ cup red wine

4 tbsp tomato purée/paste

1 tbsp dark soy sauce

salt and freshly ground black pepper

50 g/2 oz/1 cup fresh breadcrumbs

1 tbsp freshly chopped parsley

basil sprigs, to garnish

Preheat the oven to 190°C/375°F/Gas Mark 5, 10 minutes before baking. Drain the haricot/navy beans. Place in a saucepan with 1 litre/1³⁄₄ pints/1 quart fresh water. Boil rapidly for 10 minutes. Reduce the heat and simmer gently for 45 minutes. Drain the beans, reserving 300 ml/¹⁄₂ pint/1¹⁄₄ cups of the liquid.

Heat 1 tablespoon of the oil in a flameproof casserole dish and add the garlic, onions, carrots, celery and red pepper. Cook gently for 10–12 minutes until tender and starting to brown. Add a little water if the vegetables start to stick. Add the mushrooms and cook for a further 5 minutes until softened. Add the herbs and stir briefly. Stir in the red wine and boil rapidly for about 5 minutes until reduced and syrupy. Stir in the reserved beans and their liquid, tomato purée/paste and soy sauce. Season to taste with salt and pepper. Mix together the breadcrumbs and parsley with the remaining oil. Scatter this mixture evenly over the top of the stew. Cover loosely with kitchen foil, transfer to the preheated oven and cook for 30 minutes. Carefully remove the foil and cook for a further 15–20 minutes until the topping is crisp and golden. Serve garnished with basil sprigs.

## Difficulty Rating: 2 points

# Spanish Baked Tomatoes

## Serves 4

**Ingredients**

175 g/6 oz/³/₄ cup wholegrain rice

600 ml/1 pint/2¹/₂ cups vegetable stock

2 tsp sunflower/corn oil

2 shallots, peeled and finely chopped

1 garlic clove, peeled and crushed

1 green pepper, deseeded and cut into small cubes

1 red chilli, deseeded and finely chopped

50 g/2 oz/¹/₂ cup button/white mushrooms, finely chopped

1 tbsp freshly chopped oregano

salt and freshly ground black pepper

4 large ripe beef tomatoes

1 large/extra-large egg, beaten

1 tsp caster/superfine sugar

basil leaves, to garnish

crusty bread, to serve

Preheat the oven to 180°C/350°F/Gas Mark 4, 10 minutes before baking. Place the rice in a saucepan, pour over the vegetable stock and bring to the boil. Simmer for 30 minutes, or until the rice is tender. Drain and turn into a mixing bowl.

Add 1 teaspoon of sunflower/corn oil to a small nonstick pan and gently fry the shallots, garlic, pepper, chilli and mushrooms for 2 minutes. Add to the rice with the chopped oregano. Season with plenty of salt and pepper.

Slice the top off each tomato. Cut and scoop out the flesh, removing the hard core. Pass the tomato flesh through a sieve and add 1 tablespoon of the juice to the rice mixture. Stir in the beaten egg and mix. Sprinkle a little sugar in the base of each tomato, then pile the rice mixture into the shells.

Place the tomatoes in a baking dish and pour a little cold water around them. Replace their lids and drizzle a few drops of sunflower oil over the tops. Bake in the preheated oven for about 25 minutes. Garnish with the basil leaves and season with black pepper and serve immediately with crusty bread.

## Difficulty Rating: 2 points

# Italian Baked Tomatoes with Curly Endive & Radicchio

## Serves 4

### Ingredients

1 tsp olive oil

4 beef tomatoes

salt

50 g/2 oz/1 cup fresh white breadcrumbs

1 tbsp freshly snipped chives

1 tbsp freshly chopped parsley

125 g/4 oz/1¼ cups button/white mushrooms,
  finely chopped

salt and freshly ground black pepper

25 g/1 oz/¼ cup fresh Parmesan cheese, grated

### For the salad:

½ curly endive lettuce

½ small piece radicchio

2 tbsp olive oil

1 tsp balsamic vinegar

salt and freshly ground black pepper

Preheat the oven to 190°C/375°F/Gas Mark 5, 10 minutes before baking. Lightly oil a baking sheet with the teaspoon of oil. Slice the tops off the tomatoes, remove all the tomato flesh and sieve into a large bowl. Sprinkle a little salt inside the tomato shells. Place them upside down on a plate while the filling is prepared.

Mix the sieved tomato with the breadcrumbs, fresh herbs and mushrooms and season well with salt and pepper. Place the tomato shells on the prepared baking sheet and fill with the tomato and mushroom mixture. Sprinkle the cheese on top and bake in the preheated oven for 15–20 minutes until golden brown.

Meanwhile, prepare the salad. Arrange the endive and radicchio on individual serving plates and mix the remaining ingredients together in a small bowl to make the dressing. Season to taste.

When the tomatoes are cooked, allow to rest for 5 minutes, then place on the prepared plates and drizzle over a little dressing. Serve warm.

## Difficulty Rating: 1 point

# Stuffed Onions with Pine Nuts

## Serves 4

**Ingredients**

4 onions, peeled

2 garlic cloves, peeled and crushed

2 tbsp fresh brown breadcrumbs

2 tbsp fresh white breadcrumbs

3 tbsp sultanas/golden raisins

3 tbsp pine nuts

50 g/2 oz/½ cup grated low-fat hard cheese

2 tbsp freshly chopped parsley

1 egg, beaten

salt and freshly ground black pepper

Preheat the oven to 200°C/400°F/Gas Mark 6, 15 minutes before baking. Bring a pan of water to the boil, add the onions and cook gently for about 15 minutes. Drain well, allow the onions to cool, then slice each one in half horizontally. Scoop out most of the onion flesh but leave a reasonably firm shell.

Chop up 4 tablespoons of the onion flesh and place in a bowl with the crushed garlic, breadcrumbs, sultanas/golden raisins, pine nuts, most of the grated cheese (leaving some to sprinkle on top) and parsley. Mix the breadcrumb mixture together thoroughly. Bind together with as much of the beaten egg as necessary to make a firm filling. Season to taste with salt and pepper.

Pile the mixture back into the onion shells and top with the remaining cheese. Put on an oiled baking sheet and cook in the preheated oven for 20–30 minutes until golden brown. Serve immediately.

## Difficulty Rating: 1 points

# Cheese and Onion Oat Pie

## Serves 4

### Ingredients

1 tbsp, plus 1 tsp sunflower/corn oil

25 g/1 oz/¼ stick butter

2 medium onions, peeled and sliced

1 garlic clove, peeled and crushed

150 g/5 oz/2 cups porridge oats

125 g/4 oz/1 heaped cup mature Cheddar cheese, grated

2 medium/large eggs, lightly beaten

2 tbsp freshly chopped parsley

salt and freshly ground black pepper

275 g/10 oz (about 1 medium-large) baking potato, peeled

Preheat the oven to 180°C/350°F/Gas Mark 4. Heat the oil and half the butter in a saucepan until melted. Add the onions and garlic and cook gently for 10 minutes, or until soft. Remove from the heat and tip into a large bowl.

Spread the oats out on a baking sheet and toast in the hot oven for 12 minutes. Leave to cool, then add to the onions with the cheese, eggs and parsley. Season to taste with salt and pepper and mix well.

Line the base of a 20.5 cm/8 inch round sandwich tin/layer-cake pan with greaseproof/waxed paper and oil well. Thinly slice the potato and arrange the slices on the base, overlapping them slightly. Spoon the cheese and oat mixture on top of the potato, spreading evenly with the back of a spoon. Cover with foil and bake for 30 minutes.

Invert the pie onto a baking sheet so that the potatoes are on top. Carefully remove the tin and lining paper.

Preheat the grill/broiler to medium. Melt the remaining butter and carefully brush over the potato topping. Cook under the preheated grill for 5–6 minutes until the potatoes are lightly browned. Cut into wedges and serve.

## Difficulty Rating: 2 points

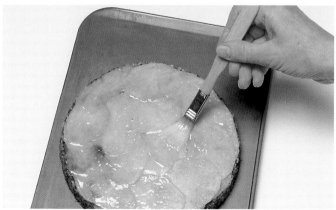

# Sicilian Baked Aubergine

## Serves 4

### Ingredients

1 large aubergine/eggplant, trimmed and cubed

2 celery stalks, trimmed

4 large ripe tomatoes

1 tsp sunflower/corn oil

2 shallots, peeled and finely chopped

1½ tsp tomato purée/paste

5 large green pitted olives

5 large black pitted olives

salt and freshly ground black pepper

1 tbsp white wine vinegar

2 tsp caster/superfine sugar

1 tbsp freshly chopped basil, to garnish

mixed salad leaves, to serve

Preheat the oven to 200°C/400°F/Gas Mark 6, 15 minutes before baking. Place the aubergine/eggplant in an oiled baking tray. Cover the tray with kitchen foil and bake in the preheated oven for 15–20 minutes until soft. Remove the aubergine from the oven and leave to cool.

Place the celery and tomatoes in a large bowl and cover with boiling water. Remove the tomatoes from the bowl when their skins begin to peel away. Remove the skins, then deseed and chop the flesh into small pieces. Remove the celery from the bowl of water, chop finely and reserve.

Pour the sunflower/corn oil into a nonstick saucepan, add the chopped shallots and fry gently for 2–3 minutes until soft. Add the celery, tomatoes, tomato purée/paste and olives. Season to taste with salt and pepper. Simmer gently for 3–4 minutes.

Add the vinegar, sugar and cooled aubergine to the pan and heat gently for 2–3 minutes until all the ingredients are well blended. Remove from the heat and leave to cool, then garnish with the chopped basil and serve cold with salad leaves.

## Difficulty Rating: 2 points

# Layered Cheese & Herb Potato Cake

## Serves 4

### Ingredients

900 g/2 lb (4–5 medium) waxy potatoes

3 tbsp freshly snipped chives

2 tbsp freshly chopped parsley

225 g/8 oz/2 cups grated mature Cheddar cheese

2 large/extra-large egg yolks

1 tsp paprika

125 g/4 oz/2¾ cups fresh white breadcrumbs

50 g/2 oz/½ cup almonds, toasted and roughly chopped

salt and freshly ground black pepper

50 g/2 oz/½ stick butter, melted

mixed salad or steamed vegetables, to serve

Preheat the oven to 180°C/350°F/Gas Mark 4, 10 minutes before baking. Lightly oil and line the base of a 20.5 cm/8 inch round cake tin/pan with lightly oiled baking parchment. Peel and thinly slice the potatoes and reserve. Stir the chives, parsley, cheese and egg yolks together in a small bowl and reserve. Mix the paprika into the breadcrumbs.

Sprinkle the almonds over the base of the tin. Cover with half the potatoes, arranging them in layers, then sprinkle with the paprika–breadcrumb mixture and season to taste with salt and pepper.

Spoon the cheese and herb mixture over the breadcrumbs with a little more seasoning, then arrange the remaining potatoes on top. Drizzle over the melted butter and press the surface down firmly.

Bake in the preheated oven for 1¼ hours, or until golden and cooked through. Let the tin stand for 10 minutes before carefully turning out the cake and serving in thick wedges. Serve immediately with salad or freshly steamed vegetables.

## Difficulty Rating: 1 point

# Melanzane Parmigiana

## Serves 4

**Ingredients**

900 g/2 lb (2 medium) aubergines/eggplants

salt and freshly ground black pepper

5 tbsp olive oil

1 red onion, peeled and chopped

½ tsp mild paprika

150 ml/¼ pint/⅔ cup dry red wine

150 ml/¼ pint/⅔ cup vegetable stock

400 g/14 oz can chopped tomatoes

1 tsp tomato purée/paste

1 tbsp freshly chopped oregano

175 g/6 oz/1½ cups mozzarella cheese, thinly sliced

40 g/1½ oz/½ cup coarsely grated Parmesan cheese

fresh basil sprig, to garnish

Preheat the oven to 200°C/400°F/Gas Mark 6, 15 minutes before baking. Cut the aubergines/eggplants lengthways into thin slices. Sprinkle with salt and leave to drain in a colander over a bowl for 30 minutes.

Meanwhile, heat 1 tablespoon of the oil in a saucepan and fry the onion for 10 minutes until softened. Add the paprika and cook for 1 minute. Stir in the wine, stock, tomatoes and tomato purée/paste. Simmer, uncovered, for 25 minutes, or until fairly thick. Stir in the oregano and season to taste. Remove from the heat.

Rinse the aubergine slices thoroughly under cold water. Pat dry on absorbent paper towels. Heat 2 tablespoons of the oil in a griddle pan and cook the aubergines in batches, for 3 minutes on each side, until golden. Drain well on absorbent paper towels.

Pour half of the tomato sauce into the base of a large ovenproof dish. Cover with half the aubergine slices, then top with the mozzarella. Cover with the remaining aubergine and pour over the remaining tomato sauce. Sprinkle with the grated Parmesan. Bake in the preheated oven for 30 minutes, or until the aubergines are tender and the sauce is bubbling. Garnish with a sprig of basil and cool for a few minutes before serving.

## Difficulty Rating: 2 points

# Aubergine Cannelloni with Watercress Sauce

## Serves 4

### Ingredients

4 large aubergines/eggplants

5–6 tbsp olive oil

350 g/12 oz/1¹/₂ cups ricotta cheese

75 g/3 oz/³/₄ cup grated Parmesan cheese

3 tbsp freshly chopped basil

salt and freshly ground black pepper

**For the watercress sauce:**

75 g/3 oz/³/₄ cup watercress, trimmed

200 ml/7 fl oz/³/₄ cup vegetable stock

1 shallot, peeled and sliced

pared strip lemon rind

1 large thyme sprig

3 tbsp crème fraîche/sour cream

1 tsp lemon juice

**To garnish:**

watercress sprigs

lemon zest

Preheat the oven to 190°C/375°F/Gas Mark 5, 10 minutes before baking. Cut the aubergines/eggplants lengthways into thin slices, discarding the side pieces. Heat 2 tablespoons oil in a frying pan and cook the aubergine slices in a single layer in several batches, turning once, until golden on both sides.

Mix the cheeses, basil and seasoning together. Lay the aubergine slices on a clean surface and spread the cheese mixture evenly between them. Roll up the slices from one of the short ends to enclose the filling. Place seam–side down in a single layer in an ovenproof dish. Bake in the oven for 15 minutes, or until golden.

To make the watercress sauce, blanch the watercress leaves in boiling water for about 30 seconds. Drain well, then rinse in a sieve under cold running water and squeeze dry. Put the stock, shallot, lemon rind and thyme in a small saucepan. Boil rapidly until reduced by half, then remove from the heat and strain.

Put the watercress and strained stock in a food processor and blend until fairly smooth. Return to the saucepan, stir in the crème fraîche/sour cream and lemon juice and season to taste with salt and pepper. Heat gently until the sauce is piping hot.

Serve a little of the sauce drizzled over the aubergines and the rest separately in a jug. Garnish the aubergine cannelloni with sprigs of watercress and lemon zest and serve immediately.

## Difficulty Rating: 4 points

# Rice-filled Peppers

## Serves 4

**Ingredients**

8 ripe tomatoes

2 tbsp olive oil

1 onion, peeled and chopped

1 garlic clove, peeled and crushed

½ tsp muscovado/dark brown sugar

125 g/4 oz/¾ cup cooked long-grain rice

1 tbsp freshly chopped oregano

50 g/2 oz/⅓ cup pine nuts, toasted

salt and freshly ground black pepper

2 large red and 2 large yellow peppers

**To serve:**

mixed salad

crusty bread

Preheat the oven to 200°C/400°F/Gas Mark 6, 15 minutes before baking. Put the tomatoes in a small bowl and pour over boiling water to cover. Leave for 1 minute, then drain. Plunge the tomatoes into cold water to cool, then peel off the skins. Quarter, remove the seeds and chop.

Heat the olive oil in a frying pan and cook the onion gently for 10 minutes until softened. Add the garlic, chopped tomatoes and sugar. Gently cook the tomato mixture for 10 minutes until thickened. Remove from the heat and stir the rice, oregano and pine nuts into the sauce. Season to taste with salt and pepper.

Halve the peppers lengthways, leaving the stems on. Remove the seeds and cores, then put the peppers in a lightly oiled roasting tin/pan cut-side down and cook in the preheated oven for about 10 minutes. Turn the peppers so they are cut-side up. Spoon in the filling, then cover with foil. Return to the oven for 15 minutes, or until the peppers are very tender, removing the foil for the last 5 minutes to allow the tops to brown a little.

Serve half a red pepper and half a yellow pepper per person with a mixed salad and plenty of warm, crusty bread.

**Difficulty Rating:** 3 **points**

# Pastini–stuffed Peppers

## Serves 6

**Ingredients**

6 red, yellow or orange peppers, tops cut off and deseeded
salt and freshly ground black pepper
175 g/6 oz/1½ cups pastini/tiny pasta shapes
4 tbsp olive oil
1 onion, peeled and finely chopped
2 garlic cloves, peeled and finely chopped
3 ripe plum tomatoes, skinned, deseeded and chopped
50 ml/2 fl oz/¼ cup dry white wine
8 pitted black olives, chopped
4 tbsp freshly chopped mixed herbs, such as parsley, basil and
　　oregano or marjoram
125 g/4 oz/1 cup mozzarella cheese, diced
25g/1 oz/¼ cup grated Parmesan cheese
fresh tomato sauce, preferably home-made, to serve

Preheat the oven to 190°C/375°F/Gas Mark 5, 10 minutes
before baking. Bring a pan of water to the boil. Trim the bottom
of each pepper so it sits straight. Blanch the peppers for 2–3
minutes, then drain on absorbent paper towels.

Return the water to the boil, add ½ teaspoon salt and the pasta
shapes and cook for 3–4 minutes, until *al dente*. Drain thoroughly,
rinse under cold running water, drain again and reserve.

Heat 2 tablespoons of the olive oil in a large frying pan, add the
onion and cook for 3–4 minutes. Add the garlic and cook for 1
minute. Stir in the tomatoes and wine and cook for 5 minutes,
stirring. Add the olives, herbs, mozzarella and half the Parmesan.
Season to taste. Remove from the heat and stir in the pasta.

Dry the insides of the peppers with absorbent paper towels,
then season lightly. Arrange the peppers in a lightly oiled
shallow baking dish and fill with the pasta mixture. Sprinkle with
the remaining Parmesan cheese and drizzle over the remaining
oil. Pour in boiling water to come 1 cm/½ inch up the sides of
the dish. Cook in the preheated oven for 25 minutes, or until
cooked. Serve immediately with freshly made tomato sauce.

## Difficulty Rating: 3 points

# Courgette Lasagne

## Serves 4

### Ingredients

2 tbsp olive oil

1 onion, peeled and finely chopped

225 g/8 oz/2½–3 cups mushrooms, wiped and thinly sliced

3–4 courgettes/zucchini, trimmed and thinly sliced

2 garlic cloves, peeled and finely chopped

½ tsp dried thyme

1–2 tbsp chopped basil or flat-leaf/Italian parsley

salt and freshly ground black pepper

1 quantity prepared white sauce (*see* page 304)

350 g/12 oz precooked lasagne sheets

225 g/8 oz/2 cups grated mozzarella cheese

50 g/2 oz/½ cup grated Parmesan cheese

400 g/14 oz can chopped tomatoes, drained

Preheat the oven to 200°C/400°F/Gas Mark 6, 15 minutes before baking. Heat the oil in a large frying pan, add the onion and cook for 3–5 minutes. Add the mushrooms, cook for 2 minutes, then add the courgettes/zucchini and cook for a further 3–4 minutes, or until tender. Stir in the garlic, thyme and basil or parsley and season to taste with salt and pepper. Remove from the heat and reserve.

Spoon a third of the white sauce onto the base of a lightly oiled large baking dish. Arrange a layer of lasagne over the sauce. Spread half the courgette mixture over the pasta, then sprinkle with some of the mozzarella and some of the Parmesan cheese. Repeat with more white sauce and another layer of lasagne, then cover with half the drained tomatoes.

Cover the tomatoes with lasagne, the remaining courgette mixture and some mozzarella and Parmesan cheese. Repeat the layers, ending with a layer of lasagne sheets, white sauce and the remaining Parmesan cheese. Bake in the preheated oven for 35 minutes, or until golden. Serve immediately.

## Difficulty Rating: 3 points

# Coconut–baked Courgettes

## Serves 4

**Ingredients**

3 tbsp groundnut/peanut oil

1 onion, peeled and finely sliced

4 garlic cloves, peeled and crushed

½ tsp chilli powder

1 tsp ground coriander

6–8 tbsp desiccated/shredded coconut

1 tbsp tomato purée/paste

700 g/1½ lb/6 cups courgettes/zucchini, thinly sliced

freshly chopped parsley, to garnish

Preheat the oven to 180°C/350°F/Gas Mark 4, 10 minutes before baking. Lightly oil a large, shallow ovenproof gratin dish. Heat a wok, add the oil and, when hot, add the onion and stir–fry for 2–3 minutes, or until softened. Add the garlic, chilli powder and coriander and stir–fry for 1–2 minutes.

Pour 300 ml/½ pint/1¼ cups cold water into the wok and bring to the boil. Add the coconut and tomato purée/paste and simmer for 3–4 minutes; most of the water will evaporate at this stage. Spoon 4 tablespoons of the spice and coconut mixture into a small bowl and reserve.

Stir the courgettes/zucchini into the remaining spice and coconut mixture, coating well. Spoon the courgettes into the oiled gratin dish and sprinkle the reserved spice and coconut mixture evenly over the top. Bake, uncovered, in the preheated oven for 15–20 minutes, or until golden. Garnish with chopped parsley and serve immediately.

**Difficulty Rating: 1 point**

# Baked Macaroni Cheese

## Serves 8

### Ingredients

450 g/1 lb/4¼ cups macaroni

75 g/3 oz/⅔ stick butter

1 onion, peeled and finely chopped

40 g/1½ oz/⅓ cup plain/all-purpose flour

1 litre/1¾ pints/1 quart milk

1–2 dried bay leaves

½ tsp dried thyme

salt and freshly ground black pepper

pinch cayenne pepper

pinch freshly grated nutmeg

2 small leeks, trimmed, finely chopped, cooked and drained

1 tbsp Dijon mustard

400 g/14 oz/4 cups mature Cheddar cheese, grated

2 tbsp dried breadcrumbs

2 tbsp freshly grated Parmesan cheese

basil sprig, to garnish

Preheat the oven to 190 C/375 F/Gas Mark 5, 10 minutes before cooking. Bring a large pan of lightly salted water to a rolling boil. Add the macaroni and cook according to the packet instructions, or until al dente. Drain thoroughly and reserve.

Meanwhile, melt 50 g/2 oz of the butter in a large, heavy-based saucepan, add the onion and cook, stirring frequently, for 5–7 minutes, until softened. Sprinkle in the flour and cook, stirring constantly, for 2 minutes. Remove from the heat, stir in the milk, return to the heat and cook, stirring, until it is a smooth sauce. Add the bay leaves and thyme to the sauce and season to taste with salt, pepper, cayenne pepper and freshly grated nutmeg. Simmer for about 15 minutes, stirring frequently, until thickened and smooth. Remove the sauce from the heat. Add the cooked leeks, mustard and Cheddar cheese and stir until the cheese has melted. Stir in the macaroni, then tip into a lightly oiled baking dish. Sprinkle the breadcrumbs and Parmesan cheese over the macaroni. Dot with the remaining butter, then bake in the preheated oven for 1 hour, or until golden. Garnish with a basil sprig and serve immediately.

## Difficulty Rating: 3 points

# Baked Macaroni with Mushrooms & Leeks

## Serves 4

### Ingredients

2 tbsp olive oil

1 onion, peeled and finely chopped

1 garlic clove, peeled and crushed

2 small leeks, trimmed and chopped

450 g/1 lb/4½ cups assorted wild mushrooms, trimmed

75 g/3 oz/⅔ stick butter

50 ml/2 fl oz/¼ cup white wine

150 ml/¼ pint/⅔ cup crème fraîche/sour cream or
    whipping cream

salt and freshly ground black pepper

350 g/12 oz/3⅓ cups short-cut macaroni

75 g/3 oz/1⅔ cups fresh white breadcrumbs

1 tbsp freshly chopped parsley, to garnish

Preheat the oven to 220°C/425°F/Gas Mark 7, 15 minutes before baking. Heat 1 tablespoon of the olive oil in a large frying pan, add the onion and garlic and cook for 2 minutes. Add the leeks, mushrooms and one third of the butter, then cook for 5 minutes. Pour in the white wine, cook for 2 minutes, then stir in the crème fraîche/sour cream or cream. Season to taste with salt and pepper.

Meanwhile, bring a large pan of lightly salted water to a rolling boil. Add the macaroni and cook according to the packet instructions, or until *al dente*.

Melt half the remaining butter with the remaining oil in a small frying pan. Add the breadcrumbs and fry until just turning golden brown. Drain on absorbent paper towels.

Drain the pasta thoroughly, toss in the remaining butter, then tip into a lightly oiled 1.5 litre/2½ pint/1½ quart shallow baking dish. Cover the pasta with the leek and mushroom mixture, then sprinkle with the fried breadcrumbs. Bake in the preheated oven for 5–10 minutes, or until golden and crisp. Garnish with chopped parsley and serve.

## Difficulty Rating: 2 points

# Gnocchi Roulade with Mozzarella & Spinach

## Serves 8

**Ingredients**

600 ml/1 pint/2½ cups milk

125 g/4 oz/¾ cup fine semolina or polenta

25 g/1 oz/¼ stick butter

75 g/3 oz/⅔ cup Cheddar cheese, grated

2 medium/large egg yolks

salt and freshly ground black pepper

700 g/1½ lb/23 cups baby spinach leaves

½ tsp freshly grated nutmeg

150 g/5 oz/1⅓ cups mozzarella cheese, grated

2 tbsp freshly grated Parmesan cheese

freshly made tomato sauce, to serve

Preheat the oven to 240°C/475°F/Gas Mark 9, 15 minutes before baking. Oil and line a large Swiss roll tin/jelly roll pan (23 x 33 cm/ 9 x 13 inch) with nonstick baking parchment.

Pour the milk into a heavy–based pan and whisk in the semolina or polenta. Bring to the boil, then simmer, stirring continuously with a wooden spoon, for 3–4 minutes, or until very thick. Remove from heat and stir in the butter and Cheddar cheese until melted. Whisk in the egg yolks and season to taste with salt and pepper. Pour into the lined tin. Cover and allow to cool for 1 hour.

Cook the baby spinach in batches in a large pan with 1 teaspoon of water for 3–4 minutes, or until wilted. Drain thoroughly, season to taste with salt, pepper and nutmeg, then allow to cool.

Spread the spinach over the cooled semolina mixture and sprinkle over just over half of the mozzarella and half the Parmesan. Bake in the preheated oven for 20 minutes, or until golden.

Allow to cool, then roll up like a Swiss roll. Sprinkle with the remaining mozzarella and Parmesan, then bake for another 15–20 minutes until golden. Serve immediately with freshly made tomato sauce.

## Difficulty Rating: 4 points

# Cannelloni with Tomato & Red Wine Sauce

## Serves 6

### Ingredients

2 tbsp olive oil

1 onion, peeled and finely chopped

1 garlic clove, peeled and crushed

250 g/9 oz carton ricotta cheese

50 g/2 oz/scant ⅓ cup pine nuts

salt and freshly ground black pepper

pinch freshly grated nutmeg

250 g/9 oz fresh spinach lasagne

25 g/1 oz/¼ stick butter

1 shallot, peeled and finely chopped

150 ml/7 fl oz/⅔ cup red wine

2 x 400 g/14 oz cans chopped tomatoes

½ tsp granulated sugar

50 g/2 oz/½ cup mozzarella cheese, grated, plus extra to serve

1 tbsp freshly chopped parsley, to garnish

fresh green salad, to serve

Preheat the oven to 200°C/400°F/Gas Mark 6, 15 minutes before baking. Heat the oil in a heavy-based pan, add the onion and garlic and cook for 2–3 minutes. Cool slightly, then stir in the ricotta cheese and pine nuts. Season the filling to taste with salt, pepper and the nutmeg.

Cut each lasagne sheet in half, put a little of the ricotta filling on each piece and roll up like a cigar to resemble cannelloni tubes. Arrange the cannelloni seam-side down in a single layer, in a lightly oiled 2.25 litre/4 pint/2¼ quart shallow ovenproof dish.

Melt the butter in a pan, add the shallot and cook for 2 minutes. Pour in the red wine, tomatoes and sugar and season well. Bring to the boil, lower the heat and simmer for about 20 minutes, or until thickened. Add a little more sugar if desired. Transfer to a food processor and blend until a smooth sauce is formed.

Pour the warm tomato sauce over the cannelloni and sprinkle with the grated mozzarella cheese. Bake in the preheated oven for about 30 minutes, or until golden and bubbling. Garnish and serve immediately with a green salad.

## Difficulty Rating: 3 points

# Cannelloni with Gorgonzola Sauce

## Serves 2–3

**Ingredients**

50 g/2 oz/¹/₂ stick salted butter

1 shallot, peeled and finely chopped

2 rashers streaky/fatty bacon, no rind, chopped

225 g/8 oz/2¹/₂ cups mushrooms, wiped and finely chopped

2 tbsp plain/all-purpose flour

125 ml/4 fl oz/¹/₂ cup double/heavy cream

6 sheets fresh egg lasagne

40 g/1¹/₂ oz/¹/₃ stick unsalted butter

150 g/5 oz/1¹/₄ cups Gorgonzola cheese, diced

150 ml/¹/₄ pint/²/₃ cup whipping cream

assorted salad leaves, to serve

Preheat the oven to 190°C/375°F/Gas Mark 5, 10 minutes before baking. Melt the salted butter in a heavy-based pan, add the shallot and bacon and cook for about 4–5 minutes. Add the mushrooms to the pan and cook for 5–6 minutes, or until the mushrooms are very soft. Stir in the flour, cook for 1 minute, then stir in the double/heavy cream and cook gently for 2 minutes. Allow to cool.

Cut each sheet of lasagne in half. Spoon some filling onto each piece and roll up from the longest side to resemble cannelloni. Arrange the cannelloni in a lightly oiled shallow 1.5 litre/2¹/₂ pint/1¹/₂ quart ovenproof dish.

Heat the unsalted butter very slowly in a pan and, when melted, add the Gorgonzola cheese. Stir until the cheese has melted, then stir in the whipping cream. Bring to the boil slowly, then simmer gently for about 5 minutes, or until thickened. Pour the cream sauce over the cannelloni. Place in the preheated oven and bake for 20 minutes, or until golden and thoroughly heated through. Serve immediately with assorted salad leaves.

## Difficulty Rating: 2 points

# Ratatouille & Pasta Bake

## Serves 4

### Ingredients

1 tbsp olive oil

2 large onions, peeled and finely chopped

400 g/14 oz can chopped tomatoes

100 ml/3½ fl oz/⅓ cup white wine

½ tsp caster/superfine sugar

salt and freshly ground black pepper

40 g/1½ oz/⅓ stick butter

2 garlic cloves, peeled and crushed

125 g/4 oz/1 heaped cup mushrooms, wiped and thickly sliced

700 g/1½ lb/6 cups courgettes/zucchini, trimmed and thickly sliced

125 g/4 oz fresh spinach lasagne

2 large/extra-large eggs

2 tbsp double/heavy cream

75 g/3 oz/¾ cup mozzarella cheese, grated

25 g/1 oz/¼ cup pecorino cheese, grated

green salad, to serve

Preheat the oven to 190°C/375°F/Gas Mark 5, 10 minutes before cooking. Heat the olive oil in a heavy-based pan, add half the onion and cook gently for 2–3 minutes. Stir in the tomatoes and wine, then simmer for 20 minutes, or until a thick consistency is formed. Add the sugar and season to taste with salt and pepper. Reserve.

Meanwhile, melt the butter in another pan, add the remaining onion, the garlic, mushrooms and courgettes/zucchini and cook for 10 minutes, or until softened.

Spread a little tomato sauce in the base of a lightly oiled 1.4 litre/2½ pint/1½ quart baking dish. Top with a layer of lasagne and spoon over half the mushroom and courgette mixture. Repeat the layers, finishing with a layer of lasagne.

Beat the eggs and cream together, then pour over the lasagne. Mix the mozzarella and pecorino cheeses together, then sprinkle on top of the lasagne. Place in the preheated oven and cook for 20 minutes, or until golden brown. Serve immediately with a green salad.

## Difficulty Rating: 2 points

# Index